Human Feelings

Explorations in Affect
Development and Meaning

Human Feelings

Explorations in Affect
Development and Meaning

edited by

Steven L. Ablon

Daniel Brown

Edward J. Khantzian

John E. Mack

THE ANALYTIC PRESS

1993   Hillsdale, NJ   London

Copyright © 1993 by The Analytic Press, Inc.
  All rights reserved. No part of this book may be reproduced in any form: by photostat, microform, retrieval system, or any other means, without the prior written permission of the copyright holder.

Published by The Analytic Press, Inc.
365 Broadway, Hillsdale, NJ 07642

Typeset in Zapf by Lind Graphics, Upper Saddle River, NJ

Library of Congress Cataloging-in-Publication Data

Human feelings : explorations in affect development and meaning /
  edited by Steven Ablon . . . [et al.].
      p. cm.
    Includes bibliographical references and index.
    ISBN 0-88163-144-2
    1. Emotions. 2. Affect (Psychology) I. Ablon, Steven L.
  BF511.H85 1993
  152.4—dc20   93-14309
                                                       CIP

Printed in the United States of America
10 9 8 7 6 5 4 3 2 1

In memory of our friends and colleagues,
Sarah Haley and Jerome Sashin,
whose untimely deaths
in the course of this project we deeply mourn.

CONTENTS

ACKNOWLEDGMENTS

We are grateful to the family members, friends, and colleagues who carefully read and criticized this manuscript and made many valuable suggestions. Individual members of the Harvard Affect Study Group especially want to thank Dr. Gridth Ablon, Dr. Doris Bargen, Cliff Cohen, H. H. The Dali Lama, Dr. Paul David, Michael Dysart, Dr. Michael Forte, Dr. John Gedo, Dr. Jules Glenn, Marushka Glissen, Rene Goodale, Dr. Allen Gurwitt, Professor Allen Guttman, Dr. Judith Huizenga, Dr. John Kafka, Dr. Henry Krystal, Dr. Samual Kaplan, Dr. Rona Knight, Dr. Joyce McDougall, Dr. William Meissner, Theodore Melnechuk, Dr. Michael Miller, Dr. Malkah Notman, Dr. Nancy Feingold-Palmer, Dr. Randall Paulsen, Dr. Jalna Perry, Dr. Susan Rosbrau Reich, Bonnie Sashin, Dr. Lisa Selin, Dr. Martha Stark, Dr. Patricia Wright, and Kalsang Yeshe.

We also want to acknowledge the generous support of the Rockefeller Foundation and the parents and students in the public school systems of Milton, Norwood, and Watertown, Massachusetts for making possible the gender role research. We wish to extend special thanks to the American Institute of Indian Studies, which funded, in part, the research on advanced meditators in South Asia. We want to thank the staff of the Office of Cultural Affairs for the Tibetan Government in exile.

The Harvard Affect Study Group is particularly indebted to Helen Modica and Patricia Carr, who have been characteristically diligent and devoted to supporting this project. A special thanks is extended to Joan

Marconi-Gilles for her patience and good spirits in putting all the chapters into the same word processing format and for preparing the final manuscript and bibliography for submission. We also want to thank the Psychiatric Service of The Cambridge Hospital for its encouragement of the Harvard Study Group. We are grateful to The Analytic Press and especially Dr. Paul Stepansky, Eleanor Starke Kobrin, and Joan Riegel for their invaluable help and support. Thanks too to Paula Williams for her careful copy editing and to Leah Kramer for her painstaking preparation of the index.

CONTRIBUTORS

Steven L. Ablon, M. D. (editor)—Training and Supervising Analyst, Boston Psychoanalytic Institute; Associate Clinical Professor of Psychiatry, Harvard Medical School at Massachusetts General Hospital.

Leslie R. Brody, Ph.D.—Associate Professor and Director, Clinical Psychology Doctoral Program, Psychology Department, Boston University.

Daniel Brown, Ph.D. (editor)—Director, Daniel Brown Associates, Cambridge, MA; Assistant Professor of Psychology, Harvard Medical School at The Cambridge Hospital.

Sarah Haley, L.C.S.W. (deceased)—formerly on staff at Boston VA Medical Center.

Alexandra Murray Harrison, M.D.—Acting Chief of Child Psychiatry, The Cambridge Hospital; Assistant Clinical Professor of Psychiatry, Harvard Medical School at The Cambridge Hospital.

Daniel Jacobs, M.D.—Training and Supervising Analyst, The Boston Psychoanalytic Institute; Assistant Clinical Professor of Psychiatry, Harvard Medical School at Beth Israel Hospital.

Edward J. Khantzian, M.D. (editor)—Associate Clinical Professor of Psychiatry, Harvard Medical School at The Cambridge Hospital; Associate Chief of Psychiatry, Tewksbury (MA) Hospital.

John E. Mack, M.D. (editor)—Professor of Psychiatry, Harvard Medical School at The Cambridge Hospital; Founding Director, Center for Psychology and Social Change (formerly Center for Psychological Studies in the Nuclear Age).

Alfred Margulies, M.D.—Associate Professor, Harvard Medical School; Faculty, Psychoanalytic Institute of New England, East, Massachusetts Institute of Psychoanalysis, and Boston Psychoanalytic Institute.

Alexander C. Morgan, M.D.—Instructor in Psychiatry, Harvard Medical School at The Cambridge Hospital; Faculty, Boston Psychoanalytic Institute and the Massachusetts Institute for Psychoanalysis.

Allen J. Palmer, M.D.—Faculty, Boston Psychoanalytic Institute; Clinical Instructor in Psychiatry, Harvard Medical School at Beth Israel Hospital.

Jerome I. Sashin, M.D. (deceased)—formerly Lecturer in Psychiatry, Harvard Medical School; Faculty, Psychoanalytic Institute of New England, East.

Stephanie Smith, M.A., M.S.W.—Candidate, Boston Psychoanalytic Institute; Lecturer in Psychiatry, Harvard Medical School at The Cambridge Hospital.

Bessel A. van der Kolk, M.D.—Chief, Erich Lindemann Trauma Clinic, Massachusetts General Hospital; Associate Professor of Psychiatry, Harvard Medical School.

INTRODUCTION

Steven L. Ablon

Feelings are a basic and essential part of being human. For the infant at the beginning of life, emotions are central to all aspects of human development and to the dialogue with caretakers. Feelings are omnipresent, infusing every aspect of human experience. We rely on feelings to evaluate authenticity, to bridge the worlds of possible realities, and to reorganize and refine, even to create, our observations.

Confronted not only with the centrality of affect but also with the complexity and confusion of thinking and writing about affect, the Harvard Affect Study Group was formed, bringing together people with different kinds of training, and from different disciplines, who shared a passionate interest in the study of affect. The Harvard Affect Study Group sought research directions that were personally compelling for each of us and that would not only summarize and build on past contributions but also lead us to new frontiers. To this end, we recognized the importance of group process and decided to explore affect in a group setting. The Harvard Affect Study Group has met twice a month over the past five years. During this time, a sense of collective safety developed that would be tested repeatedly. We came to feel secure enough to risk talking about things that for other audiences or publications we would not ordinarily be willing to do. Most of all, the sudden death from cancer of two of our members, Sarah Haley and Jerry Sashin, has acted as a central catalyst for this book. Loss and the cycles of birth, development, and death bring the most powerful affective experiences of our lives, and we not only thought about them together but also lived through them.

From the beginning, the Study Group was responsive to personal feelings and experiences ranging from the ups and downs of daily life to international problems; in this way, we tried to be open to the current affective situations of ourselves and the smaller and larger communities of which we are a part. The group had frequent side conversations about something a group member had read or on topics we were interested in, including current events. As we let these conversations evolve sometimes at the expense of considering a planned topic, we discovered an increasing ease in sharing our reactions—joy, enthusiasm, worry, unhappiness—that fostered feelings of safety about our theoretical and clinical explorations. This sense of safety also reflected a playful process in the group and facilitated creativity and freedom.

The interdisciplinary makeup of the study group is integral to the evolution and content of this book. When the group was formed, it was the original intention to bring together people with a diversity of experiences and theoretical viewpoints. Thus the group came to include developmentalists, academics specializing in gender research and linguistics, and adult and child psychoanalysts and therapists. Members brought various long-standing interests in areas such as addiction, trauma, creativity, play, adolescence, empathy, family dynamics, and nonordinary states of consciousness. These different areas of interest combined to produce new perspectives resulting in both confusion and new possibilities for integrations as the group was stimulated to think about the transformative communicative aspects of affect.

As the group progressed in the work on this volume, we came to think more deeply about our own lives in historical perspective. We discussed how, since the Middle Ages, certainly since the 17th century, the Western scientific enterprise has been an essentially masculine undertaking, emphasizing a Cartesian objectivist, self–other, cognitive kind of approach to the human phenomenon. Gradually the world has shifted from the belief that experience could be understood purely intellectually and scientifically, and there is a currently increasing awareness of the spiritual, moral, and human issues that need to be both understood and experienced directly. Affect is the medium of that experience.

For reasons that are complex and that have to do with such matters as global crises and deepening knowledge of what helps people transform and change, society in general and this book in particular are making greater efforts to explore the depths of what has been, in our Western tradition, a largely female enterprise. I refer to the exploration of the core affective experience of what it is to be human, to be open, to be receptive, to express feelings, to show one's hurts, to explore wounds, and to share the depths of feelings. Until the past decade, very little attention was paid to gender differences. Masculine and feminine experiences were treated alike, and more frequently than not, only masculine experience was studied.

In recent years, consideration of feeling as the archetypal core of human "being," as the heart of human suffering and transformation, has encouraged men to integrate their feminine sensibility into their sense of self. This is reflected in the content herein and especially in the realization that this project is not just a cognitive exercise in the empirical analysis of affect. Rather, it is an integration of two approaches to knowledge. We have attempted to be affective in the expression of affect rather than purely cognitive about affect. In that sense, the work has been guided as much by our being willing and able to "feel our way along" with these issues as by the rigorous thinking that grows out of our professional backgrounds and interests.

Because feelings are inherent in the human condition, coloring every aspect of human experience, the topic of feeling can be usefully explored only by attending to the specific contexts in which different feelings emerge, and this book brings together the related topics or modes of inquiry pursued by study group members. Each section begins with an introductory discussion highlighting its focus and describing how each section is related to the rest of the book. We hope such a format clarifies how the study group's ongoing dialogue brought about a unifying and integrative perspective on the development and nature of affect.

The book builds on the foundation of the first section, "Theoretical Considerations." The following section, "Affect and the Clinical Process," builds on that base. "Trauma, Addiction, and Psychosomatics" and "Trans-formations of Affect" range beyond developmental and therapeutic con-siderations into neurobiology, the mind–body continuum, and the spheres of epistemology, creativity, and social organization. The final section, "New Directions," further extends the frontiers of exploration into nonordinary states of consciousness, and the vicissitudes of well-being. We invite the reader to accompany us on this journey, feeling and thinking with us, and, we hope, experiencing, as we did, the excitement and eagerness that come with new discoveries and changing integrations.

As I noted at the outset, the Harvard Affect Study Group, out of which this volume developed, has provided a facilitating environment in which the sensibilities and interests of individual members have been recog-nized, nurtured, and brought into creative interaction with the sensibili-ties and interests of colleagues from different disciplines. By way of exemplifying the philosophy of inquiry that informs this project, let me, in conclusion, share with the reader this contributor's personal vision of the vicissitudes of affect across the life cycle. To this end, I turn to E. B. White's (1952) *Charlotte's Web*. There are several reasons for this choice. First, I am enthusiastic about our efforts in the sciences and in the arts to bring together the theoretical and the specific (Bruner, 1986). Although our effort in this book reaches for overarching metaphors and concepts, it derives from the details of human experience. These details, what James Joyce called the "epiphanies of the ordinary," are captured powerfully by White in the detailed language and sensibility of his description of life on the Zuckermans' farm. *Charlotte's Web* is a song of people, animals, nature, the passing of seasons, the beauty and pain of life, and life's ever-changing patterns. In addition, *Charlotte's Web* is one of the most popular children's books, for both children and adults, in the past 40 years. It is read at home, performed at schools, and watched on film. Its popularity connects it to the rapidly moving cultural context of a section of contemporary Western civilization and its preoccupations and imagination.

Charlotte's Web has been a powerful story for me even more in adulthood than when I was a child. I invariably feel very sad reading *Charlotte's Web*, and I continue to find new elements in this sadness. I think of my daughter playing Wilbur, the pig, in a fifth-grade school play. I am reminded of my childhood, of sad and lonely times on the farm, and of the comfort and companionship of the animals. *Charlotte's Web* also touches on transience, on holding in my memory moments full of feeling, moments of beauty and pain contained in memory like childhood's past as life rushes onward. Finally, I turn to *Charlotte's Web* because it is a children's story. Like myths, fairy tales, fiction, and art, children's stories capture in an emotionally distilled way what matters most to people. Children often have more immediate access to their feelings, and they struggle to come to terms with these feelings in relation to an increasingly complex awareness of life. *Charlotte's Web* has to do with the experiences and feelings of animals. Animals in a basic, perhaps even evolutionary way, provide access to our deepest experiences and feelings in life and represent archetypal energies. Through the medium of animals, we reach beyond the human in dealing with the most profound matters of birth, death, and rebirth. Also by reflecting on *Charlotte's Web* I hope to exemplify some of how this volume struggles to engage the world of feelings in our work and play.

Charlotte's Web begins with the father, Mr. Arable, going out to kill one of the newborn pigs, the runt of the litter. His eight-year-old daughter, Fern, is horrified and runs after her father. Mr. Arable says, "I know more about raising a litter of pigs than you do. A weakling makes trouble. Now run along!" (p. 3). Fern replies, "The pig couldn't help being born small, could it? If *I* had been very small at birth, would you have killed *me?*"

(p. 3). Although Mr. Arable says no, Fern tells him, "This is the most terrible case of injustice I ever heard of" (p. 3). At this point Mr. Arable's feelings lead to a change in perspective. White writes, "A queer look came over John Arable's face. He seemed almost ready to cry himself" (p. 3). He changes his mind and tells Fern, "All right . . . You go back to the house and I will bring the runt when I come in. I'll let you start it on a bottle, like a baby. Then you'll see what trouble a pig can be" (p. 3). Fern's identification with the little pig stirs up powerful feelings in her, and her feelings make an impact on her father, so he changes his mind even though he "knows more about raising a litter of pigs" (p. 3).

This brief scene opening *Charlotte's Web* touches on some central issues to be explored in our book, such as affect and character and affect and gender. Mr. Arable has his theories about raising animals. He believes that "A weakling makes trouble" (p. 3). Mr. Arable has a matter-of-fact, confident character style suggested by his statements such as, "I know more about raising a litter of pigs than you do" and "Then you'll see what trouble a pig can be" (p. 3). His theories are organized to help him manage feelings such as murderousness. In addition, Mr. Arable is gruff in his speech, but this appears to be a defensive style designed to cope with his own tenderness and guilt that seem quite near the surface in his description of his seeming "almost ready to cry himself." At the same time, identification, empathy, and the complexity of emotional states make Mr. Arable and Fern's feelings so moving.

Mr. Arable gives Fern the pig. "He's yours . . . saved from an untimely death. And may the good Lord forgive me for this foolishness" (p. 4). There's the foolishness of saving the pig, or, as the story unfolds, of not saving it. The first chapter ends with a description of Fern thinking about the pig (whom she has named Wilbur) while she is at school. The teacher asks her the capital of Pennsylvania. Fern replies dreamily, "Wilbur." The other students giggle and Fern blushes. Fern is preoccupied with her little pig, and language reveals the pig's powerful link to feeling and its own, not easily identifiable, connection to communication and logic.

Fern spends a lot of time with Wilbur. She watches him, strokes him, feeds him, walks him in her doll carriage, and puts him to bed. White describes the associated feelings of joy and enchantment. "Every day was a happy day, and every night was peaceful" (p. 11). Fern's feelings about Wilbur perhaps reflect her experience and longing for her baby days, which are further and further behind her. When Wilbur is five weeks old, arrangements are made to sell him to Fern's uncle, Homer Zuckerman, who has a barn and raises pigs. Fern can walk down the road and visit as often as she likes. Fern visits Wilbur almost every afternoon. White describes life at the farm, which is a central aspect of the book that White calls "his hymn to the barn" (Sale, 1978, p. 258). Fern "sat quietly during the long afternoons, thinking and listening and watching Wilbur. The sheep soon got to know her and trust her. So did the geese, who lived with the sheep. All the animals trusted her, she was so quiet and friendly" (p. 15).

When Wilbur is two months old, he begins to feel lonely and bored, one might say depressed, "I'm less than two months old and I'm tired of living" (p. 16). Wilbur, with encouragement from the other animals, escapes from the barnyard but finds "I'm really too young to go out into the world alone" (p. 24). Gradually, Wilbur realizes he "didn't want food, he wanted love. He wanted a friend—someone who would play with him" (p. 27). Templeton, the rat, responds, "I prefer to spend my time eating, gnawing, spying, and hiding" (p. 29). Templeton is addicted to food and organizes his life around this.

Charlotte A. Cavatica, a spider, speaks to Wilbur and becomes his friend. Wilbur learns that his new friend "Charlotte is fierce, brutal, scheming, bloodthirsty" (p. 41). Charlotte describes how she catches flies and eats them: "Delicious. Of course, I don't really eat them. I drink them—drink their blood. I love blood" (p. 39). It seems friends have complicated feelings, not just joy and peace but also murderousness, destructiveness, and fear. It is interesting that Charlotte, who like a good therapist, supports, acknowledges, bears, and identifies feelings, also is fierce and bloodthirsty. She is us, and when we acquaint ourselves with the dark destructive parts along with the loving, which Charlotte has and is, we attain an integration that facilitates growth and creativity. Similarly, the goose and the gander are worried about Templeton, who "had no morals, no conscience, no scruples, no consideration, no decency, no milk of rodent kindness, no compunctions, no higher feeling, no friendliness, no anything. He would kill a gosling if he could get away with it—the goose knew that. Everybody knew it" (p. 46). White reminds us that life is full of trauma and terrible overwhelming experiences and feelings.

At this point, the central theme of death, dying, and killing becomes even more prominent. Wilbur learns from the old sheep that he will be killed and turned into smoked bacon and ham. Wilbur is terrified, but Charlotte reassures him that she will save him and tells Wilbur she is working on a plan. Charlotte makes a web above Wilbur with "SOME PIG!" written in it in block letters. News of this mysterious and miraculous event and about the very unusual pig soon spreads all over the county. As a result, people sense remarkable qualities in Wilbur, and he feels very special. In groups, affects such as, in this case, interest and pleasure, are magnified, transformed, and experienced differently by both the individuals and the group as a whole. Feelings in this case such as anxiety or fear provide the motivation for the animals to work together, as the old sheep explains to Templeton, the rat, "Wilbur's food is your food; therefore

Wilbur's destiny and your destiny are closely linked. If Wilbur is killed and his trough stands empty day after day, you'll grow so thin we can look right through your stomach and see objects on the other side" (p. 90).

Charlotte tells the other animals in the barn that her trick of writing "SOME PIG!" in the web is working. At the same time, Charlotte, without dwelling on it, argues that in many ways it is not a trick. She says to Wilbur, "You're terrific as far as *I'm* concerned . . . and that's what counts. You're my best friend, and *I* think you're sensational. Now stop arguing and go get some sleep!" (p. 91). Also, the writing in a spider's web or just the web "each thin strand . . . decorated with dozens of tiny beads of water" (p. 77) is magical and draws its impact from the way each character in the book and each reader's feelings determine meaning, importance, and reality. We rely on affective connectiveness to assess authenticity, to bridge the worlds of different interpretations of reality, and to reorganize and refine our observations. It is these aspects of affect that play a central role in motivating and bringing structure to creativity and transformation in art, music, literature, and other creative efforts. Feelings and creativity not only save Wilbur's life but also make it meaningful. A central theme in *Charlotte's Web* is that feelings between people, between animals, about nature, and about the world make life precious, wonderful, and painful. The messages in the spider's web remind us that if we are truly experiencing our feelings, we must remain open-minded, and we must scientifically gather the experience and information before we try to distinguish tricks from reality.

When Charlotte next writes "TERRIFIC!" in a web over the pigpen, Wilbur really feels "terrific," and the Zuckermans decide to take Wilbur to the county fair. During this time, Mrs. Arable becomes concerned about Fern because she spends so much time at the barn sitting, listening, and watching the animals. When Mrs. Arable consults Dr. Dorian, the family doctor, about Fern and her ideas about spider webs and about animals talking, Dr. Dorian replies, "I don't understand everything, and I don't intend to let it worry me" (p. 110). Dr. Dorian appears wise not only in his ability to tolerate uncertainty but also in his awareness of development. When he is told that Fern is eight years old, Dr. Dorian says, "I think she will always love animals. But I doubt that she spends her entire life in Homer Zuckerman's barn cellar" (p. 111). White reminds us that affective experience and expression change during development and that the freedom to play is a vehicle for mastery, creativity, and progressive development throughout life. Dr. Dorian also asks Mrs. Arable, "How about boys—does she know any boys?" He adds, "Let Fern associate with her friends in the barn if she wants to. I would say, offhand, that spiders and pigs were fully as interesting as Henry Fussy" (p. 111). The differences and similarities between boys and girls is a secondary theme in *Charlotte's*

Web. The reader gets to know Fern much better than her brother, Avery, of whom Mrs. Arable says, "Of course, he gets into poison ivy and gets stung by wasps and bees and brings frogs and snakes home and breaks everything he lays his hands on. He's fine" (pp. 111–112). All at the same time, *Charlotte's Web* emphasizes the importance of an integration of the male and female approaches to knowledge and affect, the empirical cognitive tendencies of men, and the intuitive affectively receptive approaches of women.

Soon, "The crickets sang in the grasses. They sang the song of summer's ending, a sad, monotonous song" (p. 113). Wilbur looks even better as a result of special care and attention. Charlotte writes "RADIANT" in a web above Wilbur's pen and Wilbur "did everything possible to make himself glow" (p. 114). Even though it is egg-laying time, Charlotte accompanies Wilbur to the county fair. At the fair, Fern rides happily on the ferris wheel with Henry Fussy. Charlotte writes "HUMBLE" in her web over Wilbur's pen, and Wilbur wins a special prize at the fair. Now Wilbur means so much to the Zuckermans that they would never harm him. Charlotte weaves her egg sac, from which 514 little spiders will hatch in the spring, and Wilbur carries it back to the barn hidden in his mouth, in a blend of nurturance, love, and aggression. Charlotte dies at the deserted fairground. Echoing the powerful feeling of aloneness in death, White writes, "No one was with her when she died" (p. 171).

The spiders hatch and most of them sail away, but each year a few stay in the doorway with Wilbur. *Charlotte's Web* weaves together many themes: a closeness to nature, birth and death, joy and sadness, the changing of seasons, and the passing of time. White explores the centrality of feelings in human beings' struggles to attain harmony with one other and the rest of the natural world. *Charlotte's Web* concludes with the refrain "Life in the barn was very good—night and day, winter and summer, spring and fall, dull days and bright days. It was the best place to be, thought Wilbur, this warm delicious cellar, with the garrulous geese, the changing seasons, the heat of the sun, the passage of swallows, the nearness of rats, the sameness of sheep, the love of spiders, the smell of manure, and the glory of everything" (p. 183). At the same time, Wilbur "never forgot Charlotte. Although he loved her children and grandchildren dearly, none of the new spiders ever quite took her place in his heart. She was in a class by herself. It is not often that someone comes along who is a true friend and a good writer. Charlotte was both" (p. 184). Charlotte embodies the full range of human polarities, which we all contain but which are so explicitly embodied in her particular loving, creative, enabling, and, at the same time, devouring and bloodthirsty nature. It is my hope that this book, like Charlotte, will at times be "a true friend and a good writer" helping with each reader's own explorations into the experiences, meanings, and transformations of human feelings.

REFERENCES

Bruner, J. (1986), *Actual Minds, Possible Worlds*. Cambridge, MA: Harvard University Press.
Sale, R. (1978), *Fairy Tales and After*. Cambridge, MA: Harvard University Press.
White, E. B. (1952), *Charlotte's Web*. New York: Harper & Row.

THEORETICAL CONSIDERATIONS

The first section of this volume is devoted to developmental theories of affect. No comprehensive theory of affective development across the life span exists in the literature. Yet in the past decade there has been a great deal of interest in affect and affective development. A variety of affect development theories have appeared in the literature, some based on child observation studies and some on clinical observations. Most of the theories are limited to affect development in infancy and do not address affect development in latency, adolescence, or adulthood. The chapters in this section were written to address these gaps in the literature.

Daniel Brown, in "Affective Development, Psychopathology, and Adaptation," describes a comprehensive and integrative theory of affect development from early infancy through adulthood, basing the chapter on developmental-lines theory, an integration of psychoanalytic clinical-developmental theory, and a rapidly growing body of empirical findings from child observations and child experimental studies. According to Brown's model, there are at least eight major developmental tasks along the normal line of affective development: affect expression, affect experience, affect tolerance, affect verbalization, affect defense, affect orientation, transformation of affect, and consciousness of affect processes. These tasks span from infancy (affect expression and affect experience) to childhood (affect tolerance, verbalization, and defense) to latency (affect orientation) to adolescence (transformation of affect) and to adulthood (consciousness of affect processes). A strength of this model is its extension to latency, adolescence, and adulthood. The developmental task posed at each stage in the structuralization of affect is discussed in detail along with supporting clinical theory, child observation, and empirical data.

Brown shows how his theory of affective development can be applied to clinical situations. He understands psychopathology as a failure of affective development, describing four primary levels of affective psychopathological organization: psychosis, personality disorder, neurosis, and relative health (the psychopathology of everyday life). Each is associated with a failure to master one or more of the tasks along the line of affective development.

One limitation of Brown's developmental model for affect is that it focuses on immediate affective states. Allen Palmer, in "Affect and Character," addresses the related issue of enduring affective structures. According to his review of the psychoanalytic theories of affect and character development, repetitive sequences of affect can lead to greater continuity and stability of affective states over time. Central to Palmer's thinking is the concept of structuralization of affect. Repetitive sequences of affective states, or evolving core affective dispositions, become integrated with ideational, memory, and regulatory structures and also with self and object representations. The outcome is the formation of stable character style with a unique affective tone or affective signature.

Neither Brown's nor Palmer's chapter adequately addresses the complex issue of individual differences in affective development. Leslie Brody, in "On Understanding Gender Differences in the Expression of Emotions: Gender Roles, Socialization, and Language" thoroughly reviews the existing literature on sex role and gender differences in affective development, and presents some of her own current research on this important topic. Although methodological limitations in many of the studies on gender differences have limited this area of inquiry, nevertheless a clear pattern emerges from the many studies. Brody presents consistent research findings that boys and girls significantly differ in emotional expression. Generally, girls are more intensely emotionally expressive than boys, except in the expression of anger, and boys tend to express emotions more in action-oriented behaviors than girls do. Brody appreciates that these gender differences arise from various sources, such as genetics, biological constitution, and socialization. She believes, however, that socialization makes the main contribution to gender differences. Empirical findings, for example, suggest that emotions are discussed and displayed by parents in one way with boys and in a different way with girls. It seems that parents socialize the emotional development of boys and girls in quite different ways between them. Brody discusses historical differences in gender roles that contribute to this differentiated socialization.

Taken as a unit, these three chapters define the domain of affective developmental theory with respect to the immediate experience of affective states, enduring affective structures associated with character traits, and individual differences in affective development. The next section will show how these dimensions of affect can be applied to clinical situations and other areas of experience.

Chapter 1

AFFECTIVE DEVELOPMENT, PSYCHOPATHOLOGY, AND ADAPTATION

Daniel Brown

THE CONCEPT OF DEVELOPMENTAL LINES

There is growing consensus that adult psychopathology can be understood with reference to normal child development. This point of view is represented currently by a movement in psychoanalysis known as developmental lines thinking (A. Freud, 1965), structural psychoanalysis (Baker, 1990; Gedo and Goldberg, 1973) or developmental psychopathology (Sroufe and Rutter, 1984). The field represents an integration of the rapidly proliferating literature on child observational and experimental studies on one hand and a variety of psychoanalytic theories on the other, namely, object relations theory (Horner, 1979; Jacobson, 1973; Kernberg, 1968, 1976; Mahler, Pine, and Bergman, 1975), self psychology (Bach, 1977; Kohut, 1971; Lichtenberg, 1975; Ornstein, 1974; Stolorow and Lachmann, 1980), ego psychology (Blanck and Blanck, 1974), affective development theory (Brown, 1985; Emde, 1983; Greenspan and Lourie, 1981; Sroufe, 1979b), and integrative psychoanalytic theory (Blanck and Blanck, 1974; Gedo, 1984; Gedo and Goldberg, 1973). Human development is seen as a series of phase-specific tasks, the successful mastery of which leads to the emergence of more and more complex psychic structures. Psychopathology is viewed as a failure to master expected developmental tasks or predicted structural achievements.

A comprehensive theory of affective development has not yet appeared, although a number of models for the developmental line of affect have appeared in the literature, particularly in the last decade (Bridges, 1932; Emde, 1983; Greenspan and Lourie, 1981; Kagan and Greenspan, 1986; Lane and Schwartz, 1987; Lewis and Brooks, 1978; Piers and Curry, 1985; Sander, 1975; Sroufe, 1979b, 1984; Stern, 1985). Each of these differs in its conceptualization of and perspective on the stages of affective development. Few of these models are comprehensive in scope in that the developmental stages beyond preschool years are rarely described in any detail.

At this time, there is enough convergence in the thinking about these recently appearing models for affective development to justify an integrated and comprehensive model for normal affective development. The model described here builds on the previous works and is integrative in its attempt to synthesize a rapidly growing body of empirical findings from child observation and child experimental studies with psychoanalytically based theories of developmental psychopathology. The model is comprehensive in its attempt to elaborate the stages of affective development from infancy to adulthood.

THE STAGES OF AFFECTIVE DEVELOPMENT
IN THE NORMAL CHILD

Affect Expression

Some theorists have argued that affect is innate because a complex array of affective expressions is observable shortly after birth (Demos, 1982; Izard, 1977; Tomkins, 1962, 1963, 1968). Other theorists have proposed models for a sequential unfolding of discrete stages of normal affective development (Emde, 1983; Greenspan and Lourie, 1981; Lane and Schwartz, 1987; Lewis and Brooks, 1978; Sander, 1975; Sroufe, 1979a,b,c, 1984; Sroufe and Jacobvitz, 1989). According to them, affective experience is contingent on the development of self-observational capacity and upon the maturation of cognitive capacities. Even though genetic and developmental perspectives on affect are a matter of considerable controversy, the nature and nurture positions need not entirely contradict each other. The genetic theories are based on observations of infant affective expression, the developmental theories on inferences about infant subjectively felt affective experience. Both pertain to different aspects of affect, expression, and experience, respectively. The position taken in this chapter is that the capacity for affective expression may be innate, but the capacity for affect experience unfolds in the course of development.

Research strongly suggests that the equipment for affective expression is innate. The normal infant is biologically endowed with a repertoire of specific, basic, programmed response patterns, which are made up primarily of sets of discrete facial muscles but which may also include visceral (autonomic, glandular) elements. Infants' facial response patterns are highly specific, so that Tomkins has considered the face to be the "organ of affect" (Tomkins, 1968), although this view has been disputed (Ortony and Turner, 1990). Such display patterns can be recognized accurately at birth (Demos, 1982) and can be identified accurately across cultures (Ekman and Friesen, 1986; Izard, 1971).

According to Tomkins (1962, 1963, 1968, 1970; Tomkins and McCarter, 1964), there are eight primary facial response patterns. Each of these eight affective expressive patterns occurs in both a moderate and a high-intensity version: interest-excitement, enjoyment-joy, surprise-startle, distress-anguish, fear-terror, shame-humiliation, contempt-disgust, and anger-rage (Tomkins, 1968). Izard (1977) recognizes ten primary patterns in the belief that contempt and disgust represent separate facial response patterns. He also adds guilt to his list of emotions. The first three listed as basic affects are the so-called positive emotions; the rest are the negative emotions. According to Tomkins and Izard, each of these facial display patterns is characterized by a discrete neuromuscular pattern. Each is triggered by a specific pattern of neural stimulation. For example, interest-excitement is triggered by an increase in neural stimulation, typically by change or novelty. Eyebrows turn down, and the gaze remains fixed on its object during the state of interest. Enjoyment-joy, triggered by a sharp reduction in the gradient of neural stimulation, is characterized by the muscles' forming the smiling response. Surprise-startle, triggered by a sharp increase in neural stimulation, is characterized by raising the eyebrows and blinking the eyes. Distress-anguish is triggered by sustained levels of nonoptimal stimulation and is characterized by the muscles of the crying response—the corners of the lips are pulled downward and the eyebrows become arched. Fear-terror is triggered by a too rapid acceleration in neural stimulation and is characterized by keeping the eyes frozen open in a fixed stare and exhibiting a tendency to move away from the object (and often by autonomic changes). Shame-humiliation occurs in the context of an emotional relationship and functions to inhibit interest and to reduce facial communication. It is characterized by a lowering of the head, eyes, and eyelids. Contempt-disgust is characterized by raising the upper lip in a sneer and functions to distance oneself from the object. Anger-rage is triggered by interference with goal-oriented activity and is characterized by a frown and a clenched jaw.

Tomkins (1968) believes that each of these facial display patterns is a way of automatically signaling the continuous vicissitudes of stimulation—especially when the intensity of the stimulation is too weak or too strong, when the duration of the stimulation is too long or too short (distress and anger), or when the rate of stimulation is either changing in one direction or another (surprise and fear) or maintained at an optimal level of stimulation (interest). Other facial display patterns function to inhibit interest (shame and contempt). Tomkins believes that the facial display patterns are reflexive behaviors in response to unlearned stimuli.

There is some debate as to what triggers such early affective expressions. Evolutionary theorists like Tomkins believe that the neonate is capable of rapid and spontaneous responding to the vicissitudes of stimulation through specific facial display patterns. Tomkins believes that the facial display patterns are innately activated via preprogrammed subcortical centers according to the vicissitudes of neural firing—that is, changes in the intensity and duration of stimulation. In this view, the neonate manifests direct and spontaneous changes in affective expression according to the contingencies of the internal and external stimulation. Pribram and Melges (1969, 1980) and other neurobiologists argue that it is not the amount of neural firing per se but the organization or "configuration of neural activity" that triggers affective expression. Although the relative contribution of innate programming and early learned organization remains unclear, both Tomkins and Pribram agree that the neonate is capable of rapid and spontaneous response to the vicissitudes of stimulation through the use of specific facial expressions.

Facial display patterns have a clear adaptive function: They facilitate survival by automatically signaling to the care-giving environment the need to adjust the pattern of stimulation for the neonate, whose perceptual system has not yet matured. Facial affective displays function to amplify sensory stimuli (Tomkins, 1962, 1963, 1968), to highlight the salience of vital stimulus-events, and to communicate the need for modulation of the stimulus-pattern to the care-giving environment (Demos, 1982). Affective expressions "guarantee sensitivity to whatever is new, whatever is continuous for any period of time, and to whatever is ceasing to happen," so that the neonate can find the optimal flow of stimulation that will prompt the perceptual system toward its own maturation (Tomkins, 1968, p. 330).

The eight or ten basic facial display patterns are present at and functioning from birth, but the operation of their muscle groups becomes increasingly refined and coordinated as the child grows. The infant learns to blend discrete display patterns into combinations. The eight or ten basic units function like an expressive alphabet, in which an infinite variety of complex blends become possible that allow for the expression of many subtle emotional nuances.

The expression of certain facial display patterns are either enhanced or inhibited in certain cultural milieus. The reflexive action of these basic units of facial display becomes increasingly mediated by cognitive processes later in development. Thinking about or imagining situations that evoke distinct affects is accompanied by discrete facial display patterns, not overtly noticeable to the subject or the observer but clearly detectable by electromyographic (EMG) response (Schwartz et al., 1976). Thus, for most adults, the continuous facial expression of affects is observable only subliminally, while discontinuous or discrete moments of strong affect (affective states) may be more readily observable to others

The Development of Affective Experience

Interest and Self-Regulation

The task of affective development in the first quarter of the first year of life is twofold: The external task is to actively search the environment so as to develop schemes for perceptual information. The internal task is to maintain inner homeostasis during perceptual maturation. Greenspan and Lourie (1981) have coined the terms "engagement" and "self regulation" for each of these tasks, respectively. The neurobiologist, Pribram (1980) uses the terms "participation" and "preparation," respectively, for each. He stresses the child's active role in bringing organized stability to the central nervous system. Both processes are part of an overall task of regulation of input, whether external or internal.

In the first months of life, affective development is closely associated with the maturation of the perceptual system. Therefore, Stechler and Carpenter (1967) speak of "sensory-affective intelligence" and Izard (1977) of "affective-perceptual integration" in order to capture the inseparability of perceptual and affective maturation during this phase of development. The central nervous system shows increasing development (Greenspan and Lourie, 1981). The various sense systems also mature albeit at different rates. Hearing seems to develop earlier, and seeing, touching, and so forth, thereafter. As these sensory systems mature, the infant is prepared to take in the world.

The infant shows progressive ability for sustaining periods of alert inactivity (Wolff, 1966), vigilance (Stechler and Carpenter, 1967), or interest (Izard, 1971) during the first month of life, especially in the environment of the care-giver, as the infant and care-giver adapt to each other's rhythms with the best "temporal fit" (Sander and Julia, 1966). At such times, the infant opens the eyes wide, fixes the gaze, and scans with the eyes but otherwise remains motorically inactive. The infant actively takes in sensory information. By the fourth week, the infant has developed the capacity to turn the head toward specific stimuli (Stechler and

Carpenter, 1967) and can actively search the environment for an array of new experiences. According to the incongruity hypothesis (Hunt, 1965; Kagan, 1978; Stechler and Carpenter, 1967), the infant becomes especially interested in discrepant stimuli (novel, complex, and changing stimuli) and responds with particular interest toward any stimuli initiated by the care-giver, for example, a voice or a rattle (Field, 1978). Some argue that the context in which the stimuli occur is also important even at this early age (Sroufe, 1979b). For example, a mother wearing a mask may elicit a smile from her child in a familiar home environment; the same mask worn by the mother may elicit a cry in the laboratory.

Other developmentalists argue that the infant extracts "invariant information" (Gibson, 1966; Stern, 1985) or the "configuration of neural activity" (Pribram, 1980) in its successive samplings of the world by means of gaze or locomotion and through this process develops generalized structures for the information obtained. From this perspective, the infant is believed to be especially sensitive not to the stimulus-characteristics of the environment per se but to the temporal features inherent in perceptual samplings. The child must actively participate in, not passively receive, the environment in order to construct the schemas. These developmentalists emphasize that tempo, rhythm, and movement may be important to the child because all perceptual information across sense modalities may be translated into temporal features (Stern, 1985). For example, seven-month-old infants do not recognize specific facial expressive displays accurately by categorizing them according to stimulus-characteristics alone. They accurately select a specific facial display only when accompanied by a matching auditory stimulus (Phillips et al., 1990). Infants are especially attuned to the intonation and melody of the care-giver's speech and can extract the intended affective meaning even when words are not used, or, if used, are not understood (Fernald, 1989). Conversely, the infant's spontaneous vocalizations serve to communicate meaningful information about the infant's state that are intelligible to the attentive care-giver (Papousek, 1989). The infant is capable of organizing rudimentary perceptual schemes that enable some stimulus information to become more meaningful than other.

The ability to extract and organize sensible information from the environment is in part dependent on internal regulation. According to the input dysfunction theory, information processing and activation level covary (Venables, 1964). During the extremes of hypoarousal or hyperarousal, the motor and perceptual systems become dysregulated. The infant withdraws. During moderate arousal, the infant shows increasing motor coordination, autonomic regulation, and increased perceptual organization. Active stimulus seeking in turn can contribute to increased fluctuation in the infant's internal state. Stimulus seeking creates tension, sometimes pleasurable, sometimes unpleasureable (Sroufe, 1979b, 1984). The infant–caregiver system is faced with the task of regulation through which the infant learns self-regulation in part from the care-giver's attempts to provide a good enough environment, which minimizes the extremes of hyperarousal and hypoarousal (Greenspan and Lourie, 1981). In other words, the infant learns to maintain the organization of internal state and behavior in the face of marked shifts in arousal (Sroufe, 1979a). Stern (1985) calls this process the infant's experience with the "self-regulating other." The child's capacity for self-regulation develops from a multiplicity of soothing methods used by the care-giver (Birns, Blank, and Bridger, 1966), and it also develops in part from the caregiver's attempt to provide the infant with the full range of rich sensory experiences— looking, hearing, touching, holding, and rocking—to prime the perceptual system toward its own maturation. The care-giver who intentionally talks baby talk, varies intonations, makes baby faces, and gazes into the infant at close range provides the kind of input that most easily resonates with the infant's perceptual capacities (Stern, 1985). The task for both infant and care-giver is to find the optimal range of activation at any given moment, which primes the perceptual system toward its own maturation and contributes to the increased organization of perceptual schemas. Although significant individual differences do occur, a stable pattern of an optimal level of irritability can be observed from the second week of life through the end of the first year—a pattern of irritability that is associated with fear in reaction to novel stimuli, fussing in response to soothing efforts, and distress following failed attempts to reach a desired object (Worobey and Blajda, 1989).

The psychoanalytic literature, with its concept of homeostasis, has concerned itself with the extremes of activation and tension reduction (Brenner, 1980; Rapaport, 1953). The concept of homeostasis presumes that tension builds up and presses for discharge when the baby is either inactive or threatened by overwhelming stimuli. The concept of situation-specific tensions (Sroufe, 1979b, 1984) in the developmental literature concerns itself with moderate levels of activation, based on the assumption that the infant intentionally seeks optimal tension levels. According to Sroufe, "tension is a natural consequence of the infant's engagement of normal stimulation." Tension is not always present nor does it always necessitate discharge. The infant may intentionally alter the state of excitation in order to enhance the intake of new information (Stechler and Carpenter, 1967). Although the debate between the drive and information-processing theories of activation may not be resolved fully, the psychoanalytic notion of homeostasis and the developmental notion of active seeking of optimal tension probably represent points along a continuum: from hypoarousal, to moderate arousal, to hyperarousal. Tension reduction is perhaps a goal only when the infant fails to achieve an optimal range of stimulation. Active seeking of stimulation may be the norm most of the time, even if such a search causes significant shifts in the level of arousal. The infant and care-giver are engaged in the continuous task of regulating the internal and external state to adjust the range of stimuli and to find the right level of activation to take in stimuli in an organized way. The task for both infant and care-giver is to balance the internal and external regulation of input in a way that maximizes perceptual development.

Emde's studies (1983; Emde, Gaensbauer and Harmon, 1976; Emde et al., 1978) have lent empirical support to this theory. Emde devised a multidimensional measure for the state of activation of the infant, after his studies showed that three dimensions were observable by the third month: activation (changes in expressive intensity on the face); hedonic tone (changes in the pleasurable or unpleasurable quality); and changes in the internal and external orientation (Matias, Cohn, and Ross, 1989).

It is very difficult to know the infant's subjective experience during these changes of activation. Lewis maintains that it would be incorrect to speak of affective *experience* prior to the development of self-awareness, which develops from the fourth to the eighth month of life. Tomkins (1962, 1968) and Izard (1977) describe the child's interest and excitement in the world, although they view this interest and excitement through observations of facial displays, not through the child's subjective experience. According to Izard (1977), "emotional experience *is* present at least in some rudimentary form" (p. 395). Most developmentalists believe that the infant is capable of experiencing at least a sense of aliveness (Bennett, 1983) or alertness (Wolff, 1966). Stern's (1985) notion of an "emergent self" suggests that the infant is capable of becoming aware of the very process of emerging organization and of the various transformations that the infant experiences within the body. Likewise, Stechler and Carpenter (1967) in their notion of a "pre-self" believe that episodes of alert inactivity provide an "open space" through which infants take in the world and get a sense of their own existence.

The Attachment Bond and Primary Emotional Experience

The Primary Attachment Relationship. An important shift in affective development occurs with the establishment of a solid attachment relationship between the second and seventh month (Bennett, 1983; Greenspan and Lourie, 1981; Mahler et al., 1975; Sroufe, 1979b,c, 1984). This attachment relationship once established remains stable over the next months and first few years (Stern, 1974a; Waters, 1978). Affective-perceptual integration naturally tends toward greater selective interest in and engagement with the care-giver's behaviors. The infant becomes generally more responsive to social interactions in addition to the regulation of internal states. The intensity of the bond begins with the infant's interest in making visual contact (Klaus et al., 1972). By three to four weeks, the infant already shows visual preference for the live human face (Stechler and Carpenter, 1967). The care-giver's face consistently elicits a variety of infant facial expressions, in particular the social smiling response by the end of the second and third month and laughter by the fourth and fifth month (Sroufe, 1979b, 1984). By the eighth to tenth week, a stationary face consistently elicits the social smile. Through smiling, the infant both regulates the state of tension and communicates to the care-giver. The transformation of the endogenous into the social smile represents the transition from the infant's concern with the regulation of internal tension states to the processing of information regarding social interactions (Sroufe and Waters, 1976). By one and a half years, the smile has been thoroughly transformed into a social signal, the frequency of which is dependent on the degree of attentiveness of the care-giver (Jones and Raag, 1989). In fact, over these months, affective facial displays come to serve as "social signals" (Emde et al., 1978).

The infant's now matured units of affective expression—specific facial display patterns, the gaze, the social smile, the distress cry, and cooing vocalizations—elicit a variety of maternal responses. The care-giver responds to the infant's displays with slow and clearly presented, exaggerated facial displays, vocalizations, and gazes (Stern, 1974b). A mutual exchange develops in which the infant and the care-giver strive to imitate each other's expressive gestures (Pawlby, 1977) with a wide repertoire of facial displays that are exchanged at a high rate of change (changing about every seven or eight seconds) (Malatesta and Haviland, 1982). Both engage in a mutually enhancing kind of spontaneous play (Bennnet, 1983; Stern, 1985) or "reciprocal reward system" (Emde et al., 1976). The care-giver's response also serves to regulate the infant's state by responding to the infant's expressed distress or enjoyment.

Through these reciprocal spontaneous exchanges, primarily of positive facial displays and attenuation of negative affective displays by the care-giver (Malatesta and Haviland, 1982; Malatesta et al., 1989), a powerful affective bond or attachment relationship develops (Greenspan and Lourie, 1981; Lewis and Feiring, 1989; Sroufe, 1979a/b, 1984), which is built up after thousands of gratifying experiences with the care-giver (Murphy, 1983). Greenspan and Greenspan (1985) refer to this stage as "falling in love" with the infant. According to them, the task presented to the care-giver is to "encourage a deep, rich human relationship that contains the range of emerging human feelings and is, for the most part, pleasurable and positive" (p. 41). The care-giver does this by "wooing" the infant through gentle attempts to engage the infant through glances, vocalizations, spontaneous facial displays, cuddling, and presentation of interesting objects and using the infant's elicited affective expressions as guidelines for subsequent interventions. The care-giver also protects the child from the extremes of understimulation and overstimulation by wooing and soothing, respectively.

In a "good enough infant–care-giver system" (Sander, 1975), the care-giver is available, responsive, involved, and nonintrusive (Ainsworth et al., 1978; Biringen and Robinson, 1991), contingently responds and closely matches (Malatesta and Haviland, 1982), or carefully mirrors (Kohut, 1971) the spontaneously elicited affective displays of the infant. The signs of a successful and loving exchange include the infant's ability to use the full range of the senses in the service of this exchange, an increased capacity for warmth and physical affection, and an increased ability to maintain the loving exchange for long durations and to recover from interruptions to that intense connection (Greenspan and Greenspan, 1985). Ainsworth et al. (1978) and Ainsworth (1979) emphasize the infant's increased capacity for organization. A highly individualized expressive style develops over the first years of life (Abramson, 1991). An infant who manifests "security of attachment" shows increased organization and coordination of perceptual and motor responses and consistent behavior across a wide variety of situations (Sroufe, 1979a).

As the infant and care-giver repeatedly engage in this kind of mutual exchange, the infant comes to realize that affective expressions and behaviors produce responses and learns about cause-effect relationships, taking the initiative to intentionally elicit desired responses from the care-giver. The child attempts to integrate affective expressions across senses and with greater coordination of organized motor responses (Greenspan and Greenspan, 1985). The infant may smile in order to elicit a smile back. When encountering an uncertain situation, the infant manifests social referencing (Campos and Sternberg, 1981), looking to the care-giver to elicit a facial display before proceeding with the behavior. Greenspan and Greenspan (1985) call this stage "intentional communication." Likewise, the care-giver is able to elicit desired responses from the infant, and the two develop the capacity for joint regulation (Sander, 1975), shared intentions (Stern, 1985), and intersubjective relatedness (Trevarthan and Hubley, 1978; Stern, 1985). Each strives to introduce and share new behaviors and expressions in the context of mutual sharing. These affective displays are fundamental to learning in the child (Sullivan and Lewis, 1989). An infant who manifests "confidence in communication" is able to get the care-giver to respond and communicates with increasingly mature ways over the months (Murphy, 1983). The care-giver not only carefully matches the infant's facial display but also intro-

duces a variety of new expressive displays into the interaction, which
enable the child to become familiar with a wide range of affects. By
modeling "display rules," the care-giver facilitates the process of socialization of affective expressions (Malatesta and Haviland, 1982).

Self Observational Capacity. In a good enough infant–care-giver relationship, the care-giver is reasonably attuned to the affective expressions
of the infant. Repeated experience with the care-giver's atonement or
mirroring becomes the basis of internalization of the infant's self-
observational capacity. According to Lewis and Brooks (1978), self-
awareness develops during the fourth to eighth month. The infant gradually learns that the body exists as distinct from others, that the body
experiences a variety of internal changes, and that perception of redun-
dancy in these bodily changes over time becomes the prerequisite for the
emergence of a sense of self. Stern (1985) speaks of a "core self," which
develops from the second to the sixth month out of the infant's awareness
and coherence of the increased organization of actions, perceptions, and
affective expressions. The schematic organization of the self naturally
arises out of the capacity to link experiences continuously across time, an
outgrowth of the maturation of memory.

Maturation of the Autonomic Response System. The care-giver's attunement to the infant's changing bodily states enables the infant to develop
greater and greater awareness of internal visceral experience. The autonomic nervous system shows increasing maturation. Beginning around
the third to twelfth month, the infant manifests an orienting response to
stimuli (Sokolov, 1960), fixing the gaze and turning the head while the
body remains for the most part inactive. The infant also shows predictable cardiac deceleration and an increase in blood flow to the brain during
the orienting response. By the fifth month, the autonomic response
system, especially cardiovascular response patterns, shows signs of increased organization and stabilization (Izard et al., 1991; Lewis, 1979).
Consistent and reliable measures of autonomic change can be made at this
time (Campos et al., 1978; Fox and Fitzgerald, 1990; Izard et al., 1991).
Except under certain conditions, however, these autonomic changes are
poorly synchronized with the infant's facial affective displays. Nevertheless, the infant is capable of experiencing a variety of autonomic or
viscerally based changes in internal state.

Mood Development and Early Affective Experience. Moods are not
primarily a form of affective expression. Moods represent the infant's
dawning awareness of visceral change, that is, the perception of autonomically mediated somatic experience at any given time (Schmale, 1964). In
adults, moods and self-focused attention are interrelated (Wood, Saltzberg, and Goldsamt, 1990). In the developing child, the growing capacity
for self-observation leads to mood development. Moods constitute an

early form of affective experience. Moods are a "barometer of the ego state" (Jacobson, 1971). Because the infant is developing the capacity to become aware of visceral changes, Gemelli (1949) calls this type of experience the experience of "affective tendencies."

Though moods signify a shift in emphasis from affective expression to experience, mood development nevertheless depends on the mutual affective displays between the infant and the care-giver. In Tronick, Ricks, and Cohn's (1982) still-face experiments, normal infants were observed in interaction with their care-givers, after which Tronick et al. instructed the mothers to intentionally suppress all facial displays during subsequent interactions. The infants temporarily lost their capacity to produce facial display patterns (although subsequent studies have shown that decreased expressivity is more apparent in girls and that boys become more behaviorally active [Carter, Mayers, and Pajer, 1990]) and did not fully recover for hours after the mothers resumed normal expressive displays. Tronick believes that care-givers who are unable to generate continuous affective displays (due to withdrawal or depression) may affect the infant's capacity for spontaneous affective displays, which may predispose the child to the development of depressed moods. Temporary loss of toys (Murphy, 1983) or absence of the care-giver (Murphy and Moriarty, 1976) may likewise significantly affect the child's capacity for affective expression and the nature of experienced moods. The "accumulate distillate" of infant–care-giver interaction may contribute significantly to the quality and variety of internal moods (Tronick et al., 1982; Tronick and Cohn, 1989).

The Onset of Negative Affects; The So-Called Eighth Month Anxieties. According to Campos et al. (1978), the onset of negative emotional reactions constitutes a "developmental shift." Infants show little evidence of fear before five or six months. During the second half year, definite fear of strangers, separation, looming stimuli, and novel or unfamiliar objects and surroundings emerges (Marks, 1987). The infant in the visual cliff experiment is required to crawl to the care-giver across a solid textual surface and then across a glass surface about four feet above the floor. Prior to five months, the infant shows cardiac deceleration, increased attentiveness to depth, and a decrease in crying while on the glass (deep) side. At about eight to nine months, the infant shows cardiac acceleration, decreased attentiveness, and increased crying while on the glass side (Campos et al., 1978). Similar psychophysiological response patterns have been observed for negative reactions to strangers, separation, and looming stimuli, although there is some variation in the age of onset. In these studies, heart rate acceleration is not correlated with facial displays of distress in eight- to nine-month-olds (Lewis, Brooks, and Haviland, 1978). When the child looks distressed, the heart rate may not indicate same; when the heart rate accelerates, the child may not display distress.

Visceral changes and facial expressions are not yet synchronized (Lewis et al., 1978).

The Signal Function of Affect. Affects also take on a signal function (Emde et al., 1978) at about the age of nine months. Because of the development of cognition and memory, affective expressions are not always given in response to immediate interactions with the care-giver. The child, for example, may express a distress or fearful response in anticipation of an actual feared event (Emde et al., 1978; Schur, 1955; Zaporozhets and Neverovich, 1974). Moreover, increased awareness of internal visceral change, occurring with little correspondence to external expressive displays, implies a gap between internal affective experience and external affective expression. The infant is increasingly responsive to internal visceral, especially negative-felt visceral, experience. At this stage of development, the psychoanalytic definitions of anxiety as a "response to an internal danger" (Freud, 1926) and of the signal function of affects (Allen, 1980; Rapaport, 1953) apply to the infant's experience.

The Development of Primary Emotional Experience. At this stage of development, the capacity for primary emotional experience emerges. According to the James-Lange theory of emotion (James, 1980), two conditions must be met for genuine affective experience: visceral change and subjective awareness of this change. The six- to nine-month-old child meets these criteria. Autonomically mediated visceral changes occur with greater consistency, self-observational capacity develops, and therefore the child is increasingly aware of visceral shifts and the increasingly organized patterns of visceral change within the body. By the end of this stage of development, the normal child has achieved the capacity for genuine affective experience.

Somatic-Cognitive Integration

The period roughly from nine to twelve months is best characterized as a period of integration and differentiation (Greenspan and Lourie, 1981), and early maturation of cognitive processes becomes evident. To some extent, healthy emotional development is a prerequisite to normal cognitive development (Rohm, 1972). Schemas allow the infant to anticipate. The infant can now actively search for hidden objects or anticipate a whole object on the basis of seeing part of it (Piaget, 1981). Schemas also become organized into more complex groupings through which the infant is able to link discrete but successive behaviors together into complex coordinated chains (Piaget, 1981; Stern, 1985).

Another example of integration is seen in the synchronization of the expressive/display and experiential/visceral dimensions of affect. The facial expressive display constitutes an action- tendency of which the developing child is increasingly aware. In this sense, the maturation and utilization of the facial display system naturally lead to the inner experience of affect (Fogel and Reimers, 1989). Interpersonally, the integration of affective expression and experience constitutes the outcome of careful mirroring of the child's internal state upon the care-giver's recognition of an affective display. When the mother says to the child, "Don't be frightened," the mother acknowledges the child's affective display and simultaneously draws attention to the child's internal visceral experience. As this empathic response is repeated during many infant–care-giver interactions, synchronization of affective expression and experience is increased. Infants on the visual cliff show a consistent covariation between their facial display of distress, attending behavior, and autonomic functioning, for example, heart rate acceleration by the latter quarter of the first year of life (Lewis et al., 1978).

In adults, the interrelationship of facial display and cognitive processes is well established. Highly specific facial display patterns and distinct patterns of facial EMG activity can be observed to accompany the experience of specific emotions or to follow instructions to imagine specific emotions, such as happiness or anger. Conversely, instructions to intentionally make the facial expressive display for a specific affect also generate the corresponding internal affective experience (Blumberg and Izard, 1991; Duclos et al., 1989; Laird, 1974; Schwartz, Brown, and Ahern, 1980).

Still another example of increasing integration is in the area of self-awareness. By the end of the first year, a developmental shift occurs in cognition from similarity-based attributions to category-based attributions (Inagaki, 1989). The maturing cognitive capacities bring self-awareness to a new level—what Lewis et al. (1978) call "the categorical self." Rudimentary attributes about the self such as early social categories and comparisons begin to emerge. Stern calls this the emergence of the "subjective self" through which infants acquire the distinction between their mind and the mind of others.

The psychoanalytic object-relations theorists have emphasized how the infant constructs the "representational world" (Sandler and Rosenblatt, 1962; Sandler and Sandler, 1978) from the impressions of repeated interactions with the care-giver. These representations are believed to develop during the period of primary attachment, or what is referred to as "normal symbiosis," during which the developing impressions become differentiated into a core good selfobject representation and a core bad selfobject representation. Beginning in roughly the 9- to 12-month period, the good-self and bad-self representations become integrated into a self-concept, and the good-object and bad-object representations into a representational world. While the self and object representations are maturing and becoming integrated during this phase, such developing representations are probably not genuine mental or symbolic representations (Greenspan and Lourie, 1981) but rather schemas through which self and other become seen as separate. Nevertheless, it is likely that at this stage of development, the infant begins linking affective experience with some sort of representation. Experienced affect is now associated with the emerging self or with experience with others. Through the linking of affect and representation it is possible to speak of self-object-affect units (Kernberg, 1976).

The development of schematic groupings allows the infant to render considerable specificity to internal affective experience. The range of possible visceral changes is limited, but the capacity to experience a great variety of specific affective states is vast. According to Schacter and Singer's (1962) classic definition of emotion, cognition is the means by which affective states are given considerable specificity. The maturation of cognition and its integration with affective experience result in considerable expansion of the range of specific experienced affects (Pine, 1979). By the end of the first year, the infant experiences the emergence of very specific affective states (Bridges, 1932). The developing child can make clear experiential distinctions between such affective states as happy, sad, and mad. As cognitive capacities continue to mature, the child's ability to make more and more subtle distinctions between internal emotional states improves.

By the end of the first year, the infant has more or less completed the development of genuine affective experience. Genuine affect is a complex product composed of at least four components (Kagan, 1978): (1) a discrete facial display pattern, (2) a specific pattern of autonomically mediated visceral change (Ax, 1953), (3) subjective awareness of the visceral change, and (4) a specific constellation of cognitions (Schachter and Singer, 1962) in addition to representations regarding the visceral change. Unlike moods, genuine affects are directed toward representations of self and others and are embedded in a matrix of memories and cognitions (Klein, 1967) linking the internal visceral shifts to external reality. Each of these dimensions of affect is interrelated, so that the emergent structure of affect retains its own "dynamic unity" across different behaviors and contexts (Yarrow, 1979, p. 951). The internally experienced affective state is synchronized, in a relative sense, with the expressed facial display and also with the cognitions associated with the affect (Blumberg and Izard, 1991).

Now the infant possesses a dual system for affect: a fast-acting, highly specific reflexive facial expressive system, which serves both as a means of social communication with others and as a source of feedback about external reality, and a slower-acting visceral experiential system, which can serve as a very global indicator of the state of the organism (mood) or as a highly specific and stable affective state evoked in response to the meaning an event has to the infant. The former facial display system pertains more to the quality or specificity of the emotion; the latter visceral system pertains more to the perceived intensity of emotional state (Laird, 1974; Leventhal, 1980). The one-year-old possesses the capacity for a wide array of genuine affective experiences.

The Development of a Psychological Sense of Self and the Capacity for Affect Tolerance

In the toddler years, the infant enters a new phase of development—what Mahler et al. (1975) have called the separation-individuation stage of development. These years are marked by the full maturation of the perceptual and motor systems. The child also makes great strides in the development of cognition, memory (especially representational memory), and language. With increased perceptual and motor skills, the child becomes capable of turning interest away from the attachment relationship toward an active interest in the external environment. Mahler (1961) calls this practicing subphase the "love affair with the world." The child experiences various states of elation and considerable pleasure in mastery by effectively and playfully negotiating the new world and discovering new abilities (Mahler et al., 1975; Murphy, 1983; White, 1959).

The toddler years are also characterized by great strides in cognitive development. The child develops the capacity for genuine mental representations—symbolic representations as opposed to the more rudimentary schemas (Lewis and Brooks, 1978; Greenspan and Lourie, 1981). The capacity for symbolic representation sets the stage for the integration and differentiation of the representational world (Sandler and Rosenblatt, 1962) and the development of an organized representation for the psychological sense of self (Greenspan and Lourie, 1981; Kohut, 1971; Lewis and Brooks, 1978; Mahler et al., 1975).

During this phase, the heretofore relatively autonomous lines of affective and representational development become integrated (Socarides and Stolorow, 1984–85). The symbolic self representation and object representations and the previously developed capacity for differentiated affective experience are synthesized into a common line. From this point in development and thereafter, affective states become associated with the inner experience of self and object representations. The emergent complex constellations of affective states and internal representations of experiences are primarily affective in nature and only secondarily ideational (Basch, 1976; Modell, 1980; Novey, 1961). Affect experience undergoes a change in function. It not only functions as a response to the vicissitudes of external stimulation or as a communication to the care-giver but furthermore serves as a signal for the shifts that occur within the representational world. Certain constellations of internal self repre-sentations, object representations, or both may become activated or deactivated in particular situations. The changes in affective experience correspond to shifts in internal representations as much as to shifts in external stimulation. In this sense, affective states become partially sepa-rated from external stimulation and interactions with others with whom they were originally associated. However, memory capacity during this phase of development is unstable, so the emerging organization of repre-sentations is vulnerable to fragmentation in response to the contingencies of that developmental period (Kohut, 1971). During the rapprochement crisis, which peaks at about 17–18 months, the child is increasingly aware of separateness and experiences a resurgence of stranger and separation anxiety, as well as a tendency toward affective storms, such as panic states and temper tantrums during which the various components of affect become desynchronized, and affective experience becomes disor-ganized.

In terms of affective development, the developmental task of the separation-individuation phase is one of affective tolerance, that is, of the development of the capacity to bear intense affect states and to learn self-management of moods (Mayer et al., 1991). In child studies, both the development of representational thought in the child and the quality of the care-giver's responsiveness are associated with the emergence of the capacity for *self-regulation of internal states,* and this emergent capacity is a predictor of impulse control in the older child (Kopp, 1982; Olson, Bates and Bayles, 1990; Peto, 1968).

According to psychoanalytic theory, the child learns to tolerate intense affective states through the process of what Kohut (1971) and Tolpin (1971) have called "transmuting internalization," in which the child replaces the affect-modulating function, originally provided by the care-giver, with an internal self-soothing structure. The quality of the care-giver's response to the child's affective storms is critical if the child is to internalize self- soothing structures. The care-giver serves as a source of accurate evaluation of the meaning of the child's distress signals and as a source of accurately judging the intensity of distress (Kernberg, 1976; Tolpin, 1971). In a good enough child–care-giver system, the child repeat-edly experiences the care-giver's soothing, affect-modulating responses. As the child's representational capacity matures, he or she is able to sustain an internal representation of the care-giver's soothing function for longer and longer durations. The child intentionally returns to the care-giver as a secure base when necessary. Repeated experiences of the care-giver's soothing coupled with the maturation of representational capacity results in internalization of the soothing function by "bit-by-bit accretion of psychic structure" (Tolpin, 1971).

Transitional objects (Winnicott, 1953) also play a critical role in the process of transmuting internalization. As representational capacity matures, the child endows an inanimate object such as a blanket with the care-giver's soothing function and is thereby able to sustain the illusion of soothing, at least for short intervals, during the care-giver's absence or during the experience of affective storms (e.g., panic or tantrums). The quality of the care-giver's response to the child's use of transitional objects is also important; children whose care-givers interfere with the child's transitional object attachment are more likely to develop psychopathology later in life (Free and Goodrich, 1985).

The care-giver makes several other important contributions to the child's development of affect tolerance. Greenspan and Greenspan (1985) point out that the care-giver's dosing out of gratifying or frustrating experience helps the child to learn to reconcile emotional polarity such as pleasure and frustration. The care-giver must also be affectively available to the child. The care-giver's ability to balance affective availability with soothing helps the child to learn the optimal intensity of experienced affect, free from the extremes of feeling too little or feeling too much. The care-giver's direct expression of emotion is also an important determinant of the quality of the child's developing emotional life. The care-giver models a range of discrete emotions and also models the intensity of the emotion appropriate to a given situation. There is a clear relationship between the range of the care-giver's emotional expression and the range of emotional expression and level of social-emotional development in the child (Denham, 1989).

The hallmark of the separation-individuation phase is the development of the psychological sense of self. The sense of self as an organized structure is derived from three originally separate developmental lines: the development of the body image, the differentiation of self representation and object representation, and the development of a grandiose self. By the end of the separation-individuation period, these separate developmental lines become integrated into a cohesive sense of self. Prior to this, the body-self, the self as differentiated from the object, and the grandiose self are discrete structures (Lichtenberg, 1975). Data from child observations are consistent with this theory, namely, that a concept of the self as a physical entity with identifiable characteristics is present by 14–18 months (Schneider-Rosen and Cicchetti, 1991; Stipek, Gralinski, and Kopp, 1990).

Affective experience, which is viscerally based in the body, becomes associated first with body image, then with increasingly differentiated self representation and object representation, then with the grandiose self, and finally with the integrated, cohesive sense of self. Affective experience is not necessarily associated with the self-structure until very late in the separation-individuation phase. At this point in development, affect begins to become localized within the emerging self-structure. The experiential consequence of localization is that affect becomes something experienced within the body-self, as a felt visceral experience, and the child becomes increasingly aware that affective states are a part of him or her.

Affective Concepts, Fantasies, the Labeling of Affect and Verbalization of Affect

The period roughly between 18 and 36 months is characterized by the child's increasing ability to use ideas and language concomitant to the shift from sensory-motor to preoperational thinking (Piaget, 1952). Because of the rapid maturation of cognitive processes, the child develops considerable skill in conceptualizing (Greenspan and Greenspan, 1985). Behavioral signs of this are evident everywhere, especially in the child's considerable curiosity about the world and how things function. The child is able to name different kinds of toys and knows, for example, that mother functions as feeder and dresser (Greenspan and Greenspan, 1985). As the child experiences a greater sense of agency and competence with respect to increasingly complex goal-directed behavior, there is a marked increase in pleasurable affects associated with the performance of tasks (between 24 and 36 months) (Redding, Morgan, and Harmon, 1988).

The developing skill of conceptualizing is also apparent in the organization of emotional life. Greenspan and Greenspan (1985) call this phase of development "the creation of emotional ideas" because the child is able to synthesize immediately felt emotions into complex patterns, which involve notions of self, other, self-and-other in interaction, and the emotional need state. This emergent organization is apparent when the child demands, "Daddy, horsey ride" or "Mommy, me hungry." The maturation of cognitive development sets the stage for the emergence of wishes, fantasy, and pretend play, and the child becomes capable of organizing notions of reality around needs irrespective of reality (Modell, 1968; Stern, 1985).

This phase of development is best characterized by the acquisition of language. The child's developing skill in acquiring language is directly related to the extent to which care-givers encourage the child to attend to objects, name them, show how they work, and explain their characteristics (Vibbert and Bornstein, 1989). The ability to label internal affective states and to verbalize affect typically lags behind the ability to label objects and things or to describe situations (Katan, 1961) and is related to conceptual development (Kagan, Moss, and Sigel, 1960). By the beginning of the third year, some children are able to put at least some internal experiences into words. These children are beginning to find words for being happy, sad, mad, and sometimes scared (Brody and Harrison, 1987). The extent to which the child develops this skill in labeling and articulating affects is dependent largely on having good role models. Children learn to label their feelings more accurately when the people in their immediate environment talk about feelings frequently and articulate them (Brody and Harrison, 1987). Just as the child acquires new names for objects when parents label objects in the immediate environment for the child, the child also acquires skill in labeling affects to the extent that parents label the child's ongoing feeling states as they are perceived. This state is called "pain," "hurt," "scared," and the like. Parents tend to label things before affects, discomforting and painful feelings before fear, and fear before anger and happiness (Katan, 1961). Moreover, analysis of tape recordings of the speech of mothers of young children (age 2) compared with older children (age 10) and nonmothers has shown that mothers of young children clearly adapt and modify their speech to assist the children in the acquisition of language (Snow, 1972). The speech of these mothers is therefore simple (without subordinate clauses), repetitive of key concepts, and spoken slowly and loudly (Fernald, 1989). The child's ability to learn also is contingent on the quality of the response given by the care-givers to the child's fledgling attempts to verbalize feelings. Inconsistent or distorted familial communications may impair the child's developing ability to verbalize affect (Bateson et al., 1956). In the best sense, the care-giver encourages and supports the child in putting feelings into words slowly; clearly and correctly labels a range of specific affect states as the child expresses them; and furthermore helps the child to correct and refine attempted verbalizations until the child's acquisition of a wide range of affect labels and associated affect concepts.

The child learns not only to verbalize affect but also to take feelings out of the realm of immediate action into the realm of words and thought (Furman, 1978). The child learns the capacity for delay, because verbalization of affect leads to greater control and mastery over affective states (Katan, 1961) and therefore also greatly reinforces the capacity to tolerate affects and modulate behavior (Caulfield et al., 1989). Affect experience becomes less somatic and more cognitive (Krystal, 1974, 1975, 1977; Schur, 1955, 1969). Language also serves the child as a kind of transitional mode of relatedness. When the parent leaves the child, the child can be observed to carry on a continuous monologue with the absent parent as a way of maintaining the connection (Newson, Newson, and Mahalski, 1982; Stern, 1985). The child is now capable of using words and complex gestures to express needs and feelings and can say, "Me mad," or "No bed"

(Greenspan and Greenspan, 1985). The child is also capable of mutual negotiations and meaning by carrying on a dialogue with the care-giver and
beginning to negotiate needs, a characteristic aspect of the terrible twos.

During this period of conceptual and linguistic development, a new
sense of self emerges—what Stern (1985) calls the "verbal self." By 18
months, children show the ability to become the object of their own
reflections. Lewis and Brooks-Gunn (1979) have illustrated this development in their now well-known mirror behavior experiment in which a
spot of rouge was painted on each child's face. Children younger than 18
months pointed to the mirror upon seeing their reflection in it. Around 18
months, certainly thereafter, children began to point to the rouge spot on
their own face instead of in the mirror. From 18 to 24 months, children
begin to use the pronouns I, me, and mine (Stern, 1985) and are able to
describe the self as having definable characteristics, such as "little boy" or
"yucky hands" (Stipek, Gralinski, and Kopp, 1990). The new sense of self
that emerges can be taken as the object of observation and description.

Affect Defense and the Problem
of Affect Recognition

The maturation of preoperational cognitive abilities serves as a prerequisite for the development of psychological defenses and the distortion and
disavowal of affect-laden experiences. Emotional experience becomes
embedded more and more within a matrix of fantasies, schemas, and
memories. As a consequence of improved cognitive organization—the
increased capacity for grouping and categorizing experiences into cohesive units (Greenspan and Greenspan, 1985; Piaget, 1981)—many ideas
and feelings become combined in new ways. The child may pull together
many separate episodes of frustration, for example, into a symbolic
representation of a frustrating other or, likewise, a withdrawing other.
Affective experiences may be combined or recombined in many ways. As
a result, some experiences remain salient in awareness, and others become less accessible to conscious awareness (Stern, 1985). The capacity to
represent wishes and needs in more and more elaborate symbolic modes,
for example, through fantasies, play sequences, and pretend dramas,
implies that wishes and feelings will be conveyed more indirectly and
symbolically and less in terms of immediate facial display patterns. Attrib-
uting motivation to beliefs, wishes, and desires is essentially developed by
three years of age in a way that does not differ essentially from the way
adults attribute motivation (Bartsch and Wellman, 1989). In this sense,
symbolization of affective experience through cognition and language
becomes the vehicle by which the child distorts, denies, and transcends
reality.

These symbolic condensations allow for distortion of reality and provide the soil for neurosis. Prior to the development of linguistic ability, infants are confined to reflecting the impress of reality (Stern, 1985, p. 182). The capacities for symbolization and for grouping and categorizing cognitive-affective experiences provide the necessary ingredients for the emergence of complex intrapsychic defensive structures (Brenner, 1974; Kellerman, 1980) and along with these a complex architecture of conscious and unconscious experience. Psychoanalytically oriented developmentalists have referred to this stage of child development as the formation of a "repression barrier" (Greenspan and Greenspan, 1985; Kernberg, 1976). The impact of affective experiences is no longer immediately felt or expressed in spontaneous facial display patterns. Instead, affective experiences may become distorted, disguised, or totally disavowed from consciousness.

The development of cognitive and linguistic abilities is a mixed blessing, which on one hand allows the child to differentiate and specify affective experience while on the other hand creating the problem of recognition of affects, both internally and externally. Internally, there is increasing "slippage" between the immediately experienced, felt world and the affective fantasies or ideas designed to capture it (Stern, 1985). The child develops significant blind spots in recognizing certain internal affective states. Externally, the heretofore spontaneous facial expressive displays of certain affects now may be suppressed or masked, so that others may readily misrecognize the expressive display.

Developmentalists have offered a number of explanations for why the child has increasing difficulty recognizing the full range of affective experiences in the stream of consciousness and expressing them spontaneously with unambiguous facial display patterns. Stern (1985) believes that this tendency to develop blind spots is an outcome of the way cognitive processes become organized hierarchically. Some psychoanalytic writers have emphasized the distorting nature of wishing, in the service of self-gratification, and of children's tendency to magically organize reality around their own wishes and needs (Modell, 1968). Greenspan and Greenspan (1985) emphasize the child's increasing facility with thinking and with attempts to bring emotional life into greater conformity with the constraints of reality, thereby pushing wishes into the unconscious. This is also the age (30–40 months) when the child develops the capacity for evaluative descriptions of the self, for example, those that pertain to approval/disapproval, calling attention to or away from misbehavior, or inhibiting an impulse. Self-evaluative emotions, that is, emotional reactions to transgressions, also become apparent, such as remorse, guilt, and shame (Buss, Iscoe, and Buss, 1979; Stipek, Gralinski, and

Kopp, 1990). The child preserves vulnerable self-esteem by distorting reality so that the self is still viewed favorably (Matlin and Stang, 1978).

Others emphasize factors that contribute to distortions in facial expressive displays of affect and the associated problem of accurate recognition of facial displays. Brody and Harrison (1987) and Pollak and Thoits (1989) believe that socialization greatly contributes to the accuracy or inaccuracy of recognizing and labeling affects. Children are taught to recognize facial expressions and to identify internal states the way these are labeled by adults. Moreover, facial expressions of and talking about certain affects may not be positively reinforced and may actually be discouraged in a given culture (Izard, 1971; Harkness, 1983). Overt expression of contempt or anger may not be acceptable in a given cultural group. As a result, the internal experience of contempt or anger may be relegated to the unconscious, and its spontaneous facial expression suppressed.

The family system is also an arena fraught with distortions in communication (Bateson et al., 1956). Again, between 30 and 40 months, the child is increasingly capable of grasping parental expectations and standards (Greenspan and Greenspan, 1985) and internalizes a sense of culture (Hippler, 1977). A parent may directly or indirectly communicate the message "We never show anger in this family," communicate a different message verbally and nonverbally, or give contradictory and binding communications. The child is less likely to retain the ability to accurately recognize and label the particular feeling than would be the case if the parent correctly recognizes, mirrors, and supports the expression of the feeling in question. In contrast, the expression of aggression may be modeled within a family. Children from families in which domestic violence occurs are twice as likely as children from normal families to manifest a consistent pattern of childhood aggression by preadolescence—a pattern that becomes a strong predictor of poor adjustment in adolescence and adulthood (Griffin, 1987). This is especially true if the overt expression of anger within the home occurs in the preschool years (in contrast to the school-age years), when the younger child lacks the cognitive development to buffer the overt expression of aggression in response to affective overstimulation (Cummings, Zahn-Waxler, and Radke-Yarrow, 1984). Likewise, modeling of parents' fear responses such as fear of animals or of injury, are associated with the development of similar fears in their children—fears that are likely to persist into adulthood (Marks, 1987). Cultural and familial socialization pressures introduce a significant biasing factor into the child's ability to recognize and label affects (Al-Rihini, 1985; Leff, 1973).

There is a growing body of empirical studies to support the notion of inaccurate and distorted affective recognition in childhood. In these studies, children in designated age groups are asked to attribute feelings to stories, pictures, or certain hypothetically affect-laden situations. The results indicate that within American culture, mothers typically spend less time responding to the child's negative than to positive affective expressions (Malatesta and Haviland, 1982). Five-year-olds tend to recognize happy feelings over other feelings such as sadness (Brody and Harrison, 1987; Glasberg and Aboud, 1982), and they easily confuse sad and angry feelings (Borke, 1971) and have difficulty recognizing fear (Barden et al., 1980; Harter, 1982). Boys more than girls are typically able to recognize anger (Borke, 1971). Girls more than boys have amplified facial EMG display patterns (Schwartz, Brown, and Ahern, 1980) and are generally better than boys at sending emotional messages via facial display (Buck, Miller, and Caul, 1974). When cross-cultural studies are considered, French children, for example, more accurately recognize facial expressions of disgust and contempt than American children do (Izard, 1971). The view emerging from these studies is that the ability of the four- to five-year-old or older child to recognize and label affects is subject to highly individual, gender, and cultural patterns of distortion. By five years of age, stable individual differences in the patterning of emotional expressiveness (e.g., outgoing vs. reserved) become apparent— differences that are clearly related to the family milieu, especially to the affective behavior of the same-sex parent (Bronson, 1966).

Affective Orientation: The Affective Self-in-the-World and the Interiorization and Contextualization of Affect

The Structure of Affect—The Internal World of Emotion

The fourth to the tenth years are characterized by increasing differentiation of a range of specific affective experiences (Alexander et al., 1971; Brody and Harrison, 1987). Three-year-olds are typically capable of recognizing happy, sad, mad, and sometimes scary situations. They do not recognize shame, pride, jealousy, or guilt. The capacity to recognize specific feelings appropriate to the given situation increases with age from the fourth to the tenth year, and it also varies with the intellectual level of the child (Forrai-Banlaki, 1965). According to Brody's empirical studies, cognitive development and social skills development are prerequisites to the ability to differentiate and label affects. These findings are consistent with Piaget's theory of affect (1981), according to which certain affects like pride and frustration would not be expected to appear before the child develops intentionality. Smugness and respect would not be expected before the preoperational child develops social awareness. The recognition of guilt and jealousy comes even later as the child develops a moral sense, typically emerging concomitant to concrete operational thinking (Harter, 1982).

Emotional concepts are highly evolved by eight years of age (corresponding to the emergence of concrete operational thinking). Eight-year-olds possess a highly sophisticated and interrelated lexicon to conceptualize and convey affect, and they are capable of making subtle distinctions between closely related affective states. Factor analytic studies of descriptions of a large number of discrete emotions have shown that these discrete affects cluster together in predictable ways and are organized into a structure along two axes. The first axis pertains to affective valence. Affects are more positive or negative in valence depending on whether the situation is engaging or frustrating, respectively. The second axis pertains to the level of arousal associated with the affect. Affects are organized along a dimension of decreasing or increasing arousal. Specific affects can be located in each of the four quadrants according to the valence and level of arousal associated with the affect. The internal structure for affective experience—commonly called the circumplex model of affect—is virtually identical for latency-age children (Harris, Olthof, and Terwogt, 1981; Plutchnik, 1980; Russell and Bullock, 1986; Russell and Ridgeway, 1983) and adults (Meyer and Shack, 1989; Russell, Lewickam, and Niit, 1989; Watson and Tellegan, 1985). The implication is that the differentiation of a wide repertoire of discrete affective states, as well as their integration into a conceptual structure of experience, is more or less complete by middle childhood. This structure constitutes an "internal world of emotions," which evolves over the course of development (Lane and Schwartz, 1987).

Self-Identification and Empathy

Latency is also a period in which the child develops an increasing self-identification with emotional experiences, learning to identify affective experience both as a bodily state and as a state of mind, namely, as a dimension of self-experience. When children are asked whether they experience a certain emotion, younger children describe the feeling in association with external cues: "I'm scared because he hit me" or "I'm happy because it's my birthday." From five to ten years of age, children describe feelings in progressively interiorized and intentionalized terms, both as a condition of the subjective self and as an altered state of the body: "I'm scared because my heart is pounding . . . because I want to run away." Their ability to describe the feeling as inside their body and as a series of changes in bodily state increases with age (Wolman, Lewis, and

King, 1971, 1972a,b). By adulthood, individuals are capable of reliably describing a pattern of specific changes in bodily sensations for each emotion experienced—a skill Mason (1961) called "internal sensory perception" (Pennebaker, 1982). Likewise, Harris et al. (1981) studied the attributions that latency-age children made about the source of their feelings. He found that five-year-olds tend to attribute feelings to external situations ("happy because it's my birthday . . . angry because of fighting"). Eleven-year-olds tend to attribute feelings to their internal mental state ("happy because everything is going fine"). The locus of affect shifts during the latency years so that emotional experience progressively becomes an aspect of self-experience (Eder, 1989). Likewise, parents attribute children's behavior less to situations and more to children's intentions and personality disposition during these same years (Dix et al., 1986).

A similar pattern is observed in the area of empathy development. Children as young as three years of age can accurately identify the emotions likely to be felt in a variety of situations (Borke, 1973). Yet, although young children (about four years old) are able to identify what others might feel in a variety of situations, they could not match to the same situations what they might feel (Mood, Johnson, and Shantz, 1978). By eight years of age (but not before) the child more or less is able to identify accurately the affective state of others for a variety of affect-laden situations. At that age, children can also match what they feel in the same situation and take in more cues than younger children in identifying affects, thus exhibiting reasonably appropriate affective perspective-taking in their understanding of affective situations (Waern, 1977). However, the degree of empathy depends on the transition from preoperational to concrete operational thinking (Waern, 1977) and also to some extent on both the individual child and the nature of the affect-laden situation to be identified (Borke, 1971). This achievement parallels the child's capacity to understand and adopt social roles. In this sense, Averill (1980) has defined emotion as the capacity to adopt transient social roles.

Latency is also when the child develops a range of very specific coping strategies for various emotional states. When children are asked how they could control certain feelings, younger children spoke about changing the situation in some way; older children drew upon largely cognitive strategies and had a larger repertoire of internal emotional control strategies (Brown, Covell, and Abramovitch, 1991; Sarnoff, 1976).

Flexibility of Affective Experience

Genuine flexibility of affective experience comes with the transition from preoperational to operational thinking. Using a Piagetian framework, Harter (1977, 1982) asks the question, "Through what type of cognitive filter does a child process information about his or her emotions?" Through a series of experiments, Harter demonstrates that young children (three years old) experience particular emotions like happiness or sadness in an all-or-none manner. Likewise, teachers and parents are seen as all good or all bad or all knowing or stupid. The six- to seven-year-old preoperational child can experience two discrete affective states sequentially, for example, seeing the teacher as smart and then as dumb. The eight- to ten-year-old concrete operational child is capable of experiencing two discrete conflicting or nonconflicting affective states simultaneously, for example, the same person can be smart about some things and dumb about others (Harter and Buddin, 1987; Whitesell and Harter, 1989). By that age, the child develops the capacity to experience multiple emotions of varying intensity. For example, the child may experience up to three emotions in the same situation and can differentiate the varying intensity of each (Wintre, Polivy, and Murray, 1990). The child is also capable of experiencing blends of emotions (Lane and Schwartz, 1987).

The onset of concrete operational thinking also brings about a shift in empathy development. Older children can attribute both positive and negative affective qualities to the same situation. They understand that different individuals might respond with a variety of emotions alternating within the same situation (Pancer and Weinstein, 1987; Urberg and Docherty, 1976). They also understand that another's overt expression may not portray genuine feelings (Pancer and Weinstein, 1987).

The child's capacity for empathy is, however, still subject to considerable distortion regarding what belongs to the self and what belongs to the other (Brody and Carter, 1982). Negative feelings like sadness and anger are more likely to be attributed to others, and positive feelings like happiness are more likely to be attributed to the self. The degree to which the child responds to an emotionally laden situation by helpful prosocial behavior is a function of interest and heart rate deceleration and is interfered with by negative emotional arousal (Eisenberg et al., 1990). Moreover, the child's impressions of another person show less differentiation and less abstraction the more the child is emotionally involved in the situation. The distance and perspective-taking that becomes possible at seven to nine years of age as the child develops the capacity for concrete operational thinking is subject to regression when the older child is very emotionally involved in the situation (Rosenbach, Crockett, and Wapner, 1973).

Affective Orientation: The Affective Self-in-the-World

During latency, the child moves away from a family-centered orientation to a greater appreciation of and active involvement with a wider social context (Ohrenstein, 1986; Sarnoff, 1976). One shift in affect during latency is in affective orientation. Empirical evidence suggests that such a child shows greater differentiation of and facility with affect concepts over time. Moreover, this evolving "affective awareness" becomes part of a general orientation to reality, which the older child utilizes in awareness of self and in interpretations of other people (Gilbert, 1969, p. 638). The content of the child's fears, for example, shifts from inner-oriented fears, such as ghosts, to socially oriented fears, such as peer acceptance (Sarnoff, 1976). At this point in development and hereafter, the judgment of context becomes more important than familiarity with facial expression per se in determining the accuracy of recognition of emotions (Zagorska, 1987). Children with greater knowledge of and skill in understanding emotional situations are usually seen as likable and popular among peers (Denham et al., 1990).

The developing child has considerable capacity to characterize a wide variety of situations with a widening range of differentiated affective states, which are experienced more and more as a dimension of the self and the body-self. A useful way to characterize the affective achievement of latency is the formation of a structure for the affective self-in-the-world. De Rivera's (1977) existential-structural theory of emotions is applicable to the task of affective development mastered during the latency years. De Rivera defines an emotion as "a particular way of perceiving the situation in which the person finds himself" (p. 95). An affective experience is a specific way the unique individual perceives the situation posed by the world at any given moment, and de Rivera considers the expression of affect to be an "expressive transformation" because affects invite a transformation of the person in relation to the person's world—whether that transformation be of the bodily state, the relationship to the environment, or the relationship to others. More recently, Lazarus (1991) has developed a cognitive–motivational–relational theory of emotion. He believes that emotions pertain to the "person-environment relationship." More specifically, an emotion is the means by which individuals appraise a specific situation and then develop an action-tendency to change their relationship to the situation, that is, to establish, maintain, or disrupt the relationship based on its emotional meaning to the individual. Emotions become the foundation of our orientation to the world, and especially the social world. During the latency years, affect becomes both increasingly interiorized and contextualized. Affect signifies a particular response by an increasingly complex self to the range of situations and relationships which are presented to the growing child.

Adolescence: The Transformation of Affect

There is an ongoing debate over whether or not adolescence is characterized by a distinct stage of affective development. In the psychoanalytic literature, adolescence has been described as a period of inner turmoil (Blos, 1961, 1979). The assumption commonly made is that adolescence is a period of marked emotional variability and intensity. However, there have been surprisingly few empirical studies on affect in adolescence. In order to scientifically test this assumption, the typical task used in experiments is to have adolescents monitor and report their daily experience of emotional states at random intervals using an electronic pager. Compared with younger children and adults, adolescents do not manifest significantly greater variation or lability in the emotional states (Greene and Larson, 1991; Larson and Lampman-Petraitis, 1989). With respect to intensity of affect, Diener, Sandvik, and Larson (1985) reported greater affect intensity in adolescents relative to adult members of the same family. Moreover, there is some evidence of heightened adolescent fear associated with the developmental shifts of adolescence (Ollendick, Matson, and Helsel, 1985) and an intensification of basic mood states (Csikzentmihalyi and Larson, 1984; Faupel, 1989).

When the daily variations in affective states of adolescence are subject to factor analysis, the structure of affect, namely the circumplex structure, is not essentially different from that of latency-age children or adults. In other words, adolescents show a very similar range of affect to both children and adults, roughly organized and distributed across the quadrants divided by an affective valence and an arousal axis (Greene, 1990; Russell and Ridgeway, 1983). If anything, the arousal dimension of affect decreases in importance from adolescence to early adulthood (Greene, 1990; Watson and Tellegan, 1988). These findings suggest the opposite of the view that affect intensifies during adolescence. Relative to childhood, there is "increasing stability of emotions from adolescence to adulthood" (Greene, 1990, p. 351). Overall, there is no compelling evidence in support of the view of the so-called turmoil hypothesis of normal adolescence. Although the transition from childhood to adolescence may be characterized by an intensification of certain affective states, adolescent development progresses in the direction of greater consistency and stability of affective states.

What, then, characterizes adolescent affect if the range and dimensions of affect are like those in later childhood and adulthood? Certainly the language of affect. Teenage talk is a trademark of adolescence. Adolescent development brings forth a variety of speech patterns that include an emotive language. Danesi (1989) defined this emotive language as "the tendency of adolescents to speak with intensified language markers, revealing an impulse toward the outward expression of strong feelings. "That's amaaaaaaazing!'" (Danesi, 1989, p. 314). Thus, locating what is characteristic of adolescent affect may be found less in the type and structure of affect and more in the way it is expressed.

What may be even more characteristic of adolescent affect is its transformation by cognitive maturation. Adolescence marks the transition from concrete operational thinking to formal operational thinking (Piaget, 1952). Thinking is no longer limited to concrete objects and immediately present situations. Formal thinking is the domain of the hypothetical, the possible, the imagined. Formal operational thinking propels the adolescent from the bonds of the present into the domain of the future—the infinitude of possibilities, as the existentialists say (Blinn and Pike, 1989). With respect to interpersonal relationships, the maturation of formal operational thinking allows for the sense of interconnectedness, the "culture of mutuality" (Kegan, 1982).

With respect to affect, affect is translocated from the self to the self-in-relationship, the domain where the complex unfolding of affective states in both the self and the other can be mutually recognized. The adolescent has the capacity to discern future feelings and to make distinctions between subtle nuances of emotion (Lane and Schwartz, 1987). Moreover, affective states become integrated with formal thought operations. This frees affect from its ties to immediate situations and interactions and transports it into the realm of the possible. Affect becomes integrated into elaborate philosophical and religious belief systems, sociopolitical ideologies, and modes of artistic expression such as music, painting, sculpture, and literary and dramatic expression. If we are to characterize what is unique about adolescent affective development, it is to be found not in daily affective state shifts but in the transformation of affective experience into the passions found in the symbol-systems, ideologies, and artifacts of culture, made possible by the maturation of formal operational thinking.

Adulthood: Consciousness of Affective Processes

The ordinary everyday experience of affect for the normal adult is complex. Through the course of human development, affect undergoes what Gedo and Goldberg (1973) have called "progressive structuralization" (p. 74), the result of which is a complex synthesis of perception, physiological state, cognition, and action, of which the individual is more or less aware.

In their psychoanalytic classic on human development, *Models of the Mind*, Gedo and Goldberg (1973) describe five hierarchically organized levels of structuralization, each of which appears at a phase-specific point in child development. The last two of these, the tripartite model and, especially, the topographical model, are not applicable to infantile functioning but only to "expectable functioning in adults" (p. 110). According to Gedo and Goldberg, Freud's topographic model of the unconscious, preconscious, and conscious was created specifically to explain the fully developed or "fully differentiated psychic apparatus" (p. 105) as manifested by an adult through everyday functioning. The topographic model therefore pertains less to the stages of development than to its outcome: the ordinary mental functioning of adults, notably their conscious experience of their own mind and their relationship to external reality.

If Gedo and Goldberg's line of reasoning is followed and applied specifically to affective development, some model of affect in the normal adult is called for. Presumably, such a model would pertain both to the fully structuralized affect of the adult and to the conscious experience of affect made possible by the existence of that structure. Just as Freud created the topographical model to account for how an individual observes some of the peculiar properties of ordinary conscious experience, such as dreams, jokes, and parapraxes, likewise, a model of affect is needed to account for how individuals come to observe the ordinary affective experiences of their everyday life. Human development is unique in its capacity for self-observation. Freud's topographical model is based on the assumption that humans are capable of observing the workings of their own mind—the very functioning and processes of the mind itself—at least to some extent. The developmental task for the normal adult, then, is to become conscious of the vicissitudes of everyday affect, not simply of the affective content of experience but of the very processes by which affect comes into experience—how it is experienced by the self and what it informs the self about its relationship to internal and external reality.

From the perspective of development, various components of affect have become integrated: a physiological state, awareness of that state, cognitions about that state, and expression of the affect. Yet, from the perspective of the everyday experience of affect for the normal adult, these dimensions of affect are not readily discriminated. "Cognitions and emotion are usually fused . . . although they can be dissociated in certain unusual or abnormal states" (Lazarus, 1982, p. 1019). In ordinary experience, the perception of an object/event, the emotional state, the cognitions about the event and the resultant meaning, and the response or action that follow all seem to occur simultaneously. In everyday experience, the emotion arising from the perception of an object/event may not be recognized fully—it may be more or less "disavowed" (Gedo and Goldberg, 1973). When an emotion is consciously recognized, intense likes and dislikes may be immediately experienced, as if the perception of the event and its resultant emotional state have become confounded. Moreover, the person experiencing the event may only become aware of his or her behavior—for example, the motivation to seek an object without the conscious experience of liking it or the motivation to avoid the object—

without the conscious experience of disliking it. Emotion and the action tendencies that immediately follow also are easily confounded in ordinary experience. In this sense, it is easy to understand how some theorists have defined emotion primarily as an "action disposition" (Lang, Bradley, and Cuthbert, 1990). For example, an individual may react to another with intense anger. The anger may be externalized so that the salient experience is the external behavior of the other rather than the internal experience of the emotional state. Moreover, the individual may pace about, yell, or even lash out without being aware of the anger. Ordinary experience of affect is often in terms of one or the other of two extremes— disavowal and unreflective, compulsive action.

The tasks of affective development of the normal adult are (1) to fully recognize the vicissitudes of emotional states and (2) to learn to observe and discriminate the various dimensions of affective processing, so that a given emotional state is seen as distinct from the perceived object/event from which it arises, and so that the thoughts, fantasies, and responses associated with it are also seen as distinct from the emotional state itself. In other words, Plato's "examined life" entails observing the vicissitudes of everyday affective experience so that the self is correctly informed by the affective message and so that the action that follows is deliberate, rational, and appropriate to context, not immediate-compulsive and insensitive to context.

The individual who reflects on the processes as a good phenomenologist does make more and more refined distinctions between the various dimensions of affective processes. In this respect, the so-called information processing theories of affect are especially applicable. In information processing theory, it is customary to speak of levels of processing of cognition (Neisser, 1967), memory (Craik and Lockhart, 1972), and consciousness (Hilgard, 1977). Some of these levels of processing are available to conscious experience; others are not ordinarily available.

Arnold's (1960) model of affect is one of the most elaborate information processing models of affect described in the literature. Figure 1.1 summarizes that model. According to the model, affect begins with perception of a stimulus object or event. What follows is an immediate sense judgment or "intuitive appraisal." Arnold defines an appraisal as an "action tendency" (p. 182) or, better, a reactive tendency, to either like or dislike the object/event. If further attention is given to the object/event, a "felt action tendency" results, namely, the tendency to approach or avoid the object. A variety of physiological changes accompany the action tendency. A "secondary appraisal" of the pleasantness or unpleasantness of these physiological changes automatically results in the perception of an "emotional state." The action tendency also results in an immediate impulsive

AFFECT EXPRESSION |———————— AFFECT EXPERIENCE ————————————|

	Facial Expressive Displays	Interest Self-regulation	Attachment Bond Primary Emotional Experience			Somatic-Cognitive Integration
	0 months	**2/3 months**	**4/6 months**	**6**	**8**	**9 months** **12**
		Perceptual Maturation Homeostasis Hedonic Tone	Autonomic Regulation	Moods	8-Month Signal Anxiety Anxieties	Schema Maturation Categorical Self Synchronization of Affect Components Specificity of Affect States
			Reciprocal Facial Displays Self-Observational Capacity			

PSYCHOPATHOLOGICAL MANIFESTATION

Bland Affect		Input Dysfunction	Self-Observation Deficit Visceral Perception Deficit Inappropriate Affect Expression			Splitting of Affect Components

COPING STRATEGY

Posturing & Grimacing	Autistic Withdrawal	Sensation-Seeking Behavior Need-Fear Transference		Somatic Delusions

|——————————————— PSYCHOTIC ORGANIZATION ———————————————|

Fig. 1.1. Affect Development and Psychopathology
Part 1

37

AFFECT TOLERANCE	AFFECT VERBALIZATION	AFFECT DEFENSE
Representational Maturation	Emotional Ideas Labelling & Verbalizing Affect	Emergence of Psychological Defenses
12 months	18 months	30 — 36 — 48
Separation-Individuation Phase Increase in Affect Storms Internalization of Self-Soothing Integrating Emotional Polarities Integrating Affects & Self	Conceptual Skill Wishes & Fantasy Pretend Play Language Acquisition Self as Object of Reflection	Misrecognition of affect experience Suppression of expressive facial displays	Happy, sad, mad All-at-once affects Situationally located affects

PATHOLOGICAL MANIFESTATION

Deficits in self soothing Incapacity to bear affects Failure to localize affect in the self	Alexythymia 'Dis-affected' experience	Disavowal

COPING STRATEGY

Transitional phenomena Substance abuse	Acting out	Symptom formation

BORDERLINE PERSONALITY ORGANIZATION	NEUROSIS

Part 2

AFFECT ORIENTATION ——————— AFFECT TRANSFORMATION ——————— CONSCIOUSNESS OF AFFECT PROCESSES

Concrete operational thinking
Social roles

Formal operational thinking
Possibilities

Reflecting on the workings of the mind and levels of affect processing

7 years   10 years

13 years

adult years

Interiorization of affect
Contextualization of affect
Circumplex structure—the internal emotional world
Flexibility—multiple affects of varying intensity in same situation
Perspective-taking

Transformation of affect into art, ideology, etc.
Expressive language
Mutuality
Virtual affect

Re-centering on emotional life
Distinguishing between affect and action
Awareness of levels of affective processing

PSYCHOPATHOLOGICAL MANIFESTATION

All-or-nothing affect
Externalization of affect
Decontextualization of affect (loss of meaning)

Loss of mutuality
Lack of transformation and sublimation of affect

Confounding affect and action
Lack of conscious reflection on affective processes
Lack of awareness on preattentive affective processes, e.g. the appetitive-aversive bias

RELATIVE HEALTH—THE PSYCHOPATHOLOGY OF EVERYDAY LIFE

Part 3

39

action, or a more enduring motivational state, with respect to the object. Emotions leave residues so that more enduring emotional attitudes, habits, and sentiments are learned over time, which predispose the individual to respond to certain classes of objects with characteristic emotional reactions.

Leventhal's (1980) perceptual motor theory of emotion is a more recent elaboration of an information processing model for affect. Although comparable to Arnold's model in many respects, Leventhal postulates two main stages in processing emotional information: a perceptual motor stage and a decision action stage. The perceptual motor system consists of three hierarchically organized stages: expressive motor processing, schematic processing, and conceptual processing. Expressive motor processing is said to occur in response to a given stimulus. This innate system consists primarily of facial muscle responses that activate reflexively in response to a stimulus, and it serves to generate the elemental subjective emotional state. Next, the emotional information is schematically processed in the form of specific memories organized around attachment and aversion to the stimulus. Both the perceptual motor and schematic processing systems are rapid processing systems that do not require conscious deliberation. Next, the emotional information is conceptually processed by which process the individual extracts meaning and draws conclusions about the emotional information. These appraisals become the basis for decisions and action plans. In this model, emotional information operates by a feed-forward mechanism by which otherwise rapidly processed emotional information achieves greater strength, salience in consciousness, and greater duration as an emotional state. Whereas it is more complex than Arnold's theory, Leventhal's theory contains a lot of the same elements. The difference between the two models is that Leventhal adds an earlier stage of processing—the expressive motor system—which he draws from the research on reflexive facial displays. Yet, both models share the same concern for the primacy of immediate attachment and aversion responses to stimuli, for the connection between emotion and action, and for levels of processing, some of which operate at high speeds, normally outside of consciousness in everyday experience.

Most ordinary individuals are able to observe the action or behavioral response following an emotional state. In ordinary consciousness, individuals may recognize the emotional state itself, although certain types of affects may be disavowed. The normal adult is less aware of the specific pattern of physiological changes associated with the emotional state, except in a very global way, although there are marked individual differences in the ability to accurately perceive these changes (Pennebaker, 1982). Rarely is one aware of the affect appraisal or the action tendency. In her original work, Arnold (1960), together with more recent advocates of information processing models that give primacy to affect in human information processing, notably Zajonc (1980), refers to the approach–avoidance or appetitive–aversion dimension of information processing as preattentive, precognitive, and preverbal.

Empirical studies tend to support the information processing view of affect. Frijda, Kuipers, and ter Schure (1989) studied adults' reports of 32 emotional states along the dimensions of affect appraisal and affect readiness. Appraisals and action readiness scores were highly correlated, which suggests that for the ordinary adult, affect appraisal and action tendencies are inextricably bound up with each other.

A classic debate in the study of emotions centers on the primacy of affect or cognition in human information processing. Zajonc (1980) argues that preferences (likes and dislikes) immediately follow sensory input and come before any extensive cognitive processing of the stimulus. He also believes that affect and cognition are "separate and partially independent systems." Lazarus (1982, 1991) argues that the complete experience of any emotion presupposes "cognitive appraisal." In his view, stimuli must be processed to the point that "meaning" is extracted before any emotion can occur. Lazarus locates meaning within the self and as associated with the complex cognitive structures and social symbol systems that develop over the life course. In this sense, affect is always personal and related to one's well-being.

Both views may represent partial truths, each applying to a different level in the overall organization of affective processing. Appraisal (Arnold, 1960), preference (Zajonc, 1980), and attachment–aversion are constructs that pertain to high-speed processes normally outside of conscious awareness, whereas Lazarus's concept of "meaning" applies more to higher-level conceptual processing of emotional information that is more available to the conscious experience of affect. The former concepts apply to simple input processing, the latter to complex cognitive elaboration. The confusion arises in part from the failure to distinguish between perceptual cognition and social/conceptual cognition (Leventhal, 1980). Zajonc clarifies that the immediate apperception of liking or disliking is based on simple perceptual categorization processes—something more in the domain of perceptual processing than thinking. From one perspective, Lazarus may be correct to say that cognitive appraisal or meaning making is necessary for the full experience of an emotion. From another perspective, Zajonc may be correct to say that precognitive appraisal is necessary for an understanding of how emotion comes into consciousness. As Arnold states, "[only a] phenomenological analysis of the whole sequence from perception to emotion and action" will yield such an understanding (p. 170).

Labouvie-Vief et al.'s (1989) model of adult affective maturity has recast the Zajonc-Lazarus debate into an adult development issue. Viewing affective development across the life span, Labouvie-Vief et al. see childhood as a time to adjust to the demands of external reality. This is accompanied by a "downgrading" of the subjective world and a "decentering" of objects from thought processes. The normal phase-specific task of adulthood entails a "recentering" or reevaluation of the subjective nature of reality. Adult affective development is characterized by a "redefinition of one's emotional life." The authors see adulthood as "aimed at reconnecting notions of the objective with a sense of the inner and subjective . . . the understanding of inner psychological processes deepens in adulthood" (p. 285), and they describe this developmental achievement in terms of "reflective spontaneity."

Taking a broader view of adult development, akin to Gedo and Goldberg (1973), we might say that adult development brings the potential to observe and understand the processes of our own minds. Adult affective development is the potential for self-observation and reflection on the very processes of mental functioning. Because formal operational thinking brings possibility into cognition, adult affective development may take many forms: awareness of the contents of the stream of consciousness, observation of shifts in mood and emotional state; awareness of self-talk, free association, reflection on the subjective meaning of events and one's own behavior, analysis of conscious and unconscious motivation, distinguishing feelings and fantasy from action, and observing mind–body connections.

Self-observation for some individuals may also become a discipline. Although the normal adult is unlikely to conduct such detailed self-observation, it is certainly possible to do so. The normal adult is content to know something about the meaning or personal significance conveyed in affective experiences. Students of introspection—the philosopher, the contemplative, and the psychotherapy patient—are likely to be exceptions to the rule. Such individuals represent the possibility of directly observing in a systematic manner not only the vicissitudes of affect in everyday life, but also something about the workings of the mind. These individuals may learn about the levels by which affect is processed and comes into consciousness. Such disciplined or skilled introspection may result in awareness of levels of affective processing not normally available to conscious experience, for example, the automatic perceptual bias to categorize perceived objects/events as likable or unlikable. Not only the content of emotional experience can be known but also the very processes and levels of processing by which emotional experience occurs. Moreover, students of the mind are likely to evolve a rich, elaborate, and often technically sophisticated language for subjective states (Labouvie-Vief et al., 1989) as exemplified to some extent in psychotherapy and certainly in the great cartographies of states of consciousness found in the contemplative traditions (Brown, 1977; Wilbur, Engler, and Brown, 1986).

The possibility for conscious reflective self-observation of the workings of the mind in general and of levels of processing affective information in particular is available throughout the span of adulthood. There is no evidence of structural changes associated with aging that might otherwise limit such self-exploration. Malatesta (1981) reviewed the sparse literature on aging and affective development and found no compelling evidence for a decline in affective experience with age.

PSYCHOPATHOLOGY AS FAILURE
OF AFFECTIVE DEVELOPMENT

From a developmental-lines perspective on affective development, the normally developing child is presented with an invariant sequence of phase-specific tasks, which include affective expression, affective experience, verbalization of affect, affect tolerance, affect defense, affect orientation, transformation of affect, and consciousness of affect processes, respectively. From this developmental-lines perspective, certain psychopathological manifestations could be interpreted as developmental failures along a normal continuum of affective development (e.g., Greenspan and Porges, 1984). Depending on the specific point on the continuum where the developmental failure occurs, deficits may manifest themselves in one or more areas: expression, experience, tolerance, verbalization, recognition, orientation, transformation, and consciousness of affective processes, respectively.

In order to keep the model parsimonious, it may be useful to organize our understanding of the psychopathology of affect into four primary levels of psychopathological organization: psychosis, personality disorder, neurosis, and relative healthy adulthood (i.e., the psychopathology of everyday life). Ornstein (1974) describes three discrete levels of psychopathology along a continuum: psychosis, character pathology, and neurosis. The model may have a certain appeal, but it emphasizes severe disturbance. Because the model of affect presented in this chapter comprises healthy, normal adult development, a fourth major level of organization has been added in modification of Ornstein's model, namely, the structural organization of everyday adult affective experience and its associated psychopathology. Each of these levels of psychopathology will be described from the perspective of affective development: the specific developmental stages that have not been mastered, the main psychopathological manifestations of affect associated with each developmental failure, and the main adaptive strategies characteristic of each stage.

Psychotic Organization

The psychotically vulnerable individual may manifest a variety of developmental deficits in affective expression, experience, and/or tolerance characteristic of the severely disturbed psychiatric patient. These constitute problems in the structuralization of affect. We may refer to such deficits as "structural pathology" (Baker, 1990). Table 1.1 illustrates a continuum of affective developmental deficits in psychotically vulnerable patients. The primary deficit in the schizophrenic is in the domain of affective experience. At the more extreme end of the continuum of psychopathology, some chronic undifferentiated schizophrenics manifest, in addition, deficits in the normal capacity for affect expression. At the less extreme end of the continuum, some well-organized high-functioning paranoid schizophrenics manifest some fundamental capacity for affective experience yet fail in their ability to integrate and synchronize the basic components of normal affective experience, that is, to integrate the facial expressive display patterns, the awareness of visceral experience, and the cognitions associated with the affect.

Evidence is accumulating that some deficit in affective experience (along a normal developmental continuum representing the tasks of activation, attachment and self-awareness, and somatic–cognitive integration) may be a primary deficit in the schizophrenic. Many schizophrenics manifest deficits in capacity for interest in the world and associated self-regulation. The input dysfunction theory of schizophrenia (Buss and Lang, 1965; Chapman, 1966; Lang and Buss, 1965; McGhie and Chapman, 1961; Venables, 1964) is supported by hundreds of empirical studies. These studies clearly document the disregulation of the schizophrenic's capacity for normal activation in response to incoming stimuli. In association with these deficits in the arousal system, the schizophrenic manifests deficits in the capacity to filter stimuli. Such patients filter either too much or not enough, depending on whether they are in a chronic or acute phase of the illness (Venables, 1964). Chronic schizophrenics do not appear to take in the world, and they manifest lower levels of sensation-seeking behavior relative to normals (Brownfield, 1966; Kish, 1970). Conversely, acute schizophrenics are flooded with internal and external stimuli (Chapman, 1966; Chapman and Ghieth, 1961). These fundamental activation/arousal deficits may manifest themselves in the subjective arena. Schizophrenics often experience a basic "estrangement" (Fleck, 1980) from the world and lack a sense of existing (Perry, 1980).

Most schizophrenics manifest deficits associated with the primary attachment relationship (Lucas, 1992; Meadow, 1991). Stanton (1980) commented on the obvious lack of a consistent self-observational capacity that he noted among many of his schizophrenic patients. Schizophrenics, unlike normals, are less able to notice internal changes in bodily experience. Schizophrenics have been shown to manifest significant disturbances in awareness of proprioceptive feedback from muscles and in awareness of physiological events under the control of the autonomic nervous system (Holzman, 1970). Whereas normal individuals can identify a pattern of visceral change associated with affective experiences, Pennebaker (1982) and Mason (1961) demonstrated that schizophrenics typically cannot locate the bodily sensations or differentiate the visceral changes associated with affective experience. Normal individuals who feel anxious typically report butterflies in the stomach or tightening of the muscles when angry. Schizophrenics who feel anxious or angry are typically unable to consciously register the visceral changes accompanying affect. Because this inability is often quite apparent when attempting to engage an adult schizophrenic patient in psychotherapy, some psychoanalytically oriented therapists have argued that the incapacity to consistently describe or observe the bodily visceral changes accompanying emotion is a fundamental feature of schizophrenia (Perry, 1980; Semrad and van Buskirk, 1969). Converging lines of evidence are suggestive of both a deficit in awareness and a deficit in visceral experience on which genuine affective experience is based. Perry (1980) believes the basic disturbance in schizophrenia resides in subjectively "felt emotion," not necessarily in emotional expression. Thus, a schizophrenic patient may describe vivid, angry fantasies or may burst into tears. An observing clinician might incorrectly conclude that the patient is feeling something. Yet the patient may not "feel" angry or sad in the sense of subjectively experiencing visceral changes within the body. One consequence of this basic disturbance is the schizophrenic's inability to experience a basic sense of aliveness (Perry, 1980).

The attribution of inappropriate affect is typically made about schizophrenics. From a developmental-lines perspective, inappropriate affect is a consequence of both a failed attachment relationship and possibly also a failure in the operation of the facial affective display system. According to the developmental model presented here, the second to ninth month of life for the normal child is characterized by reciprocally attuned facial affective displays. Presumably, children who later become schizophrenic and who may not have experienced the primary attachment relationship in a normal way would thereby not be expected to attune their affective expressive displays appropriately to the care-giver. What has been called "inappropriate affect" in the schizophrenic is here reinterpreted as an outcome of desynchronized infant–care-giver facial display behavior. Some child research evidence supports the view of developmental deficits in reciprocal expressive behavior. Braverman et al. (1989) studied affective comprehension and face perception in normal children and children with pervasive developmental disorders. Relative to the normal children, the children with pervasive developmental disorders were significantly impaired on tasks requiring them to match faces and match affects. They also showed greater impairment in social relations.

Although a primary deficit in the conscious registering of visceral experience or "felt emotion" may underlie schizophrenia, a number of related affective deficits may also occur depending on the severity of the schizophrenic disturbance. On the more severe end of the continuum of psychopathology, the chronic undifferentiated schizophrenic may manifest deficits in affective expression in addition to the primary deficit in affective experience. Bleuler's (1950) original description of bland affect referred primarily to deterioration in affective expression. Bleuler described the "expressionless faces" and "image of indifference" of such schizophrenic patients. Subsequent empirical observations of schizophrenics confirmed and expanded these early clinical observations. Disturbances in affective expression or "affective flattening" include lack of observable facial expression, lack of spontaneous expressive movement of the hands and body, lack of vocal inflection, and poor eye contact (Andreason, 1979). Provence and Lifton (1962) vividly portrayed this condition as the "frozen deadness" of the schizophrenic face. Because affective expression depends to a large degree on responses of innate patterns of facial muscles, disturbed affective expression may be due to genetic defects and/or early developmental failures in the feedback mechanisms necessary for the development of patterned facial expressions and their coordination with internal changes. Some manifestations of schizophrenia have a stronger biological and perhaps genetic loading than others, so it is conceivable that the underlying genetic predisposition could manifest itself in terms of defective operation of the reflexive facial display system otherwise available at birth to the normally developing child. Moreover, the therapist's use of facial expressions with severely disturbed patients may play a crucial role in establishing an affective connection with such patients (Searles, 1984–85).

Some more organized schizophrenics possess the basic components of affective experience (subjective awareness and perception of patterns of visceral changes), as well as the potential for affective expression. In them, the failure occurs in the integration of these components with ideational and representational processes. These more organized schizophrenics—often high-functioning paranoid schizophrenics—manifest a variety of psychopathological symptoms corresponding with a failure to master the developmental task of somatic–cognitive integration. The problem for the high-functioning schizophrenic is not so much to experience the affect viscerally but to integrate the various components of affect into specific affective states. Affective experiences may become split off from consciousness for the schizophrenic (Bleuler, 1950). A failure occurs in the integration of subjective awareness and other components of affect—facial expressive patterns, visceral changes, and cognitions. When Arieti (1955) spoke of "desymbolization" of affects, he might have been trying to describe what in this developmental model is seen as a failure to integrate the visceral and cognitive components of affect. Bychowski (1952) and Volkan (1976) address the problem of introjects in the schizophrenic. In this case, the visceral component of affect is relegated to a split-off representation, which carries on a quasi-autonomous existence apart from integration into the total structure of the representational world. So long as there is no integration of the four basic components of affect, genuine affective experience is impossible. Such high-functioning paranoid schizophrenics may express affect without experiencing it, experience intense bodily changes without expression, or describe vivid and bizarre aggressive or sexual images without feeling anything in the body.

Severely disturbed patients utilize a variety of adaptive strategies to compensate for the various deficits in affect. Schizophrenic patients with bland affect may display grimacing and posturing as an attempt to provide themselves with feedback. By intentionally exaggerating and exhaustively repeating certain muscle movements, they attempt to redundantly extract information to construct schematic representations for bodily experience. Schizophrenic patients who lack a sense of aliveness may utilize a variety of sensation-seeking behaviors in an effort to amplify visceral experiences to the level of awareness. The seemingly bizarre symptoms and self-destructive behaviors of these patients (e.g., auditory hallucinations, cutting and burning, compulsive masturbation) have been interpreted as adaptive attempts to utilize certain types of external sensory input to compensate for the failure in awareness of internal visceral changes, thereby providing a temporary sense of felt bodily existence or aliveness (Perry, 1980). Schizophrenics who lack the ability to become aware of internal affective states may adopt a style of relationship in which they attempt to infer affective experience based on others' response to them (Perry, 1980). Burnham, Gladstone, and Gibson (1969) referred to this style of relationship as the schizophrenic's need–fear dilemma, in which the schizophrenic needs others to define internal experience yet fears being taken over by another. Higher-level schizophrenics, who manifest deficits primarily in somatic–cognitive integration, utilize delusional thinking. Delusions, especially somatic delusions, may be adaptive attempts to represent bodily and affective states and thereby forge the integration of visceral states with complex cognitive processes.

Personality Disorders

Patients at the level of borderline personality organization manifest fundamental deficits in affect tolerance, especially those with substance abuse problems (Krystal and Raskin, 1970), and they are capable of genuine affective experience but fail mainly in their capacity to tolerate affects. Ekstein and Wallerstein (1955) likened the extreme swings from emptiness of affect to overwhelming panic to the operation of a "defective thermostat" that could no longer regulate affect intensity in the borderline child. Others have explained the vulnerability to depression in children, similarly, as due to a failure in the regulation of affect in the infant–care-giver system (Kaslow and Wamboldt, 1985). In borderline adults, affects may be experienced with great intensity and run their course without modulation (Eissler, 1953). Such patients are vulnerable to intense affect storms—rage attacks (Kernberg, 1976) and panic states. Adler (1980, 1981) views borderlines as having failed to internalize soothing mechanisms, thereby making them vulnerable to intense panic states. Some borderline patients manifest a global deficit in the capacity to tolerate affects; others manifest deficits in the capacity to bear specific affects like depression or anxiety (Zetzel, 1949, 1965). Borderlines also manifest deficits in the localization of affective states within the total self-representation. Because of the failure to achieve an integration of the body image, the self- as-differentiated-from-the-object, and the grandiose self into a cohesive sense of self (Lichtenberg, 1975), such patients may actually experience the body-self and the self as separate entities. In other words, their affective states are not necessarily experienced as belonging to the self. This is perhaps why borderlines are capable of self-mutilation as a means of relief from intolerable tension without having any realistic idea that such acts are destructive to the self. Such a failure of integration may explain why borderlines typically experience intensive affective states as "alien" to the self, almost as if they were becoming possessed.

Borderlines, who manifest primarily global and specific deficits in affect tolerance, may utilize transitional phenomena (Adler, 1981; Baker, 1981; Horton, Lovy, and Coppolillo, 1974) and object-seeking behavior as means to preserve the intactness (Bursten, 1973) of the self-representation and object representations. Borderlines also utilize cutting behaviors, sensation seeking, and substance abuse (Khantzian, 1978; Krystal and Raskin, 1970) as means to cope with intolerable affective states.

Patients with narcissistic personality disorder manifest a chronic inability to regulate self-esteem. Normal self-esteem development has been defined with respect to the linkage of and accumulation of positive affect with the self-representation; chronic self-esteem pathology, conversely, is the outcome of failing to assimilate sufficient positive affective experiences, the result of which is the continuous experience of dysphoric affect associated with the self-representation (Joffe and Sandler, 1966). Kohut (1971) has explained such self-esteem failure in terms of a persistent pattern of failed mirroring in the infant–care-giving relationship. Many of the symptoms of narcissism function in the service of self-esteem regulation (Stolorow and Lachmann, 1980), such as narcissistic object choice (Reich, 1960), the illusion of self-sufficiency (Modell, 1975), and the experience of narcissistic states (Bach, 1985).

While self-soothing is the foundation of affective tolerance, verbalization greatly enhances affective tolerance. Yet, there is a population of personality-disordered patients who manifest a primary deficit in the capacity to verbalize affective experiences. Alexithymia is common in personality-disordered patients, especially those with substance-abusing and somatizing disorders (Krystal, 1979, 1982–83; Nemiah, 1975; Sifneos, 1973). Alexithymia means having no words for emotions. Krystal (1979, 1988) has given the most extensive description of alexithymia in terms of an affective, cognitive, and relational disturbance. With respect to the affective disturbance, alexithymic patients do not readily recognize their feelings. They are typically unaware of emotions, instead becoming aware of vague physical complaints. When asked directly about feelings, they are generally unable to describe them. When using affect-laden words, they generally lack awareness of the visceral substrate of the experience, and if at all aware of physical sensations, they have a very difficult time putting these into words. Such individuals rarely can utilize emotions as signals of internal change. They have a very difficult time distinguishing one emotion from another. Nevertheless, although generally unaware of their inner emotional life, they can at times have sudden outbursts of emotional expression. With respect to the cognitive disturbance, alexithymic patients are preoccupied with the mundane details of everyday life and have a limited capacity for imagination. In their relationships, they manifest detachment. In psychotherapy, they usually have a hard time accessing feelings for the therapist. They remain seemingly indifferent, yet often quite attached if not addicted to psychotherapy.

McDougall's (1982, 1985) description of alexithymia is similar to Krystal's. She adds, however, that alexithymic patients easily confuse affect and action. When distressing feelings occur in such patients during the course of psychoanalysis, they typically act out, in the form of substance abuse, compulsive sexual behavior, accident proneness, or somaticization. Moreover, McDougall adds that such patients split the psychic and somatic components of affect, and as a result, words and thoughts used in psychotherapy become denuded of their emotional connotations. Such "dis-affected" language no longer communicates but instead serves as a defense against genuine contact in the therapy relationship.

Considerable controversy exists about the etiology of alexithymia. Sifneos (1988) and Nemiah and Sifneos (1970) interpreted alexithymia as a biological deficit in neurotransmitter metabolism so that conscious recognition of affect is blocked. They see alexithymia as the absence of feelings due to a neuropsychological deficit, not as a psychological defense against feelings. Moreover, they see psychoanalytic psychotherapy as contraindicated for the alexithymic because of the patient's difficulty in affectively investing in the therapeutic relationship. Krystal (1979) does not like the term "deficit," preferring to see alexithymia as a kind of defensive inhibition of affect. He believes that such patients can respond favorably to psychoanalytic psychotherapy when appropriate modifications are made to accommodate their difficulty in recognizing and verbalizing affect. McDougall (1985) sees alexithymia as a defense against psychotic anxieties, such as the patient's anxiety about the right to exist or to exist as a separate autonomous self.

In developmental terms, alexithymia can be viewed as a spectrum of clinical manifestations along the normal line of affective development from the normal developmental tasks of somatic–cognitive integration through the verbalization of affect (Figure 1.1). First, as the name implies, alexithymia is primarily a deficit in the verbalization of affect. The alexithymic patient has failed to master the normal developmental task of affect verbalization. Moreover, Krystal's description of "devitalization" and "emotional outbursts" and McDougall's description of "affectively denuded language" and "acting out" suggest that the alexithymic patient also has significant difficulty with affect tolerance, so that affect is experienced as too little or too much, without an optimal range of modulation. Just as in normal child development the successive tasks of affective tolerance and affective verbalization are closely related so that verbalization of affect greatly enhances the capacity for affect tolerance, it is not surprising that the problems of affect tolerance and verbalization of affect are both commonly attributed to the alexithymic patient. Because localization of affect within the self and body-self occurs at the same stage as does affect tolerance within normal affective development, it is also not surprising to find the problem of localization of affect among the attributions made about alexithymia. McDougall (1985), for example, describes the alexithymic patient as seeing his or her body as if it were a foreign object or affect as if were a state of possession. McDougall, in contrast to Krystal, goes on to describe a feature of alexithymia that is suggestive of an even earlier developmental arrest when compared with the sequence of developmental tasks along the line of normal affective development (Figure 1.1). McDougall sees the splitting of the psychic and somatic components of affect in the alexithymic patient as a central feature of alexithymia and sees this as a defensive maneuver to manage psychotic anxieties. In terms of the developmental model, the alexithymic may have considerable difficulty with localization, tolerance, and verbalization of affect because of some underlying vulnerability in the structuralization of affect, by which the components of affect become integrated. In other words, the fundamental difficulty may be with the somatic–cognitive integration of affect.

Neuroses

The problem for neurotic patients is not so much that of structuralization of affect but disavowal of affect (Freud, 1933; Gedo and Goldberg, 1973). The neurotic patient uses a variety of intrapsychic defenses, such as repression and dissociation of the self-representation as means to keep unacceptable conflictual impulses and associated affects and self-representations from consciousness (A. Freud, 1965; Gedo and Goldberg, 1973). When these defensive operations fail, anxiety symptoms emerge as a response to the internal danger of threatening impulses. Other neurotic symptoms may also emerge (phobias, conversion symptoms) as an attempt to contain the conflictual impulses (Freud, 1959). The developmental arrest of the neurotic occurs primarily at the level of accurate recognition of affects and associated fantasies and wishes.

Relative Health: The Psychopathology of Everyday Affective Life

Forward movement along the continuum of affective development is relative. The typical normal adult rarely fully masters each of the developmental stages in question. The range of psychopathology in the so-called healthy-neurotic adult corresponds to the developmental tasks from affect defense through consciousness of affective processes along the developmental continuum. Blind spots still are likely to exist and a given individual may fail consistently to recognize specific affects. Yet, the healthy neurotic probably is capable of consciously recognizing and tolerating a wide variety of affects while still finding certain affects problematic. Nevertheless, it is the exception rather than the rule to find normal adults who have fully mastered the developmental tasks of affective transformation and consciousness of affective processes. Most individuals have not, for the most part, transformed everyday affect into the passionate pursuit of ideologies or the arts. Most individuals have not developed disciplined reflection on the workings of their mind and the processes by which emotions come into immediate experience. The psychopathology of everyday life, therefore, means that everyday emotional experience is restricted largely to the immediate, present situation or interaction. Moreover, it is likely that much of daily emotional experience is self-centered, without genuine mutuality. At the heart of egocentric emotional reactions are strong likes and dislikes, preferences and opinions, which greatly bias our perceptions of and interactions with others and about which we have little understanding of the origins of such immediate attachments and aversions. Everyday emotional experience is strongly reactive and reflects clear biases. The full meaning of many of our daily emotional reactions remains a mystery to many.

Furthermore, most normal adults readily confuse affect and action. Because affect is an action tendency (Arnold, 1960; Leventhal, 1980), it is easy for the unreflective individual to automatically transform emotional experience into action and then infer the emotional experience from the perception of the resultant action. To the extent this happens, emotions are experienced less as internal states and more as impulsive behaviors. Anger is when you yell or hit. Fear is when you withdraw. Love is when you act sexual. Whereas the reflective individual knows that each of these behaviors may be motivated by a number of very different emotional states, the unreflective individual knows only the behaviors and misconstrues them as if they were direct emotional experiences. This tendency to confuse affect and action is so prevalent that it is common among even the most reflective individuals in modern Western culture. According to Tartakoff (1966), the confusion is based on our roles in modern American society namely, because of its activistic orientation. Tartakoff (1966) describes how even normal, nonneurotic adults in our culture who are especially motivated to learn about themselves by entering into psychoanalytic training typically approach psychoanalysis as a task to be actively mastered and expect special recognition for their psychoanalytic achievements in the analytic hour.

Regression Along the Continuum
of Affective Development

Progression along the continuum of affective development is not unidirectional. Even the normal, well-adjusted individual is likely to experience regressive swings at times (Krystal, 1974, 1988). Common regressive swings include more or less temporary lapses in some of the affective developmental achievements previously consolidated in the latency years and earlier in childhood. Ordinarily, the normal adult is capable of experiencing multiple emotions of varying intensity in the same situation. Under certain circumstances, this ability to grasp the subtlety and complexity of emotional experience may be lost. The individual may revert to the all-or-nothing experience of an emotion, when it is felt in extreme. The capacity to take perspective on the situation is also lost. Moreover, whereas the normal adult is capable of experiencing a very specific affect as an internal state that is appropriate to a very specific situation, affective experience under certain circumstances may become externalized and decontextualized. When feelings are aroused, it is possible to externalize or otherwise misattribute the source of the affect. Under such circumstances, affects are experienced more in terms of the situation and less in terms of the internal state. Consider the common expressions "I'm angry because you are making me feel that way" and "I feel that you are behaving badly." In the former case, the source of the anger is not seen as having much to do with the person's own unique interpretation of the situation, but, rather, is attributed to the situation itself. In the latter case, the anger is thoroughly externalized. "I feel that you are behaving badly" is not a description of an internal feeling but a description of another's action, perceived outside the individual. Moreover, affective experience may become decontextualized, and therefore its unique meaning is lost. Consider the expression "I'm really mad." The individual is clearly aware of feeling angry but is unclear about its meaning or what contributes to this appraisal. Another common type of decontextualization occurs when the individual is unaware of what he or she is feeling in the actual situation and identifies the feeling only after the fact.

Another common regressive swing is the failure to recognize certain feeling states within oneself. Most normal adults have blind spots when it comes to recognizing certain feelings. It is not unusual to simply be unaware of what one is feeling in certain situations. A related problem is recognition of one but not another emotion in a situation that stimulates multiple emotions.

According to Krystal (1979, 1982–83) "alexithymic characteristics" are commonly observed in psychoanalytic patients. Earlier, the alexithymic condition was described as a syndrome characteristic of certain personality-disordered patients. But even so-called healthy-neurotic patients encounter times in psychotherapy, and also in everyday life, when they become temporarily alexithymic. Everyday life and therapy at times evoke intensely distressing emotional states, which the individual responds to with a regressive swing along the line of affective development. According to Krystal, such regression is characterized by the "deverbalization" and "resomatization" of affect. Thus, in the face of a distressing state, the individual is at a loss for words and may experience the affect primarily as an extreme bodily discomfort. Moreover, affect experience may become delocalized. The individual loses the ability to experience the affect as a specific localized visceral reaction, instead experiencing it as a diffuse, global bodily discomfort. A more extreme regression in the capacity for localization can occur in which the affective state is no longer experienced as part of the self or the body-self. During such intense affective storms, the affect is experienced as something alien to the individual, seizing the moment as if in a state of possession. These moderately severe regressive swings suggest a temporary problem with affect tolerance. Even healthy-neurotic individuals manifest an incapacity to bear certain affects, especially when faced with highly distressing situations like grief and trauma (Krystal, 1985, 1988; Zetzel, 1949, 1965).

Under extremely distressing life circumstances (or the regression of psychotherapy), normal healthy-neurotic adults may undergo more severe regressive swings through the continuum of affective development, which may be referred to as the splitting of affective components. McDougall (1985) describes one type of split, in which the psychic and somatic components of affect are split. As already mentioned, alexithymic patients experience strongly somatized affects and emotional ideas and words devoid of felt experience precisely because the somatic and psychic components of affect are split. McDougall (1985) also sees alexithymia as a disturbance in object relations wherein the patient is unable to evoke a benign introject with respect to the analyst. Another type of split in affective components is the split between affective experience and the self-representation or object representations. Such intense affective states may become derepresented in that the affect (much like a mood) is no longer associated with internal object representations or self-representation.

Zilboorg (1933) describes another type of split with respect to obsessions, panic attack, and psychomotor tics. According to Zilboorg, three well-integrated affective components are manifest in normal anxiety reactions: ideational content, the feeling tone (awareness of visceral experience), and the motor reaction. In obsessions, the ideational content remains in consciousness, and the feeling tone and motor reaction are split off. In panic attacks, the feeling tone and motor reaction remain conscious, and the ideational content is split off. In psychogenic tics, the motor reaction manifests itself, and the ideational content and feeling tone are split off. These examples of splitting are seen as a defensive loss in the normal somatic–cognitive integration of affective components through which the usually integrated ideation, selfobject representations, visceral experience, and motor expressive components of affect become separated.

Trauma: Fragmenting Regressive Shifts

In his discussion of the normal line of self-development and associated self-pathology, Lichtenberg (1975) distinguishes between nonfragmenting and fragmenting regressive shifts. Previously attained structural gains are lost in fragmenting shifts but are not lost in nonfragmenting shifts. Lichtenberg's distinction may be a useful way to understand different types of regression not only with respect to self-development but also with respect to affective development. The regressive swings just described refer to nonfragmenting shifts in which a normal adult experiences temporary and sometimes severe regression along the continuum of affective development but does not lose the ability to experience affect in a normal way under any conditions other than those in which the regression has occurred.

Fragmenting shifts in affective development occur during and subsequent to extreme traumatization. Posttraumatic stress disorder (PTSD) is, in part, a condition that disrupts the normal capacity for affective experience in an enduring way. Krystal (1988) has written extensively on how adult experience of massive traumatization such as an experience in the Nazi Holocaust can result in severe regression along the affective development continuum, with the subsequent development of a more or less enduring condition such as alexithymia or chronic affective numbing. Although the normal adult may show temporary alexithymic characteristics and lapses in the capacity to tolerate certain affects (a nonfragmenting shift), the severely traumatized adult may develop relatively enduring pathological conditions. The capacity to modulate the intensity of affects within an optimal range may also be lost through traumatization. As a result, PTSD is often characterized by the extremes of impulses and associated affects—feeling too little or too much aggression or sexual desire (Brown and Fromm, 1986).

Psychotherapy

One of the main contributions of Gedo and Goldberg's (1973) landmark, *Models of the Mind*, is its thesis that the treatment model that guides the therapy needs to be matched to the developmental level of the given patient. With respect to affect pathology, likewise, the approaches to and goals of psychotherapy differ for each major level of psychopathological organization—psychosis, personality disorder, neurosis, and relative health. Dynamic uncovering is not indicated for the schizophrenic patient. A therapy that focuses on correcting the fundamental problem of affective experience is well matched to the level of affective deficit in such patients (Brown, 1985; Perry, 1980; Semrad and van Buskirk, 1969). With high-functioning paranoid schizophrenic patients, whose problem is less with the capacity to register the visceral substrates of affect experience consciously and more with the integration of the cognitive, visceral, and expressive components of affect in awareness, the goal may be to help the patient link memories, fantasies, and representations with visceral experience (Brown, 1985). With personality-disordered patients, approaches that emphasize the internalization of self-soothing capacities (Buie and Adler, 1982; Krystal and Raskin, 1970), tolerance of affect (Zetzel, 1949, 1965), and verbalization of affect (Krystal, 1979; McDougall, 1985) are well suited to the types of affective pathology characteristic of this group of patients. Dynamic uncovering approaches are especially appropriate for neurotic patients, whose primary problem is disavowal or the accurate recognition of affect (Allen, 1980; Gedo and Goldberg, 1973). Such therapies also emphasize working through transference distortions, that is, the modification of the links between affects and early self- and object representations.

Moreover, psychotherapy can assist healthy-neurotic patients to progress along the continuum of affective development in a number of ways: recognize and experience a wide range of subtle and often complex and interrelated emotions and emotional concepts; develop and refine a language to express emotions; understand the meaning of an affective situation; help the patient to "own" the emotional experience, that is, to see it as a vital dimension of self-experience; reduce externalization of affect so as to see affect as an internal state; assist in the contextualizing of affect, so that the patient is increasingly aware of which external events/ interactions precipitate a given emotional state; distinguish clearly between the feeling and acting on the feeling; develop appropriate verbal, transformational, and sublimatory channels for affective expression; and teach disciplined self-awareness, so that the patient reflects in the workings of his or her own mind and on how affects come into existence (Kantrowitz, 1986). In other words, psychotherapy can assist in fostering mastery of the affective developmental tasks from latency to adulthood for the many individuals in whom this line of development remains incomplete. Psychotherapy is one medium of adult affective development in the sense that it serves the purpose of disciplined conscious reflection on affective processes.

REFERENCES

Abramson, L. (1991), Facial expressivity in failure to thrive in normal infants. *Merrill-Palmer Quart.*, 37:159–182.
Adler, G. (1980), Transference, real relationship and alliance. *Internat. J. Psychoanal.*, 61:547–558.
———— (1981), The borderline-narcissistic personality disorder continuum. *Amer. J. Psychiat.*, 138:46–50.
Ainsworth, M. D. S. (1979), Infant-mother attachment. *Amer. Psycholog.*, 34:932–937.
———— Blehar, M. C., Waters, E. & Wall, S. (1978), *Patterns of Attachment*. Hillsdale, NJ: Lawrence Erlbaum Associates.
Al-Rihini, S. (1985), The effect of the family socialization pattern on children's feelings of security. *Dirasat*, 12:199–219.

Alexander, T., Stolye, J., Roberge, J. & Leaverton, P. (1971), Developmental characteristics of emotional experience. *J. Genetic Psychol.*, 119:109–117.

Allen, J. G. (1980), Adaptive functions of affect and their implications for therapy. *Psychoanal. Rev.*, 67:217–230.

Andreason, N. (1979), Affective flattening and the criteria for schizophrenia. *Amer. J. Psych.*, 136:944–947.

Arieti, S. (1955), *Interpretation of Schizophrenia*. New York: Basic Books.

Arnold, M. B. (1960), *Emotion and Personality*. New York: Columbia University Press.

Averill, J. R. (1980), A constructivist view of emotion. In: *Emotion: Theory, Research and Experience*, Vol. 1., ed. R. Plutchik & H. Kellerman. New York: Academic Press, pp. 305–340.

Ax, A. F. (1953), The psychological differentiation between fear and anger in humans. *Psychosom. Med.*, 15:433–442.

Bach, S. (1977), On the narcissistic state of consciousness. *Internat. J. Psychoanal.*, 58:209–233.

_____ (1985), *Narcissistic States and the Therapeutic Process*. New York: Aronson.

Baker, E. L. (1981), An hypnotherapeutic approach to enhance object relatedness in psychotic patients. *Internat. J. Clin. Exp. Hypn.*, 29:136–147.

_____ (1990), Hypnoanalysis for structural pathology: Impairments of self-representation and capacity for object involvement. In: *Creative Mastery in Hypnosis and Hypnoanalysis*, ed. M. Fass & D. Brown. Hillsdale, NJ: Lawrence Erlbaum Associates, pp. 279–286.

Barden, R. C., Zelko, F. A., Duncan, S. W. & Masters, J. C. (1980), Children's consensual knowledge about the experiential determinants of emotion. *J. Personal. Soc. Psychol.*, 39:968–976.

Bartsch, K. & Wellman, H. (1989), Young children's attribution of action to beliefs and desires. *Child Develop.*, 60:946–964.

Basch, M. F. (1976), The concept of affect: A re-examination. *J. Amer. Psychol. Assn.*, 24:759–777.

Bateson, G., Jackson, D., Haley, J. & Weaklan, J. (1956), Toward a theory of schizophrenia. *Behav. Sci.*, 1:251–254.

Bennett, S. L. (1983), Early emotion. In: *Affect*, ed. M. B. Cantor & M. L. Glucksman. New York: Wiley, pp. 97–114.

Biringen, Z. & Robinson, J. (1991), Emotional availability in mother–child interactions. *Amer. J. Orthopsychiat.*, 61:258–271.

Birns, B., Blank, M. & Bridger, W. H. (1966), The effectiveness of various soothing techniques on human infants. *Psychosom. Med.*, 28:316–322.

Blanck, G. & Blanck, R. (1974), *Ego Psychology*. New York: Columbia University Press.

Bleuler, E. (1950), *Dementia Praecox or the Group of Schizophrenics*, trans. J. Zinkin. New York: IUP.

Blinn, L. M. & Pike, G. (1989), Future time perspectives. *Adolescence*, 24:289–301.

Blos, P. (1961), *On Adolescence*. New York: Free Press.

_____ (1979), *The Adolescent Passage*. New York: IUP.

Blumberg, S. H. & Izard, C. E. (1991), Patterns of emotional experiences as predictors of facial expressions of emotion. *Merrill-Palmer Quart.*, 37:183–197.

Borke, H. (1971), Interpersonal perception of young children. *Dev. Psychol.*, 5:262–269.

_____ (1973), The development of empathy in Chinese and American children between the ages of three and six years: A cross-cultural study. *Developmental Psychol.*, 9:102–108.

Braverman, M., Fein, D., Lucci, D. & Waterhouse, L. (1989), Affect comprehension in children with pervasive developmental disorders. *J. Autism Dev. Disord.*, 19:301–316.

Brenner, C. (1974), On the nature and development of affect: A unified theory. *Psychoanal. Quart.*, 43:532–556.

———— (1989), A psychoanalytic theory of affects. In: *Emotion, Vol. 1*, ed. R. Plutchik & H. Kellerman. New York: Academic Press, pp. 341–347.

Bridges, K. M. B. (1932), Emotional development in early infancy. *Child Dev.*, 3:324–341.

Brody, L. & Carter, A. (1982), Children's emotional attributions to self versus other. *J. Consult. Clin. Psychol.*, 50:665–671.

———— & Harrison, R. (1987), Developmental changes in children's abilities to match and label emotionally laden situations. *Motiva. & Emotion*, 2:347–365.

Bronson, W. C. (1966), Early antecedents of emotional expressiveness and reactivity control. *Child Dev.*, 37:793–810.

Brown, D. (1977), A model for the levels of concentrative meditation. *Internat. J. Clin. Exp. Hypn.*, 25:236–273.

———— (1985), Hypnosis as an adjunct to the psychotherapy of the severely disturbed patient. *Internat. J. Clin. Exp. Hypno.*, 33:281–301.

———— & Fromm, E. (1986), *Hypnotherapy and Hypnoanalysis*. Hillsdale, NJ: Lawrence Erlbaum Associates.

Brown, K., Covell, K. & Abramovitch, R. (1991), Time course and control of emotion. *Merrill-Palmer Quart.*, 37:273–287.

Brownfield, C. A. (1966), Optimal stimulation levels of normal and disturbed subjects in sensory deprivation. *Psychologia*, 9:27–38.

Buck, R., Miller, R. E. & Caul, W. F. (1974), Sex, personality, and psychological variables in the communication of affect via facial expression. *J. Personal. Soc. Psychol.*, 30:587–596.

Buie, D. H. & Adler, G. (1982), Definitive therapy of the borderline personality. *Internat. J. Psychoanal. Psychother.*, 9:51–87.

Burnham, D. L., Gladstone, A. I. & Gibson, R. W. (1969), *Schizophrenia and the Need-Fear Dilemma*. New York: IUP.

Burnsten, B. (1973), Some narcissistic personality types. *Internat. J. Psychoanal.*, 54:287–300.

Buss, A. H., Iscoe, I. & Buss, E. (1979), The development of embarrassment. *J. Psychol.*, 103:227–230.

———— & Lang, P. J. (1965), Psychological deficit in schizophrenia. *J. Abnorm. Psychol.*, 70:2–24.

Bychowski, G. (1952), *Psychotherapy of Psychosis*. New York: Grune & Stratton.

Campos, J. J., Hiatt, S., Ramsay, D., Henderson, C. & Svejda, M. (1978), The emergence of fear on the visual cliff. In: *The Development of Affect*, ed. M. Lewis & L. Rosenbaum. New York: Plenum Press, pp. 149–182.

———— & Sternberg, C. (1981), Perception, appraisal, and emotion. In: *Infant Social Cognition*, ed. M. Lamb & L. R. Sherrod. Hillsdale, NJ: Lawrence Erlbaum Associates, pp. 273–314.

Carter, A. A., Mayers, L. C. & Pajer, K. A. (1990), The role of dyadic affect in play and infant sex in predicting infant response to the still-face situation. *Child Dev.*, 61:764–773.

Caulfield, M. B., Fischel, J. E., DeBaryshe, B. D. & Whitehurst, G. J. (1989), Behavioral correlates of developmental expressive language disorders. *J. Abnorm. Child Psychol.*, 17:187–201.

Chapman, J. (1966), The early signs of schizophrenia. *Psychiatry*, 112:225–251.

———— & Ghieth, M. (1961), A comparative study of disordered attention in schizophrenia. *J. Ment. Sci.*, 108:481–500.

Craik, F. & Lockhart, R. (1972), Levels of processing. *J. Verbal Learn. Verbal Behav.*, 11:671–684.

Csikszentmihalyi, M. & Larson, R. W. (1984), *Being Adolescent*. New York: Basic Books.

Cummings, E., Zahn-Waxler, C. & Radke-Yarrow, M. (1984), Developmental changes in children's reactions to anger in the home. *J. Child Psychol. Psychiat.*, 25:63–74.

Danesi, M. (1989), Adolescent language as affectively coded behavior. *Adolescence*, 24:311–320.

de Rivera, J. (1977), A structural theory of emotions. *Psychological Issues*, Monogr. 10, ed. G. S. Klein. New York: IUP, pp. 9–169.

Demos, J. (1982), The changing faces of fatherhood: A new exploration in American family history. In: *Father and Child: Developmental and Clinical Perspectives*, ed. S. Cath, A. Gurwitt & J. Ross. Boston: Little, Brown, pp. 425–445.

Denham, S. A. (1989), Maternal affect and toddlers' social-emotional competence. *Amer. J. Orthopsychiat.*, 59:368–376.

_____ McKinley, M., Couchoud, E. A. & Holt, R. (1990), Emotional and behavioral predictors of preschool peer ratings. *Child Dev.*, 61:1145–1152.

Diener, E., Sandvik, E. & Larson, R. W. (1985), Age and sex effects for emotional intensity. *Dev. Psycholog.*, 21:542–546.

Dix, T., Ruble, D. N., Grusce, J. E. & Nixon, S. (1986), Social cognition in parents. *Child Dev.*, 57(4):879–894.

Duclos, S. E., Laird, J. D., Schneider, E. & Sexter, M. (1989), Emotion specific effects of facial expressions and postures on emotional experience. *J. Personal. Soc. Psychol.*, 57:100–108.

Eder, R. A. (1989), The emergent personologist. *Child Dev.*, 60:1218–1228.

Eisenberg, N., Fabes, R., Miller, P. A., Shell, R., Shea, C. & May-Plumlee, T. (1990), Preschoolers' vicarious emotional responding and their situational and dispositional prosocial behavior. *Merrill-Palmer Quart.*, 36:507–529.

Eissler, K. (1953), Notes upon the emotionality of a schizophrenic patient and its relation to problems of technique. *The Psychoanalytic Study of the Child*, 7:199–251. New York: IUP.

Ekman, P. & Friesen, W. V. (1986), A new pan–cultural facial expression of emotion. *Motiva. & Emotion*, 10:159–168.

Ekstein, R. & Wallerstein, J. (1955), Observations on the psychology of borderline and psychotic children. *The Psychoanalytic Study of the Child*, 9:344–369. New York: IUP.

Emde, R. N. (1983), The prerepresentational self and its affective core. *The Psychoanalytic Study of the Child*, 38:165–192. New Haven, CT: Yale University Press.

_____ Gaensbauer, T. J. & Harmon, R. J. (1976), *Emotional Expression in Infancy. Psychological Issues*, Monogr. 37, pp. 3–85.

_____ Kligman, D., Reich, J. & Wade, T. (1978), Emotional expression in infancy. In: *The Development of Affect*, ed. M. Lewis & L. Rosenblum. New York: Basic Books, pp. 125–148.

Faupel, K. C. (1989), Adolescent psychic entropy. *Adolescence*, 24:375–379.

Fernald, A. (1989), Intonation and communicative intent in mothers' speech to infants. *Child Dev.*, 60:1497–1510.

Field, T. M. (1978), The three R's of infant–adult interactions. *J. Pediatr. Psychol.*, 3:131–136.

Fleck, S. (1980), Some observations on the nature and value of psychotherapy with schizophrenic patients. In: *The Psychotherapy of Schizophrenia*, ed. J. S. Strauss, M. Bowers, T. W. Downey, S. Fleck, S. Jackson & I. Levine. New York: Plenum Press, pp. 55–64.

Fogel, A. & Reimers, M. (1989), On the psychobiology of emotions and their development. *Monographs Society Research Child Dev.*, 54:105–113.

Forrai-Banlaki, E. (1965), Recognition of the expression of affects as a function of intellectual maturity in 7–9 year old children. *Pscichologiai Tanulmanyok*, 8:139–151.

Fox, N. A. & Fitzgerald, H. E. (1990), Autonomic function in infancy. *Merrill-Palmer Quart.*, 36:27–51.

Free, K. & Goodrich, W. (1985), Transitional object attachment in normal and in chronically disturbed adolescents. *Child Psychiat. Human Dev.*, 16:30–44.

Freud, A., ed. (1965), The concept of developmental lines. In: *The Writings of Anna Freud, Vol. 6*. New York: IUP, pp. 62–106.

Freud, S. (1926), *Inhibitions, symptoms, and anxiety. Standard Edition*, 20:159–209. London: Hogarth Press, 1959.

_____ (1933), *New Introductory Lectures on Psycho-Analysis. Standard Edition*, 22:5–182. London: Hogarth Press, 1964.

Frijda, N. H., Kuipers, P. &. ter Schure, E. (1989), Relations among emotion, appraisal, and emotional action readiness. *J. Personal. Soc. Psychol.*, 57:212–228.

Furman, R. A. (1978), Some developmental aspects of the verbalization of affects. *The Psychoanalytic Study of the Child*, 33:187–211. New Haven, CT: Yale University Press.

Gedo, J. (1984), *Psychoanalysis and Its Discontents*. New York: Guilford Press.

_____ & Goldberg, A. (1973), *Models of the Mind*. Chicago: University of Chicago Press.

Gemelli, A. (1949), Orienting concepts in the study of affective states. *J. Nerv. Ment. Dis.*, 110:198–214.

Gibson, J. J. (1966), *The Senses Considered as Perceptual Systems*. Boston: Houghton Mifflin.

Gilbert, D. (1969), The young child's awareness of affect. *Child Dev.*, 40(2):629–640.

Glasberg, R. &. Aboud, F. (1982), Keeping one's distance from sadness. *Dev. Psychol.*, 287–293.

Greene, A. L. (1990), Patterns of affectivity in the transition to adolescence. *J. Exp. Child Psychol.*, 50:340–356.

_____ & Larson, R. W. (1991), Variation in stress reactivity during adolescence. In: *Life-Span Perspectives on Stress and Coping*, ed. E. M. Cummings, A. L. Greene &. K. H. Karraker. Hillsdale, NJ: Lawrence Erlbaum Associates.

Greenspan, S. & Greenspan, N. T. (1985), *First Feelings*. New York: Viking Press.

_____ & Lourie, R. S. (1981), Developmental structuralist approach to the classification of adaptive and pathological personality organizations. *Amer. J. Psychiat.*, 138:725–735.

_____ & Porges, S. W. (1984), Psychopathology in infancy and early childhood. *Child Dev.*, 55(1):49–70.

Griffin, G. W. (1987), Childhood predictive characteristics of aggressive adolescents. *Exceptional Children*, 54:246–252.

Harkness, S. (1983), The cultural construction of child development. *Ethos*, 11:221–231.

Harris, P., Olthof, T. &. Terwogt, M. (1981), Children's knowledge of emotions. *J. Child Psychol. Psychiat.*, 22:247–261.

Harter, S. (1977), A cognitive-developmental approach to children's expression of conflicting feelings and a technique to facilitate such expression in play therapy. *J. Consult. Clin. Psychol.*, 45:427–432.

_____ (1982), A cognitive-developmental approach to children's understanding of affect and trait labels. In: *Social-Cognitive Development in Context*, ed. F. Serafica. New York: Guilford, pp. 27–61.

_____ & Buddin, B. J. (1987), Children's understanding of the similarity of two emotions. *Dev. Psychol.*, 23:388–399.

Hilgard, E. R. (1977), *Divided Consciousness*. New York: Wiley.

Hippler, A. (1977), Cultural evolution. *J. Psychohist.*, 4:419–438.

Holzman, P. S. (1970), Perceptual dysfunction in the schizophrenic syndrome. In: *The Schizophrenic Reactions*, ed. M. M. Gill &. P. S. Holzman. New York: Brunner/Mazel, pp. 216–232.

Horner, A. J. (1979), *Object Relations and the Developing Ego in Therapy*. New York: Brunner/ Mazel.

Horton, P. C., Lovy, J. W. &. Coppolillo, H. P. (1974), Personality disorders and transitional relatedness. *Arch. Gen. Psychiat.*, 30:618–622.

Hunt, J. Mc. V. (1965), Intrinsic motivation and its role in psychological development. In: *Nebraska Symposium on Motivation*, ed. D. Levine, 13:189–226.

Inagaki, K. (1989), Developmental shift in biological inference processes. *Human Dev.*, 32:79–87.

Izard, C. E. (1971), *The Face of Emotion*. New York: Appleton-Century-Crofts.

_____ (1977), *Human Emotions*. New York: Plenum Press.

_____ Porges, S. W., Simons, R. F. & Hayes, O. M. (1991), Infant cardiac activity. *Dev. Psychol.*, 27:432–434.

Jacobson, E. (1971), Norman and pathological moods. In: *Depression,* ed. E. Jacobson. New York: IUP.

Jacobson, E. (1973), *The Self and the Object World.* New York: IUP.

James, W. (1980), *The Principles of Psychology.* New York: Holt.

Joffe, W. G. & Sandler, J. (1966), Notes on pain, depression and individuation. *The Psychoanalytic Study of the Child,* 20:394–424. New York: IUP.

Jones, S. S. & Raag, T. (1989), Smile production in older infants. *Child Dev.,* 60:811–818.

Kagan, J. (1978), On emotion and its development. In: *The Development of Affect,* ed. M. Lewis & L. A. Rosenblum. New York: Plenum Press, pp. 11–42.

_____ & Greenspan, S. I. (1986), Milestones of development: A dialogue. *Zero to Three,* 6(5):1–9.

_____ Moss, H. A. & Sigel, I. E. (1960), Conceptual style and the use of affect labels. *Merrill-Palmer Quart.,* 6:261–278.

Kantrowitz, J. L. (1986), Affect availability, tolerance, complexity and modulation in psychoanalysis: Follow-up of a longitudinal, prospective study. *J. Amer. Psychoanal. Assn.,* 34:529–559.

Kaslow, N. & Wamboldt, F. S. (1985), Childhood depression: Current perspectives and future directions. *J. Nerv. Ment. Dis.,* 125:181–201.

Katan, A. (1961), Some thoughts about the role of verbalization in early childhood. *J. Soc. Clin. Psychol.,* 3:416–424.

Kegan, R. (1982), *The Evolving Self.* Cambridge, MA: Harvard University Press.

Kellerman, H. (1980), A structural model of emotion and personality. In: *Emotion,* vol. 1, ed. R. Plutchik & H. Kellerman. New York: Academic Press, pp. 349–384.

Kernberg, O. (1968), The treatment of patients with borderline personality organization. *Internat. J. Psycho-Anal.,* 49:600–619.

_____ (1976), *Object Relations Theory and Clinical Psychoanalysis.* New York: Aronson.

Khantzian, E. (1978), The ego, the self and opiate addiction. *Internat. Rev. Psychoanal.,* 5:189–198.

Kish, G. B. (1970), Cognitive innovation and stimulus seeking. *Percept. Motor Skills,* 30:95–101.

Klaus, M., Jerauld, R., Kereger, N., McAlpine, W., Steffa, M. & Kennell, J. (1972), Maternal attachment: Importance of the first post-partum days. *New Engl. J. Med.,* 286:460–463.

Klein, G. S. (1967), Peremptory ideation: Structure and force in motivated ideas. In: *Motives and Thought,* ed. R. R. Holt. New York: IUP, pp. 80–130.

Kohut, H. (1971), *The Analysis of Self.* New York: IUP.

_____ (1988), *The Restoration of the Self.* New York: IUP.

Kopp, C. B. (1982), The antecedents of self-regulation: A developmental perspective. *Dev. Psychol.,* 18:199–214.

Krystal, H. (1974), The genetic development of affects and affect regression. *The Annual of Psychoanalysis,* 2:98–126. New York: IUP.

_____ (1975), Affect tolerance. *The Annual of Psychoanalysis,* 3:179–219. New York: IUP.

_____ (1977), Aspects of affect theory. *Bull. Menn. Clin.,* 41:1–26.

_____ (1979), Alexithymia and psychotherapy. *Amer. J. Psychother.,* 33:17–31.

_____ (1982–83), Alexithymia and the effectiveness of psychoanalytic treatment. *Internat. J. Psychoanal. Psychother.,* 9:353–378.

_____ (1985), Trauma and the stimulus barrier. *Psychoanal. Inq.,* 5:131–161.

_____ (1988), *Integration and Self-Healing.* Hillsdale, NJ: The Analytic Press.

_____ & Raskin, H. (1970), *Drug Dependence.* Detroit: Wayne State University Press.

Labouvie-Vief, G., Hakin-Larson, J., DeVoe, M. & Schoeberlein, S. (1989), Emotions and self-regulation. *Human Dev.,* 32:279–299.

Laird, J. D. (1974), Self-attribution of emotion. *J. Personal. Soc. Psychol.,* 29:475–486.

Lane, R. D. & Schwartz, G. E. (1987), Levels of emotional awareness. *Amer. J. Psychiat.*, 144:133–143.

Lang, P. J., Bradley, M. M. & Cuthbert, B. N. (1990), Emotion, attention and the startle reflex. *Psychol. Rev.*, 97:377–395.

_____ & Buss, A. H. (1965), Psychological deficit in schizophrenia. *J. Abn. Psychol.*, 70:77–106.

Larson, R. & Lampman–Petraitis, C. (1989), Daily emotional states as reported by children and adolescents. *Child Dev.*, 60:1250–1260.

Lazarus, R. S. (1982), Thoughts on the relations between emotion and cognition. *Amer. Psychol.*, 37:1019–1024.

_____ (1991), *Emotion and Adaptation.* New York: Oxford University Press.

Leff, J. P. (1973), Culture and the differentiation of emotional states. *Brit. J. Psychol.*, 23:299–306.

Leventhal, H. (1980), Toward a comprehensive theory of emotion. *Adv. Exp. Soc. Psychol.*, 13:139–207.

Lewis, M. (1979), A developmental study of the cardiac response to stimulus onset and offset during the first year of life. *Psychophysiol.*, 8:689–698.

_____ & Brooks, J. (1978), Self-knowledge and emotional development. In: *The Development of Affect*, ed. M. Lewis & L. A. Rosenblum. New York: Plenum Press, pp. 205–226.

_____ _____ & Haviland, J. (1978), Hearts and faces: A study in the measurement of emotion. In: *The Development of Affect*, ed. M. Lewis & L. A. Rosenblum. New York: Plenum Press, pp. 77–123.

_____ & Brooks-Gunn, J. (1979), *Social Cognition and the Acquisition of Self.* New York: Plenum Press.

_____ & Feiring, C. (1989), Infant, mother, and mother–infant interaction behavior and subsequent attachment. *Child Dev.*, 60:831–837.

Lichtenberg, J. (1975), The development of a sense of self. *J. Amer. Psychoanal. Assn.*, 23:354–383.

Lucas, R. (1992), The psychotic personality: A psychoanalytic theory and its application in clinical practice. *Psychoanal. Psychother.*, 6:73–79.

Mahler, M. (1961), On sadness and grief in infancy and childhood. *The Psychoanalytic Study of the Child*, 16:332–351. New York: IUP.

Mahler, M. S., Pine, F. & Bergman, A. (1975), *The Psychological Birth of the Human Infant.* New York: Basic Books.

Malatesta, C. Z. (1981), Affective development over the life span. *Merrill-Palmer Quart.*, 27:145–173.

_____ Culver, C., Tesman, J. R. & Shepard, B. (1989), The development of emotion expression during the first two years of life. *Monographs of the Society for Research in Child Development*, 54:1–104.

_____ & Haviland, J. M. (1982), Learning display rules. *Child Dev.*, 53:991–1003.

Marks, I. M. (1987), The development of normal fear. *J. Child Psychol. Psychiat. Allied Discip.*, 28:667–697.

Mason, R. E. (1961), *Internal Perception and Bodily Functioning.* New York: IUP.

Matias, R., Cohn, J. F. & Ross, S. (1989), A comparison of two systems that code infant affective expression. *Dev. Psychol.*, 25(4):483–489.

Matlin, M. & Stang, D. (1978), *The Polyanna Principle: Selectivity in Language, Memory and Thought.* Cambridge, MA: Schnekman.

Mayer, J. D., Salovey, P., Gomberg-Kaufman, S. & Blainey, K. (1991), A broader conception of mood experience. *J. Personal. Soc. Psychol.*, 60:100–111.

McDougall, J. (1982), Alexithymia, psychosomatosis, and psychosis. *Internat. J. Psychoanal. Psychother.*, 9:379–388.

_____ (1985), *Theatres of the Mind.* New York: Brunner/Mazel.

McGhie, A. & Chapman, J. (1961), Disorders of attention and perception in early schizophrenia. *Brit. J. Med. Psychol.*, 34:103–116.

Meadow, P. W. (1991), Resonating with the psychotic patient. *Modern Psychoanal.*, 16:87–103.

Meyer, G. J. & Shack, J. R. (1989), Structural convergence of mood and personality. *J. Personal. Soc. Psychol.*, 57:691–706.

Modell, A. H. (1968), *Object Love and reality*. New York: IUP.

_____ (1975), A narcissistic defense against affects. *Internat. J. Psycho-Anal.*, 56:275–282.

_____ (1980), Affects and their non-communication. *Internat. J. Pyscho-Anal.*, 61:259–267.

Mood, D. W., Johnson, J. E. & Shantz, C. (1978), Social comprehension and affect matching in young children. *Merrill-Palmer Quart.*, 24:63–66.

Murphy, L. B. (1983), Issues in the development of emotion in infancy. In: *Emotion, Vol. 2*, ed. R. Plutchik & H. Kellerman. New York: Academic Press, pp. 1–34.

_____ & Moriarty, A. (1976), *Vulnerability, Coping and Growth*. New Haven, CT: Yale University Press.

Neisser, U. (1967), *Cognitive Psychology*. New York: Appleton-Century-Crofts.

Nemiah, J. C. (1975), Denial revisited. *Psychother. Psychosom.*, 64:169–186.

_____ & Sifneos, P. (1970), Affect and fantasy in patients with psychosomatic disorders. In: *Modern Trends in Psychosomatic Medicine*. London: Butterworth.

Newson, J., Newson, E. & Mahalski, P. A. (1982), Persistent infant comfort habits and their sequelae at 11 and 16 years. *J. Child Psychol. Psychiat. Allied Discip.*, 23:421–436.

Novey, S. (1961), Further considerations of affect theory in psychoanalysis. *Internat. J. Psycho-Anal.*, 43:21–32.

Ohrenstein, L. (1986), There is nothing latent about latency. *Child Adolesc. Soc. Work J.*, 3:143–150.

Ollendick, T. H., Matson, J. L. & Helsel, W. J. (1985), Fears in children and adolescents. *Behav. Res. Ther.*, 23:465–467.

Olson, S. L., Bates, J. E. & Bayles, K. (1990), Early antecedents of childhood impulsivity. *J. Abn. Child Psychol.*, 18:317–334.

Ornstein, P. D. (1974), On narcissism. *Annual Rev. Psychoanal.*, 2:127–149.

Ortony, A. & Turner, T. J. (1990), What's basic about basic emotions. *Psychol. Rev.*, 97:315–331.

Pancer, S. M. & Weinstein, S. M. (1987), The development of affective skills in school-aged children. *J. Appl. Dev. Psychol.*, 8:165–181.

Papousek, M. (1989), Determinants of responsiveness to infant vocal expression of emotional state. *Infant Beh. & Dev.*, 12:517–524.

Pawlby, S. (1977), Imitative interaction. In: *Studies in Mother–Infant Interaction*, ed. H. R. Schaeffer. New York: Academic Press, pp. 203–224.

Pennebaker, J. W. (1982), *The Psychology of Physical Symptoms*. New York: Springer.

Perry, J. (1980), Psychotherapy with schizophrenics. McLean Hospital, Belmont, MA. Unpublished manuscript.

Peto, A. (1968), On affect control. *Internat. J. Psycho-Anal.*, 49:471–473.

Phillips, R. D., Wagner, S. H., Fells, C. A. & Lynch, M. (1990), Do infants recognize emotion in facial expressions? *Infant Behav. Dev.*, 13:71–84.

Piaget, J. (1952), *The Origins of Intelligence*. New York: Norton.

_____ (1981), *Intelligence and Affectivity*. Annual Reviews Monograph. Palo Alto, CA: Annual Reviews.

Piers, M. A. & Curry, N. E. (1985), A developmental perspective on children's affects. *J. Children Contemp. Soc.*, 17(4):23–36.

Pine, F. (1979), On the expansion of the affect array. *Bull. Menn. Clin.*, 43:79–95.

Plutchik, R. (1980), A general psychoevolutionary theory of emotion. In: *Emotion, Vol. 1*, ed. R. Plutchik & H. Kellerman. New York: Academic Press, pp. 3–34.

Pollak, L. H. & Thoits, P. A. (1989), Processes in emotional socialization. *Soc. Psychol. Quart.*, 52:22–34.

Pribram, K. H. (1980), The biology of emotion and other feelings. In: *Emotion, Vol. 1*, ed. R. Plutchik & H. Kellerman. New York: Academic Press, pp. 245–269.

_____ & Melges, F. T. (1969), Psychophysiological basis of emotion. In: *Handbook of Clinical Neurology, Vol. 3*, ed. P. J. Vinken & G. W. Bruyn. Amsterdam: North Holland.

Provence, S. & Lifton, R. (1962), *Infants in Institutions*. New York: IUP.

Rapaport, D. (1953), On the psychoanalytic theory of affects. *Internat. J. Psycho-Anal.*, 34:177–198.

Redding, R. E., Morgan, G. A. & Harmon, R. J. (1988), Mastery motivation in infants and toddlers. *Infant Behav. Dev.*, 11:419–430.

Reich, A. (1960), Pathologic formed self-esteem. In: *Anne Reich: Psychoanalytic Contributions*. New York: IUP, pp. 288–311.

Rohm, H. (1972), The relation between infantile affect and intellectual development. *Praxis der Kinderpsychologie und Kinderpsychiatrie*, 21(3):89–97.

Rosenbach, D., Crockett, W. H. & Wapner, S. (1973), Developmental level, emotional involvement and the resolution of inconsistency in impression formation. *Dev. Psychol.*, 8:120–130.

Russell, J. A. & Bullock, M. (1986), On the dimensions preschoolers use to interpret facial expressions of emotion. *Dev. Psychol.*, 22:97–102.

_____ Lewickam, M. & Niit, T. (1989), A cross-cultural study of a circumplex model of affect. *J. Personal. Soc. Psychol.*, 57:848–856.

_____ & Ridgeway, D. (1983), Dimensions underlying children's emotion concepts. *Dev. Psychol.*, 19:795–804.

Sander, L. W. (1975), Infant and caretaking environment: Investigation and conceptualization of adaptive behavior in a system of increasing complexity. In: *Explorations in Child Psychology*, ed. E. G. Anthony. New York: Plenum, pp. 126–166.

_____ & Julia, H. L. (1966), Continuous interactional monitoring in the neonate. *Psychosom. Med.*, 28:822–835.

Sandler, J. & Rosenblatt, B. (1962), The concept of the representational world. *The Psychoanalytic Study of the Child*, 17:128–146. New York: IUP.

_____ & Sandler, A. (1978), On the development of object relationships and affects. *Internat. J. Psycho-Anal.*, 59:285–296.

Sarnoff, C. (1976), *Latency*. New York: Aronson.

Schachter, S. & Singer, J. E. (1962), Cognitive, social and physiological determinants of emotional state. *Psychol. Rev.*, 69:379–399.

Schmale, A. (1964), A genetic view of affects. *The Psychoanalytic Study of the Child*, 19:287–310. New York: IUP.

Schneider-Rosen, K. & Cicchetti, D. (1991), Early self-knowledge and emotional development. *Dev. Psychol.*, 27:417–478.

Schur, M. (1955), Comments of the metapsychology of somatization. *The Psychoanalytic Study of the Child*, 10:119–164. New York: IUP.

_____ (1969), Affects and cognition. *Amer. J. Psychoanal.*, 50:647–653.

Schwartz, G. E., Brown, S. L. & Ahern, G. L. (1980), Facial muscle patterning and subjective experience during affective imagery. *Psychophysiol.*, 17:75–82.

_____ Fair, P. L., Mandel, M. R. & Klerman, G. L. (1976), Facial muscle patterning to affective imagery in depressed and non-depressed subjects. *Science*, 192:489–491.

Searles, H. F. (1984–85), The role of the analyst's facial expressions in psychoanalysis and psychoanalytic therapy. *Internat. J. Psychoanal. Psychother.*, 10:47–73.

Semrad, E. V. & van Buskirk, D. (1969), *Teaching Psychotherapy of Psychotic Patients*. New York: Grune & Stratton.

Sifneos, P. E. (1973), The prevalence of "alexithymic" characteristics in psychosomatic patients. *Psychother. Psychosom.*, 22:255–262.

_____ (1988), Alexithymia and its relationship to hemispheric specialization, affect and creativity. *Hemispheric Specialization*, 11:287–292.

Snow, C. E. (1972), Mothers' speech to children learning language. *Child Dev.*, 43:549–565.

Socarides, D. D. & Stolorow, R. D. (1984–85), Affects and self objects. *Annual of Psychoanalysis*, 12–13:105–119. New York: IUP.

Sokolov, E. N. (1960), Neuronal models and the orienting reflex. In: *The Central Nervous System and Behavior*, ed. M. Brazier. New York: Josiah Macy Jr. Foundation.

Sroufe, L. A. (1979a), The coherence of individual development. *Amer. Psychol.*, 34:834–841.

_____ (1979b), Socioemotional development. In: *Handbook of Infant Development*, ed. J. Osofsky. New York: Wiley, pp. 462–510.

_____ (1979b), The ontogenesis of emotion in infancy. In: *Handbook of Infant Development*, ed. J. Osofsky. New York: Wiley, pp. 491–510.

_____ (1984), The organization of emotional development. In: *Approaches to Emotion*, ed. K. R. Scherer & P. Ekman. Hillsdale, NJ: Lawrence Erlbaum Associates.

_____ & Rutter, M. (1984), The domain of developmental psychopathology. *Child. Dev.*, 55:17–29.

_____ & Jacobvitz, D. (1989), Diverging pathways, developing transformations, multiple etiologies and the problem on continuity in development. *Human Dev.*, 32:196–203.

_____ & Waters, E. (1976), The ontogenesis of smiling and laughter. *Psychol. Rev.*, 83:173–189.

Stanton, A. (1980), Insight and self-observation: Their role in the analysis of the etiology of illness. In: *The Psychotherapy of Schizophrenia*, ed. J. S. Strauss. New York: IUP, pp. 131–144.

Stechler, G. & Carpenter, G. (1967), A viewpoint on early affective development. In: *The Exceptional Infant*, ed. J. Hellmath. Seattle, WA: Special Child Publications, pp. 163–189.

Stern, D. (1974a), The goal and structure of mother-infant play. *J. Amer. Acad. Child Psychiat.*, 13:402–421.

_____ (1974b), Mother and infant at play: The dyadic interaction involving facial, vocal and gaze behaviors. In: *The Effect of the Infant on Its Caretaker*, ed. M. Lewis & L. A. Rosenblum. New York: Wiley, pp. 187–213.

_____ (1985), *The Interpersonal World of the Infant*. New York: Basic Books.

Stipek, D. J., Gralinski, H. & Kopp, C. B. (1990), Self-concept development in the toddler years. *Dev. Psychol.*, 26:972–977.

Stolorow, R. D. & Lachmann, F. M. (1980), *Psychoanalysis and Developmental Arrests*. New York: IUP.

Sullivan, M. W. & Lewis, M. (1989), Emotion and cognition in infancy. *Internat. J. Behav. Dev.*, 12:221–237.

Tartakoff, H. H. (1966), The normal personality in our culture and the Nobel Prize Complex. In: *Psychoanalysis—A General Psychology*, ed. R. M. Lowenstein, L. M. Newman, & A. J. Solnet. New York: IUP, pp. 222–252.

Tolpin, M. (1971), On the beginnings of a cohesive self. *The Psychoanalytic Study of the Child*, 26:316–352. New Haven, CT: Yale University Press.

Tomkins, S. S. (1962), *Affect, Imagery, Consciousness, Vol 1*. New York: Springer.

_____ (1963), *Affect, Imagery, Consciousness, Vol 2*. New York: Springer.

_____ (1968), Affects: Primary motives of man. *Humanitas*, 3:321–345.

_____ (1970), Affect as the primary motivational system. In: *Feelings and Emotions*, ed. M. Arnold. New York: Academic Press.

_____ & McCarter, R. (1964), What and where are the primary affects? Some evidence for a theory. *Percept. and Motor Skills*, 18:118–158.

Trevarthan, C. & Hubley, P. (1978), Secondary intersubjectivity. In: *Action, Gesture and Symbol*, ed. A. Lock. New York: Academic Press.

Tronick, E. & Cohn, J. (1989), Infant–mother face-to-face interaction. *Child Dev.*, 60:85–92.

_____ Ricks, M. & Cohn, J.D. (1982), Maternal and infant affective exchange. In: *Emotion and Early Interaction*, ed. T. Field & A. Fogel. Hillsdale, NJ: Lawrence Erlbaum Associates.

Urberg, K. A. & Docherty, E. M. (1976), Development of role-taking skills in young children. *Dev. Psychol.*, 12:198–203.

Venables, P. H. (1964), Input dysfunction in schizophrenia. In: *Progress in Experimental Personality Research*, ed. B. A. Maher. New York: Academy, pp. 1–45.

Vibbert, M. & Bornstein, M. H. (1989), Specific associations between domains of mother–child interaction and toddler referential language and pretense play. *Infant Behav. Dev.*, 12:163–184.

Volkan, V. (1976), *Primitive Internalized Object Relations*. New York: IUP.

Waern, Y. (1977), Psychological understanding in 6–12 year old children. *Scand. J. Psychol.*, 18:21–30.

Waters, E. (1978), The reliability and stability of individual differences in infant–mother attachment. *Child Dev.*, 49:483–494.

Watson, D. & Tellegan, A. (1985), Toward a consensual structure of mood. *Psychol. Bull.*, 98:219–235.

_____ & _____ (1988), Development and validation of brief measures of positive and negative affect: The PANAS scales. *J. Person. & Soc. Psychol.*, 54:1063–1970.

White, R. (1959), Motivation reconsidered. *Psychol. Rev.*, 66:297–333.

Whitesell, N. R. & Harter, S. (1989), Children's reports of conflict between simultaneous opposite-valence emotions. *Child Dev.*, 60:673–682.

Wilbur, K., Engler, J. & Brown, D. (1986), *Transformations of Consciousness*. Boston: Shambala.

Winnicott, D. W. (1953), Transitional objects and transitional phenomena. *Internat. J. Psycho-Anal.*, 34:89–97.

Wintre, M. G., Polivy, J. & Murray, M. A. (1990), Self-predictions of emotional response patterns. *Child Dev.*, 61:1124–1133.

Wolff, P. H. (1966), The causes, controls, and organization of behavior in the neonate. In: *Psychological Issues*, Monogr. 17, ed. G. S. Klein. New York: IUP.

Wolman, R. N., Lewis, W. C. & King, M. (1971), The development of emotions. *Child Dev.*, 42:1288–1293.

_____ _____ _____ (1972a), The development of the language of emotions: IV. *J. Genet. Psychol.*, 120:65–81.

_____ _____ _____ (1972b), The development of the language of emotions: I. *J. Genet. Psychol.*, 120:167–176.

Wood, J. V., Saltzberg, J. A. & Goldsamt, L. A. (1990), Does affect induce self-focused attention? *J. Personal. Soc. Psychol.*, 58:899–908.

Worobey, J. & Blajda, V. (1989), Temperament ratings at 2 weeks, 2 months, and 1 year. *Dev. Psychol.*, 25:257–263.

Yarrow, L. J. (1979), Emotional development. *Amer. Psychol.*, 25:257–263.

Zagorska, W. (1987), Badania nad rozpoznawaniem emocji na podstawie ekspresji mimicznej i kontektu syntuacyjnego [Studies of emotion recognition based on facial expression and situational context]. *Psychologia Wychowawcza*, 30:32–39.

Zajonc, R. B. (1980), Feeling and thinking: Preferences need no inferences. *Amer. Psychol.*, 35:151–175.

Zaporozhets, A. V. & Neverovich, Y. Z. (1974), The origin, function and structure of emotional processes in the child. *Voprosy Psikhologii*, 6:59–73.

Zetzel, E. R. (1949), Anxiety and the capacity to bear it. *Internat. J. Psycho-Anal.*, 30:1–12.

_____ (1965), Depression and the incapacity to bear it. In: *Drives, Affects, Behavior*, ed. M. Schur. New York: IUP.

Zilboorg, G. (1933), Anxiety without affect. *Psychoanal. Quart.*, 2:48–67.

Chapter 2

AFFECT AND CHARACTER

Allen J. Palmer

Affects are often considered in two contradictory ways: commonly, as an enduring aspect of a person's state of mind, and theoretically, as transient in nature and unrelated to a person's character. Although affect has been conceptualized as time limited and fluid in nature, repetitive sequences of affects can be viewed as having continuity and stability over time. Our daily experience of ourselves and others confirms our commonsense understanding that we each have a predictable, prevailing affect that is a signature aspect of our character. This suggests that our theoretical conceptualizations be reexamined, taking into account affect sequences and their continuity over time. An affect sequence is here defined as the experience and expression of a variety of affects in an ordered and organized manner within a given time period. Given its organized nature, an affect sequence is capable of repetition at other points in time.

This chapter considers how repetitive experience and expression of affect sequences can serve as the basis for the predominant emotional tone of a person's character; undertakes a selective review of the psychoanalytic literature, examining the multiplicity of perspectives and conceptualizations about affects; refers to perspectives that allude to or offer a direct contribution to the nature of continuous affect states and stable affect patterns, that is, the structuralization of affect; and explores the various ways affect can be structuralized, examining the ideational, regulatory, self-representational, and object representational structures, as well as the and cognitive–memory structures in the course of development. One outcome of an integration of such complex trends is the formation of a stable character with a unique affective constellation. A clinical vignette will be presented to illustrate the presence of affect sequences, and speculation about the developmental origins of this affect pattern will be offered.

Attempts to integrate a theory of affects into existing psychoanalytic metapsychology have resulted in confusion. Many questions have been raised about how to view and conceptualize affects. Do affects arise in the id and are they considered to be equivalent to drives and, therefore, a primary source of motivation? Do affects arise in the ego and are they considered to be drive derivatives, ego states, ego functions (like signal affects)? Do affects arise in the self and are they considered to be aspects of the self-experience? Finally, are affects the most salient aspect of object relationships? Efforts at clarification have come from psychoanalysts, academic psychologists, and, most recently, developmental researchers. There is not yet a unified psychoanalytic conceptual model for affects. I begin with an examination of the nature and function of affects with the added perspective of the continuity of affect states over time. It is the latter that I consider to be the affective dimension to a person's character.

Contemporary investigators consider affect to consist of three components: a neurophysiologic core, an expressive aspect, and a experiential, that is, a somatically experienced, dimension. Experiences interact with neurophysiologic actualities as development occurs. The expressive and experiential components are conceptualized as developing greater and greater complexity during the earliest phases of an individual's life cycle. Furthermore, these components develop interdependently. As an example of the ontogenetic development, the experiential dimension first may exist as a somatic feeling state in itself (like distress), later may evolve into a feeling state that can be recognized on (like an awareness of distress), and, later still, may become linked with specific imagery (like the image of mother leaving the room) that, in turn, can be linked to other imagery and feeling states. An early infantile state of organismic distress may evolve into a more specific experience of emotional distress.

A complete developmental paradigm for affects has not yet appeared in the literature. Chapter 1 of this volume is an attempt to develop a comprehensive developmental model for affect from infancy through adulthood. Krystal (1974, 1975) has proposed a schema that postulates the development of internal structures that permit affect tolerance. Within the context of an object relationship and by way of internalizations, the child develops capacities for affect recognition and differentiation, desomatization, and verbalization of affect states. In Chapter 1 of this volume Brown has also postulated a developmental paradigm involving a progression from affect expression to affect experience, affect tolerance, affect verbalization, affect recognition, affect orientation, affect transformation, and consciousness of affect processes.

FUNCTIONS OF AFFECT

Ambiguity about the nature of affects extends to the realm of their evolutionary significance and purpose in nature. In 1872, Darwin considered the value of affect expression for survival. He proposed that animals and humans use facial expressions to express emotions and to communicate to other members of the species. He suggested that such actions are inherited, reflex, and necessary for survival (Darwin, 1872; Demos, 1982; Izard, 1971). Inheritance of affects, for survival or other purposes, by definition bespeaks a continuity of affects across generations. We might speculate that such continuities find expression in the structured affect constellations within a given individual's character. In 1923, with the introduction of his structural theory, Freud suggested that affects can also serve a signal function. They warn the ego of danger situations and promote the mobilization of defenses (Freud, 1926). Accordingly, they serve the survival needs of the individual. Believing in the inheritance of acquired traits, Freud (1926) wrote:

> If we go further and inquire into the origin of that anxiety—and of affects in general—we shall be leaving the realm of pure psychology and entering the borderland of physiology. Affective states have become incorporated in the mind as precipitates of primeval traumatic experiences, and when a similar situation occurs they are revived like mnemic symbols. . . . Biological necessity demands that a situation of danger should have an affective symbol, so that a symbol of this kind would have to be created in any case [pp. 93–94].

Modell (1984), in exploring a form of unconscious guilt that interferes with the gratification of personal wishes, offers a "biologic speculation" to explain this phenomenon. He postulates that this complex affect may represent a "prehistoric acquisition" serving the adaptive needs of the group by way of the altruism of the individual. Modell wrote:

> It is reasonable to suppose that evolution might favor the survival of those individuals who experience guilt when they behave greedily and the guilt leads to the prohibition of the wish to have everything for oneself. This form of guilt, which in man's earlier history contributed to the survival of the group, continues to be inherited and to exert its influence upon modern man . . . [pp. 79–80].

Affect has also been seen as a phylogenetically and ontogenetically fundamental form of communication and "language" between infant and care-giver in the earliest moments of life. Schactel (1959) assigns affects a central role in interpersonal communication. Demos and others believe that a primary role for affects is in the regulation of transactions between infant and care-giver, affects serving to lend saliency to experienced events (Demos, 1982; Escalona, 1968; Sandler and Sandler, 1978; Sroufe, 1979; Stechler and Carpenter, 1967). Basch (1976), drawing upon developmental studies, regards the facial expressions of infants as functioning to express emotion and to promote survival. Izard (1978), in discussing the role of affect in infant development, speaks of affect as functioning to provide continuity from past to present experiences. The implication of this is that affects serve bridging functions between discrete events and may be the medium for memory formation and continuity of felt experience in time.

Tomkins (1962, 1963), expanding on the idea of the function of affects originally described by Darwin, contends that affects function to motivate the individual. Furthermore, Tomkins notes that affects function to amplify drives and lend urgency to a wide variety of nonaffective activities (perceptual, cognitive, and motor). More recently, a number of psychoanalytic and developmental researchers (Basch, 1976; Dahl, 1979; Demos, 1982; Demos and Kaplan, 1986; Holt, 1976; Izard, 1977; Klein, 1967; Tomkins, 1962, 1963) have discarded Freud's drive–discharge theory and its role in motivation. They have replaced it with motivation concepts that place at the core either emotions themselves or emotions in combination with cognition.

EARLY PSYCHOANALYTIC VIEWS OF AFFECT: AN EMERGING VIEW ON THE STRUCTURALIZATION OF AFFECT

Affective-Ideational Structures

Freud initially equated affect with psychic energy. In 1894, in "The Neuro-Psychoses of Defense," Freud (1894) stated:

> I refer to the concept that in mental functions something is to be distinguished—a quota of affect or sum of excitation—which possesses all the characteristics of a quantity (though we have no means of measuring it), which is capable of increase, diminution, displacement and discharge, and which is spread over the memory-traces of ideas somewhat as an electric charge is spread over the surface of a body [p. 60].

In 1900, with the introduction of the metapsychological model in "The Interpretation of Dreams," Freud changed his conception of affect from one in which it is equated with psychic energy itself to one in which it is viewed as a discharge by-product of energy, which is attached to unconscious ideation. In other words, affect is a sign of drive energy invested in an unconscious wish or idea.

Freud (1900, p. 434) wrote, ". . . the ideational contents have undergone displacements and substitutions, while the affects have remained unchanged. No wonder, then, that the ideational content which has been altered by dream-distortion no longer fits the affect which has remained intact." From this vantage point, the connection is between affect and an ideational element, and the affect is unchanging over time, whereas the ideation can be transformed. Furthermore, Freud saw affects as "potentialities" for expression and unconscious ideas as "actualities" (1915). Current developmental investigators view affects as constantly available to the individual, existing as neurophysiologic actualities triggered by internal and external stimuli.

Regulatory Structures

The link of particular, yet interchangeable, ideational elements to a given affect connotes the formation of stable structures of affect-ideational units that are stable over time. With the advent of ego psychology, the conceptualization of ego structures was applied to the realm of affects. With developmental progression, ego structures would form and function to contain, channel, and transform fluid affects. Such stable structures could be viewed as the permanent scaffolding for affect discharge, thereby determining an aspect of character. The following will highlight some of the contributions from ego psychology as it pertains to the relationship of ego structures and affect.

Freud's introduction of the idea of signal affects in order to monitor internal experiences of danger and initiate defenses represented a vital activity within the newly conceptualized ego structure. Fenichel expanded on this in his 1945 discussion of three forms of anxiety: traumatic anxiety, anxiety in the service of the ego (signal anxiety), and panic when anxiety has overwhelmed the ego. Fenichel (1941), Glover (1947), and Jones (1948) also suggested that affects can signal the ego to initiate defenses against other affects. This led to the ideas of "inborn affect-discharge channels" (Rapaport, 1953, p. 501), thresholds for affect discharge, taming of affects (Fenichel, 1941; Glover, 1947), and a layering of affects (Jones, 1929). Defenses serve to bind not only drives but also affects and to bring them within the sphere of the ego.

Reider (Rangell, 1952) suggested that there is a developmental hierarchy for affects and that progression is dependent on ego development. In early life, the regulatory psychic structures are rudimentary and the affects are therefore primitive. In later development, as the internal regulatory structures become more elaborate, the affects that emerge are more complex. Valenstein (1962) noted that affects themselves can be used to defend against other affects. Referring to a "superfluity of affects," he states, ". . . this overdoing of affects is *habitual* enough in certain patients, and probably specific enough to justify the designation as a mechanism of defense" (Valenstein, 1962, p. 318, emphasis added). Extrapolating from this, we can speculate that habitual affects, like habitual defenses, contribute an important dimension to character formation.

Landauer (1938), in exploring the idea of mastery of primitive affects in the developing person, drew upon the early psychoanalytic view of affect impinging on the ego. Landauer conceptualized that a discrete affective reaction could serve mastery by becoming a continuous state. For example, a habitually cheerful person might utilize gaiety as a means to forestall despair. Expanding on Freud's view of guilt as reflecting tension between the superego and ego, Landauer introduced the idea of chronic affect states as reflecting continuous tension between the psychic structures. Landauer proposed that when one affect is used to defend against another one, the defending affect is referred to as a "super-affect." "Since a prohibited affect threatens to return again and again, the super-affect, once formed, seems to be *continuously present.* A mood or a certain type of temperament is created" (Landauer, 1938, p. 402, italics added).

Zetzel's (1949, 1965) and later Krystal's (1974, 1975) works emphasized the ego's capacity for affect tolerance. Zetzel and Krystal conceptualized the capacity to tolerate dysphoric affects such as anxiety, depression, and pain as a developmental achievement. Such ego capacities provide a habitual mode of regulating, modulating, and controlling affects.

Psychoanalytic theorists have considered "mood" from two perspectives: a dominant feeling state and a state or frame of mind. Both perspectives emphasize the transitory nature of mood. Jacobson (1953, 1957) stressed the pervasive, yet more or less temporary, nature of moods. Jacobson (1957, p. 75) stated: "[Moods] represent, as it were, a cross section through the entire state of the ego, lending a particular uniform coloring to all its manifestations for a longer or shorter period of time."

The question of continuity of a mood over time was, therefore, raised. Weinshel (1970), in referring to the first description of mood, noted, " 'The dominant emotional characteristic or cast of mind: as a man of somber mood,' is what we frequently consider to be part of character" and added, "I would prefer to consider such a 'cast of mind' as a mood; I would label it 'temperament' to indicate its relationship to character, its more enduring tendency, and its synchronicity with sense of self " (p. 314).

Weinshel (1970) stressed that moods are stable, organized psychological structures, which derive from the earliest days of life and which have contributions from the three psychic agencies. He remarked:

> These early experiences are often part of a genetic sequence in which memories of events having a comparable affective charge become organized into relatively definitive patterns; and it is not unlikely that some of the earliest affect-laden experiences may become the nuclei for organized ego states which we conceptualize as moods [p. 315].

It appears that Weinshal is proposing that experiences from earliest infancy establish affective memory traces that form a nidus around which later memories crystallize. Such a pattern of affectivity is a state or frame of mind that exists over time.

AFFECTS AND REPRESENTATIONS

Affect Core Self

It is possible that in infancy one can begin to map an affect profile, in which core affect dispositions are aroused and then expressed, by either internal (bodily) or external (interpersonal) factors and that patterns of affective expression are developed and structuralized. Temperamental factors would involve the infant's particular propensity for one or several affect (neurophysiologic) actualities, and a basic profile can be recorded. Wolff's (1966) pioneering research in infant development based on observational data on expressive-behavioral/affective states in infants indicated the presence of discrete affect states in the first days of life. The link between a neurologic core process and expressive features is implied. Tomkins's (1962, 1963) differential emotions theory, outlined in *Affects, Imagery, Consciousness*, emphasized discrete affects as unique phenomenologic and motivational processes and that affect states are inherited, biologic actualities, namely, dispositions.

External factors—the interpersonal or object relations dimension—play a crucial role in affect patterning. Within the infant–care-giver dyad, affects can be amplified, dampened, shifted, or extinguished. Thomas and Chess (1977) noted, "The child is in a perpetual state of active reorganization and cannot properly be regarded as maintaining inborn characteristics as static qualities. In this view, the constants in development are not some sets of traits but rather the *processes* by which these traits are maintained in the transaction between organism and environment" (Thomas and Chess, 1977, p. 42).

The repetitive nature of the infant–care-giver interaction could result in an elaboration or alteration of a basic affectivity constellation to form a specific affect profile. An infant may eventually spend more time in one affect state than in several others, indicating the presence of an early (within the phase of infancy) form of psychic structuralization. With ongoing ego development, including selective internalizations, a stable pattern may emerge. This would begin to occur in the earliest "protore-presentational," preverbal period of development. The stability of a given affect constellation might serve as the preideational dimension of charac-ter, unrelated to the view of libidinal zonal influences on character or defensive aspects of character.

Emde (1983) hypothesized the existence of a prerepresentational self that contains at its core an affective component. He views the affective core as being as basic as temperament and serves as the aspect of self that provides *continuity* over time. The affective core-self is believed to be in active communication with other affects and an active agent for self-monitoring and social interchange. Emde, quoting Izard (1977), indicated that the affective self provides continuity of experience across develop-ment and that this is guaranteed "since its central organization is biolog-ical and its vital relations are unchanging." It is also a structure of synthesizing information from one's environment. In ambiguous social situations, one calls upon one's affective core, and one "socially referenc-es" the other individual's affective signals to determine the affectively laden communication in question (Emde, 1983). In short, the affective core-self is viewed as one of the earliest psychic structures that is stable and continuous over time and through successive stages of development.

Affects and the Representational World

Kernberg (1982) eschews the either/or conceptual dilemma between drives and affects as the primary motivational system. Instead of thinking that affects derive from drives, he suggests that drives derive from affects. A coalescence of pleasurable affects into libidinal drives and a coalescence of unpleasurable affects into aggressive drives occur once the affects become organized into stable intrapsychic structures linking self-representation and object representations. The implication of multiple and varying affects' being organized in this way points to the development of stable structures that are continuous over time, that is, elements of character.

Sandler and Sandler (1978) note that in the development of object relationships in earliest childhood, affective experiences are central and lend saliency and meaning to experience. They indicate that in addition to instinctual forces, the child and the adult are motivated to experience affective states of pleasure, security, safety, and affirmation and to avoid, reject, or minimize states of unpleasure. This is a different notion about a pleasure principle because it is based on capturing or re-creating a feeling state within the context of an actualized object relationship or in a wish-fulfilling fantasy with an internal object representation, rather than pleasure derived from tension reduction in a drive reduction of instinctual energies. This view of affect as a motivating force has been raised by numerous researchers such as Tomkins, Izard, Holt and Klein. The construction of mental representations that are closely linked with affect states becomes the template for later external relationships or fantasied ones. Such development requires the child to have the capacity to recognize affect states, to perceive self and objects in interaction, to remember experiences, and to actively seek out or avoid certain experiences. The further development of a child's internal representations will then "act as a basis for the ongoing organization of the child's subjective experiences and motor activities" (Sandler and Sandler, 1978, p. 291).

From the perspective of "character," particular object relationships and their re-creations from an inner template motivate the individual to achieve and repeatedly reexperience given affective states. The stability of the object relationships and the impetus to reexperience given affect states will combine to provide a patterned array of modes of achieving this, be it in externally directed behaviors vis-à-vis relationships or internally oriented and affectively experienced fantasies. Created and re-created affect states within the context of a therapeutic relationship would provide the transferential basis to mobilize and discover unconscious affect-ideation patterns. The affect states may shift, but the goal may be the same, and its achievement on a prolonged basis may be achieved depending on the success of current object choices, fantasy life, drives, conflicts, defenses, or external impediments or facilitating events, that is, the stability of successful compromise formation with its object relational and affective components included. Sandler and Sandler (1978) noted:

> There is no doubt of the importance to us of an understanding of the ways in which individuals actualize the infantile object-relationships present in their unconscious fantasies through many different activities in their daily lives. These activities may show themselves in relation to other people, or may simply be present as so-called "character traits." Some character traits appear specifically designed to evoke particular responses in others, and this may give us an additional avenue of approach to the understanding of character [p. 291].

With development, affective-cognitive structures develop within an ontogeny of object relations. Somatic experience and visual imagery appear to be the forerunners of later cognitive structures to which affect adheres and gets expressed. Affects linked with ideational content, according to Kernberg (1982), always implies an object relationship.

Affective-Cognitive Structures

The development of symbolic representations and language likewise forms a network of representations, images, and ideas to which affect states coalesce. Klein (1967), in exploring preemptory ideation, including memory, noted that structured affective- cognitive-motor events form the basis of motivation. According to Klein, memory networks coalesce around affects. The associative capacity of a person enables ever more complex interconnection, reverberation, and expansion between a given affective experience with one and then many associated symbolic/ideoaffective elements. A network of associations can serve as a series of triggers for one or more linked affect states and as an organized structure that is stable in time and capable of repetition and expansion to wider associative pathways. Furthermore, it can serve to maintain a given affect pattern in time. Freud, in his work on hysteria and obsessive compulsive neurosis, discussed the linking and defensive disengagement between ideoaffective complexes and their various associations. More recently, Tomkins has referred to this spreading phenomenon as an analogue capacity, namely, that the person is capable of creating analogies, thereby transferring affect and meaning from one idea or representation to another.

With the focus on affect/behavioral interchanges between infant and mother, Stern (1985) noted the achievement of "affect attunement" based on selective and inexact imitations by the mother of the infant's expressions. Stern (1985) stated, "The channel or modality of expression used by the mother to match the infant's behavior is different from the channel or modality used by the infant. . . . What is being matched is not the other person's behavior *per se*, but rather some aspect of the behavior that reflects the person's feeling state" (p. 141). The bridging and coalescing of affects with multiple modes of expression originating in both exact and approximate imitations provide a model for affect-somatic expressive expansion and, later, affect-ideational expansion along multiple associative pathways. Once more, a coalescence of multiple affect channels can form the basis of a pattern capable of continuity and repetition.

PSYCHOANALYTIC VIEWS OF CHARACTER FORMATION

Psychoanalytic conceptualizations of character have undergone significant developments since Freud's first statement on character in 1900:

"What we describe as our 'character' is based on the memory traces of our impressions; and, moreover, the impressions which have had the greatest effect on us—those of our earliest youth—are precisely the ones which scarcely ever become conscious."

Freud (1908), in "Character and Anal Erotism," pointed out the relationship of fixed modes of expression to impulses and their somatic zonal sources. Character, in this view, was seen as either the ongoing expression of unmodified instincts or a construction of instincts modified by sublimation and reaction formation. Freud went beyond this perspective when he considered the impact of life experiences on the structuring of character in "Some Character-Types Met with in Psycho-analytic Work" (1916).

Freud (1931), in "Libidinal Types," examined character types from the standpoint of the predominant location of libido within the tripartite agencies of the mind. For example, libido located mainly in the id could influence the formation of an erotic type, whereas the obsessional type is influenced primarily by superego forces. Thus, the structural, tripartite model of the mind served as the new framework in which to consider the basis for the development character typologies. The importance of experiences that shape development of the ego, especially as they pertain to processes of identification (Freud, 1917), was the next advance in the conceptualization of character. Freud (1914), in "Mourning and Melancholia," spoke of how the shadow of abandoned objects can fall upon and transform an individual's ego. Thus, the character of the ego could be viewed, in part, as a reflection of abandoned object cathexis. Identification processes influencing ego-ideal and superego formation added yet further complexity to the concept of character formation.

Abraham (1921, 1924, 1925), extending Freud's contributions, conceptualized character as the formation of certain traits derived from the vicissitudes of libidinal development and its particular stages and modes of expression. He stressed both the changeable nature of character due to such influences as regression and progression and the shifting orientations present with the expression of one or the other side of ambivalence. Reich (1933) forwarded the view of traits' forming as a result of defensive reactions to impulses. With a shift in emphasis swinging over to the side of defensive functions, Reich gave weight to external factors, especially the suppressive activities of parents and the child's identifications and defensive repression of drive expression. He likened character formation to symptom formation yet emphasized the complexity of the achieved defensive organization and its habitual, rigid nature.

Fenichel's (1945) contribution to the conceptualization of character was his emphasis on the habitual manner in which the ego organizes and harmonizes the multiple internal id and superego demands and external reality demands. Thus, the ego in its synthetic activities functions as a stable, integrating force within the individual (Nunberg, 1931). Hartmann (1939, 1950) introduced the ego adaptation view of character, adding the important consideration of ego constitutional variables alongside the familiar contribution of drive-based constitutional variables. The conflict-free ego factors had been now added to the familiar conflict-based ego contributions. Hartmann (1939, 1950) and Jacobson (1954) led the way to the next level of conceptualization of character by noting that character is greatly influenced by a synthesis of ego functions and self-representations and object representations. For example self-representations, object representations, and self-representations in relation to object representations combine to form a complex, stable organization.

Moore and Fine (1990) defined character as: "The enduring, patterned functioning of an individual. As perceived by others, it is the person's habitual way of thinking, feeling, and acting. Understood psychodynamically, character is the person's habitual mode of reconciling intrapsychic conflicts" (p. 37). Moore and Fine (1990) emphasized the role of compromise formation in character formation with the development of stable patterns of thinking, feeling, and acting. Although they have considered individual differences at birth along with intrauterine factors and developments in the first years of life, they emphasized the role of the resolution of oedipal conflicts and consolidated superego formation in the development of character. This chapter emphasizes the preoedipal organization of affective elements into stable patterns, consolidating into what may be termed as an individual's affective "signature" with its unique, enduring tone and range.

CASE VIGNETTE

In our therapeutic efforts to know our patients, as in most interpersonal interactions, we come to experience the other person's character style and affective tone. Over time, we become sufficiently familiar with the person's affect-communications such that with each encounter we anticipate the potential range of affects of the other and the affective dialogue in which we are likely to engage. In a sense, we develop a representation of the other person (and ourselves in relationship to that person) that is colored by our prior knowledge of the person's predominant affect and range of expression. The following case vignette of an eight-year-old boy illustrates the presence of, elaboration of, and triggers for stable affect sequences.

An eight-year-old boy of serious demeanor, evidenced by a blank facial expression, entered analysis for the treatment of facial tics and obsessive-compulsive rituals. Verbal communication was minimal, consisting of brief bursts of reality-oriented questions or commands to engage in action-oriented play. Outwardly, he showed little reaction to friendly greetings or questions that focused on his nonverbal communication of bringing small objects from home and hiding them from my sight.

He repeatedly engaged me in competitive contests requiring fine motor agility, for instance, the stacking of small, odd-shaped blocks. Comments on my part about to the dichotomy of control and dyscontrol being enacted in our competitive play breached the silence between us but did not alter his affect expression of intense seriousness. The occasional failure to place an object in a desired way would be accompanied by an affective shift from seriousness to irritation and a rush to activity. Questions attempting to discern his feelings were rebuffed by silent activity. His success in defeating me in the game often brought a sudden smile to his face that was quickly erased and replaced by an angry frown. When he appeared angry, he'd escalate his motoric activity level, becoming careless in his actions and in his adherence to the rules of the game. In response to my noting his change in play, he'd answer, "Who cares?" and would abandon the contest by throwing the blocks in the air. He would then escalate his actions by scattering papers, markers, and cards around the office, all the while appearing intensely angry.

The above pattern of affects and behavior was repeated daily for several months. Yet he would occasionally punctuate his activities with questions that provided a verbal entrée into his inner affect experience and its accompanying ideation. For example, after winning a contest, he asked the name, age, and problems of a patient he had seen leaving my office and whether I was jealous of his victories. With further repetitions of the throwing sequence, he angrily blurted out that he wanted to leave me with "a big mess to clean up." This affect sequence was repeated over several months and seemed to add detail to his overall affective tone of seriousness: blank expression, focused aggression, irritation leading to anger, or happiness leading to anger and then anxiety/fear.

The trigger for the hostile-aggressive competitive play may have been his anger and jealousy of my relationship with the other patient, whereas his annoyance and amplified anger were the outcome of his sense of weakness in defeat and in being unable to control the blocks in his desired manner. I wondered whether his question also indicated a transference experience derived from his jealousy of his mother's closeness with his younger brother and his father. Furthermore, the question may have indicated his anxiety in defeating me and his fear of retribution. The trigger for his momentary pleasure was his triumph over me in the game, yet this was replaced by anxiety/fear and a further escalation of his anger.

With repetitions of the throwing sequence, he indicated at least one of his motivations for his actions by saying he wanted to leave me with "a big mess to clean up." Thus, he elaborated on the meaning of his action and its connection to anger and conflicts on a preoedipal level of psychosexual development. Further elaboration on his wish to leave me with a mess ensued in his associations about my relationship with other patients and urgent demands to be given special toys and snacks. Anger was replaced by sadness, and I postulated as to prior experiences of intense neediness and excessive control, derivative of experiences of feeling displaced in a primary object relationship.

This vignette indicates how this boy's predominant affect tone of seriousness was an enduring aspect of his character. Furthermore, his predominant tone was the result of a constellation of patterned affects. Examining the boy's serious nature—a chronic affect tone and aspect of his developing character—we discover complex affect-action-ideational sequences. Even though certain changes occurred through the course of treatment, particularly elaboration of the underlying dynamics and affect-ideational elements fueling motoric-behavioral sequences, his overall affect tone remained unchanged. We might speculate on the relevance of his history to the development of these sequences, in particular the nature of his earliest object relationships and discrete developmental events. Born with an active disposition and an enjoyment of movement, he did not like being held by his mother for any length of time. Parental attempts at keeping his playing with food to a minimum resulted in tension during his early eating experiences. Parental efforts at offering choices of clothing were met with opposition. Struggles over dressing activities ensued. When the parents expressed their frustration, he would react with fright and then compliance. One arena that was free of such conflict, that brought great pleasure, and that facilitated enjoyable assertion was gross motor play.

The boy sustained three traumatic injuries while playing outdoors over the course of his second and third years of life. Each injury necessitated a brief, yet painful and restrictive medical procedure. In addition, he was separated from his parents during the procedures. The distress he felt at his mother's pregnancy, her inability to lift and carry him while pregnant due to a pinched nerve in her neck, and the birth of a brother was expressed in an upsurge of aggressive play and loud, disruptive behaviors. He then reacted to behavioral shaping with improved self-control and behavioral change. Tic symptoms developed soon thereafter and a sober demeanor gradually unfolded. Strategies offered to him by his parents to help manage his distress around symptom expression and experience of lost control have included suppression of disturbing ideation and associated affects and substitutive ideation or activity. He has used compulsive defenses and the persona of a powerful person to prevent tension rises and unwanted, preemptory motoric and ideational expression.

It is my impression that he had repeated experiences in which interest and pleasurable assertion were suddenly accompanied and then replaced by tension at varying levels of intensity, resulting in anxiety and efforts at behavioral control. The shift in affect was accompanied by an emphasis on self-control. He reacted to certain early parental ministrations with pleasure and joy and, to others, with tension and opposition. A rise in tension accompanying external limitations on his assertion may have served to activate vulnerabilities in his neurobiologic inhibitory/ expressive systems, resulting in motor tics. Furthermore, the traumatic experiences served as an impetus for him to inhibit his motoric activity and affective expression, as did his experience of his mother's pregnancy, his brother's birth, and the aftermath. It is my impression that these complex developmental and interpersonal factors in which inhibition of behavior and affect predominated contributed to this boy's sober character. Whereas certain therapeutic aspects and their technical counterparts are alluded to in this vignette, the predominant focus of the vignette is on illustrating the presence of an enduring affect tone while numerous changes have been set in motion by the therapeutic process.

DISCUSSION

In a consideration of the relationship of affects to character development, it might be useful to touch upon and contrast the two divergent conceptualizations that make up the contemporary debate on affect theory within psychoanalysis. The first point of view as postulated by Brenner (1982) and drawing centrally from psychoanalytic data, contends that affects exist as the sum total of ideas and sensation, the former consisting of thoughts, memories, mental representations of objects, and one's own sensations, wishes, and fears, and the latter consisting of sensations of pleasure, unpleasure, or combinations of the two. Brenner (1982) states:

> Their [affects] antecedents are sensations of pleasure and unpleasure, the most important of which are the sensations associated with the lack of gratification of a drive derivative, so-called drive tension, and with the gratification of a drive derivative, i.e., with drive discharge. Such sensations of pleasure and unpleasure are the undifferentiated matrix from which the entire gamut of the affects of later life develop [p. 49].

Furthermore, Brenner notes that sensations of pleasure and unpleasure are constitutionally determined and do not undergo a developmental progression, whereas the progressive development of "ideas" underlies the differences between primitive and mature affects.

According to Harrison (1986, p. 204), the linking of experiences of pleasure/unpleasure and ideation can be inferred in infants as early as three to four months old, when ". . . the infant's capacity to act purposefully, with evidence of joyful feelings (which suggest the existence of 'idea,' however vague), and the infant's capability to anticipate that the purposeful activity will lead to those feelings." Accordingly, the infant's experience of affect (inclusive of an ideational component) occurs within the developing rudimentary ego long before the acquisition of language. Thus, Harrison sees an integration of neonatal research and Freud's structural theoretical point of view.

The second point of view, drawing on infant observational studies, contends that a number of discrete affects are present at birth and in earliest infancy and are devoid of ideational content yet form the basis of communication. The affects that are communicated are not assumed to be part of the infant's awareness at birth or soon thereafter. An affect core self develops within the context of interchanges with the primary caretaker. The earliest phase of affect development would be characterized as presymbolic, preideational, and, primarily, prerepresentational. From this perspective, one could speculate on the nature of the early structuralization of affects. Brown, in Chapter 1, presents a structural model in which affect-ideorepresentational complexes are formed in the course of development.

One model for the structuralization of affects could be conceptualized as follows: Once an affective core self is formed, linkages would be forged to other affect states as dictated by internal and external experiences. As core and associated affect states coalesce, a stable network and pattern of affectivity would be created. Sequences of affects within an affect network and between affect networks form the basis of these patterns. The repetitive, and perhaps preferred, expression of such patterns across time then establishes continuity of affect states, forming the early foundation of affect-in-character.

Subsequent development of perception, cognition, ideation, representation, memory formation, time sense, and defenses born of conflict would overlay, intermingle, and elaborate core affect patterns. Expansion of affect patterns, in greater and greater complexity, would occur as new associations are formed beyond the initial skeletal pattern. Interconnecting patterns would then provide continuity in time through subsequent phases of development. Internalizations are seen as adding to and modifying established affect patterns.

It would appear that affect is a "psychic structure" only in a biologic sense, inasmuch as neurophysiologic core processes create affect actualities whether labeled globally as pleasure and unpleasure or discretely as anger, sadness, and fear (negative affects) or surprise, interest, or joy (positive affects). An analogy might be drawn to the nature, or "structure," of a fluid. Affects, given internal or external triggers, can be expressed and as development progresses, subjectively experienced. Affects can serve communication purposes (interpersonally and intrapsychically) and according to Tomkins can serve as a source of motivation. Ontogenesis of the person in the scope of interpersonal experiences with primary affective care-givers will ultimately results in the linking of affect states with somatic, ideational, regulatory, and representational complexes or other symbolic formations. These intimately linked factors form a stable organization or profile of interconnecting affective-ideational units. Similar to Freud's (1894) statement of affect's spreading itself "over the memory traces of an idea like an electric charge over the surface of the body" (1894, p. 75) affects can serve to color and highlight various representational, ideational,and symbolic structures.

One might speculate that affects contribute to the stability of psychic structure and vice versa. Furthermore, we might speculate that affects are structuralized along the lines of an open-systems model resulting in a unique "architecture." For example, partial overlap of contiguous affect-ideation complexes may create bridges that have a transitional affect-ideational property of their own, facilitating movement from one affect-ideational constellation to another. Furthermore, overlap may create complex, compound affect states or lend subtle shading and meaning to a primary affect-ideorepresentational complex. As an open system existing in a developmental continuum, external influences, internalizations, and drive-based forces impinge, reverberate, and add varying quantities of stimulation and variation to the overall structure.

The general organization of affect-somatic-regulatory-ideorepresentational elements in this model could be seen as contributing to a pattern of preferred affectivity, relatively stable over time. A person may explore or reach into novel affect states yet cycle back and attempt to integrate the novel with the core or baseline affect pattern. A pattern of preferred affectivity, having homeostatic functions, would create the basis for a person's affect "signature," namely, an individual's unique, predominant affect tone, range, and constellation.

REFERENCES

Abraham, K. (1921), Contributions to the theory of the anal character. In: *Selected Papers of Karl Abraham*. New York: Basic Books, pp. 370–392, 1953.

_____ (1924), Influence of oral erotism on character-formation. In: *Selected Papers of Karl Abraham*. New York: Basic Books, pp. 393–406, 1953.

_____ (1925), Character formation on the genital level of the libido. In: *Selected Papers of Karl Abraham.* New York: Basic Books, pp. 407–417, 1953.

Basch, M. F. (1976), The concept of affect: A re-examination. *J. Amer. Psychoanal. Assn.,* 24:759–777.

Brenner, C. (1982), *The Mind in Conflict.* New York: IUP.

Dahl, H. (1979), The appetite hypothesis of emotions: A new psychoanalytic model of motivation. In: *Emotions and Personality in Psychopathology,* ed. C. E. Izard. New York: Plenum Press, pp. 201–225.

Darwin, C. (1872), *The Expressions of the Emotions in Man and Animals.* Chicago: University of Chicago Press, 1965.

Demos, E. V. (1982), Affect in early infancy: Physiology or psychology? *Psychoanal. Inq.,* 1:533–574.

_____ & Kaplan, S. (1986), Motivation reconsidered: Affect biographies of two infants. *Psychoanal. Contemp. Thought,* 9:147–223.

Emde, R. N. (1983), The prerepresentational self and its affective core. *The Psychoanalytic Study of the Child,* 38:165–192. New Haven, CT: Yale University Press.

Escalona, S. (1968), *The Roots of Individuality.* Chicago: Aldine.

Fenichel, O. (1941), The ego and the affects. In: *The Collected Papers of Otto Fenichel,* 2nd Series. New York: Norton, pp. 215–227, 1954.

_____ (1945), *The Psychoanalytic Theory of Neurosis.* New York: Norton.

Freud, S. (1894), The neuro-psychoses of defense. *Standard Edition,* 3:45–61. London: Hogarth Press, 1962.

_____ (1900), *The Interpretation of Dreams.* Standard Edition, 5. London: Hogarth Press, 1953.

_____ (1908), *Character and anal erotism. Standard Edition,* 9:167–175. London: Hogarth Press, 1959.

_____ (1915), The unconscious. *Standard Edition,* 14:166–204. London: Hogarth Press, 1957.

_____ (1916), Some character-types met with in psycho-analytic work. *Standard Edition,* 14:309–333. London: Hogarth Press, 1957.

_____ (1917), Mourning and melancholia. *Standard Edition,* 14:243–258. London: Hogarth Press, 1957.

_____ (1923), The ego and the id. *Standard Edition,* 19:12–59. London: Hogarth Press, 1961.

_____ (1926), *Inhibitions, Symptoms, and Anxiety. Standard Edition,* 20:87–172. London: Hogarth Press, 1959.

_____ (1931), Libidinal types. *Standard Edition,* 21:215–220. London: Hogarth Press, 1961.

Glover, E. (1947), Basic mental concepts: Their clinical and theoretical value. *Psychoanal. Quart.,* 16:482–506.

Harrison, I. B. (1986), A note on the nature and the developmental origins of affect. In: *Psychoanalysis—The Science of Mental Conflict,* ed. A. Richards & M. Willick. Hillsdale, NJ: The Analytic Press, pp. 191–208.

Hartmann, H. (1939), *Ego Psychology and the Problem of Adaptation.* New York: IUP, 1958.

_____ (1950). Comments on the psychoanalytic theory of the ego. *The Psychoanalytic Study of the Child,* 5:74–96. New York: IUP.

Holt, R. R. (1976), Drive or wish? A reconsideration of the psychoanalytic theory of motivation. In: *Psychology versus metapsychology, Psychoanalytic essays in memory of George S. Klein,* ed. M. M. Gill & P. S. Holzman. *Psychological Issues,* Monogr. 9:158–197. New York: IUP.

Izard, C. E. (1971), *The Face of Emotion.* New York: Appleton-Century-Crofts.

_____ (1977). *Human Emotions.* New York: Plenum Press.

_____ (1978), On the ontogenesis of emotions and emotion-cognition relationships in infancy. In: *The Development of Affects,* ed. M. Lewis & L. Rosenblum. New York: Plenum Press, pp. 398–413.

Jacobson, E. (1953), The affects and their pleasure-unpleasure qualities in relation to the psychic discharge processes. In: *Drives, Affects and Behavior,* ed. R. Lowenstein. New York: IUP.
_____ (1954), The self and the object world. *The Psychoanalytic Study of the Child,* 9:75–127. New York: IUP.
_____ (1957), Normal and pathological moods: Their nature and function. *The Psychoanalytic Study of the Child,* 12:73–113. New York: IUP.
Jones, E. (1929), Fear, guilt and hate. In: *Papers on Psychoanalysis.* Baltimore: Williams & Wilkins, pp. 304–319, 1948.
Kernberg, O. F. (1982), Self, ego, affects and drives. *J. Amer. Psychoanal. Assn.,* 30:893–917.
Klein, G. S. (1967), Preemptory ideation: Structure and force in motivated ideas. In: *Motives and Thought, Psychoanalytic Essays in Honor of David Rapaport,* ed. R. R. Holt. *Psychological Issues,* Monogr. 5:80–130. New York: IUP.
_____ (1976), *Psychoanalytic Theory.* New York: IUP.
Krystal, H. (1974), The genetic development of affects and affect regression. *The Annual of Psychoanalysis,* 2:98–126. New York: IUP.
_____ (1975), Affect tolerance. *The Annual of Psychoanalysis,* 3:179–219. New York: IUP.
Landauer, K. (1938), Affects, passions and temperament. *Internat. J. Psycho-Anal.,* 19:388–415.
Modell, A. H. (1984), On having more. In: *Psychoanalysis in a New Context.* New York: IUP, pp. 71–82.
Moore, B. E. & Fine, B. D. (1990), *Psychoanalytic Terms and Concepts.* New Haven, CT: Yale University Press.
Nunberg, H. (1931), The synthetic function of the ego. In: *Practice and Theory of Psychoanalysis.* New York: IUP, 1955.
Rangell, L. (1952), Panel: The theory of affects. *J. Amer. Psychoanal. Assn.,* 8:300–315.
Rapaport, D. (1953), On the psychoanalytic theory of affects. *Internat. J. Psycho-Anal.,* 34:177–198.
Reich, W. (1933), *Character-Analysis.* New York: Orgone Inst. Press, 1949.
Sandler, J. & Sandler, A. M. (1978), On the development of object relationships and affects. *Internat. J. Psycho-Anal.,* 59:285–296.
Schachtel, E. G. (1959), *Metamorphosis.* New York: Basic Books.
Sroufe, L. A. (1979), The ontogenesis of emotion in infancy. In: *Handbook of Infant Development,* ed. J. Osofsky. New York: Wiley, pp. 491–518.
Stechler, G. & Carpenter, G. (1967), A viewpoint on early affective development. In: *The Exceptional Infant, Vol. 1,* ed. J. Hellmuth. Seattle, WA: Special Child Publications, pp. 163–189.
Stern, D. N. (1985), *The Interpersonal World of the Infant.* New York: Basic Books.
Thomas, A. & Chess, S. (1977), *Temperament and Development.* New York: Brunner/Mazel.
Tomkins, S. (1962), *Affects, Imagery, Consciousness, Vol. 1.* New York: Springer.
_____ (1963), *Affects, Imagery, Consciousness, Vol. 2.* New York: Springer.
Valenstein, A. (1962), The psycho-analytic situation: Affects, emotional reliving, and insight in the psycho-analytic process. *Internat. J. Psycho-Anal.,* 43:315–324.
Weinshel, E. (1970), Some psychoanalytic considerations on mood. *Internat. J. Psycho-Anal.,* 51:313–320.
Wolff, P. H. (1966), The causes, controls and organization of behavior in the neonate. In: *Psychological Issues,* Monogr. 17. New York: IUP.
Zetzel, E. (1949), Anxiety and the capacity to bear it. In: *The Capacity for Emotional Growth.* New York: IUP, pp. 33–52, 1970.
_____ (1965), On the incapacity to bear depression. In: *The Capacity for Emotional Growth.* New York: IUP, pp. 82–114, 1970.

Chapter 3

ON UNDERSTANDING GENDER DIFFERENCES IN THE EXPRESSION OF EMOTION

Gender Roles, Socialization, and Language

Leslie R. Brody

There is increasing evidence that, in this culture, females express a wide variety of emotions more intensely than do males, both verbally and through nonverbal facial expressions. Why such gender differences exist is an exceedingly difficult and complex question to answer (Hall, 1987). Undoubtedly, biological factors, including genetic, hormonal, and neuropsychological variables, as well as social factors, including differing gender roles and the power and status differences between the two sexes, contribute to gender differences in emotion. Both biological and social factors in turn affect parent and peer socialization processes, which differ powerfully for each sex and which create different affective environments for boys versus girls (Brody, 1985; Hall, 1987; Maltz and Borker, 1982). Socialization differences may be the most proximate and direct cause of gender differences in emotional expressiveness. However, they can be understood only in the context of the biological and social factors previously alluded to. For example, the socialization of boys' and girls' expressiveness may differ because girls are biologically predisposed to verbalize language earlier than are boys, or because boys' nonverbal and behavioral affect expressions are more intense when they are infants, causing caretakers to respond differently to them. Socialization differences are also influenced by cultural and historical factors and may be perpetuated in a process by which each generation identifies with and internalizes the values, behaviors, and parenting styles of previous generations (Hall, 1987).

Emotions can be expressed in four basic ways: verbally, behaviorially (e.g., "acting out"), through nonverbal facial expressions, and through physiological arousal (increased heartbeat rate, galvanic skin response, respiration, temperature) (Adelmann and Zajonc, 1989; Brody and Hall, in press). This chapter will treat the verbal expression of emotion, although I will allude to the other modalities to support some of my arguments. In particular, I will not review the evidence that females are more facially expressive of emotion than are males, although supporting data for this assertion are well established and widely cited (Brody and Hall, in press; Hall, 1984; Schwartz, Brown, and Ahern, 1980).

Further, my emphasis on reviewing data concerning the verbal expression of feelings (a modality used more by females) largely reflects a relative deemphasis in the recent literature on the ways in which males express and manage their feelings. Data collected in the 1970s suggested that males tend to be "internalizers" of emotion; that is, they manifest emotion in their levels of physiological arousal and not in their facial expressions (Buck, Miller, and Caul, 1974). In contrast, females tend to be "externalizers" of emotion; that is, they manifest emotion in facial expressions and not in levels of physiological arousal. These data are complicated by the fact that when researchers look at these patterns within individuals of both sexes, as opposed to comparing groups of subjects, positive and not inverse relations emerge among physiological arousal, facial expression, and self-reports of emotional experience (Adelmann and Zajonc, 1989). Cacioppo et al. (1992) argue that only a small subset of the population can reliably be classified as externalizers or internalizers. Thus, some studies suggest that males express emotion with higher levels of physiological arousal than do females, but the data do not present a clear picture. Ironically, recent data on emotional physiological arousal are not useful in clarifying the nature of existing gender differences because such data are often collected using samples that are exclusively female. The stated justification for the use of only female samples is that females produce more reliable psychophysiological measures of emotional arousal than do males (Schwartz et al., 1980).

Finally, I will focus on the expression of emotions, as distinguished from the experience and the recognition of emotions. Experience and expression are quite difficult to disentangle empirically, even though experience is often easy to distinguish phenomenologically from expression. Once you ask people to tell you what they are experiencing, you are already asking them to express it, thus confounding the two. Research that attempts to look at experience and expression independently has found that gender differences are more salient in the latter (Brody and Hall, in press).

I make several arguments about expressiveness. First, I argue that females in this culture tend to be both more verbally and more facially expressive of a wide variety of emotions than are males. In contrast, males tend to express emotions more through behaviors and actions than do females. This argument is qualified by findings indicating that gender differences in expressiveness vary with age, culture, situation, cohort, and the type of emotion expressed. Second, I argue that there are powerful differences in the socialization of male and female emotional expressiveness, which undoubtedly contribute to gender differences in later affective functioning and which may be, at least in part, reactions to infant gender differences in reactivity and affective expression. Third, I argue that the direction of gender differences for specific emotions, for example, that men express more anger but less shame than women do, is consistent with the idea that each sex is socialized to adapt to differing gender roles, in other words, that there are systematic relationships between gender roles and emotional expressiveness. Fourth, I argue that gender differences in the development of verbal language contribute to gender differences in emotional expressiveness, with girls developing verbal language earlier and maintaining language superiority throughout development. I illustrate some of these points with reference to gender differences in the incidence of alexithymia, and I conclude with some speculations concerning the clinical implications of this work.

I am writing about emotions within the framework of a functionalist perspective: that emotions serve an adaptive purpose both interpersonally and intrapsychically. One can view emotions as being activated largely when notable change is perceived or when expected events are violated or confirmed (Fischer, Shaver, and Carnochan, 1989). Interpersonally, they can serve as communications that, depending on one's model of personality, can signal the existence, satisfaction, or frustration of drives or needs, as well as the state of the self-system, its relatedness or nonrelatedness to others, and its impending actions. Intrapsychically, emotions can serve as tension regulators in the face of conflict (Lewis, 1983), and they can also motivate behavior. Each emotion is associated with patterned action tendencies or organized plans for bringing about a change in relation to the appraised events. For example, the experience of anger, activated by frustration in reaching a goal, may set into place a series of behaviors that are adapted to remove a block to a goal, to reduce intrapsychic tension, and to interpersonally warn others of imminent aggression (Malatesta, 1988, gives other examples).

Gender differences in emotional functioning can exist in any phase of this model. Because the two sexes have different gender roles, they have differing motivations, conflicts, social expectations, and experiences against which they evaluate "notable change." They may also differ in the kinds of patterned action tendencies each feeling sets into motion (Malatesta, 1988).

SEX DIFFERENCES: WHAT IS THE EVIDENCE?

Following are the methodological constraints of the existing research, which are important to note before interpreting data. People tend to see the same expressions as angry when they believe the person is male, and sad and scared when they believe the same person is female (Condry and Condry, 1976), so research on sex differences in facial expressions becomes particularly suspect when the coders are not blind to the subjects' sex. Moreover, the sex of the observers who are rating emotional expressions has been found to influence their emotion ratings and therefore needs to be controlled (Cunningham and Shapiro, 1984). Other biases occur in studies in which people are asked to rate emotional experiences using self-report inventories, which are subject to impression management. For example, men may say they experience fewer feelings because that is what sex-role stereotypes dictate males are supposed to say. Thus, people's emotional self-reporting should always be explored in relation to their tendency to engage in impression management, meaning to respond in socially desirable ways. In addition, sex differences in emotional functioning should be generalized only across different types of measurement, such as physiological indices, codings of facial expressions, or self-report measures, when the measures have been found to relate to each other. For example, much of the research on gender differences in neuropsychological correlates of emotion seems to be task specific (Stalans and Wedding, 1985), and research based on any one type of measure does not support a generalized interpretation of gender differences in brain–affect relationships.

In general, in the literature that I review, social desirability tendencies are not taken into consideration when self-report measures are used, coders are not blind to the subjects' sex, nor is the sex of raters controlled. Hence, conclusions based on this research should be very tentative.

A review article I wrote in 1985 (Brody, 1985) discussed gender differences in a number of areas of emotional functioning, including emotional expressions (physiological, facial, and verbal expressions), emotional experience, affect recognition (the ability to recognize the nonverbal facial expressions of others), defenses and display rules, and the socialization of affect. I concluded that within the methodological constraints of the existing literature, there was evidence that females reported experiencing more happiness, sadness, and fear than did males (and therefore expressed more of these feelings as well), whereas males reported experiencing more anger than did females. From an early age, females were socialized to express more emotions than were males, with the exception of anger. Furthermore, females seemed to be both better encoders and decoders of emotion than were males: they were both more accurate at recognizing nonverbal facial expression of emotion than were males and also tended to express emotions using facial expressions in ways that were more recognizable to others than did males. Males, in contrast, tended to express emotions with physiological reactions that were not observable to others. Finally, females seemed to defend against or cope with emotions by using internalizing defenses, for example, turning against the self, whereas males used externalizing defenses, such as turning against the other. The evidence for gender differences in emotional expression was much stronger than the evidence for experience, partly for the reason I mentioned to earlier, that is, that experience is difficult to measure independent of expression. Finally, I emphasized that these gender differences in emotional functioning were culturally and situationally specific, varying both in different situations as well in different subcultural groups.

Recent studies suggest that males and females continue to understand, express, and cope with feelings differently. Males seem to use more direct behaviors or "acting out" to express their feelings (especially anger). For example, Whitesell, Robinson, and Harter (1991) reported that boys and girls didn't differ in their ratings for self-reported anger, but they did differ in coping strategies: boys used hitting and other expressive strategies, and girls used both avoidant strategies—such as getting away and doing work—and some approach strategies. Quite similarly, Fabes and Eisenberg (1991) found that in their preschool sample, boys sought retaliation more in response to anger, whereas girls defended themselves nonaggressively. Furthermore, Strayer (1986) found that when asked to generate explanations for feelings, girls used more interpersonal strategies than did boys.

The literature on defense mechanisms also indicates males' propensity for the expression of feelings through actions. Across many studies, it has been found that females use the defenses of turning against the self and reversal more than do males, whereas males use turning against the other and projection more than do females (Cramer, 1991). Similarly, 6- to 12-year-old girls are more likely to use internalizing and appeasing types of defenses in a wide variety of emotionally laden situations than are boys. In situations involving direct, interpersonal conflict, girls were less open than boys about expressions of dislike or contempt (Hay, 1989).

In contrast to males' expression of feelings through behaviors, the results of many studies support the idea that females express feelings in both facial and verbal modalities more intensely than do males. Gender differences in the frequency of emotions expressed in these two modalities have also been found, but they are not quite as clearly documented as intensity differences (Brody and Hall, in press). The results for gender differences in the intensity of specific emotions, especially anger, are equivocal and are affected by the type of situation being responded to and the subject's age, cultural background, and, possibly, cohort membership, that is, the period in history in which the person grew up.

Females report more intense emotional experiences than do males, especially more intense distress, fear, sympathy, embarrassment, sadness, shame, and guilt over a wide range of ages. For example, adult females report more intense positive and negative emotional experiences than do males using a self-report task, the Affect Intensity Measure, which correlates with both physiological indices of emotion and behavioral measures and reports by others (Diener, Sandvik, and Larsen, 1985). Eight-, 11-, and 19-year-old females report more distress and more sympathy than do males in both a sympathy- and distress-inducing procedure (Eisenberg et al., 1988). Furthermore, at all ages and using a variety of self-report measures, females report themselves to be more fearful than do males (Blier and Blier-Wilson, 1989; Brody, 1985; Brody, Hay, and Vandewater, 1990; Croake, Myers, and Singh, 1987; Highlen and Gilles, 1978; Highlen and Johnston, 1979; Kirkpatrick, 1984).

Females also report and display the emotions associated with dysphoric self-consciousness more than do males, including shame, guilt, and embarrassment. Using a behavioral self-report inventory that describes shame-based versus guilt-based alternatives to various situations, Tangney (1990) found that females reported both more shame- and guilt-based experiences than did males. Consistent with this work are sex differences reported by Stapley and Haviland (1989), indicating that adolescent girls reported more shame, sadness and distress than did adolescent boys, as well as work by Lewis et al. (1989), indicating that 2-year-old females displayed more embarrassment in embarrassing situations than males did. Whereas females reported and expressed more of these negative self-conscious emotions than did males, Tangney (1990) found that college-age men reported more pride (a positive self-conscious emotion) than did women.

Some studies continue to find that anger is expressed more by males than by females. Gordis, Smith, and Mascio (1991), testing children in kindergarten through the sixth grade, found that when asked to generate and explain the story character's feelings, males produced more anger responses, whereas females produced more sadness responses. Consistent with these findings is a naturalistic observation study in which four-and-a-half-year-old boys were observed to become significantly more angry than were same-age girls in free-play situations (Fabes and Eisenberg, 1991). A study of emotions reported in response to situations found that 8-year-old males reported more intense anger in response to sad situations than did females, and male adolescents reported more intense anger in response to loving situations than did females. However, in the same study, contrary to these patterns, female adolescents rated anger more intensely in sad situations than did males; and anger in angry situations was rated equally intensely by the two sexes (Wintre et al., 1990).

Many of these sex differences may be culturally, age, and situationally specific. For example, contradictory to the literature on more reports of fear by females is one study that indicated that 2-year-old males displayed more wariness (defined as behavioral inhibition and gaze aversion to a stranger) than did females, suggesting either developmental changes or situational specificity in gender differences in fear-related expressions (Lewis et al., 1989). That gender differences vary by age is also highlighted by Wintre, Polivy, and Murray (1990), who showed that adolescents displayed more gender differences than did younger age groups in the quality and intensity of emotions reported in situations designed to elicit multiple emotions (loving, angry, happy, sad, and fearful). Male adolescents reported less intense emotions than did females, but they also reported more varied emotions than did the adolescent females. Finally, although anger is usually expressed more by males than by females, infant girls were found to display more anger toward mothers than were infant boys in a separation-reunion task, a finding that Malatesta et al. (1989) attribute to closer bonding between mothers and daughters. All of these studies indicate that there may be both developmental changes and situational specificity in gender differences in emotional expression (e.g., boys may be fearful of strangers, girls of separation).

Cultural variations in gender differences were noted when Sommers and Kosmitzki (1988) asked a sample of American and German adults a series of six questions about emotions, among which was the question "Which emotions do you experience regularly and often?" The authors found greater sex differences in general among the American sample, with sex differences in fear reported only for the Americans, not the Germans (i.e., the American men more often reported that fear was an emotion to be avoided). Furthermore, the reporting of anger among the two samples of women was reversed: American women reported more anger the older they got, and German women reported less anger the older they got. Finally, German men reported experiencing gratitude more often than did the American men.

In my own work, I looked at gender differences in the self-ratings of 18 different emotions in a sample of adults ranging in age from 27 to 63 years.[1] The participants in the study consisted of 110 wives and 92 of their husbands. The couples were primarily Caucasian, with a wide variety of ethnic and religious backgrounds, including Indian, Portuguese, Irish, Jewish, Catholic, and Italian, and a wide range of socioeconomic backgrounds. The wives were significantly younger than were the husbands (37.9 years vs. 40.25 years), and the range in age of the sample was 27 to 63 years. Participants had been married or living together for at least three years previous to the onset of the study.

The sample was asked to rate the intensity of 18 different feelings they would experience in response to 48 different stories, including angry, annoyed, ashamed, bored, contemptuous, disgusted, embarrassed, envious/jealous, frightened, grateful, happy, hurt, nervous/apprehensive, pitying, respectful, sad, surprised, and warm. The 18 emotions were chosen both on the basis of results from a pilot sample, which indicated that these were the most frequent emotions experienced about these stories and on the basis of the literature on gender differences in emotional expressions (Brody, 1985). Although we were asking subjects to rate their emotional experiences, our measure relied on their verbal expression and discrimination of feelings, and therefore the most accurate description of what we were measuring is emotional expressiveness.

Each emotion was rated on a six-point scale consisting of not at all, slightly, somewhat, moderately, very, and extremely. The 48 stories were developed in extensive pilot work and were written to depict eight different types of situations, with six stories in each of the eight situations. Four of the situations evoked specific feelings: anger, envy, fear, and warmth; and four of the situations portrayed sex-role stereotyped behaviors without intending to evoke specific feelings, including situations that depicted female socially desirable behaviors (affection, kindness, and sympathy), male socially desirable behaviors (independence, adventurousness, and strength), female socially undesirable behaviors (nagging, gullibility, and spinelessness), and male socially undesirable behaviors (violence, coarseness, and cynicism). For each of the sets of six stories (within the eight types of situations), three were written with male characters who provoked the feeling, and three were written with female characters who provoked the feeling. For example, two of the fear scenarios were: "You left your car in an empty parking lot at night; when you go to pick up the car, you notice a strange man/woman standing near the car," and "You're walking alone at night and notice that a woman/man you don't know is walking behind you and may be following you."

Another measure included in the study was the Marlowe-Crowne Social Desirability Scale, a 34-item self-report scale designed to measure the degree to which individuals need to present themselves in a socially

[1]This study was funded by a Gender Roles grant from the Rockefeller Foundation.

desirable manner or the degree to which they engage in "impression management" and, possibly, self-deception as well (Crowne and Marlowe, 1960; Gergen and Marlowe, 1970).

What were the results? Controlling for socially desirable responding on the Marlowe-Crowne, and using a Sex × sex of story protagonist multivariate analysis of variance, there was a significant sex difference across the 18 emotions, as well as a significant difference in emotional reporting as a function of whether the story protagonist was male or female. Although the multivariate Sex × story protagonist interaction was not significant, some of the univariate interactions were. Means and F-values for each of the 18 emotions reported toward both male and female protagonists are displayed in Table 3.1. Of the 18 emotions, eight showed significant sex differences: annoyance, disgust, sadness, warmth, happiness, hurt, fear, and nervousness. Anger also tended to be significantly different for men and women. In every case, women reported

Table 3.1. Women's and Men's Reported Feelings Toward Males and Females[a]

	Women Toward:				Men Toward:				Univariate F-values		
	Males		Females		Males		Females		Sex	Sex × Prot	Prot
	M	SD	M	SD	M	SD	M	SD	df:(1,89)	(1,89)	(1,89)
Anger	.14	.55	−.08	.39	.00	.38	−.10	.41	3.21^t	3.15^t	18.88***
Annoyed	.08	.44	.01	.57	−.01	.45	−.13	.45	4.18*	.69	6.55*
Ashamed	.03	.49	−.03	.37	−.03	.35	−.03	.37	.21	.94	.90
Bored	−.02	.31	−.09	.23	.07	.56	.01	.73	2.03	.03	2.73
Contempt	.00	.44	−.09	.35	.12	.60	−.03	.38	2.72	.79	15.59***
Disgust	.10	.56	.04	.54	.02	.47	−.13	.34	4.55*	1.40	8.78**
Envy	−.03	.33	.01	.33	.04	.47	−.02	.34	.17	3.88*	.07
Embarrassed	.05	.41	−.01	.46	−.03	.37	−.05	.47	1.44	.25	1.37
Fear	.18	.41	−.04	.31	−.05	.34	−.18	.26	21.62***	1.93	55.09***
Gratitude	.00	.31	−.01	.38	−.03	.41	.00	.49	.05	.33	.18
Happy	.04	.39	.07	.43	−.08	.38	−.04	.45	4.65*	.01	1.98
Hurt	.06	.45	.01	.46	−.10	.28	−.10	.30	6.58*	.87	1.25
Nervous	.14	.49	.01	.49	−.09	.32	−.17	.38	14.23***	.49	14.32***
Pity	−.01	.41	.08	.45	−.06	.38	−.03	.41	2.22	.89	4.36*
Respect	.05	.40	.02	.39	−.08	.51	−.04	.57	2.09	1.69	.15
Sad	.07	.44	.05	.45	−.13	.34	−.07	.41	9.47**	1.64	.20
Surprise	−.03	.61	.01	.54	−.08	.43	.08	.59	.00	4.64*	10.63**
Warmth	.10	.46	.09	.49	−.15	.40	−.07	.55	9.03**	2.87^t	1.43

[a]These results are based on a repeated measures Sex (2) × Sex of story protagonist (2) MANOVA, with sex of subject being a repeated measure, since husbands and wives were not independent of each other. The means are based on z - scores.

Multivariate F for Subject Gender: (18,72) = 3.66, p < .001

for Sex of protagonist: (18,72) = 7.06, p < .001

for Interaction of Gender × Protagonist: (18,72) = 1.30, n.s.

^{t} = p < .10; * = p < .05; ** = p < .01; ***p < .0001.

more intense feelings than did men. For the feelings of anger, envy, warmth, and surprise, however, the gender differences tended to be protagonist specific. Men and women tended to be equally angry at women, but women tended to be more angry at men than men were. Women reported feeling equally warm and surprised toward men and women, whereas men reported more warmth and surprise toward women than toward men. Men tended to be most surprised when female characters appeared in situations intended to be fear inducing, such as a female's emerging from a dark alley. Women also reported more envy toward women, whereas men reported more envy toward men. These results for envy are in direct contrast to psychoanalytic hypotheses that women envy men because of anatomical differences. The results are also in contrast to feminist revisions of psychoanalytic theories, that women envy men because men have higher status and power than they do. Instead, the data suggest, in accordance with social psychological theories, that people envy those to whom they comparatively evaluate themselves, that is, same-sex individuals.

These results confirm previous research that gender differences in anger are situationally specific, and they differ further depending on the sex of the person who is eliciting the feeling. Blier and Blier-Wilson (1989) also found that the sex of the target person affected subjects' emotion responses. College-age males reported lower confidence in expressing anger to females than did female subjects, and females reported significantly more confidence in expressing affection and liking to males than did male subjects.

Men were the object of more negative feelings on the part of both sexes than were women. More anger, contempt, disgust, fear, nervousness, and annoyance were reported toward males than toward females, given the same situations. Perhaps these negative feelings are a function of changing gender roles, in which both men and women are more actively aware of the greater power held by males and the potential for abuse of that power. Alternatively, perhaps both men and women are uncomfortable saying anything negative about women, meaning that they feel it is socially unacceptable to reveal, or perhaps experience, negative feelings about women. This may partially serve an adaptive function for the culture, because the unacceptability of negative feelings toward women may help to protect them from harm (Brody, 1985).

More pity and surprise were reported in response to women's behavior than men's behavior. Perhaps the greater pity toward women is due to women's lower status and power in this culture. Surprise seemed to be expressed in situations in which women were violating normative sex role expectations, such as walking in dark alleys by themselves.

In sum, the available literature tends to confirm that women are more intensely verbally expressive of emotions than are men, but this expressivity is situationally, age, and culturally specific as well as specific to certain feelings. Several studies indicate that in this culture, males express feelings such as anger and pride, that is, emotions associated with differentiating from others and possibly competing with them, more than do females, whereas females express feelings related to social bonding, self-consciousness, and vulnerability, including fear, nervousness, pity, warmth, sadness, guilt, shame, and embarrassment, more than do males.

My own research indicates, however, that gender differences in the expression of feelings depend on the situation being responded to as well as on the sex of the person who is the object of that feeling. For example, women report more intense feelings than do men, including more intense anger, although their anger is directed specifically at males and not at other females. Men tend to report more warmth when the target person is female and not male. Thus, men may be equally expressive of the emotions related to social bonding (e.g., warmth) when the object of their affection is other women, whereas women may be equally expressive of the emotions related to competition and differentiation (e.g., anger) when the object of their emotion is men, not women. It may be that gender differences in expressivity in this culture arise partially from the fact that the two sexes often interact in situations which are sex differentiated, women spending more time in the company of other women than men do and vice versa. In other words, because it is socially unacceptable to express anger toward women and not toward men, people who spend more time in the company of women would tend to express anger less often than those who spend more time in the company of men. The empirical literature indicates that at least for latency-age children, same-sex interactions do predominate over opposite-sex interactions (Maltz and Borker, 1982), and gender differences in peer interactions may greatly affect emotional expressiveness.

Hall (1987), drawing on the work of Maltz and Borker (1982), persuasively argues that the origins of gender differences in emotional functioning may be due to the fact that girls tend to play in intimate, small groups that value verbal communication and cooperation and that minimize hostility and overt conflict. Boys, in contrast, tend to play in larger, hierarchically organized groups in which criticism, teasing, and status-oriented competition are commonplace. Such differences would lead girls to learn to value the expression of emotion (although not direct anger) and boys to learn to value the expression of only those emotions related to competition.

In addition to same-sex peer group socialization, both males and females may identify with and internalize the emotional expressiveness of same-sex adult models: an intergenerational modeling of gender differences. Moreover, by smiling more and being more physically affectionate to preschool girls than to boys, teachers may influence girls to be more emotionally expressive than boys (Botkin and Twardosz, 1988). Finally, there is increasing evidence that parents may socialize the emotional functioning of boys and girls very differently.

GENDER DIFFERENCES IN THE SOCIALIZATION OF EMOTION

The work on the socialization of emotion is remarkably consistent in indicating that, in this culture, emotions are verbally discussed more with girls than with boys (with the possible exceptions of anger and related emotions, such as disgust and contempt) and that parents display a wider range of emotional facial expressions to girls than to boys starting at very early ages.

Studies of gender differences in mothers' dyadic interactions with their young infants (aged 2 1/2 to 22 months; Malatesta et al., 1989) indicate that mothers showed more expressivity and positive affect to girls than to boys in a play session, especially to girls who were securely attached. Girls were thus exposed to a wider range of emotions than were boys. (Mothers did not respond differently to sons and daughters under conditions of child distress.) Malatesta and Haviland (1982) report similar findings for younger children: they found that mothers of three- to six-month-olds smiled more at their daughters. Similarly, Parnell's (1991) work indicates that mothers expressed more positive affect to their 32-month-old daughters than to their 32-month-old sons.

Gender differences in maternal responsivity to infant emotion may be a reaction to innate gender differences in emotional expressivity. That is, if boys are more facially and behaviorally expressive of emotions during the neonatal period, mothers may try to contain their sons' affect by displaying less affect around them. (There is some evidence that boys are more irritable and display more gross motor behavior than do girls; Fogel, 1984). In an intriguing study in which coders were not aware of the sex of the infant, Cunningham and Shapiro (1984) found that infant boys were more intensely emotionally expressive than were infant girls. This may induce mothers to respond differently to boys and girls, which may in turn affect boys' and girls' emotional functioning, which subsequently changes the nature of the mothers' responses, and so on, in a continual series of reciprocal exchanges as outlined by transactional systems models of development (Sameroff, 1975).

Possibly because boys are more intensely expressive, mothers may find their expressions easier to interpret and respond to. Girls may have to amplify their facial expressions in order to ensure that they are under-stood, and they may have to learn to recognize subtle facial expressions of others in order to make sure that they have accurately communicated their feelings. In contrast, boys may learn to control, or possibly inhibit, their early emotional arousal, especially facial expressiveness. This may, in the long run, cause girls to be more facially and verbally expressive of feelings, as well as to be more sensitive to the expressions of others, than are boys.

Tronick and Cohn (1989) present data that can be interpreted as consistent with this line of reasoning. They measured behavioral matching (the degree to which infants and caretakers were in the same state at the same point in time) and synchrony (the degree to which infants and mothers were able to move together focusing on changes over time) in three-, six-, and nine-month-olds. Mother–son dyads were more likely to be in matching states than mother–daughter dyads at all ages and also had higher synchrony scores at six and nine months than did mother–daughter dyads. Although Tronick and Cohn (1989) indicate that these results contradict Chodorow's hypothesis that mothers are more em-pathic toward daughters than toward sons, the results may have less to do with empathy than with the possibility raised above: that boys' expres-sions are easier to read than are girls', and that their expressions are thus matched more easily. These data all suggest (quite speculatively) that girls have to amplify affects in order to be understood, and they thus learn to be more emotionally expressive than are boys during the course of development. In order to test this hypothesis, more research is needed that explores within-sex differences in the intensity of infants' emotional expressions as related to maternal responsiveness and as predictive of later verbal and nonverbal emotional expressiveness.

Data on the socialization of preschoolers' affect are remarkably consis-tent with the infant data presented above. In a creative and ground-breaking study, Greif, Alvarez, and Ulman (1981) demonstrated that given the same wordless storybook, parents developed stories differently for their preschool sons versus daughters. Fathers in particular used more emotion words with their daughters than with their sons, although mothers minimized discussing anger with their daughters. Schell and Gleason (1989) reanalyzed Greif's data, using language-based computer techniques, and found that fathers spoke more emotion words to daugh-ters; mothers did so as well, but not to a significant extent. The authors found that of all parent–child dyads (e.g., father–daughter, mother–son), father–daughter dyads used the highest incidence of emotion words. Only one category of emotion words was not spoken more frequently to girls than to boys: disgust.

In an often-cited study, Dunn, Bretherton, and Munn (1987) showed that mothers spoke more about emotions to their 18- to 24-month-old daughters than to their sons, and that by 24 months, girls were producing more emotion words than were boys. Related findings have been reported by Fivush (1989), who investigated mother–child conversations between 30- to 35-month-old children and their mothers about children's past experiences. She found some tendency for mothers to use more positive than negative emotion terms with their daughters, but approximately equal numbers of positive and negative emotion words with their sons. When mothers of daughters did use negative emotion words, they attributed them to other people. In contrast, mothers of sons attributed negative emotions to the children themselves. These white, middle-class mothers never spoke about anger with their daughters but did with their sons; and they spoke about sadness more with their daughters than with their sons. Another interesting finding was that with daughters, mothers focused and elaborated on the emotion state itself, rather than discussing the cause and consequence of the emotion as they did with their sons, thus possibly teaching their sons to control their feelings while teaching their daughters to be sensitive to the feeling itself. Further data consistent with these patterns have been reported by Radke-Yarrow and Kochanska (1990), who demonstrated that mothers responded in gratifying ways (e.g. attentive concern) to their 2- to $3\frac{1}{2}$-year-old sons' expressions of anger. In contrast, they ignored or tried to inhibit their same-age daughters' expressions of anger. (Depressed mothers differed in these gender-differentiated interaction patterns, with daughters' anger eliciting more attentive involvement from depressed mothers than did sons' anger.)

Although the data on gender differences in school-age children's emotional functioning are limited, one study corroborates infant and preschool trends by indicating that school-age girls anticipate more positive reactions from mothers for expressions of sadness than for anger, and school-age boys anticipate negative reactions from both fathers and mothers for expressions of sadness (Fuchs and Thelen, 1988).

All of these socialization differences suggest that mothers and fathers socialize their sons and daughters differently and, as Ruddick (1982) suggests, in accordance with the prevailing norms of the culture. Parents try to create children who will be appreciated by the wider culture and be accepted by it. One of the major ways through which acceptability is judged may be how well individual boys and girls (and later, men and women) conform to culturally defined gender roles. The importance of gender roles in relation to sex differences in emotional functioning will be discussed next, with the caution that what is culturally defined as an acceptable gender role may vary significantly as a function of changes in cultural and historical context.

GENDER ROLES AND EMOTIONAL EXPRESSIVITY

A Theoretical Overview

I have previously argued that since the two sexes need to adapt to different interpersonal and intrapsychic roles, it follows that their emotional functioning should differ (Brody, 1985). There are many ways in which the two sexes differ in their social roles in this culture: women have lower status and power (Miller, 1976), express less physical aggression (Hyde, 1986), and do more family and child caretaking than do men. In their higher status and power position, men have traditionally been the providers for their families and at least in this culture, are often required to compete with other men for those provisions. From a functionalist perspective, these differing roles should lead to differences in emotional experience. For women, rearing children adaptively would require minimizing the expression of anger and maximizing the ability to recognize nonverbal facial expressions; relating to a more aggressive sex might engender fear and anxiety and might also minimize anger, since one would not want to be attacked. Expressing warmth and happiness would lead to social bonding, which would be adaptive for its protective functions (e.g., against aggression from others), for its instrumental functions (e.g., child caretaking), and for its intrapsychic functions (e.g., facilitating empathic attunement with significant others). For men, maximizing anger and minimizing the expression of fear, guilt, sadness, and hurt would all be adaptive for a competitive environment in which the aggression motivated by anger might lead to obtaining more resources, in which feeling fearful or hurt might preclude winning a competition, and in which feeling guilty or sad might lead to taking care of another, rather than seeking resources for oneself.

One of women's primary roles in this culture has been that of child caretaking. In her intriguing work on the kind of thinking that mothering requires, Ruddick (1982) analyzes a mother's role: to preserve her child's life, to foster her child's growth, and to shape a child who is acceptable to self and others in the culture, someone who is appreciated by others. What kinds of emotions are adaptive for these roles? Certainly a capacity for empathy or what Ruddick terms attentive love, feelings of warmth, respect, pride in others, and the ability to recognize and be sensitive to the feelings of others to whom you are trying to make your child acceptable. In addition, because mothers are confronted with the fragility and constantly changing nature of the life they are trying to preserve (and over which they often have very little control), Ruddick notes that mothers may often develop a sense of humility, cheerfulness, and resilient good humor. Or, alternatively, they may develop a feeling of fearfulness and excessive control.

The traditional provider role for fathers demands that fathers be ambitious, clever, aggressive, and impatient (Demos, 1982). These characteristics are antithetical to those required for good child rearing. To this day, even in dual-career couples, fathers spend one fifth to one quarter as much time interacting with their children than do mothers (Lamb and Oppenheim, 1989), and the quality of their interaction differs markedly from that of mothers. Research on father language has indicated that fathers use more direct imperatives with their children, more threats, and more pejorative language, especially with their sons (e.g., "You dingaling"). They also interrupt the speech of their children more than mothers do and speak to their children using more cognitively demanding speech (Gleason, 1989). The language that fathers use with their children is quite consistent with the kinds of roles the fathers are expected to play.

Because emotions are also adaptive for intrapsychic development, it would be helpful to look at theories about gender differences in intrapsychic functioning that might be related to emotional functioning. In particular, Chodorow (1982) argues intrapsychic gender differences arise from the cultural norm that women differentiate from a same-sex caretaker and thus retain a sense of connectedness to others and that men differentiate from an opposite-sex caretaker, causing them to be more separate from others as well as more rigid in their masculine identity. The rigidity is due to the fact that men's identification is frequently with a stereotype of masculinity, rather than with a father who is genuinely available for interaction and identification. Chodorow's theory suggests that women should experience and express all of the emotions associated with social bonding more easily than do men—warmth, respect, sadness, hurt, shame, loneliness, and the like—and men should experience and express the emotions associated with differentiation more so than should women—contempt, annoyance, anger, disgust, rejection, pride, scorn, and honor.

Many feminist psychoanalytic and object relations theorists have written about the impact that lower status and power have on female psychological development in this culture (Miller, 1976). Groups with lower status and power should experience feelings of envy, gratitude, fear, hurt, respect, and anger toward higher status groups, whereas higher status groups should experience contempt, guilt, pity, scorn, and possibly anger toward lower status groups. Research has in fact indicated that reports of fear are related not only to being female but also to being nonwhite, young, and less educated—all "subordinate" types of characteristics (Clemente and Kleinman, 1977; Croake et al., 1987; Dodd and Mills, 1985; Parker, 1986). Although status and power differences undoubtedly contribute in subtle and powerful ways to female and male emotional functioning, the data that relate status to emotional functioning are far from clear and are often opposite to what one might predict (Brody and Hall, in press). For example, higher status men actually reported themselves to be more fearful than did lower status men (Brody and Flanagan, submitted).

These various perspectives on the interpersonal and intrapsychic roles and experiences to which males and females adapt all converge on the types of emotions one would expect men and women to differentially experience and express. Women should express emotions associated with vulnerability, social bonding, caretaking, and lower status (e.g., fear, hurt, embarrassment, shame, warmth, respect, gratitude, anxiety, and guilt), and men should express emotions associated with differentiation, power, competition, and moral authority (e.g,, anger, contempt, disgust, pity, scorn, pride, and honor). Although Lewis (1985) argued that men should experience guilt more than do women, theories based on adaptations to gender role would predict more guilt on the part of women (i.e., that guilt may arise from a disruption of attachment, more critical for the gender roles of women, and, moreover, that in adapting to male gender roles involving competition, men should report less guilt). Many of the gender differences found in the research I have previously reviewed are consistent with these ideas but further suggest that gender differences are situationally and culturally specific. Inasmuch as gender roles exist within a historical and cultural context and are not invariant across time and place, it is not surprising that gender differences in emotion vary as a function of age, culture, and situation. Even Chodorow's theory is predicated on the assumption that women are the primary caretakers; in cultures in which this is not the case, some of the gender differences discussed above would not emerge.

Historical changes in gender role–affective relationships are evident in changes in the kinds of advice about anger and intimacy that popular magazines gave to women from 1900 to 1979 (Cancian and Gordon, 1988). In the early part of the century, the magazines advised traditional values, including the ideas of self-sacrifice, avoiding conflict, and minimizing anger, whereas in more recent times, they promote self-development and open communication of negative and positive feelings, including anger. Even in modern magazines, however, women are seen as responsible for maintaining intimate relationships, a role that has remained invariant all through the 20th century.

Similarly, definitions of fathering have changed over the years, and such historical changes have almost certainly affected male emotional functioning. Demos (1982) has written of the changing nature of social expectations regarding fathers' roles. At the end of the 17th century, when fathers still worked at home, they had multiple roles vis-à-vis their children: they were moral overseers, teachers, guidance counselors, benefactors, progenitors, companions, and care-givers. With the rise of industrialism in the 19th century, when fathers began working outside the home, men and women began to occupy markedly different spheres, and fathers' contacts with their children began to wane. The role of fathers shifted to become more that of disciplinarian and moral authority to children, with rough-and-tumble play being the kind of interaction that predominated. These historical changes and expectations undoubtedly influenced the types of emotional functioning that were adaptive for fathers and men in this culture.

Empirical Evidence

What is the research evidence that gender roles systematically relate to emotional functioning, even within each sex? Are different gender roles associated with unique emotions? If so, men and women who have cross-sex gender roles should express more of the emotions that are adaptive to those gender roles and that are usually associated with the opposite sex. That is, men who have primary responsibility for child rearing should also manifest some of the emotions associated with that role, such as empathy, warmth, and fearfulness. Similarly, women who compete as family providers should manifest more anger, disgust, and contempt and less of the emotions characterized as "vulnerable." Indeed, in a study of men who were the primary caretakers for their children, Risman (1987) found that both mothers and fathers who interacted more with their children reported higher intimacy than did fathers or mothers who interacted less. Primary caretaking fathers and dual-paycheck mothers reported almost identical levels of feminine stereotyped traits, including attributes such as communality and nurturance.

A growing body of research indicates that there are systematic relations between gender role attributes and the quality and intensity of emotional expression for both sexes, especially for gender-role-related personality attributes, such as being communal and nurturant (stereotypically feminine) as opposed to independent and active (stereotypically masculine). For example, feminine-sex-typed men and women report higher levels of nervousness than do either androgynous or masculine-typed groups, as measured by a self-report nervousness inventory (Bander and Betz, 1981). Men and women with feminine-sex-typed personality traits, as measured by the Bem Sex Role Inventory, had the highest fear scores on the Wolpe Fear Inventory (Dillon, Wolf, and Katz, 1985). Several studies have indicated that masculine-sex-typed subjects are less emotionally expressive and less intimate in the content of their self- disclosures than are feminine-sex-typed subjects (Lewis and Mc-Carthy, l988; Narus and Fischer, 1981; Orlofsky and Windle, 1978). Work by Ingram et al. (l988) indicates that femininity in both men and women is associated with the amplification of negative affect in general and is possibly associated with both depression and anxiety. In my own work with school-age children, gender role identity as measured by both gender-role-related personality traits and toy preferences was a more significant predictor of a wide range of feelings, including fear, anger, disgust, envy, happiness, and hurt, than was biological sex (Brody et al., 1990). Masculine-related traits and toy preferences (measured by self-report) were connected to the emotions of disgust and anger, whereas feminine related traits and toy preferences were connected to vulnerable feelings, including fear, warmth, and hurt.

In exploring the relation between gender-role attributes and emotional expressivity in adults, I have been considering not only gender role traits but also gender role behaviors and attitudes in relation to emotional expressivity. In the same sample of couples discussed earlier, I also assessed gender role traits (masculinity, femininity, aggressiveness, and emotional invulnerability or emotional toughness), using Spence, Helmreich, and Stapp's (1974) Personality Attributes Questionnaire. I assessed sex-role attitudes with the Attitudes Toward Women Scale (Spence and Helmreich, 1972), which consists of items that assess sex-role ideology, ranging from liberal, or nontraditional, attitudes toward women's roles to traditional attitudes. Sex-role behaviors were assessed by rating the sex-role stereotypic nature of the participants' occupations, as well as the number of hours participants were employed per week. Occupations were rated on whether they were stereotypically performed by and associated with women (e.g., nurse, teacher) or by men (e.g., scientist, businessman, engineer) and were subsequently coded as either stereotypically masculine or feminine.

Correlations between scores on gender-role variables and reported fear and nervousness revealed that men who did more stereotypic female household tasks (e.g., laundry, child care, meal preparation) reported greater nervousness, whereas women who did more household tasks stereotypically associated with men, (e.g., yardwork) reported less nervousness and fear. For both sexes, working in traditionally female occupations (e.g., nurse, teacher) tended to be related to increased fear toward both sexes. Similarly, for women, more stereotypic female traits (e.g., nurturance) related to increased fear, and stereotypic masculine traits (e.g., aggression) related to decreased fear and nervousness for both men and women. Some of these results raise the familiar chicken-or-egg question: Do people who are initially more fearful or anxious choose more feminine-stereotyped occupations and tasks to perform, or does performing such occupations and tasks (many of which are service oriented) lead to more fear? Conversely, do women low in fear choose more masculine stereotypic tasks to perform, or does doing such tasks tend to reduce levels of fear? Since feminine roles involve taking care of others, fear may be adaptive, because the people one is responsible for, such as children and elderly parents, are ultimately vulnerable, fragile, and not under one's control (Ruddick, 1982). Affective attunement may also be adaptive for a caretaking role, because interpersonal relationships involve a wide range of affects and emotional intensities.

In order to group people into gender-role "types" using all of their gender-role variables (e.g., occupation, traits), a cluster analysis on all of the gender role variables was performed, which identified six conceptually meaningful clusters of subjects using Ward's method based on Euclidian distance measures. Cluster 1 (27 males, 5 females) was identified as traditionally masculine; cluster 2 (35 females, 2 males) was identified as a feminist group working in part-time stereotypic female occupations; cluster 3 (30 males, 3 females) was identified as a masculine group who worked long hours and had average attitudes toward women's roles (that is, neither strongly feminist nor strongly traditional); cluster 4 (17 females, 30 males) was identified as an androgynous group who endorsed feminist attitudes and who worked in a mix of traditional and nontraditional occupations 40 hours per week; cluster 5 (17 females) was identified as a feminine traditional group who were working part-time in mostly female stereotypic occupations and who reported very traditional attitudes toward women's roles; finally, cluster 6 (22 females) was identified as a feminine group whose primary occupation was that of homemaker, who scored on the feminist end of the scale on attitudes toward women's roles.

These groups differed in status as measured by income, education, and type of occupation. The homemakers (cluster 6) and traditional working women (cluster 5) had the lowest status; the long working hours masculine group (cluster 3) and the androgynous group (cluster 4) had the highest status.

How did these groups differ on emotion? A 6 (cluster) × 2 (sex of story protagonist) multivariate analysis of variance on all 18 emotions revealed significant univariate main effects or interactions for five of the emotions: fear, warmth, anger, nervousness, and gratitude. (The multivariate main effects for cluster and the multivariate cluster × protagonist interaction were not significant, and thus the univariate results should be interpreted cautiously). Table 3.2 displays each cluster's mean scores for the five emotions with significant univariate F-values. The data indicate that group 3, the masculine group who worked long hours, reported significantly less warmth than did other groups; the homemakers reported

Table 3.2. Clusters' Reported Feelings Toward Males and Females[a]

Cluster	Warmth[b] Toward M	Warmth[b] Toward F	Fear[b,c] Toward M	Fear[b,c] Toward F	Nervousness[b] Toward M	Nervousness[b] Toward F	Anger[c] Toward M	Anger[c] Toward F	Gratitude[c] Toward M	Gratitude[c] Toward F
1 Masculine (27 Males; 5 Females) M	-.13	-.13	-.10	-.04	-.09	-.11	.05	-.14	-.05	-.03
SD	.57	.49	.18	.48	.34	.44	.48	.27	.43	.33
2 Working feminist (35 F; 2M) M	.01	-.07	.11	-.13	.18	.03	.09	-.15	.06	-.04
SD	.49	.48	.41	.16	.50	.40	.34	.26	.41	.42
3 Long working hours masc (30 M; 3 F) M	-.29	-.19	-.01	-.22	-.04	-.22	-.02	.01	-.13	-.04
SD	.27	.31	.43	.15	.37	.32	.39	.53	.29	.63
4 Androgynous (17 F, 30 M) M	.03	.12	.05	-.18	-.07	-.11	.06	-.07	.00	.00
SD	.57	.67	.35	.20	.30	.44	.75	.47	.33	.43
5 Traditional feminine work part-time (17 F) M	.03	.06	.47	.17	.44	.26	.41	-.02	.24	.00
SD	.44	.45	.62	.50	1.04	1.04	.75	.46	.46	.18
6 Homemakers (22 F) M	.31	.18	.18	-.04	.11	-.01	.13	-.03	.15	.03
SD	.41	.53	.28	.29	.26	.36	.47	.37	.53	.39

[a]These data are based on z-scores for each emotion. A Cluster (6) × Sex of Story Protagonist (2) MANOVA was performed on the z-scores. Multivariate effects for Cluster were $F(5,90) = 1.20$, p = .11. Multivariate effects for the Cluster × protagonist interaction were $F(5,90) = 1.20$, p = .11.

[b]Univariate effects for the main effect cluster were significant as follows: Warmth: $F(5,182) = 3.89$, p < .005; Fear $F(5,182) = 6.51$, p < .001; Nervousness $F(5,182) = 4.00$, p < .001.

[c]The interaction of cluster × sex of protagonist was significant as follows: Anger $F(5,182) = 3.28$, p < .005; Fear $F(5,182) = 3.75$, p < .005; Gratitude $F(5,182) = 2.09$, p < .07.

significantly more warmth than did other groups. Working women with traditional attitudes reported more fear and nervousness than did other groups. There were also some interesting interactions with sex of story protagonist: the traditional working women reported more anger and fear toward men than toward women, whereas the other groups reported anger and fear equally toward men and women. Interestingly, the traditional working women also tended to report more gratitude toward men than toward women, whereas the other clusters reported these emotions equally toward men and women.

These results demonstrate that gender role is indeed associated with emotion. At the beginning of the chapter, I mentioned theories of emotion that suggest that emotions arise from the violation of expectations (Fischer et al., 1989). The group of working women with traditional attitudes reported more fear and anger than did other groups, especially toward males. They may have their expectations disconfirmed more than the other groups because of the discrepancies between their attitudes and their behavior; namely, they don't believe they should be working. Perhaps they direct toward men more of the negative feelings arising from this discrepancy because they perceive men to have more power with respect to work roles than women do. Alternatively, perhaps this group's initial fear of and anger toward men results in the adoption of traditional gender-role attitudes as a means of protection.

Traditional working women also reported more gratitude toward men than toward women. Gratitude toward men seemed to be elicited in situations in which males were acting in unexpected ways, that is, ways that are more typical for females: nurturing, kind, or affectionate. Gratitude has also been viewed as an emotion that facilitates social relationships and bonding and that is usually associated with feminine gender-role stereotypic traits. Those with low status are expected to feel grateful toward those with high status (Kemper, 1978; Sommers and Kosmitzki, 1988).

That homemakers reported more warmth and that people with masculine gender-role identities who worked long hours reported less warmth are not surprising if one takes the view that emotions reflect enduring personality dispositions and behaviors (Malatesta, 1988) and that emotions are adaptive for the roles people function in.

In summary, much of what has been cast as sex differences in emotional functioning can be recast as gender-role differences. The importance of gender role in relation to emotional functioning is usually masked, because the majority of men have stereotypic masculine gender-role traits and behaviors, and the majority of women have stereotypic feminine gender-role traits and behaviors. Thus, even though gender role may have powerful effects on emotional functioning, when it is not explored independently of sex, the more powerful effects of gender role will be disguised by sex differences. Clearly, more research is needed in which the effects of gender role and sex are studied for their independent contributions to emotional functioning.

ORIGINS OF INDIVIDUAL DIFFERENCES IN GENDER ROLE FUNCTIONING

Although it is clear that gender role traits, behaviors, and attitudes do systematically relate to emotional expressiveness, the harder issue is how to explain the origins of such gender-role variables. Are they socialized? For example, are stereotypically feminine men, that is, men who are more nurturing and communal in their functioning, socialized differently from other men? Conversely, are stereotypically masculine women, those who are more agentic and possibly aggressive, socialized differently from other women?

Or, alternatively, are gender-role personality traits genetically based? Lewis (1985) argued that the tendency to nurture was probably biologically based and more genetically tied to women than to men. Behavioral genetics research has suggested a heritable component of gender-role-related personality traits, as measured by the Comrey Personality Scale (Ahern et al., 1982). Needs for dominance and nurturance, traditionally linked to males and females, respectively, have also been found to have a genetic component. The heritability index estimated for all of these personality attributes is 20–26% (Ahern et al., 1982). Thus, although the data concerning gender-role traits from behavioral genetics studies are limited, the data suggest that gender-role-related traits may not be due solely to socialization practices. (It is important to note, however, that there is little evidence or even reason to suggest that the gender-role-related attitudes that have been found to relate to emotional functioning are genetically based.)

What biological processes might influence gender differences in gender-role attributes and affective functioning? Many neuropsychologists are studying gender differences in cerebral lateralization in an effort to understand gender differences in emotional functioning. A popular theory is that males process information, including affective information, with more pronounced cerebral lateralization than do females (i.e., females use both hemispheres more symmetrically). However, research has indicated that, for both sexes, different types of affective tasks (e.g., recognizing facial expressions, expressing emotions verbally vs. nonverbally) require different processing skills and are associated with different areas of the brain. Gender differences in cerebral lateralization are not consistent or reliable across tasks and studies (Meyers and Smith, 1987). Bleier (l991) convincingly argues that the empirical evidence for gender lateralization differences is lacking and that the available data are flawed by hidden or distorted assumptions and interpretations. Furthermore, given the data on the plasticity of the human brain, it is just as likely that gender differences in the nature of environmental inputs influence any existing neurological gender differences in brain development as the other way around (Bleier, l991).

Gender differences in hormonal processes have also been linked to differences in emotional functioning and may affect gender-role stereotypic traits. Susman et al. (1987) found that sad and anxious affect in adolescent boys were related to hormones associated with puberty, including testosterone–estradiol ratios, levels of testosterone–estradiol binding globulin, and androstenedione. Brooks-Gunn and Warren (1989) found that negative affect in adolescent girls was associated with rapid rises in hormone levels. Hormones accounted for only 4% of the variance in negative affect, however, and social factors, such as negative life events, accounted for far more of the variance: 8–18%. Thus hormones may contribute (although perhaps only slightly, relative to social variables) to the development of emotional expressiveness and perhaps to the development of stereotypic gender-role-related traits as well.

The literature thus suggests that socialization influences, hormonal factors, genetic factors, and neuropsychological factors may all contribute to individual differences in gender roles and hence to aspects of emotional functioning that are influenced by gender roles. However, data on the determinants of gender role are only just beginning to emerge, remaining far from conclusive about the relative contributions of any of these variables. More research on these determinants would be illuminating and intriguing.

GENDER, LANGUAGE, AND SOCIALIZATION

The aforementioned research suggests that there are clear gender differences (possibly attributable to gender-role differences) in emotional functioning, which result in females' and males' learning to use "emotion language" differently, in both verbal and nonverbal modes of expression. Girls learn to express feelings through words and facial expressions (except, possibly, disgust and anger), whereas boys may learn to express feelings through actions and behaviors (Brody and Hall, in press; Hall, 1984). Alternatively, perhaps boys never learn to substitute words for (or use words in addition to) the nonverbal expression of feelings.

Selma Fraiberg, in her classic and widely read book *The Magic Years*

(1959), summarizes psychoanalytic notions about the developmental correspondence between language and action, which she terms "word magic":

> ... The words, the names of objects, are capable of substituting for the objects themselves, mental experience substitutes for a real experience, and by doing so a painful emotion, anxiety, is overcome. ... Words substitute for human acts and the uniquely human achievements of control of body urges—delay, postponement and even renunciation of gratification—are very largely due to the higher mental processes that are made possible by language [pp. 114–115].

It is certainly within the framework of Fraiberg's argument that learning words for feelings can substitute for expressing those feelings in other ways. I was struck with the power of this argument when my 12-month-old daughter began to substitute the word "bite" instead of actually biting when she was frustrated or angry.

Is there any research to support the hypothesis that the verbal expression of emotion serves to substitute for its nonverbal expression? Over a period of time, Bloom and colleagues (Bloom, Beckwith, and Capatides, 1988; Bloom and Capatides, 1987) studied 12 infants who were 9 months to 2 years old. Their work suggests not only that infants' emotional expressiveness may indeed be influenced by their language learning but also that the onset of verbal language doesn't decrease nonverbal emotional expressions relative to earlier levels; rather, the failure to learn verbal language increases nonverbal emotional expression. At 9 months, both early and late language learners had similar levels of nonverbal emotional expressiveness. Only the later word learners increased in the frequency and total time spent in nonverbal emotional expression, whereas the early word learners showed no changes in their nonverbal affect expression. These findings support the notion that nonverbal and verbal expressions are directly related, and what it suggests is that children who learn words early curtail an increase in the level of nonverbal emotional expression, whereas those who do not learn words early increasingly learn to express feelings nonverbally. The affect socialization literature indicates that those children are more likely to be boys.

Bloom et al. (1988) did not explore gender differences in the relation between affect and language (only six boys and six girls were included in the study), but what is provocative is that we know that girls develop language skills earlier than do boys (Gleason, Hay, and Cain, 1989). Girls' earlier language skills, perhaps due to subtle neuropsychological sex differences, perhaps due to the kinds of socialization influences discussed earlier (which in fact may give rise to neuropsychological differences

[Bleier, 1991]), may give them an edge in putting their feelings into words and not acting them out as boys tend to do (Fabes and Eisenberg, 1991).

The literature on alexithymia sheds further light on the relationships between nonverbal and verbal expressions of feelings. Alexithymia, a widely debated psychiatric syndrome, consists in difficulties in verbalizing and describing emotions, with limited abilities to fantasize. For example, Taylor (1987) writes that alexithymic individuals might have outbursts of rage or sobbing but would not be able to elaborate verbally on what they were feeling. The fact that alexithymia has been associated with psychosomatic disorder, posttraumatic stress disorder, substance abuse, and sociopathic personality (Sifneos, 1988), many of which involve the acting-out of impulses, supports the notion that nonverbal and verbal forms of emotional expression may substitute for each other. Alexithymia is more common in males than in females (Smith, 1983; Taylor, 1987), and, similarly, many of the disorders it is associated with (except some psychosomatic disorders) are more common in males than in females. These data support the idea that females learn to express feelings verbally and males learn to express them through behavioral means.

Stern (1985) argues that with the emergence of verbal language comes accountability to others, in that the communication of shared experiences and meanings becomes possible: "In learning a new word, a baby isolates an experience for clear identification and at the same time becomes accountable to mother for that word." Language thus provides a new way of being connected to others. It is compelling that in emphasizing internal feeling state words more to daughters than to sons, parents may influence girls to become more accountable for their internal feeling states and more interpersonally connected to other people than are boys. Lewis (1985) similarly argues that female language superiority may be fostered by (and in turn foster) women's attachments to others. She further hypothesizes that women's language superiority may be an evolutionary adaptation in that it fosters the "vocal or nonharmful" control of the infant for the child-caretaking role.

Stern (1985) also distinguishes between language-based experiences, which are public and for which one is accountable to others, and nonverbal experiences, which are private and deniable to others. He states that those experiences that are deniable to others may become more and more deniable to the self, merging into the unconscious. This suggests that boys, who are less socialized in the verbal language of emotions than are girls, may begin to deny feelings to both self and others. Denial in the sense that Stern is using it suggests both that boys may be unaware of their feelings and that they may defend against their feelings using other defenses.

Differences in defense use may partially mediate gender differences in emotional expression. For example, if males defend against anger by turning against others or projecting it onto others and if females turn the anger against themselves (perhaps in the form of depression or self-punishment), males will express what is interpreted to be anger more than do females (Cramer, 1991). The expressivity difference may thus be due to the way the feeling is managed and not to differences in the initial experience. This line of reasoning becomes important clinically when evaluating someone who doesn't express anger or sadness: does he or she have a deficit in emotional experience, or is he or she defending against the verbalization of emotional expression? Stern's argument suggests that in not verbalizing experiences, the infant begins to have deficits with respect to such experiences, losing all awareness of them. Unfortunately, existing research has not been sophisticated enough either to distinguish between deficit and defense or to look at the ways in which they might interact. For example, in my own research, the finding that males express warmth when the target is a woman but not a man suggests that males may learn that certain feelings are unacceptable in specific situations. Do they actually feel warmth but learn not to express it, or, alternatively, are they unable to feel warmth toward men, defending not just against expression but also against experience? Perhaps more qualitative data will be able to shed further light on this question.

In sum, it seems that females learn to be verbally and facially expressive of emotions, whereas boys may learn to express emotions through behavior and action. These differences may arise because of gender differences in emotion socialization differences, which may in turn be based on or interact with subtle neuropsychological and genetic differences in the propensity for language learning. As I have tried to describe, language-based differences in emotional functioning may have implications for emotional functioning far beyond a person's emotional vocabulary, influencing, among other things, one's relationships to others, one's self-awareness, and one's nonverbal behaviors. Gilchrist (1987) notes in her journals, "We live at the level of our language. Whatever we can articulate we can imagine or understand or explore" (p. 30). Similarly, Hare-Mustin and Marecek (1988), citing Bruner and Wittgenstein, write that "language inevitably structures one's experience of reality as well as the experience of those to whom one communicates."

CONCLUSIONS

The data on gender differences in emotional expressiveness indicate that females are more intensely verbally and facially expressive of a wide variety of emotions than are males. Males are more intensely emotionally expressive through actions and behaviors than are females. Sex differences in the intensity of verbal emotional expressivity are especially marked for emotions that are adaptive for stereotypic gender roles. Thus, females express more intense fear and hurt, related to stereotypic feminine vulnerability; more intense warmth and guilt, related to stereotypic feminine social bonding; and more intense shame and embarrassment, related to low status and power. The few emotions that are in some contexts expressed verbally more by males than by females are related to stereotypic male gender roles, including differentiation and competition (e.g., anger and pride). Further, there is some evidence that males and females with stereotypic cross-gender-role traits and behaviors report emotions more consistent with their gender roles than with their biological gender. Individual differences in gender-role functioning, including type of occupation and behavior, may result in differing emotions. For example, a group of working women with traditional attitudes toward women's roles reported more fear and nervousness than did women with other kinds of gender roles. In addition, men who worked in traditionally female occupations reported more fear than did other men. Thus it may be the case that gender roles (which can also be thought of as social roles) are the more powerful determinants of sex differences in emotional functioning and may make a more significant contribution to emotional expressivity than does biological gender.

Gender differences in specific emotions have been found to differ as a function of age, culture, cohort, and the specific situation that elicits the emotion, including the gender of the person to whom the emotion is being expressed. For example, in this culture, women report more anger toward men than toward women, whereas men report anger equally toward men and women; men report more warmth toward women than toward men, whereas women report warmth equally toward women and men. These target-specific emotions indicate that emotional expressiveness is heavily influenced by what is culturally acceptable and normative. Both males and females may be capable of expressing emotions more associated with the opposite sex when the context permits it. For example, in present-day Germany, men report more fear and gratitude than American men do (Sommers and Kosmitzki, 1988). That gender differences in emotional expressivity are different in different cultures is consistent with the argument that gender differences in emotion are related to adaptations to gender roles, because gender roles vary with respect to age, culture, and situation.

I have suggested that gender differences are multidetermined and may be a function of gender differences in the affect socialization process, including parent, peer, and teacher socialization influences, as well as the language socialization process. A transactional developmental model (that is, reciprocal dyadic or systems interactions that vary over time) may well account for early gender differences in the affect socialization of boys versus girls. Such a model views development as a series of bidirectional influences over time between an individual (with innate temperamental and other constitutional response tendencies) and that individual's context (including parents, teachers, socioeconomic status). Each part (or partner) in the series of interactions reciprocally influences and changes other parts. Using such a model to understand early affect socialization, I have posited the following series of transactions. First, because neonatal boys may have more intense affective expressions than do neonatal girls, boys' expressions may be easier for caretakers to match than girls'. Girls may have to learn to amplify the intensity and clarity of their emotional expressions in order to convey their feelings, because their early facial expressions are more muted. Further, caretakers may enter a relationship with their newborns with a set of gender-role-differentiated expectations that may differentially influence their interaction patterns with their sons and with their daughters. As a result of both their differing expectations for sons versus daughters, as well as in response to the early temperamental differences between their sons and their daughters, parents may emphasize emotions when interacting with their daughters, while de-emphasizing, or attempting to contain, emotions in their sons.

Taking the model one step further, girls' early language facility may also influence parents to talk to them about a wide variety of feeling states (with the exceptions of anger and disgust) from a very early age. Girls may therefore enter later peer relationships more prepared to articulate emotions; boys enter later peer relationships more prepared to mute their feelings. The quality of boys' peer relationships seems to further minimize the expression of feelings, with the exception of those feelings that are adaptive for the hierarchical, competitive games found to be characteristic of boys' play, such as anger and disgust. Such gender differences in the quality of peer relationships would further influence as well as be influenced by other socialization differences (e.g., teachers and the media) to affect gender differences in emotional functioning.

To summarize, it may well be that gender differences in emotion socialization result from a complex series of interactions between early subtle neuropsychological, genetic, and hormonal differences between boys and girls (especially the propensity for expressive language), which reciprocally affect the quality of caretaker and peer affective responsivity. Gender differences in peer and caretaker socialization are influenced not only by innate response and temperamental tendencies but also by expectations about gender roles. Eventually, females and males learn to use emotions and affect language differently, which may lead them to become differentially accountable to others as well as differentially aware of their own feeling states.

CLINICAL IMPLICATIONS

Perhaps the way in which the literature on gender differences in expressivity can be most useful to clinicians is in creating new meanings and new frames of reference about gender roles and emotion, which can serve to validate patients' experiences. Hare-Mustin and Marecek (1988) discuss the concept of deconstruction, that is, understanding the underlying and hidden meanings in a narrative, as critical for the psychotherapy process. Until recently, the power of gender roles in shaping patients' experiences was largely neglected by mental health professionals, which served to keep the experiential component of those roles in patients' lives hidden from awareness. Therapists who can validate their patients' gender-role-based experiences are undoubtedly more empathic and ultimately of more help to their patients, because the context in which males and females develop plays such an important role in their emotional development.

Extreme adaptation to gender roles has often been interpreted as psychopathology (Lewis, 1985). For example, for many years, a commonly accepted view of women in both psychiatry and clinical psychology was that they were "hysterical," overly emotional and excitable, and "histrionic." Many feminist writers have pointed out that women can be described this way only if male behavior is normative, that is, that male lack of expressivity is the standard, and female expressivity is seen as pathological, as "too much" relative to that standard (Hall, 1987). More recently, female expressivity has been viewed as the healthy norm, due largely to the efforts of feminist clinicians, researchers, and scholars (Hare-Mustin and Marecek, 1988), and the pendulum has begun to swing the other way, so that men's relative inexpressivity is seen as "deficient" or "defensive." In particular, recent themes in family therapy have centered on the "resistant" husband/father, that is, the male client who does not articulate or express emotion and is therefore more difficult for the therapist to engage.

If, instead, one views female expressivity and male inexpressivity as arising from a historical and social context in which people are socialized to adapt to gender roles, then relative comparisons between the two sexes become less important. With an understanding of how "gender-related meanings" (Hare-Mustin and Marecek, 1988) are embedded in our concepts of psychopathology, both males and females (and mothers and fathers) might be subject to less blame and be seen in a less pathological light by the therapeutic community. Rather, each sex would be seen as adapting to a different set of gender-role-based socialization patterns.

Understanding the cultural and socialization influences on the gender roles each partner plays in an emotional exchange (whether it be patient–therapist, wife–husband, or parent–child) would help patients to cast their behavior and that of their partners in a new light. For example, an appreciation of the types of patterns reviewed in this chapter might be used to help couples understand the gender-based patterns of communication in their marriage. Notarius and Johnson (1982) found that wives tended to reciprocate their husbands' positive and negative emotions with further emotional expressions, which in turn produced more responses from their husbands. In contrast, husbands responded to their wives' positive emotions with affectively neutral responses and to their wives' negative emotions with no consistent response patterns, thus cutting off an exchange. A perspective on gender-based patterns might help to decrease blame in such exchanges and to widen both participants' perspectives on some of the reasons underlying their behavior. With increased awareness may come an increased likelihood for change.

The research reviewed in this chapter also highlights that individual differences in stereotypic gender-role-related attributes (e.g., nurturance) are more important than biological gender in affecting emotional development. Thus, although therapists should be aware of how powerful gender and gender roles are in affecting development, they should not be blinded by gender into making erroneous assumptions about patients' personalities. Individual differences, and the gender-role characteristics of each individual patient, continue to be of primary importance. Finally, the existing research on gender differences, by demonstrating the cultural, age, and situational specificity of emotional expression, holds forth the promise that affective expression can be taught, or retaught, for both sexes in a new interpersonal relationship, the psychotherapeutic one. The psychotherapeutic relationship provides a new context in which the transactional series of exchanges involved in the emotional socialization process can take place; it is a context in which emotional functioning can be socialized in new and, it is hoped, less dysfunctional ways.

REFERENCES

Adelmann, P. K. & Zajonc, R. (1989), Facial efference and the experience of emotion. *Ann. Rev. Psychol.*, 40:249–280.

Ahern, F. M., Johnson, R. D., Wilson, J. R., McClearn, G. E. & Vandenberg, S. G. (1982), Family resemblances in personality. *Behav. Genet.*, 12:261–280.

Bander, R. S. & Betz, N. E. (1981), The relationship of sex and sex role to trait and situationally specific anxiety types. *J. Res. Personal.*, 15:312–322.

Bleier, R. (1991), Gender ideology and the brain. In: *Women and Men: New Perspectives on Gender Differences*, ed. M. Notman & C. Nadelson. Washington: American Psychiatric Press, pp. 63–73.

Blier, M. J. & Blier-Wilson, L. A. (1989), Gender differences in self-rated emotional expressiveness. *Sex Roles*, 21:287–295.

Bloom, L., Beckwith, R. & Capatides, J. (1988), Developments in the expression of affect. *Infant Behav. Dev.*, 11:169–186.

———— & Capatides, J. D. (1987), Expression of affect and the emergence of language. *Child Dev.*, 58:1513–1522.

Botkin, D. & Twardosz, S. (1988), Early childhood teachers' affectionate behavior. *Early Childhood Res. Quart.*, 3:167–177.

Brody, L. R. (1985), Gender differences in emotional development. *J. Personal.*, 53:102–149.

———— & Flanagan, L. (submitted), Fear, status, and gender-role stereotypic occupations, personality attributes, and household behaviors.

———— & Hall, J. A. (in press), Gender and emotion. In: *Handbook of Emotions*, ed. M. Lewis & J. Haviland. New York: Guilford Press.

———— Hay, D. H. & Vandewater, E. (1990), Gender, gender role identity and children's reported feelings toward the same and opposite sex. *Sex Roles*, 3:363–387.

Brooks-Gunn, J. & Warren, M. P. (1989), Biological and social contributions to negative affect in young adolescent girls. *Child Dev.*, 60:40–55.

Buck, R., Miller, R. E. & Caul, W. F. (1974), Sex, personality and physiological variables in the communication of affect via facial expression. *J. Personal. Soc. Psychol.*, 30:587–596.

Cacioppo, J. T., Uchino, B. N., Crites, S. L., Snydersmith, M., Smith, G., Berntson, G. & Lang, P. J. (1992), Relationship between facial expressiveness and sympathetic activation in emotion: A critical review, with emphasis on modeling underlying mechanisms and individual differences. *J. Personal. Soc. Psychol.*, 62:110–128.

Cancian, F. & Gordon, S. (1988), Changing emotion norms in marriage. *Gender Soc.*, 2:308–342.

Chodorow, N. (1982), Family structure and feminine personality. In: *Women, Culture & Personality*, ed. M. Rosaldo & L. Lamphere. Stanford, CA: Stanford University Press, pp. 43–66.

Clemente, F. & Kleinman, M. B. (1977), Fear of crime in the U.S.: A multivariate analysis. *Soc. Forces*, 56:519–531.

Condry, J. & Condry, S. (1976), Sex differences: A study of the eye of the beholder. *Child Dev.*, 47:812–819.

Cramer, P. (1991), *The Development of the Defense Mechanisms*. New York: Springer.

Croake, J. W., Myers, K. M. & Singh, A. (1987), Demographic features of adult fears. *Internat. J. Soc. Psychiat.*, 33:285–293.

Crowne, D. & Marlowe, D. (1960), A new scale of social desirability independent of psychopathology. *J. Consult. Psychol.*, 24:349–354.

Cunningham, J. & Shapiro, L. (1984), Infant affective expression as a function of infant and adult gender. Unpublished manuscript, Brandeis University.

Demos, J. (1982), The changing faces of fatherhood. In: *Father and Child*, ed. S. Cath, A. Gurwitt & J. Ross. Boston: Little, Brown, pp. 425–445.

Diener, E., Sandvik, E. & Larsen, R. (1985), Age and sex effects for emotional intensity. *Dev. Psychol.*, 21:542–546.

Dillon, K. M., Wolf, E. & Katz, H. (1985), Sex roles, gender, and fear. *J. Psychol.*, 119:355–359.

Dodd, D. K. & Mills, L. L. (1985), FADIS: A measure of the fear of accidental death and injury. *Psychol. Rec.*, 35:269–275.

Dunn, J., Bretherton, I. & Munn, P. (1987), Conversations about feeling states between mothers and their children. *Dev. Psychol.*, 23:132–139.

Eisenberg, N., Schaller, M., Fabes, R. A., Bustamante, D., Mathy, R., Shell, R. & Rhodes, K. (1988), Differentiation of personal distress and sympathy in children and adults. *Dev. Psychol.*, 24:766–775.

Fabes, R. A. & Eisenberg, N. (1991), Children's coping with interpersonal anger. Presented at the biennial meeting of the Society for Research in Child Development, Seattle, WA.

Fischer, K. W., Shaver, P. & Carnochan, P. (1989), A skill approach to emotional development: From basic to subordinate category emotions. In: *Child Development Today and Tomorrow*, ed. W. Damon. San Francisco: Jossey-Bass, pp. 107–136.

Fivush, R. (1989), Exploring sex differences in the emotional content of mother–child conversations about the past. *Sex Roles*, 20:675–691.

Fogel, A. (1984), *Infancy: Infant, Family and Society.* New York: West.

Fraiberg, S. (1959), *The Magic Years.* New York: Charles Scribner's Sons.

Fuchs, S. & Thelen, M. (1988), Children's expected interpersonal consequences of communicating their affective state and reported likelihood of expression. *Child Dev.*, 59:1314–1322.

Gergen, K. & Marlowe, D. (1970), *Personality and Social Behavior.* Reading, MA: Addison-Wesley.

Gilchrist, E. (1987), *Falling Through Space.* Boston: Little, Brown.

Gleason, J. (1989), Sex differences in parent–child interaction. In: *Language, Gender, and Sex in Comparative Perspective*, ed. S. Philips, S. Steele & C. Tanz. Cambridge, MA: Cambridge University Press, pp. 189–199.

_____ Hay, D. & Cain, L. (1989), Social and affective determinants of language acquisition. In: *The Teachability of Language*, ed. M. L. Rice & L. Schiefelbusch. Baltimore: Paul H. Brookes, pp. 171–186.

Gordis, F., Smith, J. & Mascio, C. (1991). Gender differences in attributions of sadness and anger. Presented at the biennial meeting of the Society for Research in Child Development, Seattle, WA.

Greif, E., Alvarez, M. & Ulman, K. (1981), Recognizing emotions in other people: Sex differences in socialization. Presented at the biennial meeting of the Society for Research in Child Development, Boston, MA.

Hall, J. A. (1984), *Nonverbal Sex Differences.* Baltimore, MD: Johns Hopkins University Press.

_____ (1987), On explaining gender differences. In: *Review of Personality and Social Psychology. Vol. 7*, ed. P. Shaver & C. Hendrick. Newbury Park, CA: Sage Publications, pp. 177–200.

Hare-Mustin, R. T. & Marecek, J. (1988), The meaning of difference. *Amer. Psychol.*, 43:455–464.

Hay, D. (1989), Children's use of defense: Developmental and individual difference. Unpublished doctoral dissertation, Boston University.

Highlen, P. S. & Gilles, S. F. (1978). Effects of situational factors, sex and attitude on affective self-disclosure with acquaintances. *J. Counsel. Psychol.*, 25:270–276.

_____ & Johnston, B. (1979), Effects of situational variables on affective self-disclosure with acquaintances. *J. Counsel. Psychol.*, 26:255–258.

Hyde, J. S. (1986), Gender differences in aggression. In: *The Psychology of Gender*, ed. J. S. Hyde and M. Linn. Baltimore, MD: Johns Hopkins University Press, pp. 51–66.

Ingram, R., Cruet, D., Johnson, B. & Wisnicki, K. (1988), Self-focused attention, gender, gender role, and vulnerability to negative affect. *J. Person. Soc. Psychol.*, 55:967–978.

Kemper, T. (1978), *A Social Interactional Theory of Emotions.* New York: Wiley.

Kirkpatrick, D. R. (1984), Age, gender and patterns of common intense fear among adults. *Behav. Res. Ther.*, 22:141–150.

Lamb, M. & Oppenheim, D. (1989), Fatherhood and father–child relationships. In: *Fathers and Their Families*, ed. S. Cath, A. Gurwitt & L. Gunsberg. Hillsdale, NJ: The Analytic Press, pp. 11–16.

Lewis, E. T. & McCarthy, P. R. (1988), Perceptions of self-disclosure as a function of gender-linked variables. *Sex Roles*, 19:47–56.

Lewis, H. B. (1983), *Freud and Modern Psychology, Vol. 2.* New York: Plenum Press.

_____ (1985), Depression vs. paranoia: Why are there sex differences in mental illness? *J. Personal.*, 53:150–178.

Lewis, M., Sullivan, M. W., Stanger, C. & Weiss, M. (1989), Self-development and self-conscious emotions. *Child Dev.*, 60:146–156.

Malatesta, C. Z. (1988), The role of emotions in the development and organization of personality. In: *Nebraska Symposium on Motivation: Socioemotional Development*, ed. R. Thompson. Lincoln: University of Nebraska Press, pp. 1–55.

_____ Culver, C., Tesman, J. & Shepard, B. (1989), The development of emotion expression during the first two years of life. *Monographs of the Society for Research in Child Development*, 50:1–2, Serial No. 219.

_____ & Haviland, J. M. (1982), Learning display rules. *Child Dev.*, 53:991–1003.

Maltz, D. M. & Borker, R. A. (1982), A cultural approach to male–female miscommunication. In: *Language and Social Identity*, ed. J. Gumperz. Cambridge, MA: Cambridge University Press, pp. 195–216.

Meyers, M. B. & Smith, B. (1987), Cerebral processing of nonverbal affective stimuli. *Biological Psychol.*, 24:67–84.

Miller, J. B. (1976), *Toward a New Psychology of Women.* Boston, MA: Beacon Press.

Narus, L. R. & Fischer, J. L. (1981), Sex roles and intimacy in same and other sex relationships. *Psychol. Women Quart.*, 5:444–455.

Notarius, C. I. & Johnson, J. S. (1982), Emotional expression in husbands and wives. *J. Marriage Fam.*, 44:483–489.

Orlofsky, J. L. & Windle, M. T. (1978), Sex role orientation, behavioral adaptability and personal adjustment. *Sex Roles*, 4:801–811.

Parker, K. D. (1986), Black–white differences in perceptions of fear of crime. *J. Social Psychol.*, 128:487–494.

Parnell, K. (1991), Toddler interaction in relation to mother and peers. Unpublished doctoral dissertation, Boston University.

Radke-Yarrow, M. & Kochanska, G. (1990), Anger in young children. In: *Psychological and Biological Approaches to Emotion*, ed. N. L. Stein, B. Leventhal & T. Trabasso. Hillsdale, NJ: Lawrence Erlbaum Associates.

Risman, B. J. (1987), Intimate relationships from a microstructural perspective. *Gender Soc.*, 1:6–32.

Ruddick, S. (1982), Maternal thinking. In: *Rethinking the Family*, ed. B. Thorne & M. Yalom. New York: Longman, pp. 76–94.

Sameroff, A. (1975), Transactional models in early social relations. *Human Dev.*, 18:65–79.

Schell, A. & Gleason, J. B. (December 1989), Gender differences in the acquisition of the vocabulary of emotion. Presented at the annual meeting of the American Association of Applied Linguistics, Washington, DC.

Schwartz, G. E., Brown, S., & Ahern, G. L. (1980), Facial muscle patterning and subjective experience during affective imagery. *Psychophysiol.*, 17:75–82.

Sifneos, P. E. (1988), Alexithymia and its relationship to hemispheric specialization, affect and creativity. *Hemispheric Specialization*, 11:287–292.

Smith, G. R. (1983), Alexithymia in medical patients referred to a consultation/liaison service. *Amer. J. Psychiat.*, 140:99–101.

Sommers, S. & Kosmitzki, C. (1988), Emotion and social context. *Brit. J. Soc. Psych.*, 27:35–49.

Spence, J. T. & Helmreich, R. L. (1972), The attitudes toward women scale. *Journal Supplement: Abstract Service Catalog of Selected Documents in Psychology*, 2:66–67.

_____ _____ & Stapp, J. (1974), The personal attributes questionnaire. *Journal Supplement: Abstract Service Catalog of Selected Documents in Psychology*, 4:43.

Stalans, L. & Wedding, D. (1985), Superiority of the left hemisphere in the recognition of emotional faces. *Internat. J. Neurosci.*, 25:219–223.

Stapley, J. & Haviland, J. (1989), Beyond depression: Gender differences in normal adolescents' emotional experience. *Sex Roles*, 20:295–309.

Stern, D. (1985), *The Interpersonal World of the Infant*. New York: Basic Books.

Strayer, J. (1986), Children's attributions regarding the situational determinants of emotion in self and others. *Dev. Psychol.*, 22:649–654.

Susman, E., Inoff-Germain, G., Nottelmann, E. D., Loriaux, D. L., Cutler, G. B. & Chrousos, G. P. (1987), Hormones, emotional dispositions, and aggressive attributes in young adolescents. *Child Dev.*, 58:1114–1134.

Tangney, J. P. (1990), Assessing individual differences in proneness to shame and guilt. *J. Personal Soc. Psychol.*, 59:102–111.

Taylor, G. (1987), Alexithymia: Culture and class relationships: A symposium. *Transcultural Psychiatric Res. Rev.*, 24:85–95.

Tronick, E. & Cohn, J. (1989), Infant–mother face-to-face interaction. *Child Dev.*, 60:85–92.

Whitesell, N. R., Robinson, N. S. & Harter, S. (April 1991), Anger in early adolescence: Prototypical causes and gender differences in coping strategies. Presented at the biennial meeting of the Society for Research in Child Development, Seattle, WA.

Wintre, M. G., Polivy, J. & Murray, M. (1990), Self predictions of emotional response patterns. *Child Dev.*, 61:1124–1133.

Part II

AFFECT AND THE LIFE CYCLE

This section is devoted to an understanding of emotions in psychotherapy. Moreover, each of its five chapters describes a patient in different stages of the life span. In this sense, each chapter can be viewed from two perspectives: first as an example of an application of affect theory to the clinical process through a case presentation, and second, as an illustration of normal–phase specific affective developmental issues confronting the individual in each stage of the life span.

Steven Ablon, in "The Therapeutic Action of Play and Affect in Child Analysis," describes the analysis of a 5-year-old and a 12-year-old. In each case illustration, Ablon attempts to demonstrate how play is used as a primary means to master affect. In the case of the 5-year-old boy, therapeutic play allows the boy to master unintegrated violent and sexual fantasies. In the case of the 12-year-old boy, therapeutic play allows him to work through intensely painful affects associated with the death of his mother. According to Ablon, play and fantasy are the phase-appropriate means by which children lend organization to powerful affects, fantasies, and traumatic experiences. Play and fantasy act as means in the intersubjective sphere of the therapeutic relationship to enhance the integration of the child's intensely painful experiences and feelings.

Alexandra Harrison, in "Affective Interactions in the Families with Young Children," expands the context of traditional child psychoanalysis into the arena of family interaction. She discusses the case of a 5-year-old girl whose presenting problem of temper tantrums was associated with unresolved oedipal conflicts. Harrison reminds us that traditional intrapsychic interpretation of the oedipal conflict fails to address adequately the impact of such conflict on all members of the family system. In this case, Molly's temper tantrums pose significant problems for her mother, father, and 8-year-old sister. The reaction of each respectively complicated Molly's attempt to resolve her phase-appropriate developmental oedipal strivings. Using affect-script theory, Harrison shows how families such as Molly's react to her problem behavior by constructing a family myth to manage the behavior which threatens family coherence. Such myth making minimizes the impact of uncomfortable affective states that are evoked in family members. Through a combination of child therapy and family treatment, Harrison explores the family myth associated with Molly's intense affect. By enhancing the family's capacity to tolerate affects, Molly's ability to play is restored, and she is able to resolve the oedipal conflict.

Stephanie Smith, in "Problems with Affect Tolerance in the Analysis of an Adolescent Girl," addresses the issue of affective development in middle adolescence. She sees middle adolescence as a phase in which preoedipal conflicts and associated affects are reworked through a process of grieving early infantile objects and the grandiose self. From the perspective of affect development, the maturation of formal operational thinking sets the stage for the emergence of complex and subtle affective states and for the reversibility of affective states. Smith illustrates these dimensions of adolescent affective development through a detailed case discussion of the psychoanalysis of a 14-year-old girl who suffered multiple losses and moves and experienced repeated failure of maternal caretaking. According to Smith's understanding, psychoanalysis of middle adolescents should be focused primarily on the development of affective tolerance. Successful working through of the vicissitudes of the transference was enhanced by the analyst's sensitive focus on affect both with the patient and in conjoint sessions with the patient's mother and the patient together.

Alfred Margulies, in "Empathy, Virtuality, and the Birth of Complex Emotional States," addresses the issue of empathy in psychotherapy and psychoanalysis with adults. According to Brown's model for affective development described in Chapter 1, the task of adult affective development includes recognition of the vicissitudes of complex emotional states and the various levels of affective processing. Margulies likewise assumes that the inner experience for the normal adult is exceedingly complex and rich. Margulies reminds us that empathy is not simply a process of discovering or uncovering what is there in the patient's experience, but a process of creating something new. Because of the complexity of inner experience, therapeutic empathy serves to enhance what is possible or virtual in the patient and makes it actual and manifest. Whether the therapeutic approach emphasizes the here-and-now or unconscious state, in each case, therapeutic intervention creates and shapes the patient's inner experience. With respect to affect, the therapist helps to identify and label affects, provides external structure when it is lacking in the patient, and helps the patient to link complex emotional states together. Margulies illustrates this complex interactive process through a brief case discussion. In this sense, adult psychotherapy serves in the phase-appropriate task of mastering adult affective development, mainly to become more aware of affective experiences and processes but also to give form to inner experience and affective experience.

Alexander Morgan, in "Affect in the Elderly—Do Older People Feel Differently?" addresses the all too neglected issue of emotional experience in the elderly. Morgan challenges unfortunate stereotypes that the elderly experience feelings differently, are inflexible, and cannot change. What little research is available on affective development in the elderly shows that their affective development is not so different from development in younger adults. Morgan discusses the therapy of a woman in her 80s. The first phase of the woman's treatment examines her many somatic complaints. The second phase of her treatment explores her grief and rage regarding the breakup of her daughter's marriage. The third and last phase of the treatment focuses on the quality of her self-experience, specifically on a detailed exploration of her affective states. Morgan points out that the patient was able to develop new affective sequences during treatment. In addition, Morgan shows not only that the elderly can significantly change their affective experiences in psychotherapy but also that the developmental tasks posed for the elderly are not essentially different from those for younger adults, namely to explore the vicissitudes and complexities of one's own inner emotional life.

Chapter 4

THE THERAPEUTIC ACTION
OF PLAY AND AFFECT
IN CHILD ANALYSIS

Steven L. Ablon

I remembered one morning when I discovered a cocoon in the bark of a tree, just as a butterfly was making a hole in its case and preparing to come out. I waited a while, but it was too long appearing and I was impatient. I bent over it and breathed on it to warm it. I warmed it as quickly as I could and the miracle began to happen before my eyes, faster than life. The case opened, the butterfly started slowly crawling out and I shall never forget my horror when I saw how its wings were folded back and crumpled; the wretched butterfly tried with its whole trembling body to unfold them. Bending over it, I tried to help it with my breath. In vain. It needed to be hatched out patiently and the unfolding of the wings should be a gradual process in the sun. Now it was too late. My breath had forced the butterfly to appear, all crumpled, before its time. It struggled desperately and, a few seconds later, died in the palm of my hand. That little body is, I do believe, the greatest weight I have on my conscience. For I realize today that it is a mortal sin to violate the great laws of nature. We should not hurry, we should not be impatient, but we should confidently obey the eternal rhythm (Kazantzakis, 1952).

This chapter examines in the analytic setting the nature of the health promoting qualities of play and play's fundamental link to affect. A central aspect of the process is providing the therapeutic environment in which the analyst is the child's steadfast companion and follower while the analyst maintains a lively self-analytic capacity. In this context, the integrative functions of play emerge more clearly, as does the value of not interpreting or interfering with the unfolding of the play.

Many attempts have been made to understand the therapeutic action of play in psychoanalysis. Particular attention has been focused on repetition and mastery of trauma and conflict through changing passive experiences into active ones. Freud (1920) observed, "In the case of children's play we seemed to see that children repeat unpleasurable experiences for the additional reason that they can master a powerful impression far more thoroughly by being active than they could by merely experiencing it passively" (p. 35). Variations on this theme are abreaction or catharsis of overwhelming affect and problem solving through play. Again, to quote Freud (1920), "It is clear that in their play children repeat everything that has made a great impression on them in real life, and that in doing so they abreact the strength of the impression and, as one might put it, make themselves master of the situation" (pp. 16–17).

The importance of mastery of affect is emphasized by Waelder (1933). "The repetition compulsion, then, purely empirically, is not a blind primal impulse which demands, 'Repeat!' It is a pressure exerted by unfinished processes, and it is a constant striving to assimilate" (p. 216). Waelder understands play to be a process like a repetition compulsion, which also has a teleological function. "This function is not so much the preparation for future activities in adult life as it is the assimilation of the mass of excitations from the outer world, which affect the organism too severely or too suddenly to permit of their immediate disposal" (p. 218). The elaboration of fantasies, wishes, and fears in play involves problem solving and mastery similar to the process of dreaming and telling the manifest content of dreams (Ablon and Mack, 1980). In a similar way to dreams, play facilitates an appreciation of the nuances and transitions involved in reality orientation. As Waelder (1933) points out, this is similar to Freud's understanding of grieving.

> Mourning is the suffering entailed by this task of separation. This task, however, is accomplished under the sway of the repetition compulsion. The lost object constantly comes to mind; fresh accesses of ungratified affection are freshly painful. In this constantly repeated resurgence of the painful experience a gradual assimilation occurs simultaneously with the course of normal grief. The affect fades away little by little [p. 219].

The process of reworking past difficulties and painful experiences has been discussed in terms of reconstruction and enactment. Also emphasized is the importance of freedom from superego constraints during play as the child tries on various roles usually prohibited by social norms and the child's conscience.

Technically, the analyst's traditional interventions have included facilitation of the therapeutic alliance, analysis of defense, and clarification and interpretation of the transference, defined as a recapitulation of previous fantasies, feelings, and conflicts about parents as they are expressed in relation to the analyst. Also, identification with the analyzing function of the analyst, bringing unconscious conflict into awareness, and interpersonal forces such as providing a holding environment and strengthening of the ego have been discussed. Play in the analytic setting allows the child to bring forward and explore feelings that are most troublesome and important. In the process, the child expands an organizing aspect of the psyche and brings order to the chaos of preconscious and unconscious affect as it is worked and explored in symbolic terms in play. Such assimilation of affects and experience past and present into an organizing aspect of the mind has a powerful therapeutic effect in its own right without reconstructive interpretation. The process does not detract from the therapeutic effect of play in relation to verbalized insight, reconstruction, and interpretation of the transference. The balance and prominence of the therapeutic impact of these experiences depend on the individual child and the complex vicissitudes of the child's constitution, life experiences, development, and psychic structure.

Many child analysts have experienced analyses in which children have improved in a dramatic and enduring way, although the play remained displaced and not related verbally and directly to the important people in the child's life. In these situations, analyses have proceeded without insight's being verbally or consciously structured. Neubauer (1987) lucidly describes the same observation: "I have often been surprised at the progress children in analysis can make without 'primary interpretations.' I mean by the term those interpretations that address themselves to the patient's relationship to primary objects" (p. 6). In these analyses, the child may make many drawings without discussing them, play structured board games with powerful themes that are not discussed directly in relation to the child's life, or remain silent and sometimes openly antagonistic to the analyst while occupying himself with books or magazines. Perhaps these aspects of analyses are not emphasized because the analyst fears his interventions are not sophisticated or important enough to warrant the child's being brought to him rather than to any good-hearted adult playmate. In fact, my view is that an analytic situation that allows the child to use play for symbolic but not directly verbalized organization and synthesis of affects and as a result to resume the progressive development is extremely difficult and taxing. A position of neutrality in which the analyst is interested in allowing the play to expand, and the child is "encouraged to continue" (Stern, 1985, p. 151) and perhaps eventually to understand some of what is being communicated, is difficult to maintain.

The analyst needs to see both the defense and the communication in the child's play and to tolerate the powerful affects that emerge in the play and in the relationship. These affects include anger, sadness, helplessness, humiliation, worthlessness, sadism, intense sexuality, and dependence on the analyst, and they raise taxing countertransference stresses. Difficulty in sitting with these painful affects can lead to defensive efforts by the analyst such as intellectualization, premature intervention, manipulation, limit setting, and other activities that bring closure to the child's explorations. For example, a boy of 14 was silent in analysis and spent his analytic hours choosing between a series of magazines he stored in the office. These magazines ranged from *Mad* magazine, to *Popular Mechanics*, to *Car and Driver*, to *Rolling Stone*. He'd snarl whenever I tried to engage him. When I suggested the frequency of meetings be decreased, the patient, who had improved remarkably, became despondent and suicidal. The establishment and maintenance of an analytic situation depends on the analyst's sitting with the child's painful affects and trying to help him bear them. This occurs when the analyst does not intervene to avoid these affects, but it also depends on how the analyst helps to establish the analytic setting and how the analyst responds to events in the analysis that diverge from play in terms of having reality consequences such as acts that would endanger the analyst or the child or do damage to the office or time constraints such as refusing to leave at the end of an hour. Fortunately, our child analysands are quite forgiving of our struggles such as inattentiveness, insensitivity, inexact interpretations, and interpretations based on our need to understand, to feel valued, or not to feel helpless.

With this perspective in mind, I shall describe periods in the analysis of a five-year-old boy and of a twelve-year-old boy that perhaps will illustrate the therapeutic action of play and affect in psychoanalysis at different ages in terms of the expansion of the organizing assimilative function of the ego.

CLINICAL MATERIAL

First Case

John began analysis at age five because of stuttering, preoccupations with violent fantasies, and angry physical and verbal outbursts toward his parents; his sister, who was four years younger; and his friends. John's parents had separated when he was 11 months old; they divorced when he was 23 months old. His mother and father each remarried approximately a year after the divorce. During the separation and divorce there was much animosity between John's parents, which occasionally led to angry verbal outbursts between them. John lived with his mother and stepfather and visited his father on weekends twice a month. Shortly after his sister was born, during a weekend visit, John's father said he would not bring John home, and John began to stutter. The stuttering persisted and became worse.

John was a bright, energetic, appealing child with a marked stutter, who came enthusiastically to his analytic hours. At the beginning of the analysis, John's play involved violent, dangerous adventures in which the hero had an assistant such as Dr. Watson and Sherlock or Robin and Batman. When Batman would attack his enemy Joker, John would stutter more severely, show me a small cut on his hand, and talk at length about how the hero was invincible and how bullets merely bounced off him. Gradually in his play, the themes shifted to his rivalry with his sister, Sarah. John told a story about a boy who stabs and kills his sister with a knife and kills his parents and many people; finally, the doctor shoots him six times in the chest with a lugar. John said he thinks about killing all the time and then changed his mind and said he "never thinks about killing, a thousand times never, three thousand times never." John noticed the book *Children Who Hate*. He said, "Children hate because no one lets them crash, smash and be angry." He began to play "Horace good and bad who lives in a four-room apartment with Doris his sister in a plaid dress." In the play, Doris was buried in clay, submerged in containers of water, and thrown around the office before Horace came to her rescue. These themes preceded the following hours from the third month of analysis.

John came into the office and retrieved a rope he had hidden from the hour before. I thought John was more consciously aware of wanting to begin where he had left off in the last hour. He said he wanted to play Batman and Robin. He seemed to be reaffirming our partnership and closeness particularly in the face of his being increasingly aware of his anger and aggression. John played at having Batman and Robin throw all the other figures out of the dollhouse. Batman and Robin then changed identities, slept, had a bath, ate breakfast, and watched television together. I thought that John was exploring the dyad, the two of us interchangeable. The mood was very pleasant and happy, perhaps because John wished to reexperience the early months with his mother before the disruption of her anxieties and depression. I was unsure where we were headed and simply took an interest in the play and encouraged John to elaborate it further.

Batman saw Joker and threw Joker down a hole in the radiator cover, which John said was a pit with electric eels at the bottom of it. Then John told me I was not to watch something Batman and Robin were going to do on the toilet. I sensed that although it was not conscious yet, John was becoming clearer about what he wanted to communicate and was letting me know not to see it before he did and thus spoil his sense of discovery. While Batman and Robin were trying to pull Joker out of the pit, John told me a story about a visit to a local farm and how he saw the chickens pooping every place. He told me that some little kids he knows love to throw poopies around and make a mess. John's play had gained momentum and he was increasingly excited. He said that he has seen poopies fall out of his sister's diaper. I said that poopies can be very interesting and exciting, hoping to let John know that I appreciated the powerful feelings he was experiencing and that I was prepared to go forward with him. It seemed that in the context of the dyad, he could bear and understand these feelings, the dyad in the office and as he had longed for it with his mother. John said that when he was little he stuck his finger in his bum and tasted his poopies and it was good. Then John said that he wanted a "C." I understood from previous hours that this meant a cookie. John also got a book and asked me to read it to him. I thought that he and I understood that we were communicating about powerful feelings from the past reexperienced now, and I said I thought he was telling me about very important feelings he was having now and had had as a little boy. John said that he was not sure whether he could come to his hour on Friday. I sensed that John was now overwhelmed. There was a problem in our communication, perhaps the way it had been with his mother, and I felt he was worried that I would withdraw from him. I said I wondered if he was worried that I was upset with him and didn't want to see him because he had been telling me about tasting and playing with his poopies. This did not feel satisfactory, and although John left without great distress at the end of the hour, I felt dissatisfied with my response. Now I think John was frightened by the intrusiveness and disruption made by my remarks about his telling me important feelings he had had as a little boy. I think I was trying to organize and distance us from this material.

Two hours later, I began to have more understanding of what John was struggling with. John wanted to play that Spiderman, Batman, and Robin were searching for a person who stole things. In the play, Joker was caught and thrown down the pit. Now there was a triad, and the theme of a person who stole things was emerging. John said that Superman had been thrown down the pit and had to be treated and put in bed in the dollhouse and that an ambulance was called. I thought John was communicating about his helplessness and his need of treatment for what had been stolen from him. While Superman was in bed, John wanted to throw the action figures back and forth with me. When he missed a catch, he angrily said "Butt" or "Bum." We seemed to both know we were involved with things' being stolen and missed. I thought of the stolen mother, her breast, but especially John's body, his bum, and his feces. Sometimes

John's throws were hard, and when I wondered whether those throws were hard and angry throws, John said no. John was intense and angry. I had hoped to acknowledge the anger and help him bear it, but I interfered with John's own realization and sense of discovery. I was worried about being hurt by John's hard throws and named the anger prematurely to interrupt it.

John looked at a Pink Panther coloring book and said that another child had colored in it. He said he was hungry. He colored in a picture of the Pink Panther's saying "Ouch, ouch" because Pink Panther's arm was being hurt. I thought that I was not letting John color in the affect himself, thus stealing from him and disrupting our communication so that he again felt hungry. At the end of this hour, John asked for a paper plane he had made in previous sessions and remembered that he broke into pieces the one I had made. At the end of the hour, John found it very hard to leave until he had made some repairs on his plane and added a second laser gun. I sensed that we were elaborating our communications about loss and being stolen from and that John's anger was displaced from me to my plane that he had broken into pieces. The intensity of the anger and aggression required reparation before John could leave. I did not comment further, not being sure what would be helpful and feeling confident that if I did not interfere, John's communication with himself and me would bring further organization to these fears, feelings, and fantasies.

In his next hour, John played that C3PO and R2D2 were rescuing a person who lived in a house. Superman and C3PO flew about the office together. John told me that they spend two days together and go to the movies. When I said how happy they are together, John added that it was great that I see him four days a week instead of once a week like when we first met. He said that it's a great idea. I felt that John was declaring his love for me in the face of his rage but also that he was confirming my impression that he wanted me to follow his flight pattern and not interfere because of my own anxieties. Then John told me that a mouse had gone down the pit and that it needed to be rescued by pouring water into the pit. He pretended to pour water on a cat the way he once poured water on his dog, Chestnut. His dog had got a cold but was better when they gave the dog medicine. John emphasized that cats don't like water. I waited, sensing that John was moving between destructions and repair prior to taking off.

John again wanted to play catch with me and when he missed, he got angry, threw harder, and said, "Butt, butt." He also shot a rubber band in my direction. Then he returned to the dollhouse and told me that a stove had exploded, that this was the end of the mother, and that Superman and Jor-el (Superman's father) were left together. John returned to the game of catch, the back and forth, the dialogue. I shared with John that I now understood that it was my fault, my bad throws, that caused him to miss. This seemed to allow him to elaborate further his murderousness toward me with the rubber band and his murderousness toward his mother. Jor-el and Superman went on an adventure. They found Joker, who thought he was hearing voices and was brought to see me. I was supposed to cure him by shooting him in the head with a laser gun, but the cure lasted only two days because Superman tricked him by calling out, "Hey you," and making him think he was hearing voices again. John told me it all has to do with a bad dream and that it can be helped by talking about it the way he did with me. I sensed that John worried that I might still be too anxious to allow him to elaborate on his murderousness and cruelty, and he reassured me that I was helping him. John then wanted to attach a transmitter to Jor-el. This involved threading a string and tying it around Jor-el's waist. He cut the string too short and had me cut it too short also but without apparent anxiety. During this process, he had me spell "Is there a doctor in the house?" When I was interested in the question, John told me that I was the doctor, and I was to help him with the transmitter. Taking an interest in John's question, not needing to know if there was a doctor in the house, was the result of my reorienting myself so that I was available to receive John's conscious and unconscious affective transmissions.

At the beginning of his next hour, John was surprised to see the dollhouse and said he was going to tell me he looked and it was missing. We continued to explore the theme of things missing, even a house missing. John said he was awake last night; it wasn't a dream, and he heard footsteps. It was scary; it was Frankenstein. When he looked outside, the candle was blown out. It wasn't Frankenstein but just a regular raccoon that had done it. John said he wasn't sleeping. It wasn't a dream. He asked "Is there a doctor in the house?" He seemed to be elaborating both the terror and monstrous rage that he felt when something is missing, when a life is snuffed out, such as for an anguished child with a depressed mother. I thought that this was speculation, one of many viewpoints that could bring some organization to John's powerful feelings and fantasies. I tried to leave this open for John, and I tried to tolerate the powerful feelings and confusion, allowing John in his own time and way to bring whatever organization he created. I felt the terror and rage that I was the mother behind the doctor in the house. There was a cat after a mouse, and I should pour water on the cat and chase it away.

John said he watches *"Tom and Jerry"* on television in the morning. He asked me if I had watched *"Tom and Jerry"* when I was little. John told me he has a babysitter who doesn't let him do things. He calls her a "hag." She doesn't wear pants. When I expressed an interest in this, he said that girls have a penis, a little one, a small one. John began playing James Bond 007, and I was to be Jim Ace 004, his chauffeur. We made friends with a third man, whom we invited to the house because he had no home. The man had a friend who was killed by a man who had escaped from prison five days ago. The man was Righty Left, Luke Skywalker, Jaws. James Bond fought and beat him. I left for later in the analysis the verbalization of the Frankenstein in John. At this point, it was not clear enough in his consciousness, but the symbolic expression of these powerful feelings in the play made possible the subsequent expansion of our communication involving the sadism of cat-and-mouse games, the overstimulating but prohibiting hag, and the castration and murder. John went to the bathroom. When he returned, he told me that when he goes it burns; his father looked at it and it was cloudy. He told John to drink more water, and now it was like a waterfall. Did I know that his sister, Sarah, had an operation yesterday and had her tonsils out? He and Sarah played catch with a poop. Penises smell like a poop. At the end of the hour, John had Superman race Jor-el and win. Before leaving at the end of the hour, John wanted to put all the toys away in the dollhouse. He went to the bathroom perhaps to see if he was intact, perhaps because he worried he could not contain the flood of additional feelings and fantasies. Nevertheless, John seemed to remind me that he could put these feelings and fantasies away at the end of the hour, that in our play—the communication and synthesis of affect and meanings—there was a doctor in the house.

In these hours, John functioned as both the participant and the observer. He increasingly took on my role as a person who noticed, who said there were things to be observed and looked at. Clarifying what was noticed and observed let clarification function as being on the road to interpretation. In John's play, powerful affects and themes were displaced and externalized and then, in a back and forth way, progressively acknowledged, organized, and internalized. For example, when John noticed the book *Children Who Hate*, he understood by that time that I was interested in why children hate. He knew what he and I were there for and he talked about his hate. In his play, John showed me how children can enjoy themselves and how they can hate. In this way, there was a recapitulation of conflict and powerful affect in the transference with mutative aspects. This applies to John's playing games that were displaced from the toilet, indulging in it with me as the transference figure rather than his mother, his father, or his fastidious grandmother.

In his play about Batman and Robin changing identities, sleeping together, having a bath, eating breakfast, and watching TV, John explored his longing to be close to his father and sorted out how he might not have to copy everything about him. In addition, John increasingly elaborated and explored the oedipal themes, the competition between Jor-el and his son, Superman, phallic and masturbatory themes, and the penis that burns and can make a waterfall. John's fantasies about girls' having a penis and his sister's having her tonsils out as well as the regression involved in the penis's smelling like a poop were part of a symbolic reworking and clarification of these powerful concerns. As the analysis progressed, John's play facilitated increasing organization and clarity on the way to a verbal mastery of his competition with his father, his masturbatory fantasies, and his wishes to have intercourse with his mother as he understood it from primal scenes, as well as the subsequent fear of castration and attack by his father. John's play allowed him to recapture at an explanatory level powerful preconscious and unconscious affects, conflicts, and fantasies. In this way, play in analysis provided in an affective realm an organizing, integrative interplay between experience and insight.

Second Case

Craig began analysis at age 11 because of increasing passive–aggressive struggles that dated back to his mother's death from brain cancer when he was 4. Craig's hours reflected his guilt about his angry and aggressive feelings and his fear that such feelings would drive people away. At the beginning of his analysis, Craig played card games and made self-defeating moves. He talked about getting revenge for losing, and then he became worried that I would be angry and dislike him. Craig talked about violent, sadistic movies and books involving revenge. At the same time, Craig's denial about his mother's death was expressed in terms of fantasies about her spirit's being an observing presence. In this context, Craig talked about his hunger for material possessions as well as for his stepmother's brownies, and he wondered how many children I saw. As his empty feelings and his hunger for his mother began to be more prominent in the transference, Craig began to complain about how his analytic hours deprived him of other activities. During card games, he would sadistically tease me. When he talked about a bad boy at school who had sex on his mind all the time, he became worried about how his clothing stuck out in front.

In the eighth month of analysis, Craig became involved in playing the game Clue. Over approximately a three-week period, Craig developed his own version of the game. I knew immediately from his keen interest and relish for this game of murder that he understood the game to be an important vehicle for communicating with me about his most pressing concerns. Many themes evolved. For example, Mrs. Peacock murdered Colonel Mustard and shot herself. She was alive again and murdered all the people who tried to catch her except Mr. Green. He caught her twice but had no bullets and she escaped. He caught her again and shot her.

From a rich but confusing tapestry of multiple murders and returns to life, themes of a woman murderer and murdered and a woman's committing suicide emerged.

At this point, Craig wanted to make cards that explained why people committed these murders. He decided on four cards: insane, revenge, for the fun of it, and hate. Although Craig was agreeable to selecting and elaborating on these categories, I was keener about it because of my anxieties about the chaotic and gruesome production of murderous, destructive, and sadistic feelings. As I appreciated that Craig was not affectively invested in these categories, I became aware of my anxieties and was able to resume allowing Craig to develop his communication in his own way. As the game progressed, Craig was Inspector Green, and he had two associates. They discovered that Colonel Mustard had murdered a husband and wife in bed after a party. They had thrown champagne on Colonel Mustard, that was why. He killed because of hate. After four murders, Inspector Green chopped off Colonel Mustard's head. He also shot a woman in the head because she was not dead. He put her out of her misery.

I made no interventions except occasionally to sum up the basic narrative and feelings involved but to not extend the material beyond the surface presentation. In this way, I put some of the play into words, let Craig know I was interested, and was carefully following his communications, and was ready to continue his explorations with him but would try not to intrude or foreclose these elaborations. Gradually, the game evolved into three men against three women. When the men killed the last woman, they were promoted a rank. Craig was concerned that this made him sound like a "male chauvinist." He said this was true also because the men in his game have guns, and the women have knives. The women do not know how to shoot the guns well anyway. A sexy Asian woman, Miss Scarlet, was designated as the bad one, and eventually she began to win these murderous battles. Craig was telling me about his attitude toward women and the differences between men and women, but affectively this seemed secondary to his increasing preoccupation with and excitement about the bad sexy Miss Scarlet.

At the beginning of his next hour, Craig said he called to tell me that Mary, the woman who drives him to his appointments, could not pick him up yesterday. He asked whether I have a secretary or was the phone on an answering service. It didn't sound like an answering machine. I understood that Craig was bringing to the theme of murder his feelings of abandonment and that gradually he was becoming more aware that these feelings were directed toward me. When he said he couldn't come, she asked why; he said his driver forgot to pick him up. He said even if it were the truth, he wouldn't say he didn't feel like coming to his appointments.

Actually, he went sledding and skiing, and he was glad he didn't have to come. I sensed that Craig was telling me not to intrude and ask him questions and that once that has been established, he can tell me about abandoning me.

Craig added that Mary had ruined her coat and was shopping and forgot to pick him up. When Craig called to ask where she was, the old lady Mary lives with said Mary was out for lunch and had gone shopping with a friend. Craig seemed to be elaborating on the feelings of abandonment and that what people say to explain it can be very confusing. I suspected that this related to Craig's mother and her death, but I said nothing about my ideas, being certain it would disrupt or stop the play. Mary told Craig that he comes into my office at the back of the house but Craig thought since the driveway and the entrance doors were on the same side it must be the front. Craig looked out the window and said that that must be the backyard. He said it was big, and the front yard wouldn't be fenced in. Craig's interest in how you tell the front entrance from the back had many possible meanings, but the relationship to the present material was difficult for me to ascertain other than its connection to the theme of women's giving him important misinformation.

Craig said he was in a play tonight and in a chorus. A friend who can't act got the main part. There were two library teachers in charge. The one who arranged the play gave the parts to her classes, and he had to fight to get even a small part as a janitor. Since she arranged it, that seemed fair. Craig wanted to play Clue. He rolled the dice, got a one, and said it shows how he always gets poor luck. He played the part of Mrs. Peacock. He won, boasting that he was a good detective because he watched my face and watched where I wrote things down on the scorecard. As Craig talked about the unfairness of the library teacher and his poor luck but how he was a good detective, I had the conviction that his detective work was bringing him closer to an important communication about abandonment, unfairness, and poor luck. Craig then wanted to play "our game." His people captured General Scarlet. She could be killed by being blown to nothing with a bazooka. Then she would have no grave for other gangsters to visit. Or she could be killed with a machine gun. That would spread her blood all over. Another way would be to use a pistol to blow away her head and her stomach. As Craig elaborated and savored the way Miss Scarlet could be killed, feelings of hatred, cruelty, and, through projective identification, terror and repulsion were apprehended. Craig decided instead she would be shot with a poison dart that stings like a wasp or a million times worse than that as the poison got into your blood. I sensed that with Miss Scarlet, the past rage, terror, destruction, pain, and horror of his mother's cancer and chemotherapy were in his awareness, and I brought this up with him. I said it sounded like the chemotherapy medicine they gave his mother was like a poison. Craig listened and continued, perhaps elaborating the power of his lost mother and his wish to recapture parts of her and her power. Craig said it was the women, the bad group who have ranks like general, colonel, and captain. Craig set traps and caught the women, and he captured all their weapons.

Craig came for his next hour and told me that he just had a snowball fight. He had sneaked into the other kids' fort when they were not there and crushed and smashed all their snowballs. It was a lot of fun. He wanted to play our game of Clue, the men against the women. Craig moved quickly from the destruction in his daily life to the game of Clue. There was a pleasure and enthusiasm for destruction and murder. The women were shot for having committed first-degree murder. Miss Scarlet was captured, and on pain of death she agreed to be Mr. Green's slave. She was promoted to his assistant. The other people tried to kill her out of revenge because she killed one of them. Actually, she'd been ordered to bring Colonel Mustard back from the dead as part of her being a slave and she did it. Each time she was about to be shot or poisoned, Inspector Green rescued her. Then she turned against him, killed the three women, and tried to kill Inspector Green, but he killed her. It turned out that she had been a double agent all the time. With great intensity, Craig played out Miss Scarlet the slave, and it came as a shock when she turned against Mr. Green. There was a feeling not just of terrible betrayal but also of despair that she was a double agent all the time. I did not link this intense enactment to Craig's mother. The enactment provided powerful affective organization but did not seem consciously available yet.

Then Craig wanted to sit first in my place on the floor and then in my chair. He said he was the psychiatrist. He would like to be a lawyer first and a psychiatrist second, because becoming a psychiatrist took so many years. He conducted an interview in which I was to say that I got along fine at home but not in school. I was to say that I had good friends but my teacher and the students were mean to me because they knew that I went to a psychiatrist and they thought that meant I was crazy even though that wasn't really true. Craig changed places with me the way he did when we share these painful feelings in the play and in projective identification. He wanted to be sure I could stand to be in his place and would not refuse this play. I said that the feelings we had been playing about murder and revenge and his mother's death made him worried that he was crazy. At the end of the hour, Craig was reluctant to leave. I felt it was not because of anxiety, but, rather, because he felt that the horror, pain, abandonment, terror, and rage had been experienced and assimilated between us as it had not in his experience of the past, and he did not want to lose this so soon.

In this play, Craig was able to elaborate his fantasies about killing and reviving his mother, his confusion about her violent, angry outbursts when she was very ill, the poisonous chemotherapy, and her tortured, painful death. Craig was also able to explore his feelings of being betrayed by his mother, a double agent who seemed to be loyal but turned on him, his concerns that I would turn on him and abandon him, and his fears that his sadistic and sexual fantasies would overwhelm him and would drive me to abandon him. At the same time, Craig clarified his sense of having been responsible for his mother's death, his concern about what a demonic and bad person he was, and his sense that he should be punished and tortured in return. Craig's shifting sexual identification and his fears of women and of being damaged and castrated were also apparent.

DISCUSSION

As illustrated in the hours from the analyses of John and Craig, play in the analytic situation provides a new stage on which the child can attempt to find organization for affectively powerful aspects of his experience and inner life. The analyst accepts role assignments and is the empathic interacter in the play and dramas. The analyst's situation as someone who accepts without attempting to deflect the affect, who experiences the play as a revelation, and who appreciates the exploratory aspect of the effort supports what is perhaps a preexisting faculty for dealing with trauma and powerful affect using the vehicle of play. Winnicott (1963) highlights this preexisting faculty.

> The state of affairs in an analysis in which the analyst is permitted by the patient to reach to the deepest layers of the analysand's personality because of his position as subjective object, or because of the dependence of the patient in the transference psychosis; here there is danger if the analyst interprets instead of waiting for the patient to creatively discover. . . . If we wait we become objectively perceived in the patient's own time, but if we fail to behave in a way that is facilitating the patient's analytic process (which is equivalent of the infant's and the child's maturational process) we suddenly became not-me for the patient, and then we know too much, and we are dangerous because we are too nearly in communication with the central still and silent spot of the patient's ego-organization [p. 189].

At such times, rather than the most accurate of interpretations' facilitating insight and play, we frequently observe the child's becoming much less willing to share his feelings and fantasies.

Sander (1979) emphasizes this maturational process within both the child and the analyst.

There is an unavoidable uncertainty that the analyst is left with and must endure, recognizing and permitting the patient's private and unfound center while facilitating the integrative process necessary for his initiation of new adaptive organization that springs from it and cannot be carried out without it. The recognizing and enduring of this confrontation with uncertainty, paradoxically, is the fruition of the analyst's knowledge and certainty, a facilitation of the maturational process within which the analyst's own development is ongoing [p. 345].

Bettelheim (1976), in his studies of the meaning and importance of fairy tales, also recognizes the child's faculties for dealing with trauma and powerful affects by play and fantasy.

A child needs to understand what is going on within his conscious self so that he can also cope with that which goes on in his unconscious. He can achieve this understanding, and with it the ability to cope, not through rational comprehension of the nature and content of his unconscious, but by becoming familiar with it through spinning out daydreams—ruminating, rearranging and fantasizing about suitable story elements in response to unconscious pressures. By doing this, the child fits unconscious content into conscious fantasies, which then enable him to deal with that content [p. 7].

Bettelheim (1976) stresses the importance of the child's making his or her discoveries, which is also a crucial element in play.

Adult interpretations, as correct as they may be, rob the child of the opportunity to feel that he, on his own, through repeated hearing and ruminating about the story, has coped successfully with a difficult situation. We grow, we find meaning in life, and security in ourselves by having understood and solved personal problems on our own, not by having them explained to us by others [pp. 18, 19].

Implicit in this view of the therapeutic action of play and affect in child analysis is a belief in the innate capacity for organization and synthesis on the part of the growing organism, the child, and the adult. Furthermore, play in its intimate connection with affect provides a potentially powerful vehicle for mastery and growth. This potential is part of human nature, what Ogden (1989) refers to as *"psychological deep structure . . .* a structural, psychological readiness to organize experience along specific, predetermined lines" (p. 145). In addition, as Tompkins (1962, 1963) observes in infants, the affect of interest motivates learning. By and large, the affect of interest plays a prominent role for the child and the analyst. A related issue is that of self-observation and self-regulation. In play, the increasing awareness of the activity and process of the play helps to facilitate a self-regulatory process. As the child recognizes the symbolic dialogue in the play and changes it, there is the development of a metadialogue.

The extent and importance of symbolic affective expression on a nonverbal level have been increasingly appreciated. From a neurophysiologic point of view, Schwartz (1987) argues that psychoanalysis does not consist of hermeneutics only but rather is powerfully tied to neurobiology. This is based in part on the observation

> that much of the clinical data which analysts interpret has origins in purely *motor* phenomena. As skilled clinicians recognize, emotion seems often to reveal itself through little signs—a change in vocal tone or inflection, for obvious example—that have an apparently greater than chance association with particular feelings—a snarl with contempt or a sudden hush with embarrassment [p. 476].

Activity or motoric expression is an important element of play. The related neurophysiologic underpinnings of affect and motoric expression catalyze the synthetic, therapeutic function of the symbolic expression of affects in play.

Stern's (1985) exploration of the infant's subjective experience and the development of the infant's senses of self is also relevant to the therapeutic action of play that transpires outside of verbal relatedness. "It is important to note that the domain of intersubjective relatedness, like that of core-relatedness, goes on outside of awareness and without being rendered verbally. In fact, the experience of intersubjective relatedness, like that of core-relatedness, can only be alluded to; it cannot really be described (although poets can evoke it)" (p. 27). In addition, Stern's work is consistent with the observation that play in child analysis involves different domains of development at all times. "All domains of relatedness remain active during development. The infant does not grow out of any of them; none of them atrophy, none of them become developmentally obsolete or get left behind. And once all domains are available, there is no assurance that any one domain will necessarily claim preponderance during any particular age period" (p. 31).

These issues concerning the therapeutic action of play and affect in child analysis also apply to adult analysis and analytic psychotherapy. The term "Spielraum" was used by Freud to describe the importance of room for play in the thoughts and feelings in an adult analysis. In explorations of "curative effects," Valenstein (1981) comes to similar questions regarding insight and interpretation. "To what extent is neurosis ultimately attributable to a failure of integration? Rather than insight having the direct 'curative' effect, it is probable that the enhancement of integration . . . enables one to deal consciously with problems at a secondary process level" (p. 314). In response to Hadamard (1945) and his research for his book *The Psychology of Invention in the Mathematical Field,* Albert Einstein emphasized the importance of emotions and combinatory play in discovery, discovery that shares much with therapeutic action.

> The words or the language, as they are written or spoken, do not seem to play any role in my mechanism of thought. The psychical entities which seem to serve as elements in thought are certain signs and more or less clear images which can be "voluntarily" reproduced and combined. There is, of course, a certain connection between those elements and relevant logical concepts. It is also clear that the desire to arrive finally at logically connected concepts is the emotional basis of this rather vague play with the above mentioned elements. But taken from a psychological viewpoint, this combinatory play seems to be the essential feature in productive thought—before there is any connection with logical construction in words or other kinds of signs which can be communicated to others. The above mentioned elements are, in my case, of visual and some of muscular type. Conventional words or other signs have to be sought for laboriously only in a secondary stage, when the mentioned associative play is sufficiently established and can be reproduced at will [pp. 142–143].

In exploring the therapeutic action of play in child analysis, the viewpoint is developed that play is intimately linked to an innate capacity for organization and integration on the part of the growing, adapting, changing child and adult. In addition, because play offers ready access to intense affects, play is a powerful vehicle for facilitating mastery and growth. As a result, an important challenge is how to facilitate and not disrupt play in the therapeutic situation. The major disruption to the unfolding of play often derives from our attempts to avoid powerful feelings arising in ourselves during the play. From this perspective, I would add that perhaps all play is integrative. When we view play as endless repetition and symbolization without any movement toward growth or mastery, we often have not yet been able to understand or tolerate the struggle or communication involved. For example, if a child seems dissociated from his or her repetitive play and its affects, this is not unbeneficial but rather a use of play to master and communicate about the reasons and uses of this kind of dissociation while evoking in the therapist highly informative but very taxing feelings of isolation, helplessness, and abandonment.

REFERENCES

Ablon, S. L. & Mack, J. E. (1980), Children's dreams reconsidered. *The Psychoanalytic Study of the Child,* 35:179–217. New Haven, CT: Yale University Press.
Bettelheim, B. (1976), *The Uses of Enchantment.* New York: Knopf.

Freud, S. (1920), Beyond the pleasure principle. *Standard Edition*, 18:3–64. London: Hogarth Press, 1953.

Hadamard, J. (1945), *The Psychology of Invention in the Mathematical Field*. Princeton, NJ: Princeton University Press.

Kazantzakis, N. (1952), *Zorba The Greek*. New York: Simon & Schuster.

Neubauer, P. B. (1987), The many meanings of play: Introduction. *The Psychoanalytic Study of the Child*, 42:3–9. New Haven, CT: Yale University Press.

Ogden, T. H. (1989), *The Primitive Edge of Experience*. Northvale, NJ: Aronson.

Sander, L. W. (1983), Polarity, paradox and the organizing process in development. In: *Frontiers of Infant Psychiatry, Vol. 1*, ed. J. D. Call, E. Galenson & R. L. Tyson. New York: Basic Books, pp. 333–346.

Schwartz, A. (1987), Drives, affects, behavior—and learning: Approaches to a psychobiology of emotion and to an integration of psychoanalytic and neurobiologic thought. *J. Amer. Psychoanal. Assn.*, 35:467–506.

Stern, D. N. (1985), *The Interpersonal World of the Infant*. New York: Basic Books.

Tomkins, S. (1962), *Affect, Imagery, Consciousness. Vol. I*. New York: Springer.

——— (1963), *Affect, Imagery, Consciousness. Vol. II*. New York: Springer.

Valenstein, A. (1981), Insight as an embedded concept. *The Psychoanalytic Study of the Child*, 36:307–315. New Haven, CT: Yale University Press.

Waelder, R. (1933), The psychoanalytic theory of play. *Psychoanal. Quart.*, 2:208–224.

Winnicott, D. W. (1963), Communicating and not communicating leading to a study of certain opposites. In: *The Maturational Processes and the Facilitating Environment*. New York: IUP, pp. 179–192.

Chapter 5

AFFECTIVE INTERACTIONS IN FAMILIES WITH YOUNG CHILDREN

Alexandra Murray Harrison

This chapter discusses the family interactions that can support or obstruct the affective experience of individual family members because affective experience is considered important for one's sense of oneself as an individual and also as critical to the developmental process. The focus is on the interactions I observed in meetings with a five-year-old girl and her family that interfered with the natural development and resolution of oedipal stage conflicts.

The ways in which families interfere with family members' having their own feelings are well documented in writings using the Group Relations Theory model of family functioning (Shapiro, 1982, 1985; Shapiro and Carr, 1991). This model derives from Bion's theory of small groups and conceptualizes regression in response to threatening affect generated by the movement of a family member into a new developmental position (Bion, 1961; Shapiro, 1985). Whether as an autonomous pattern around which the explanatory narrative is constructed or as a communicator and stressor, affect is an organizer and a motivator.

In his "script theory," Tomkins postulates that sequences of affects that occur in certain interpersonal and experiential contexts become associated with unconscious stories in the developing child (Tomkins, 1978). Studies in observational and epidemiological research have demonstrated the reactions of children to the affective displays of their parents, whether in the form of behavior, language, or facial expression and tone of voice (Beardslee et al., in press; Beebe and Sloate, 1982; Demos, 1982; Field, 1977; Osofsky, 1982; Osofsky and Eberhart-Wright, 1988; Stern, 1988).

Parents also have affective reactions to their young children's behavior, which powerfully influence their responses to them. For example, mothers of toddlers have often described to me the anxiety or hurt they feel in response to their child's normal aggressive exploratory or assertive behavior, causing them either to withdraw or to overcontrol their child. The meaning the child may construct from this interaction—"If I assert myself against my mother, she will leave me or try to dominate me"—will clearly resonate with similar stories in the mother's own past. Yet doesn't the father have a role? What about siblings? How can this kind of formulation be developed to include the family as a whole?

In this chapter, a sequence of family meetings of the Smith family tests the following hypothesis: When a family member presents a developmental challenge to the rest of the family, the family will attempt to integrate the person's new behavior into the family "myth," or belief system. If the feelings involved are too threatening to the family as a group, the family changes its explanation of this behavior to one that better allows them to manage the affect. In the course of this change, the developmental task itself may be influenced. In this particular case, I discuss a five-year-old's effort to find within her family support for her oedipal-stage conflict and the responses of family members to this challenge.

One might ask what can be gained by exploring this hypothesis, since formulations about regression from oedipal-level conflict to preoedipal conflict are standard fare in psychoanalytic thinking. My answer is that observations of families as they respond to this type of stress, as they move between these two sets of conflicts, are not so common. Such observations offer possibilities for constructing more complex models for these processes and for relinquishing the reductive thinking that leads to judgmental stereotypes and empathic failures in our clinical work and writings.

CLINICAL CASE

Molly Smith was five years old when her parents consulted me about her temper tantrums. They told me that she screamed so loudly that no one in the family could bear it and that she fought bitterly with her eight-year-old sister, Jenny. It was Mrs. S, however, whom Molly chose as the target for most of her oppositional and provocative behavior. Her struggles with her mother sometimes appeared to dominate their relationship and were associated with a regression into babyishness on Molly's part.

It is important to note that Molly was a successful student and was well liked by her peers. Thus I initially hypothesized that her symptomatic behavior was (1) organized around something going wrong in the family and (2) still dependent on the family context for its manifestation. I have chosen this case specifically because of the strong personal resources within the family, which allows one to focus more easily on the fine-tunings of the family interactions and to identify oedipal-level conflict. That is not to say that preoedipal issues about loss and nurturance were not dominant themes in the Smith family meetings, but only that the interface between these two conflictual levels was clearer than in families with greater degrees of disorganization or more rigid defensive behaviors.

The Smith family had in fact suffered a series of losses, including death, family moves, and illnesses. The family had moved to the Boston area from a foreign country when Mrs. S was pregnant with Molly and Jenny was three years old. Mr. S was an American, and Mrs. S a native of the foreign country. The couple had met when they were both working in the same office for an international company. The move was occasioned by a favorable job change for Mr. S, but it required Mrs. S both to give up the high-powered and satisfying job she had in the other city and to leave her family and the country of her birth. The move was also coincident in time with the tragic death of Mrs. S's father, to whom both Mrs. S and Jenny were very close. Mr. S's job demanded his full attention immediately, and thus the weight of establishing the family in their new home and taking care of a small child fell to Mrs. S, who was pregnant and grieving.

When Molly was born, the extreme fatigue Mrs. S had experienced during the pregnancy remained unremitting, and eventually a diagnosis of a nonspecific autoimmune condition was made. Her symptoms caused her to need a nap during the afternoons and sometimes drained her of her patience and made her irritable. On top of all this, Mr. S developed an internal malignant tumor, which was diagnosed several years after the move, and he underwent surgery and other treatments before being given a clean bill of health.

Both parents were attractive, accomplished people. Mrs. S was an articulate storyteller and related the family history sometimes with tears in her eyes and in a quiet, sad voice. Her husband watched his wife with respectful concern, adding details here and there. I made an initial formulation that Mrs. S was depressed, her depression precipitated by her losses in the move, by her father's death, and by her husband's illness and actualized by the turning inward of her anger at the two men she loved, who had "abandoned" her but who also were so dangerously vulnerable. It was easy to imagine links between her chronic illness and her depression, between her depressed "unavailability" and Molly's temper tantrums, and between the family's anger at Molly and their fear of getting at their ill mother. Finally, it was a short step from these formulations to a hypothesis about Molly's oedipal development's being complicated by her fear of aggressive competition with her vulnerable mother. This set of formulations is not an unusual one in cases of behavior problems in young children seen by child therapists.

Yet this formulation restricts itself primarily to two members of the family of four. Such limitation seems important if we consider what we know about group process and the complex interactions that occur among all members of a group (Hoffman, 1981; Minuchin, 1975; Minuchin, Rosman, and Baker, 1978; Shapiro and Carr, 1991; Zilbach, 1986). What actually went on in the family that got in the way of Molly's enjoying this time in her life? What effect did Molly's behavior have on the other family members, and what were the communications among them that mediated this effect? It was with these questions in mind that I approached my first family meeting, an account of which follows.

First Family Meeting

Mr. S was late for the first family meeting. I invited Mrs. S and Molly and Jenny into the playroom. The three of them talked about what might have happened to Mr. S, and Jenny decided to make a sign for him that said, "Dad, come right in!" to put on the door. Molly made a picture of Jenny and told her mother that it was Jenny when she was a baby. I inquired about other times when Dad was away. Jenny said she didn't like it when he was gone, and Molly said she loved it when he came home. I asked her what happened when Dad came home, and she made a vigorous, expansive gesture with her arms as her face lit up with pleasure. "It's exciting," I suggested. She nodded. Jenny added, "It's like an earthquake!" I responded, "An earthquake! What happens in an earthquake?" "The house shakes!" Jenny said. "The house rumbles!" Molly cried. I asked, "Have you ever been in an earthquake?" Both girls shook their heads. Mrs. S spoke. "Jenny has, but she doesn't remember. She used to wake up in the middle of the night and cry, and we wouldn't know there had been an earthquake, but the next day we would find out there had been."

There followed a discussion about dreams. Molly volunteered that she had had a scary dream. Mrs. S encouraged her to tell it but Molly declined, saying she couldn't remember it. Mrs. S then told a childhood dream of hers, in which her parents turned into stick figures. Jenny contributed a dream she had heard of in which a girl had to put catsup on a doorknob each morning to keep her brother alive. Apparently encouraged by her mother's and sister's accounts of dreams, Molly told her dream of "a big party and someone was going to sleep over" and then "Mom and Dad left" and "robbers came and tried to kidnap us!"

Mr. S arrived at this point, and the three were clearly pleased to see him. He responded warmly to the delighted greeting of his two daughters. Mr. S explained that he at first had lost the combination to the lock on my door. Mrs. S summarized the meeting so far. At the mention of earthquakes, Mr. and Mrs. S began to review the history of the family in the country of X. Jenny's status was secure in this discussion, as she described memories of the family home there. Molly tried to compete, offering details that were corrected by her parents as memories from photographs or from other family members' accounts.

As Mrs. S described her career to me, Mr. S turned to Jenny, who was drawing a picture of the family home in X. Molly interrupted her mother with a question about a dollhouse doll. "Is it a boy or a girl?" she asked. She decided herself that it must be a boy and added, "Imagine if a boy were born with long hair!" Jenny responded with a devaluing remark about Molly's "babyish" idea. Mrs. S picked up Molly's comment, saying, "Wasn't there a parking lot?" (referring to a toy garage). "Boys always have that (particular toy). I always wanted that."

As part of the discussion of the family history, Mr. and Mrs. S described their choice of names for their daughters. Molly had been named for Mrs. S's father. At mention of this, Molly started to talk baby talk and moved her chair closer to her mother. Jenny moved from her chair to the floor and began to set up the dollhouse. As the parents talked about the beginning of their family life in X, both girls began to play quietly together with the dollhouse, setting up an orderly family scene. Molly jumped up and took the toy camera. "I'm going to take a picture of everybody!" she cried. "Me too!" said Jenny, after she was finished.

Mother changed the subject by saying she wanted to talk about a problem Molly had the other day in leaving her friend's house, which exemplified the behavior that caused so much trouble. It had been time to go home, and Molly was refusing to put on her coat and come with Mother, who had come to collect her. An interesting conversation ensued. Mother said to Molly, "If you don't come now, you cannot come again next week as planned." Then, hoping to demonstrate to Molly the deleterious effect of her behavior on her friendship, she appealed to the friend, saying something like, "Jane, don't you want Molly to behave so that she can come back next week?" Jane pleaded, "Choose me, Molly! Choose me!" Molly, however, had steadfastly stuck to her defiant position, telling her friend, "Goodbye, Jane. At least I have your picture."

Throughout Mrs. S's relating the story, Molly was talking baby talk loudly and banging the toy hammer on the nails in the tool bench. "BAM!

BAM! BAM!" Mr. S made several verbal attempts to quiet her, each one getting progressively angrier and louder. His anger seemed to be an overreaction to Molly's provocation. Finally, in exasperation, he grabbed the hammer away from her. With impressive ingenuity, Molly continued banging with her head. "You can't take away my head," she pronounced.

The end of the meeting saw Mrs. S's asking Molly to repeat "what she's been saying all the time lately," and Molly responding obligingly, "I don't care!" Then Mr. S accused Molly of "hurting your mother's feelings" with that talk, but Mrs. S corrected him, saying, "It doesn't hurt my feelings." This point of disagreement was not pursued. Instead, Jenny complained wistfully about Molly's "acting like a baby to get her way."

Discussion of First Meeting

How could we understand this first meeting? Mr. S's lateness is a communication: His absence is an important feature of whatever the problem is. But his anticipated arrival is also part of the problem. It is an exciting event for both the girls, which gives them "earthquakelike" feelings and which also stirs competition between them. Molly reacts to Jenny's taking first place in welcoming father by drawing a picture of Jenny as a baby.

The choice of the earthquake metaphor has potential for rich elaboration. It certainly alerts us to the presence of danger. But in a playful way it also introduces the happy excitement of these girls about their father. So there is a choice to play, and a choice to protect oneself. Here it seems that Mrs. S's remarks swing the balance away from pleasurable affects and toward anxiety and fear. In her story, a child warns the family of impending danger. Even while the adults are insensitive to powerful destructive forces deep within, a child cries out, calling attention to them.

There followed the discussion of dreams. Both girls tell dreams that contain the theme of threatened loss of a family member linked with what appear to be exciting and sexually stimulating images. In the girls' dreams, the "loss" seems less important than the thrilling feelings associated with danger. Putting catsup on a doorknob to keep it "alive" and being "kidnapped by robbers" are both sexual themes. Mother's dream, on the other hand, contains the loss theme in conjunction with dematerialized bodies. In this sequence, as in the previous one, Mrs. S's depression presents a powerful challenge to her daughters' enjoyment of oedipal fantasies.

Mr. S then appeared and the family was complete. They proceeded to tell their family history. While Mrs. S was talking about her career, Mr. S's subtle move away from her to Jenny called my attention to conflict within the marriage. Was Mr. S responding to what he perceived as his wife's unavailability, represented by the story of her important career in her own country? Or was he feeling guilty about having taken her away from her family and about his fantasy of having deprived her so that he might have more? The partnership of Jenny and Mr. S in this meeting may have illustrated both Mr. S's use of closeness to his older daughter to avoid the painful feelings of loss associated with the move and the family effort to find relief in idealized memories of family life in their first home.

Molly's question about the gender of the doll interrupted Mrs. S's description of her job and Mr. S's whispered comments to Jenny about her picture. Did her curious remarks have a relationship to what was going on at that time in the meeting? Molly's focus on the gender differ- ence introduced a new symbolic meaning of loss, the loss of the "male member," or castration. In stressing the girl's long hair, she was perhaps defensively reacting to a common fantasy of little girls that they originally had a penis and that it was taken away. The remarks might also have represented a defense against the aggressive impulses associated with the have-not position. In this sense, she was returning to the dream themes of the robber and the sister who had her brother's fate in her hands. On a preoedipal level, she was expressing a prototypical narcissistic complaint, her grudge against her mother for not giving her everything.

Mrs. S developed further the theme of loss, the loss of a girl in relation to a boy. In her remarks about "always having wanted that," namely, what boys "always have," Mrs. S allied herself with Molly in feelings of loss: loss of father and loss of male attributes—career, penis—represented in terms of being female and devalued.

The subject of the grandfather's death seemed to stir Molly to regress further in an effort to "not leave" Mother. Then, as the parents' story moved into an account of the family's early life, the affects expressed suggest an idealization, an idealization reflective of the subjectively re- called time around the birth of the first child. The idealization also fit the blissful "memories" of a young child with her mother. The girls' dollhouse play was consistent with this harmonious fantasy. As if in an attempt to preserve this ideal family, Molly and Jenny "took a picture" of it.

On an unconscious level, Molly seemed to present an oedipal challenge to the family: "Can I find the enjoyable closeness to my father I want? Can I get enough distance from my mother to be free to complain about what she didn't give me and to play at getting it for myself?" But this demand for closeness with Father and distance from Mother generates a set of negative reactions from the other family members. First, Mother re- sponds as if saying, "I cannot tolerate anyone leaving me again. When my husband leaves, I can't get angry at him because he is too vulnerable, just as my father was when he left me. When my daughter defies me, it feels like another loss." Jenny seems to be saying, "I had to stop being a baby too soon. I am jealous of Molly's power over everyone by virtue of being the baby." Father seems to be saying, "Something pushes me to fight with my little daughter instead of playing with her. I am afraid to get angry at my vulnerable wife, and I have to protect her from the girls' getting at her. It is better to get angry at Molly for causing the trouble."

When Father turned on Molly in anger and accusation, he missed the opportunity to symbolically move to her side, to help her understand her behavior with Mother and with Jane. He missed the chance to support his wife in an attempt to find an alternative explanation to the "not caring" one. Instead, he joined the initial attack by Mother for "not coming home" and by Jenny for "acting like a little baby." Clearly, everyone in the family—not just Mother—had some stake in maintaining this perception of Molly as abandoning and as dependent and demanding. In this way, the abandoning parent and the abandoned child are both represented by Molly, and neither the parents nor Jenny need accept responsibility for these attributes. They can criticize them in Molly. Thus burdened, Molly's attempt to take a step forward was defeated, and she was reduced to the position of the humiliated oedipal child.

Let us review our initial hypothesis using this clinical material. In this case, Molly is trying to take a step forward in her development and presents a challenge to her family. The challenge involves becoming more involved with her father in an excited playful way and becoming more distant and competitive with her mother. This behavior stresses Mother by making her feel painfully abandoned by Molly, as she was by Molly's grandfather, and as she has been by her husband, both because of her repressed hostility toward him and because of her fear that he would die of his illness. Mother's self-denying behavior gives a clue about her intolerance of her own dependent needs and thus her rejection of the child who is so demanding that hers be met. The behavior challenges Father by causing Mother to become depressed and to threaten him with abandonment both through her current withdrawal and through his fear about her illness. Also, Molly's behavior reminds him of his own dependent and demanding feelings toward Mother, feelings he not only dislikes but sees as destructive. Finally, Jenny resents Molly's moving into her special role in relation to her father at the same time she is angry at her for usurping her position as her mother's baby.

Perhaps if the Smith family had fewer reasons to be stressed by Molly's oedipal behavior, for example, if the parents did not both have serious illnesses, the family might have been able to meet the affective challenge. They might have interpreted Molly's behavior as typical 5-year-old little girl behavior. Father might have enjoyed some seductive play with Molly but would at the same time have strengthened his loving alliance with Mother. Mother might have felt less alone and would have better tolerated Molly's demanding and devaluing treatment of her. Jenny would still have felt resentful but would have also felt supported by her parents in managing her negative feelings toward her sister and putting them in perspective. In this situation, however, the parents' illnesses seemed to make the challenge intolerable, and they interpreted Molly's behavior in the light of their own disavowed painful feelings as both the abandoning parent and the abandoned child.

Later Family Meetings

Some of these themes were developed in subsequent sessions. In the next family meeting, a discussion of Molly's "bad behavior" led to the subject of Mrs. S's being particularly stressed at the moment. My questioning about this stress finally led to a reluctant acknowledgment of Mrs. S's illness. The family clearly was afraid to talk about this. I said something like, "I would feel mad if I came home from school tired and cranky and my mom was tired and cranky too. I'd think, 'Where is she? I need her *now!*' " This remark of mine was followed by an uneasy silence. I continued, "But then if I saw she was sick, it would be hard for me to get mad. I'd *feel* mad, but I'd worry about her, and I'd feel bad that I was hateful toward my poor, sick mother." Silence again, but easier. The kids returned to their play. I announced the end of the session. Everybody started to get up and get ready to leave. Jenny, who was sitting by the garage, took a car and rolled it experimentally down the ramp. Then she put the mother dollhouse doll in the car and sent it crashing down the ramp. She looked up, grinned, and walked out of the room with a light step.

The next time, Mrs. S and the girls came without Mr. S. Mrs. S immediately brought up the subject of her availability or lack of it, which had been introduced in the previous meeting. She said that she was afraid she would be around less for her family during the next few weeks, because a friend of the family, who was "like a father" to Mr. S, was gravely ill and she wanted to make herself available to his wife during this trying time. She added that when Mr. S had been ill, three years before, a friend of hers had stayed with her during the difficult hours in hospital waiting rooms, which had meant a great deal to her. Now she wanted to do the same thing for another woman. The girls, of course, were fascinated by this subject and asked many questions about both time periods, such as "How old was I when Daddy was sick?" "Did Daddy have the same thing as Jim?" and "Who was your friend who stayed with you?"

As they talked, Molly gave her mother a pretend "sandwich" she made of pieces from a game, and Jenny was fixing up the dollhouse. Mrs. S responded, "No, Jim's problem isn't at all the same as Daddy's. We knew Daddy wouldn't die." In this interesting construction, Mrs. S's answer might have been followed by another question about Daddy or by another question about Jim. Both men had cancer. Since Mrs. S had just said that there wasn't a question of Mr. S's dying, the more urgent question would focus on the other man. Indeed, Jenny asked, "Is Jim going to die?" Mother said, "I don't think he's going to make it."

In association to this remark, Mrs. S began to talk about how irritable Molly had been when she picked her up from school. In order to open up the pattern of focusing attention on Molly's defiance as a defense against threatening affect, I asked *Jenny* what *she* did when she got home from school that day. Jenny said that she was dropped off by friends and that her mother came to the driveway to meet her. She said to her mother, "How was the play?" referring to a school play she had had a part in, and her mother "didn't answer her." So she went into the house and saw Molly, who said hello to her, apparently in a "more affectionate mood" than usual, and went into her room. Jenny followed Molly into her room, and Molly "yelled" at her. When she had finished with her account of the events, Mrs. S said that that wasn't *exactly* what she remembered. For one thing, Jenny had asked her, "How was it?" without explaining what "it" was.

Although I did not interpret the transference at that point, I caught the reference to a woman friend who stayed with the mother to help her bear the anxiety of her husband's illness. I said that Jenny must have come home looking for something from her mother that had to do with the play, something to take away a bad feeling. So she set Mother up in a way—not on purpose—probably not even knowing she was doing it. When her mother didn't make her feel better, Jenny looked to Molly for a solution. Either Molly would give her comforting "affection" or Molly would make a fight with her and distract her from her worries. At this point, Mrs. S interjected, "I think I know what was making Jenny upset about her play. Her father had to cancel out on it. He had to go to the hospital to get some tests." Apparently, Mr. S had had a recurrence of symptoms, which indicated the continued presence of his malignancy. His absence at the family meeting was due to his still being at the hospital taking tests. "Now I understand what Jenny meant," I said. "Jenny didn't mean 'How was *it?*' She meant 'How was he?' "

In the last family meeting before the summer break, Mr. S came on time, and the three others were late. Mrs. Smith explained they were late because Jenny was delayed in coming home. No one complained about Jenny's lateness. Mother continued that Jenny had a lot of free time before she went to camp. I thought that this was a strange way to put it, since I knew Jenny had never been to sleepaway camp before, and I would have thought that it was her going away that was noteworthy, rather than the time before she went away. Interestingly, Father picked up on Jenny's free time, also. I pointed out the way the family had focused attention *away* from Jenny's going away while telling me about her going to camp. Molly came to me with a dollhouse doll in her hand and complained irritably, "You put that lady in a different outfit!" as if she were complaining about my challenge to the family's usual defensive response. Mother then talked to Jenny about when "the lady" said she was to arrive at camp, telling her "You could arrive at four o'clock or two, so it really depends on you," focusing on Jenny's volition in the act of leaving the family.

Mother then congratulated Molly on her "good mood" since school stopped. Molly proclaimed that she and Jenny had hardly been fighting at all. Then they proceeded to have an argument, which culminated in a complaint by Molly that Jenny and her friend had "walked through" a project she was doing on the floor. Mother burst out at Molly, "Do you want her to disappear? You just want her to not be there . . . ever!" Molly, Jenny, and Mother got into a rousing fight, while Father sat quietly by. Things calmed down. Then Father interrupted the peace to challenge Molly about her expressed wish to exclude Jenny from a group activity with Molly's friends. At this point, I suggested that the family seemed to be making a concerted effort to protect themselves against losing a family member, because when the issue came up in relation to Jenny's going to camp, they kept distracting attention away from it by focusing on some "bad behavior" of Molly's, particularly her wish to make someone in the family "disappear." Mother nodded. I asked them if Jenny's going to camp could be making them think of another loss.

Mother said that when she was 5, her father had been in a bad auto accident. I remembered that that was the same age Jenny was when Mr. S had his operation. Mother continued to talk, telling about how she felt when she and her mother waited in the little town where the accident had occurred, so that they could be with her injured father. It took him months to recover, and there were times when they were not sure he would survive. "That was the loneliest feeling I ever had," Mrs. S said. "When I think of loss and being alone with kids, I think of that time." Molly added empathically, "Because he was hurt." Both children had been listening, spellbound. I pointed out that when the family faced their fears of loss and talked about them together, they had more capacity to manage them than they thought they did. It was a short distance from this to an acknowledgment that the loss they really feared was loss of Mr. S. Mr. S said that the tests he had taken were all negative, but that he had been frightened. Mrs. S said that she had been frightened too.

The Individual Treatment

In the fall, the family reported they had had a good summer and that Molly was doing well. Later that year, however, they contacted me again, complaining about the same oppositional behavior. This time, Molly insisted on seeing me alone. In the first visit, she drew a picture of a snowman, all dressed up in hat and scarf. She added the snow, but the snowflakes she drew looked more like snowballs, and the thick black outlines quickly obliterated the centers, apparently turning them into fat raindrops. Molly was dismayed and said that she had spoiled her picture. She attempted the same scene a second time, with the same result. I thought that she was communicating her self-image as a bad girl who turned happy times into stormy ones. She demonstrated her creative potential, however, in the third picture. She first made a third try at the cheerful snow scene. When the snow again came out as raindrops, she made a black rain cloud overhead, drew a line down the center of the page, and made a cheerful springtime scene on the second half of the page. Finally, she drew a thick black line all around the edges of the picture, making a frame. This, I decided, was an excellent step toward accommodating the good girl and the bad girl self-representations in one picture.

In the early sessions, Molly was suspicious that I would expose her badness. I was careful to play alongside her and not demand that she reveal to me anything threatening. Another direction my interventions took was to relieve her superego pressure. I always took a tolerant attitude when, in displacement, she introduced me to her unacceptable babyish, greedy, demanding, and angry attitudes. I would express interest in a friend who would behave in a greedy or hostile way and say, "So and So must have a reason for behaving like that." A few "friends" emerged as prototypes of various negative attributes. I would always inquire about them with interest and concern.

The games we played were usually constructions of paper, tape, buttons, yarn, or colored fabrics. Initially, these constructions seemed to follow a theme of "everything" images contrasted with "nothing" images. Once we constructed a giant bakery display window out of stacks of multicolored buttons. This time the "nothing" perception was left to my imagination. Another time we made a giant Christmas tree out of colored paper and made elaborate gifts under it for all the family members. Molly made up a story out one family member who would "not make it" for Christmas and who therefore would not get a present. The sadness about the idea of who would "not make it" was hidden behind the explanation that bad children don't get toys from Santa Claus. Which person in the family would the unfortunate be? she wondered. Because the phrase "not make it" recalled her mother's term for someone who was dying, I wondered whether Molly meant that someone could die. She rejected this interpretation but drew closer to me in the play.

We drew pictures together. She drew many things; I always drew the two of us playing together. She seemed to need me to be actively playing at her side, supporting the pleasurable experience of the play.

It was also clear that as Molly began to relax, she began to feel free to define herself in a number of ways. She distinguished herself from various friends in terms of likes and dislikes, habits, appearance, and abilities in the stories she would bring me from school. She belonged to a group of friends, she told me. She would play with one friend when she was in this kind of mood, that friend when she was in another mood. Interesting to me was that the stereotyped "friends"—not her real friends, as it turned out—changed not at all, whereas Molly herself seemed to blossom. She also began to attack me in devaluing ways. She would draw pictures of me and pointedly ask for the gray crayon . . . to color my hair. She would measure herself against me and wonder how long it would take her to surpass me in height. I would say, "You *love* to tease me. You love to make fun of me." At first she would anxiously deny it. Then, when she saw that I found this wish of hers perfectly acceptable and even worth playing about, she started to agree with me. She told me, "One thing I like about you is that you have such a good sense of humor. I have fun playing with you." "I have fun playing with you too," I said. And I meant it.

At the same time this was happening, Molly had begun to show real musical talent, which was recognized at school and at home. Her identification as a troublemaker was preempted by that as a musician, and this ushered her into latency with new grace and self-esteem. What relative roles this musical gift and the individual treatment had in her maturational progress played, I will never know. At the same time, however, I had several meetings with her parents together and a number of meetings with each parent alone in order to discuss the family dynamics elucidated in the family meetings of the previous year. These later meetings were, I believe, critical in terms of supporting the family's growth, because they interrupted some of the destructive patterns the family tended to move into. Both parents recognized these patterns as we reviewed them, and we took our understanding of them further by discussing them in this new context.

SUMMARY

We began with a working hypothesis about the inhibition or facilitation of individual change based on the responses of family members to the person trying to change. Affects were identified as the currency of these interchanges. Using the clinical case of a 5-year-old girl who was struggling with oedipal conflict, the hypothesis was explored primarily through the material of family meetings and then followed up with material from an individual treatment. The metaphor of an earthquake in the first family meeting provided the thematic focus for the potentiality for change, for development. The metaphor included two meanings the family gave to the affective states involved in this developmental process—one exciting and pleasurable, and the other hostile and frightening. The family's inability to serve as a container for the "earthquake" affect precluded the freedom needed to play through to some resolution of the oedipal conflict, the freedom to play the grandiose "everything" self-image as well as the contrasting have-not self-image and to find some tolerable solution. When this ability to play was restored, Molly's development proceeded. The ability to play was supported by the individual therapy, by Molly's newly discovered musical talent, and by her family's enhanced capacity to tolerate the affects involved. The family's new ability to do this allowed each family member to better acknowledge his or her own feelings, and it freed Molly from her family role of expressing the affects associated with abandonment. She was thus supported in her efforts to define herself as a complicated person in her own right. In her metaphor, Molly found a way to include stormy weather and sunny days within the same frame, a good forecast for tomorrow. It is hoped that similar conceptual models that attempt to understand the same complex processes will continue to lead us further from reductive stereotypes and closer to formulations that respect the contributions of every individual in the family. And the clinicians who use these models in their work with families would do well to keep their attention focused on the affect in the meetings, because when families are afraid to feel, they lose the critical capacity to play.

REFERENCES

Beardslee, W. R., Hoke, L., Wheelock, I., Rothberg, P., van de Velde, P. & Swatling, S. (1992), Initial findings on preventive interventions for families with affective disorders. *Amer. J. Psychiat.*, 149-10:1335–1340.
Beebe, B. & Sloate, P. (1982), Assessment and treatment of difficulties in mother–infant attunement in the first three years of life. *Psychoanal. Inq.*, 1:601–625.
Bion, W. R. (1961), *Experiences in Groups and Other Papers.* London: Tavistock Pub. Ltd.
Demos, V. (1982), Affect in early infancy: Physiology or psychology. *Psychoanal. Inq.*, 1:533–575.
Field, T. M. (1977), Effects of early separation, interactive deficits and experimental manipulations on mother-infant face-to-face. *Child Dev.*, 48:763–771.
Hoffman, L. (1981), *Foundations of Family Therapy.* New York: Basic Books, Inc.
Minuchin, S. (1974), *Families and Family Therapy.* Cambridge, MA: Harvard University Press.
_____ Rosman, B. L. & Baker, L. (1978), *Psychosomatic Families.* Cambridge, MA: Harvard University Press.
Osofsky, J. (1982), The development of the parent–infant relationship. *Psychoanal. Inq.*, 1:625–643.

_____ & Eberhart-Wright, A. (1988), Affective exchange between high risk mothers and infants. *Internat. J. Psycho-Anal.*, 69:221–233.

Shapiro, E. R. (1982), The holding environment and family therapy with acting out adolescents. *Internat. J. Psychoanal. Psychother.*, 9:209–226.

_____ & Carr, A. W. (1991), *Lost in Familiar Places*. New Haven, CT: Yale University Press.

Shapiro, R. L. (1985), Family dynamics and object-relations theory: An analytic group-interpretative approach to family therapy. In: *Group Relations Reader 2*, ed. A. D. Colman & M. H. Geller. A. K. Rice Institute Series. Springfield, VA: Goetz.

Stern, D. N. (1988), Affect in the context of the infant's lived experience. *Internat. J. Psycho-Anal.*, 69:233–239.

Tomkins, S. S. (1978), Script theory: Differential magnification of affects. Nebraska Symposium on Motivation, pp. 201–236.

Zitbach, J. J. (1986), *Young Children in Family Therapy*. New York: Brunner, Mazel.

Chapter 6

PROBLEMS WITH AFFECT TOLERANCE IN THE ANALYSIS OF AN ADOLESCENT GIRL

Stephanie Smith

This chapter discusses questions raised by the analysis of Sarah, a middle adolescent. Anxiety about potentially overwhelming feeling states dominated her treatment for several years, and development of affect tolerance became an important focus of our work. The focus on affect tolerance contributed to prevention of both a therapeutic impasse and the breaking off of analysis. Instead, there was an improved working alliance, which enabled the analysis to deepen. During treatment, Sarah developed a greater capacity for self-observation, exploration, and the uncovering of unconscious fantasy, which increased her capacity to tolerate regression, experience internal conflict, and work in the transference.

My experience with Sarah prompted inquiry into the nature of affect and affect development in the middle years of adolescence. Was Sarah's difficulty with affect tolerance unique and related to the traumatic events of her life, or was this a common phenomenon for at least some female adolescents? In either case, what are the implications for technique?

Chused (1990) comments on the adolescent's use of externalization and the tendency of adolescents to resist the development of transference and to flee treatment. This chapter investigates the role of affect tolerance and its relation to the development of transference in adolescence. How might

An earlier version of this chapter appeared in *Child Analysis: Clinical, Theoretical, and Applied,* Vol. 4 (1993) published by the Cleveland Center for Research in Child Development.

the analyst's attention to developmental problems with affect enhance the adolescent's capacity to experience internal conflict, tolerate regression, and work in the transference? Following a review of the pertinent literature are a description of the early phases of Sarah's treatment and a discussion of the technical interventions. One unusual feature was introduced: Sarah's mother joined us for one session every third week. These conjoint sessions, which continued for almost two years, contributed to a working alliance and helped to facilitate Sarah's development and her capacity for affect tolerance.

REVIEW OF THE LITERATURE

Traditional psychoanalytic views describe adolescence as a time of emotional turmoil and disequilibrium. Geleerd (1957) compares this period of development to an active volcanic process in which continuous eruptions take place from within and keep the earth's crust from solidifying. Turmoil has traditionally been viewed as usual and necessary for movement toward consolidation of the adult personality. Current researchers agree that adolescence is a period of time requiring multiple changes (biological, social, and psychological, but they do not find that the general population of adolescents can be described as being in a time of major emotional dysfunction or vulnerability (Hauser and Smith, 1991). Although the current research suggests that turmoil may be a sign of psychopathology, this still represents an area of controversy due to the lack of adequate observational data regarding affect development in adolescence and adulthood (Brown, this volume; Hauser and Smith, 1991).

Blos (1962) asserts that adolescence is a time of major psychological restructuring and involves decisive turns in psychic development. The quality of the object search changes. There is a move toward a heterosexual organization and away from the pregenital and bisexual position. The middle adolescent experiences inner emptiness, grief, and sadness, which constitutes part of the mourning process that is essential to the gradual achievement of liberation from incestuous ties. This process takes time and repeated reworking.

The break with the inner infantile objects shakes the adolescent to the center (Blos, 1962). Katan (1951) describes a final displacement of the incestuous desires toward the parents, calling this developmental experience "object removal" in order to stress its finality and irreversibility (see also Furman, 1988). Blos (1979) sees this period as a normal transitional phase that adolescents typically handle with narcissistic withdrawal and overvaluation of the self at the expense of reality testing. An adolescent experiences intense need to concretely avoid the parents, who are still experienced as incestuous and projects and externalizes internal states onto the environment. Simultaneously, there is intense hunger for the parents, which finds expression in transitory, idealized, narcissistic love relationships. These relationships in particular serve as displacements for the love felt toward the same-sex parent. Blos (1979) views the coming to terms with the homosexual and pregenital components of pubertal sexuality as a primary developmental task of adolescence and believes that sexual identity formation is predicated on the completion of this process. Identification with the same-sex parent must occur before heterosexual love can be achieved.

Blos (1962) states that during this time, defenses are unstable, transitory, and aimed at counteracting the intense, inner pressures and weakened hold on reality. Many adolescents adopt behavior that permits a divorce of feeling from action, and may exert frantic efforts to remain reality bound. Blos (1962) adds that the middle adolescent will induce ego states of affective intensity to allow the ego an experience of self and thus protect the integrity of a sense of boundaries and cohesion. There is often a move toward affective states marked by exuberance and elation to defend against the pain of the necessary affects associated with mourning. Modell's (1990) description of the "manic defense" may be relevant to these states of elation and exuberance. Modell describes the manic defense as an attempt to live in the everlasting present, where there is no past or future, no loss or death. It is a flight from inner reality (Modell, 1990; Winnicott, 1958).

Although there is difference of opinion as to when a child can grieve, theorists agree that an ability to grieve is possible in adolescence. This allows the adolescent to choose new love relationships instead of resorting to the displacement of incestuous yearnings. Acquiring the ability to mourn has a profound effect on a number of ego functions: It is a prerequisite to an individual's ability to give up various aspects of infantile omnipotence and to diminish grandiose views of the self. More subtle and complex forms of self-awareness can develop; and, most important, a new capacity for judgment and reality testing can emerge (Furman, 1978; Krystal, 1988; Wolfenstein, 1966).

Krystal (1988) states that in order for these developments to take place, affects must be adequately verbalized, desomatized, and differentiated. Otherwise, they become too threatening and overwhelm the existing psychic organization and functioning: they are so close to the infantile affects that they pose the danger of the return of infantile psychic trauma.

Brown (this volume) proposes a developmental line of affects and states that during toddlerhood and Mahler's stage of separation-individuation, the developmental task in terms of affect is affect tolerance, that is, the development of the capacity to bear intense affective states and begin to learn self-management of moods. He emphasizes the importance of the caregiver's responsiveness and ability to model responses for the child. He states that affective experience, which is viscerally based in the body, becomes associated first with body image, then with the increasingly differentiated self-representation and object representations. A related task is developing the ability to localize affective experience within the emerging representational self-structure. He also describes the period between 18 and 36 months as a time of cognitive shift and in terms of acquisition of language. He emphasizes that the extent to which the child is able to learn to label and articulate affective experience is largely dependent on having good role models. The capacity to verbalize affects lifts feelings out of the realm of immediate action and helps the child to learn the capacity for delay (Furman, 1978). Verbalization of affects leads to greater control and mastery of affective states (Katan, 1961) and therefore also greatly reinforces the capacity to tolerate affects and modulate behavior.

Brown also states that by the close of latency, the child would have the capacity (dependent on cognitive development and social skills) to tolerate, differentiate, and label specific affective experiences. There should also be the capacity to experience affect states as one's own and as part of oneself. He questions the range of studies that imply that differentiation of a full range of affective experiences is more or less complete by the ages of 10 or 12. Brown proposes that there are further developments in adolescence and adulthood and adds that adequate observational data do not exist regarding adolescent affect development to conclude otherwise.

A crucial aspect in the shift of psychic organization is the adolescent's new capacity for conceptual thinking and theory building. Piaget's theory of formal operations describes the new capacity to hypothesize and make connections. Multiple possibilities now predominate, rather than only the concrete reality of the moment. There can be more than one truth and reality in addition to a new capacity to reflect on the past and the future (Piaget and Inhelder, 1958). This has implications for the adolescent's capacity for differentiation in terms of internal and external experience with a new experience of emotion and fantasy life. Steingart speaks of an advance from self-image to more abstract self-ideation that still can retain and use developmental imagery and perhaps sensations (Steingart, 1969). There are also implications for the adolescents' capacity to have increasingly complex and subtle affect states as well as to think about their feelings and those of others.

At present, affective development and cognitive organization are generally thought to be mutually and reciprocally interactive (Brenner, 1982; Pine, 1979; Saari, 1978). According to Schafer, in regard to adolescents, affects serve as powerful organizers of experience, and they contribute in profound ways to ego development. Increased acceptance, tolerance, and integration of feeling states contribute to increasing differentiation of specific, sharply defined, and stable representations (Schafer, 1973).

Hauser and Smith (1991) cite Fisher, who perceives adolescents as particularly vulnerable to contextual factors because of their newly acquired cognitive capacities. These recent attainments are quickly reversed by environmental failure, reversing at the same time previous attainments established during the more stable childhood period. Fisher's notion of contextual responsiveness does not imply one-to-one correspondence with actual people or events. The research findings demonstrate that children's perceptions of parental behaviors are likely to coincide more with how the child experiences the behavior than with neutral observers' perceptions of the same behaviors and that children's perceptions have a strong relationship with self-esteem. Citing Susman and Brooks-Gunn, they suggest that cognitive changes may actually be as much of a destabilizer as are the hormonal vicissitudes of adolescence (Hauser and Smith, 1992).

REFERRAL AND INITIAL INTERVIEW

Sarah was referred by her mother's analyst when almost 14. Her grades had begun to deteriorate, and she was more openly expressing complaints about her mother as well as general unhappiness. She was described by all as relatively well adjusted but was the type of vulnerable child whose difficulties might easily be overlooked.

Sarah appeared for her first interview in an elegant red sweater and jeans. She sat with her arms folded tightly across her chest. She was attractive and lively but spoke in a controlled manner without much feeling. Sarah seemed to be unusually insightful, articulate, and composed for her years. She began by saying, "I've never been in therapy because I could always get by. I've really had a hard life. I need help now because my grades are going down and I'm not happy. I'm good at telling you my problems because I've had plenty of time to think about them: I've been alone a lot. I'm glad to have someone to talk to because my mother isn't interested. She pretends sometimes but she has so many problems of her own that I have to keep an eye on her and take care of her."

The story that unfolded revealed multiple losses and moves. The central theme was having to grow up in the context of adults with significant problems and highly maladaptive ways of managing feelings of pain and isolation. Sarah's greatest concern was her relationship with her mother. She described Mrs. L as moody, withdrawn, or attacking when angry; self-absorbed; and periodically threatening suicide. Sarah said she felt guilty and thought she was too much for her mother to handle. She worried that she was a burden and that Mrs. L did not want her. Memories and present descriptions of her mother sounded both realistic and devalued. Sarah said that she wanted to change her mother, improve their relationship, and feel loved and wanted.

Sarah also told me about Mark, who died when she was 11. Mark was the man who had raised her along with her mother. He was highly idealized and remembered as the loving, responsible, and responsive parent.

HISTORY

Like Sarah's, Mrs. L's problems had also became apparent in middle adolescence and were characterized by acting out and attraction to a counterculture and communal life-style. Her analyst understood this behavior as an attempt to escape intolerable isolation and depression. In late adolescence, Mrs. L gave birth to Sarah but did not marry John, the biological father. Instead, she married Mark, who had stood by her. The three of them lived in questionable, unstable situations, including a bizarre cult, until Mrs. L separated from Mark and finally divorced him. Mark had significant difficulties, would become seriously depressed, and was involved with drugs. Although he could be warm, caring, and exciting, he could also be extremely difficult and unreliable. When Sarah was 7, Mrs. L returned with Sarah to the city of her birth and lived in an apartment near her own parents. She entered treatment, put her life together professionally, and tried to create a home for her daughter. Although Mrs. L was burdened by significant emotional difficulties, she had in fact attempted to care for Sarah to the best of her ability.

According to both Mrs. L and Sarah, Sarah did well, until adolescence, without major symptoms or a breakdown in functioning. There was no evidence from mother or child of specific developmental delays, defects, major illnesses, or hospitalizations. Both Sarah and her mother emphasized Sarah's competence at home and school as well as her capacity to relate to adults and children in a pleasing manner. Sarah did remember feeling alone and being a good girl in her search for love and approval.

When Sarah was 11, Mark died of a drug overdose and there was the possibility of suicide. Mrs. L left Sarah with her parents and traveled alone to attend the funeral. Sarah responded with indifference to being left at home, and her functioning appeared unchanged through this period. During the fourth year of treatment, she came to understand that she had unconsciously managed to maintain the belief that Mark was still alive while freely speaking about the actual events of his death. When Sarah turned 13, Mrs. L decided to tell her about her biological father, John. Sarah's response was to call John and arrange a meeting. John agreed to the arrangement but canceled at the last minute. Sarah was visibly upset and couldn't understand why he didn't want to see her.

PSYCHOTHERAPY

Sarah initiated treatment more than a year later. I suspect that her ability to ask for therapy was related to the fact that Mrs. L had begun and remained in analysis. Mrs. L's treatment was an acknowledgment that something was wrong with her and gave some legitimacy to Sarah's resentment. Also, with someone else in the picture to take care of Mrs. L, Sarah could begin to acknowledge her own anger and feelings of deprivation and loss. Sarah also told me about her mother's and her concern that she might repeat her mother's adolescence and begin to take drugs and become sexually promiscuous.

Sarah was seen twice a week for seven months. I also met separately with Mrs. L approximately every six weeks. Sarah's initial response to me was positive, and she could easily tell me her concerns as well as facts about present and past. She never missed an appointment. She brought in pictures and wanted to share her experiences with me. Her descriptions were all in words and controlled. She could state without reservation her pleasure in having someone to talk to and told me that she was beginning to improve rapidly. During this period, it became clear that the price of good functioning had been ego constriction involving the overuse of defenses such as intellectualization, isolation of affect, denial, and avoidance in an attempt to ward off painful and frightening affect states, fantasies, and memories. Sarah could be angry and express resentment toward Mrs. L. She said, "Mother wants me to be happy so that she doesn't have to bother with me." Within this context, she brought her first dream: "I had a tear [pronounced as a rip—not crying] in my eye that was very ugly; I was happy when I heard it could get fixed. I told my mother, who wasn't so happy but took me to the doctor anyway." Sarah shared the dream with her mother, who said that it was a therapy dream and suggested that she tell her therapist. Sarah could acknowledge that she worried about what she might see in therapy, that the dream reflected her sadness, her fear that something was wrong with her, and her wish to get fixed. Her main concern, however, was Mrs. L's response to the dream: "Tell your therapist." Sarah experienced this as a rejection contained within a message that her mother was not interested and was sending her to someone else. In fact, Sarah felt a double rejection; her mother had turned her over to me, and I couldn't be her mother either. She feared that she would discover that Mrs. L didn't care, and she worried she would become too dependent on me. She said, "Mother can't live without analysis."

She agreed when I suggested that the wish to get fixed might also be a worry. She made links to growing up and concluded, "Adults don't have it so good." She described her concerns about the future and her feeling that "changes are usually bad." For Sarah, change meant news of death or a move to a new, upsetting situation. She also said, "I have to grow up but I don't know how: so much has happened to me."

Although her associations appeared to reveal an anxious, frightened little girl who felt murderous, guilty, and unlovable, she could not stay in touch with these feeling states and fantasies. I did wonder whether I was observing only lifelong patterns or also posttraumatic symptoms. Although in her daily life she was active and lively and told me with enthusiasm and exuberance about her school friends and various young men, it became apparent to me that these actions were not primarily in the service of progressive development. Instead, she revealed a continual search for a substitute for the early parent and rigid defenses against the experiences of early yearnings, frustration, and anger. Although while Sarah spoke I also heard the theme of her loss of two fathers, she was fully concentrated on her mother.

During this time, Sarah became increasingly aware of her concerns and wishes and felt cornered by her conflicts. I suggested analysis, and Sarah struggled and alternated between wanting to work in greater depth and being too busy. Deliberations about analysis underlined both her difficulty in identifying with her mother and her heightened concerns abut dependency and autonomy.

The change to four sessions weekly occurred several months after an experience at school in which a young man called her an airhead. Sarah was in tears and acted surprised when I wondered aloud what might have made him say such a thing. Sarah thought she could appear "spacey" sometimes. I asked her whether the fact that she kept so much locked up inside and out of awareness might sometimes make her appear attractive and bubbly, but without much substance. Sarah cried and nodded. At least for the moment, She seemed to appreciate the enormous cost of her problems in terms of her personality and capacity to have relationships and live her life.

PSYCHOANALYSIS

Sarah came to see me four times a week for the following three years. Within weeks, there was a dramatic change. The increase in frequency of sessions put increased pressure on her defenses and intensified frustrated yearnings for a preoedipal relationship. Her difficulties in forming a relationship and her relative inability to tolerate negative affect states and accompanying fantasies brought out rage, ambivalence, and guilt. Reflection and discussion all but disappeared, and she now externalized and concretized her experience. She began to miss sessions, experienced me and her sessions as torture, and insisted that her real relationship with her mother was the whole problem.

The form of Sarah's descriptions changed: she now brought a flood of frightening fantasies and memories and described multiple nightmares. One dream began with an image of her mother in a grey business suit; suddenly she saw instead a scary lady vampire with large fangs. She ran into the cellar to hide from her. Suddenly, for a split second, her mother was hiding from the vampire with her. Then Sarah was alone again. In another dream, Sarah was with her friend's brother. Someone walked up to them and slit the young man's throat. Sarah woke up "so scared." She told me that she was angry, frightened, and very critical of me. I tried to talk with her about her fears of regression and treatment, but she denied these. She was furious with me and accused me of causing her pain and not protecting her. She complained that sessions interfered with sports; it was my fault that she couldn't play. She hadn't wanted to come today because she was having so much fun with friends. She blamed me for causing her nightmares and ruining her social life. She explained that she could manage her problems herself and said, "I could even study last night because I put my radio on." She was comforted when I said that it sounded as if she felt so alone with her pain. Her response was a sad "Nobody knows my pain," and she quickly added that coming to see me wasn't good for her.

She told me that Mark had an interest in vampires and also that he used to chop up banana slugs with a huge knife. She also complained that her mother was dating someone Sarah thought was a jerk and that she thinks her mother's having sex with him. Her tone was anxious and excited, and her associations were first to her strep throat and then to a horrible lump in her throat when she thinks about it. Then she said she forgot to take her strep throat medication; no one had reminded her and somebody should have. I asked her if she felt that I, like Mother, didn't care or look after her because I didn't help her to avoid her scary thoughts and because I spoke with her about them instead of doing something like reminding her to take her medicine. She screamed, "I don't need analysis; it hurt less when I skipped a session and went to get my ears pierced!"

One day she came for only the last five minutes. She was laughing and said she had been flirting with one of the popular boys after school. She had really wanted to come today to tell me about the plans she and her friends had for a party. She started to describe her interest in the young man and suddenly burst into tears. She said, "I've been having nightmares and I get so scared that I'm afraid to go to sleep. I want to tell you my dreams and what I'm feeling, but I can't stand it and I can't tell you because it's too much! I can't get away from it anymore. I just want to sleep!" She became frightened and increasingly devalued me, herself, and the analysis. Themes were expressed as enactment and were not open for discussion. She repeatedly attempted to involve me in battle, and her material continued to reveal her experience of me as an overstimulating and dangerous parental figure. She insisted that the problems were only in reality and demanded joint sessions with her mother. She didn't want to imagine what the meetings with Mother would be like; we should just have them. She refused the idea of a separate therapist because her aim was to have only joint sessions. She denied having a loyalty conflict and denied concern with what she might find out or what could happen between us.

Sarah's regression in the sessions involved a loss of observing capacities, an increase in the use of externalization, and a wish for concrete solutions that would reinvolve her mother as an empathic and caring person and aid in the service of blocking affect and avoiding her internal experience. Feeling states were painful, terrifying, and potentially overwhelming and could not serve a signal function. The regression highlighted her difficulties with affect tolerance and self-management of moods. Sarah was surprised by her own response, which increased her anxiety that something was wrong with her and that she was like her mother.

Sarah's response to analysis presented a confusing diagnostic picture. I was impressed by the fact that although she was having nightmares, the increased intensity did not result in serious acting out or a wish to completely stop therapy. She also maintained her level of functioning in daily life. I understood the regression as her response to traumatic events, as a result of developmental failure, and as an attempt to solve her adolescent dilemma and struggle to resolve conflicts with autonomy, identity, and sexuality. The reworking of preoedipal conflicts was complicated by the effects of her relationship with her mother, the death of Mark, the rejection by Jack, and by multiple losses and moves. Pathological maternal identifications that could interfere with adolescent development became apparent as they were "lived out" in the sessions with no possibility for observation or interpretation. Although the material was highly condensed, there was clearly an intense negative maternal transference, and I represented the frustrating, depriving, torturing, seductive, unreliable, rejecting, and murderous mother. Simultaneously, Sarah identified with and conveyed through action her sense of Mother as fragile, in emotional pain, and easily overwhelmed. Sarah, like Mother, felt both tortured and murderous and attempted to defend, protect both of us, and maintain herself by either verbally attacking me or missing sessions. Part of what became actualized (Sandler, 1976) was the feeling that we were too much for each other. Feeling and talking in each other's presence felt cruel and potentially destructive. I began to wonder whether analysis was too painful and whether it would be productive, or would repeat, as well as become an additional trauma for Sarah. At this point, I could easily have made a clinical decision to alter her treatment and stop the analysis, based on an enactment and my countertransference response.

A predominant theme in Sarah's analysis had been that she had no one to talk to or depend on and that it was dangerous to depend on people because they were too preoccupied to listen, care, and protect; could leave; and could even die. The specific focus was her mother, whom she blamed for everything and who Sarah felt had failed to provide her with a normal, stable life. Indeed, Mrs. L's preoccupation, affective lability, and difficulty in talking about feelings meant that she couldn't be sufficiently attuned and available for Sarah so as to help Sarah learn to tolerate affects and regulate feeling states. One can speculate from Sarah's history that this was also true during her early years and could have contributed to developmental failure and difficulties in the area of affect tolerance. Sarah's material suggested that her response was to bottle up her frustration and resentment in an attempt to remain attractive to Mrs. L, avoid abandonment, and protect each of them from their destructive wishes toward the other.

Many topics were unspeakable, and Mrs. L kept a secret: she did not tell Sarah about her natural father. Also, Sarah suspected that her mother was trying hard to conceal ambivalent and destructive wishes toward her daughter. Sarah explained the confusing and unclear reality with her own projections and blamed herself.

Sarah's transference revealed that it was taboo to tell; it was far too dangerous. Sarah experienced the treatment as her being seduced to feel and to tell. Working with me was experienced as disloyal to Mrs. L, dangerous, and also very threatening in the disclosure of her deepest yearnings. The transition to analysis brought an end to the use of precocious defenses and temporarily increased her use of externalization and projection as well as her expectation of retaliation. It also increased her confusion, and there were times when I felt she could not maintain the as-if quality involved in a therapeutic alliance, instead experiencing me as the real mother. She appeared, at times, to have lost the capacity to differentiate between inner life and outer reality and also between past and present.

Continued analysis and further development of transference depended on Sarah's ability to tolerate affects while sustaining the ability to observe herself and to access memories and fantasy life. She would also need to feel safe to tell within the context of our relationship. This required the ability for differentiation and some capacity to view me as different from her experience of Mrs. L. It would also involve some modification of, and separation from, pathological identifications with representations of her mother as overwhelmed, destructive, and helpless. Although this would be the work of the analysis, there had to be sufficient alteration to allow the analysis to proceed.

Sarah's wish to meet with Mrs. L combined elements of developmental need and defense. She wanted to improve their relationship and hoped that with a therapist present, they might be able to talk to each other. She also was trying to avoid her inner life by bringing in the real mother and protecting herself from both me and her mother by not being alone with either of us. I understood later in the analysis that the creation of a triangle was also an attempt to revive Mark both as a denial of his death and as a wish to involve the father in her attempts at separation.

Although I had never included a parent of an adolescent in an analytic session, I felt it was important to honor Sarah's request, pay attention to developmental need, and respect her defenses. I also felt it would be essential for Sarah and her mother to tell and to know without either of them becoming overwhelmed. I hoped that it would alter and improve their relationship and also facilitate the ego development that would enable the analysis to continue.

I suggested that we continue the analysis and also include Mrs. L in a session. Sarah's response was to complain bitterly: she wanted to stop the analysis and have three-way meetings with her mother. I noticed that she did not invite Mrs. L to join us and also that she actually began to more regularly attend sessions. What became clear was Sarah's worry that her mother didn't care, would refuse to come, and wanted to fob her off onto a therapist. Sarah wondered what she meant to Mrs. L and whether there was a place for her. During this time, analysis provided a place for Sarah and met some of her needs for dependency and safety. I tried to remain present, interested, helpful, and open to any feelings or topics that would arise. I also tried to encourage her to describe how she felt, which ultimately enabled interpretive work. This was in the face of Sarah's many attempts to disrupt the relationship.

One day Sarah arrived 15 minutes late and was preoccupied with several fights she and her mother had had the night before. She complained that her mother never noticed her unless she did something wrong and that her mother avoided taking responsibility for her own problems by saying that she was doing her best. Sarah continued for some time and then fell silent. I said, "You sound very angry with your mother." Sarah started to sob and said, "I'm angry that I have to talk to Smitty because my mother doesn't care and won't listen." She was silent and then said, "I guess I am angry. I don't like to tell you that I'm angry." I said that I wondered whether she could even let herself know that she felt angry. She continued to cry and said, "I'm so afraid that I am going to hurt my mother's feelings. I can't be angry; I'm not angry; maybe I am." She sobbed and was silent. I finally repeated, "I'm so afraid I'm going to hurt my mother if I know I feel angry." Sarah said, "I want my mother" and continued to cry.

I was an adult who did not retaliate. Analysis provided Sarah with an experience of having the opportunity to express herself and share with me without negative consequence. Within three months, our work enabled Sarah to risk inviting Mrs. L to join us. Her mother's first response was refusal: she didn't want to come because it would be too much and she would be overwhelmed. What follows is material from a session following the refusal. There is an important shift in the material: Sarah spoke of her sadness and poor self-esteem. Also, there was evidence of symbolic rather than concrete expression and capacity for regression in the service of the ego.

Sarah came 15 minutes late. She sat down and blamed the trains and the fact that she had to talk to her friends after school. She said, "I suppose I could have called Grandmother for a ride. Oh, where are the pens." Sarah sat and sketched for the first time since the transition to analysis. She told me that she was angry because her mother didn't want to come. She said she would feel too overwhelmed. Sarah confided that she hadn't made it clear how much it mattered because then it would really matter if Mother said no. Sarah said, "She acts like it's not her fault that she can't come, like she doesn't have any responsibility." Sarah drew scribbles and suddenly said, "Oh, it's a man; well, half man and half duck. Oh yes, and some daffy daffodils. Why, these drawings came out of my scribbles, like out of nowhere!" I said, "Out of nowhere?" She giggled and said, "My unconscious." Sarah said that she used to grow daffodils as a child. She also told me she was beginning to realize that all the friends at school didn't help and that she wanted to understand why there is always a black cloud over her head. She said that she was never happy. When I asked what she meant, she said that she didn't know because she didn't let herself think long enough to find out. She kept busy, but she was worried and didn't feel all right. Then she told me that this picture was different from any ever before because it had long brush strokes. Then she drew a daffy daffodil that she said was squished and ugly, and she showed it to me. She asked if I liked it. Before I could answer, she told me that she always needed to have people tell her that they think she is pretty. I remarked that she hadn't given me any time to say anything. She was silent. I asked her if maybe she wanted to talk about the part of her that she feels is daffy, squished, and ugly. Her response was, "All kids think they aren't lovable and don't like themselves." I asked if feeling this way about herself was in any way connected with her mother's refusal. Sarah seemed surprised, looked down, and sadly replied, "Maybe." There was a tear in her eye.

Sarah was more determined than ever before and was now able to persist and insist that her mother join a session. Mrs. L told Sarah that she was discussing her apprehensions with her analyst. Mrs. L had also told me of her concerns in one of our meetings. After some months, Mrs. L telephoned to tell me that she would attend. She would come only out of obligation because she imagined that the session would be beyond her "highest level of bearable pain."

The session was difficult because Sarah was able to be confronting and accusing and wanted to know all the facts about both of their lives. She was able to tell her mother that she thought she didn't care and requested that Mrs. L be less preoccupied and more interested in her. She also wanted Mrs. L to share more of herself. Although Mrs. L appeared formal and constricted, her attempts were admirable. She answered her daughter's questions to the best of her ability. She also told Sarah that she would do her best but that she had limitations. She was working hard in her own analysis, but Sarah would have to accept her struggles as well. Both agreed that the meeting was helpful. Mrs. L stated clearly that Sarah was to continue analysis and felt that she could handle joining one of Sarah's sessions once in three weeks. Mrs. L seemed more relaxed when she left and said with a smile, "That wasn't so hard." Sarah would have preferred more frequent meetings but was very pleased by the outcome.

Sarah initially felt that the analytic hours were a waste compared to the meetings with her mother. During the individual sessions, she complained principally about having to have analysis. Slowly, however, she began to find it interesting to talk with me about her observations about Mrs. L and their interaction. Although many themes developed, an important theme for this discussion is that Sarah began to realize that there was a discrepancy between her actual mother and the mother she imagined and expected; she began to observe her own attempts to perpetuate certain negative interactions and views of her mother; she unhappily began to acknowledge that various images of Mother were highly idealized and devalued. Slowly she understood that avoiding analysis protected the sustaining fantasies both that she could have the idealized mother she carried around inside and that Mrs. L would change in the sessions and become like Sarah's internal image. This interfered with the possibility of noticing her mother's positive aspects. Both she and Mrs. L could only be

devalued in comparison with these images and expectations, which contributed to Sarah's low self-esteem, the depth of her disappointment, and
her feelings of deprivation.

In one conjoint meeting, Sarah listed complaints, and Mrs. L agreed to
comply with change. Three weeks later, Sarah arrived late for the joint
meeting. She rushed in and burst out crying. She exclaimed, "Mom has
been wonderful since we last met. (She used up a whole box of tissue
during the hour.) "How can I feel like I hate her when she is like this?
Everyone tells me I have to talk about what's happened to me. I usually
think it's really stupid, but I wonder when she tries and I still hate her! The
problem is my mother. No, it's me; I've failed her, or maybe I just think I
have. I need to sort this out, but I'd rather play tennis and be in plays. It
must be a great thing to be a therapist and be told all day that you're
needed; all those patients caring more about you than you care about
them. I just hate this!"

The example illustrates the ways in which Sarah began to clarify,
differentiate, and sort out the confusion between inner and outer. Her
individual sessions slowly began to feel, as Sarah said, "less toxic," and her
increasing capacity to work in the transference was coupled with increasingly rich and creative ways of bringing material. She began to draw,
write stories, and express feelings, memories, and fantasies with greater
comfort. Her increased capacity for affect tolerance allowed self-
observing capacities in the face of feelings of sadness, anger, and guilt.
This allowed for a continued analytic process and for her emotional
growth and development.

DISCUSSION

In Sarah's case, a focus on development of affect tolerance promoted ego
development. This approach helped to prevent a therapeutic impasse,
facilitated the development of transference, and enabled the analysis to
deepen. Increased structuralization resulted in a greater capacity to bear
affects, acknowledge inner experience and conflict, and begin to mourn.
This, in turn, resulted in Sarah's greater reality testing and acceptance of
limitations in herself and others. Analysis eventually enabled Sarah to
negotiate the tasks of middle adolescence and proceed with her development.

Sarah's attempts to negotiate phase-specific adolescent conflicts were
complicated by traumatic life events; most salient were the effects of
intermittently neglectful and traumatic patenting and Mark's death. Analysis revealed that Sarah's difficulties with affect tolerance were linked to
representations of Mrs. L and included aspects of Mrs. L's maladaptive

ways of managing pain and isolation. Pathological identifications with Mrs. L were used in a restitutive attempt to negotiate adolescent conflicts. Further analysis revealed that pathological and devalued identifications were also used defensively to maintain an idealized image of Mark and the denial of his death.

Although posttraumatic symptoms might provide some explanation, the analysis revealed evidence of underlying developmental failure in the area of affect tolerance. Based on the transference and the history, one can speculate that there were failures in caretaking and resulting difficulties during Sarah's toddler and preschool years. The developmental tasks of this phase include separation-individuation, development of autonomy, and resolution of anal-phase conflicts. The tasks in terms of affect development involve beginning to develop the capacity to bear and verbalize intense affective states and to learn self-management of moods. Problems at this time would have ramifications for subsequent structuralization and also for the reworking of preoedipal conflicts and identifications in adolescence. We know that Sarah's adaptive but costly prepubertal response was precocious development and ego constriction. Mark's death, Jack's rejection, and the onset of puberty put increased pressure on rigid defenses, created symptoms, and revealed developmental failure.

In psychotherapy, I became a stabilizing force, and Sarah continued to maintain the same inner balance and defensive style. The intensity of analysis put pressure on Sarah's defenses and intensified her frustrated yearnings for a preoedipal tie. The resulting regression put Sarah in touch with her feelings. The analysis provided a holding environment (Winnicott, 1960), which provided for some of Sarah's needs for dependency and safety while she anxiously alternated between fury and withdrawal. My efforts emphasized helping Sarah learn to experience and talk about what she felt rather than what it meant. It was also essential to remain present, interested, and open to any topics that would arise.

Furman (1991) states that most child analytic patients are not in touch with their feelings not because they have not developed the ability to feel but because their feelings arouse so much unpleasure or anxiety that they defend against them. Interpretation of these defenses produces unpleasure or anxiety and does not usually bring back the warded-off feeling, much less the ability to tolerate and use it, and it can lead to further defense. Furman further states that the task of helping the child to value, bear, and contain feelings is achieved by feeling with the child. Developmentally, a child learns to know his own feelings when the parents feel with him in a contained, step-by-step manner. Furman feels that this achievement has wide-ranging effects on all ego functions, especially on the organizing ability. She emphasizes that an independent, reliable testing of outer reality grows out of knowing and trusting inner reality, sensations, and feelings.

Sarah's wish to meet with Mrs. L combined elements of developmental need and defense. Conjoint sessions provided the possibility for each of them to find out that they could know and tell without becoming overwhelmed. It allowed Sarah the opportunity to sort out confusion, to clarify, and to differentiate between inner representations and the reality of her mother. A crucial aspect of this process was sharing her observations with me in the individual sessions and having the opportunity to reflect, together with some who had actually shared the experience, on what she had felt and perceived. Conjoint sessions enabled Sarah to experience different and more positive images of Mrs. L with which to identify. Their relationship also improved, which was important to both of them and for Sarah's continued development.

Shapiro suggests that a family focus may be useful during a phase of the adolescent's individual treatment, that is, if in the family meetings, affects and impulses can be sufficiently contained for their origins to be understood. He lists four factors that contribute to the usefulness of family therapy: (1) the stage of adolescence itself and the shared family regression that recapitulates and allows for the reworking of earlier conflicts, (2) the adolescent's continuing need for family support during this period, (3) the powerful effects of new experience with the parents on the adolescent's still flexible character structure, and (4) the possibility of reintegration of projected and acted-out conflicts leading to modification in parental functioning. The family therapy hopefully leads to greater internalization of conflict and a gradual cessation of family therapy (Shapiro, 1982).

Sarah's insistence on my involvement precluded the possibility of separate conjoint meetings. Creating this triangle enabled Sarah to face unbearable loyalty conflicts while simultaneously protecting herself by not being alone with either of us. I served enabling, mediating, and containing functions.

Although I was aware that I was participating in an enactment with multiple meanings, my initial focus was on the communication of thoughts and feelings rather than on the interpretation of meaning. This resulted in Sarah's beginning to feel safe and that she had permission to know and tell. She began to tolerate the conflict involved in experiencing and talking about her feelings and thoughts. Intense affects became increasingly modulated, and Sarah began to experience a greater sense of autonomy and control.

Sarah not only began to discriminate between inner and outer perceptions of Mrs. L, but also developed a greater capacity to work in the transference. In our individual sessions, she began to share thoughts and feelings and find value in observing herself. She also began to understand that she could learn from what she thought and felt about me and that there were aspects of our relationship that represented and repeated other relationships. The introduction of the real mother into some sessions contributed to a diminution of action in favor of understanding, and it enhanced the development of transference.

I would hypothesize that many middle adolescents experience difficulties with affect tolerance and that phase-specific developmental conflicts contribute both to the resistance to the development of transference and the frequent breaking off of treatment. Treatment in middle adolescence may involve adaptation in analytic technique and involve a focus on the development of affect tolerance.

During middle adolescence, there are multiple psychological, biological, and social changes that are new and different and can be experienced as destabilizing. Defenses are aimed both at counteracting these intense, inner pressures and affective states and at concrete avoidance of the real parents and experiences that evoke hunger attached to preoedipal and oedipal representations of the parents. The result is often narcissistic withdrawal, use of intense affective states in the service of maintaining ego boundaries, and divorce of feeling from action in an effort to remain reality bound. In addition, adolescent reworking of preoedipal conflicts and identification would include revival and reworking of preoedipal aspects of affect development. For most adolescents, this involves the revival of conflicts and unresolved difficulties with affect tolerance and verbalization of affect.

The major modification in technique was the introduction of the mother, who was also in analysis, into some analytic sessions. Although this was facilitative in Sarah's case, I wonder if the imperative to introduce the real mother is common among middle adolescents or whether it primarily reflects response to past trauma and developmental failure. Should this technique be considered an adaptation to specific adolescent conflicts or a modification based on Sarah's specific developmental problems? In either event, a focus on the development of affect tolerance may be necessary in the treatment of many adolescents and related to the development of transference and the continuation of treatment.

REFERENCES

Blos, P. (1962), *On Adolescence.* New York: Free Press.
_____ (1979), *The Adolescent Passage.* New York: IUP.
Brenner, C. (1982), *The Mind in Conflict.* Madison, CT: IUP.
Chused, J. F. (1990), Externalization: A resistance in the beginning phase of adolescent

analysis. In: *On Beginning an Analysis,* ed. T. J. Jacobs & A. Rothstein. Madison, CT: IUP, pp. 127–150.

Furman, E. (1991), On feeling and being felt with. Presented at the tenth annual Marianne Kris Memorial Lecture at the annual meeting of the Association for Child Psychoanalysis, St. Louis, MO.

Furman, R. (1978), Some developmental aspects of the verbalization of affects. *The Psychoanalytic Study of the Child,* 33:187–211. New Haven, CT: Yale University Press.

_____ (1988), Object removal revisited. *Internat. Rev. Psychoanal.,* 15:165–176.

Geleerd, E. R. (1957), Some aspects of psychoanalytic technique in adolescence. *The Psychoanalytic Study of the Child,* 12:263–283. New York: IUP.

Hauser, S. T. & Smith, H. F. (1991), The development and experience of affect in adolescence. *J. Amer. Psychoanal. Assn.,* 39:131–165.

Katan, A. (1951), The role of "displacement" in agoraphobia. *Internat. J. Psychoanal.* 32:42–50.

_____ (1961), Some thoughts about the role of verbalization in early childhood. *The Psychoanalytic Study of the Child,* 16:184–188. New York: IUP.

Krystal, H. (1988), *Integration and Self-Healing.* Hillsdale, NJ: The Analytic Press.

Modell, A. H. (1990), *Other Times, Other Realities.* Cambridge, MA: Harvard University Press.

Piaget, J. & Inhelder, B. (1958), *The Growth of Logical Thinking from Childhood Through Adolescence,* ed. & trans. A. Parsons & S. Seagrin. New York: Basic Books.

Pine, F. (1979), On the expansion of affect array: A developmental description. *Bull. Menn. Clin.,* 43:79–95.

Saari, C. (1978), Cognitive and communicative features of emotional experience, or do you show what you think you feel? In: *The Development of Affect,* ed. M. Lewis & L. Rosenblum. New York: Plenum Press, pp. 361–375.

Sandler, J. (1976), Countertransference and role-responsiveness. *Internat. Rev. Psychoanal.,* 3:43–47.

Schafer, R. (1973), Concepts of self and identity and the experience of separation-individuation in adolescence. *Psychoanal. Quart.,* 42:42–59.

Shapiro, E. R. (1982), The holding environment and family therapy with acting out adolescents. *Internat. J. Psycho-Anal. Psychother.,* 9:209–225.

Steingart, I. (1969), On self, character, and the development of a psychic apparatus. *The Psychoanalytic Study of the Child,* 24:271–306. New York: IUP.

Winnicott, D. W. (1958), *Collected Papers.* New York: Basic Books.

_____ (1960), The theory of the parent-infant relationship. *Internat. J. Psycho-Anal.,* 41:585–595.

Wolfenstein, M. (1966), How is mourning possible? *The Psychoanalytic Study of the Child,* 21:93–123. New York: IUP.

Chapter 7

EMPATHY, VIRTUALITY, AND THE BIRTH OF COMPLEX EMOTIONAL STATES

Do We Find or Do We Create Feelings in the Other?

Alfred Margulies

> What an abyss of uncertainty, whenever the mind feels overtaken by itself; when it, the seeker, is at the same time the dark region through which it must go seeking and where all its equipment will avail it nothing. Seek? More than that: create. It is face to face with something which does not yet exist, to which it alone can give reality and substance, which it alone can bring into the light of day.
>
> —Proust

> [U]nconscious ideas continue to exist after repression as actual structures in the system *Ucs.*, whereas all that corresponds in that system to unconscious affects is a potential beginning which is prevented from developing.
>
> —Freud (1915, p. 178)

We treat the concept of affect as if it were a concrete, describable entity. But by its nature affect is highly nuanced and contextual. At best, the term "affect" serves as a broad indicator of a certain type of experience. In its most extreme states, it can seem most conceptually pure, for example, as in describing the experiences we call "rage," "panic," "mirth," or "rapture." Extreme states, though, are by definition not the most common experience and so are not always the best descriptors of what we mean to explore. Usually we see in-between states or complex amalgams. To paint a picture, for example, we put basic colors on the palette, but we then blend the colors to achieve variations and subtleties. Otherwise, we end up with cartoons.

Even in the limit situations of extreme states, different affects have different properties that are unique to themselves. For example, grief has a cathartic quality that panic does not. As a concept then, "affect" should properly refer to a specific affect. Given the extraordinarily subtle nuances of clinical work, we can almost never adequately describe the affective tones that we encounter in our everyday work.

It comes as no surprise then that in our attempts to feel into another's experience of the world, we come up against our inherent limitations of language and meaning. We grope toward the other through the mysterious process we dub "empathy." My contention in this chapter is that it is the implicit clumsiness of this process with its built-in tension of knowing and not knowing, of approximation and misunderstanding, that is in itself creative of new feeling experiences.[1]

THE ENIGMA OF EMPATHY

In most human interactions, there is a tacit assumption of some level of empathy; it is part of the medium of social discourse and is taken for granted. We make subtle, sometimes definitive, judgments about the other based on the minutest of gestures, smiles, and frowns—and all of this on the edge of our awareness and largely nonverbal. Often the empathic assumption comes to the fore when we find that we have been tricked (as by the good poker player) or oddly baffled (as by the person who hides from us in deeper ways, such as with autism). Good enough empathy, however, is good enough for most interactions.

In treatment, we often attain a level of attunement that borders on the uncanny (Margulies, 1993). We may even predict what the other person will next say (Havens 1978a, 1978b); we eerily anticipate one another. Yet, most of the time, we grope along or coast on our implicit knowledge of the other. Affective resonance, the bedrock of empathy, creates a strong

---

[1]This chapter derives substantially from, complements, and expands work first presented in Margulies (1989, chapter 8). Early on I had abandoned the graphical development of these ideas (indeed, the bulk of this work preceded and then was incorporated narratively into *The Empathic Imagination*), but then, with the help and encouragement of Jerome Sashin, I returned to it. This paper draws extensively on our dialogue, which was cut short by his tragic death. I am, of course, solely responsible for errors and simplifications. Dr. Ana-Maria Rizzuto, a close colleague and friend of Jerry's, offered many helpful suggestions. Dr. John Callahan, a mathematician and coauthor with Jerry, also graciously helped clarify my understanding.

interactive field on a rudimentary preverbal and bodily level, as anyone who has loved a small child or animal knows.

> Remembered bouquets long since dead . . . left in my memory the bygone charm with which I . . . burdened this new bouquet.
>
> —Henri Matisse

Empathy by its very nature is projective. I mean this not in the sense of a defensive mechanism, but merely that our own experience, even if powerfully and incontrovertibly in resonance with the other, must remain our own experience of the other's experience. We can share with, but we can never be, the other. Though we may be in remarkable affective attunement, the other's experience, with its surprising, unique shadings, will always elude us. We can only approximate another's experience from within the framework of our own.

In this sense, empathy is best seen as a process, in bits and pieces and always incomplete, ultimately impossible, spiraling on as the two participants change in their knowledge of one another. Because there can never be a vantage point for the empathizer that does not in some fundamental fashion influence the object of empathy, the process is truly that of participant observation and in its essence is very much akin to the methodological discoveries made by observers in the physical sciences.

EMPATHY AND FINDING THE SELF

That we are inevitably confronted by our own solipsism in the quest for the other raises some thorny and critical problems. As empathizers we, in a sense, always create the other in some image of our own—and we do this rapidly and even against our intentions otherwise. Our ideal remains to hold these constructions of the other within some web of tension, both knowing and not knowing.

The phenomenologists talk of "absence in presence." The term "gestalt" might also do. Both refer to the human propensity to complete in perception the design of things, though to a strong degree that "found" design is, of course, cast out onto the world by the very finders. The found design of the other can be compared to that of a virtual reality or image. Consider, for example, the three-dimensional image of a hologram—seemingly substantial, almost palpable, inherent in the holographic plate, but exquisitely sensitive to the viewer's own motions and vantage point in space. The image, although reproducible, comes alive momentarily and uniquely in the observer's consciousness, waiting to be born with each new viewing.

But I want also to capture the relativistic property of virtuality that changes with the viewer's point of view. Perhaps the simple image of a mirror reflection will serve as an analogy: I can see myself only from my vantage point. I see my eyes looking at themselves, never do I see myself looking away—though another looking at my virtual image in the same mirror can do so, because he or she is not locked into my constant relative position in space with respect to myself. The other sees aspects of my virtual image unavailable to me, though it is *my* image.

In exploring the inner life of another, a further mysterious property of the dialectic of empathic interaction emerges: What we expect of the other, the other will come to manifest. We mirror each other's expectations in a dance of mutual (though not always sympathetic) empathy. Much of this is familiar from the work of those interested in the social envelop of our work. Harry Stack Sullivan, for example, recommended that the beginning therapist pay close attention to how the patient initially responds to the therapist, how this then affects the therapist, how the therapist's response in turn feeds back to the patient, and so on in circular fashion. Horney (1937) found the machinery of the repetition compulsion in self-fulfilling interpersonal enactments. This is, after all, transference writ large into everyday life.

There are, though, subtle aspects of the empathic enterprise that have to do with the naming of experience before the person has fully come to experience that experience in and of itself. This, I think, is because experience itself is seldom fully born; it has its own nascent and undeveloped features. The various terms for affect and emotional states point in this direction.

EMPATHY'S CREATION OF ITS OBJECT
OF CONTEMPLATION

Brown (in this volume) writes of the structuralization of affect, that is, affect itself develops and grows in complexity as an entangled and parallel line of psychological maturation. Basch (1983) has been helpful in his delineation of hierarchies of affective complexities: "affect" is a somatic response that is involuntary, automatic, and autonomically mediated; "feeling" is the "conscious awareness of an affective event as a subjective experience"; "emotions" are "much more complex states in which several feelings are experienced as a unity in a relationship to the self and its goals" (pp. 117–118). Such hierarchical models guide us through a thicket of otherwise insoluble problems.

Clearly we move in both directions of elaboration in our clinical work. Complex emotional states are regularly elaborated in the interpersonal dialectic (e.g., connected via interpretation: "The experience you feel now with me seems similar to how you have felt with your mother"). Less valued in the literature is how we work from the bottom up (e.g., alexithymia and clarification: "When you have felt a headache in the past it's been at a time when you have squelched your anger; yesterday you left feeling frustrated by me"). Clarifications of affect—the painstaking process of attaching bodily experience to feeling states—is in its essence another kind of interpretation—a creation of meaning and a linking to broader experience (though such work is often seen as preparatory to higher levels of interpretation. The margins, though, blur: Clarification is often done through the medium of the transference.)

I am, of course, struggling with a part of a larger problem: what it means to build psychic structure. My point is that in the very identifying of affects (e.g., clarification) or in the broader sweep of linking complex emotional states through interpretation, we are in effect creating something new and not merely releasing or uncovering something buried away.

Some interesting problems arise (only some of which will be addressed in this chapter). What are the implications for the experiencer when the empathizer attributes a level of affective structuralization that is not yet fully there, but virtual, nascent, unborn, or thwarted? Are these "leading-the-witness" assumptions crucial to the healing power of empathy? When do they go awry? What are the complications in such interpersonal presumptions of experience?

SOME UNEXPECTED CONCEPTUAL HELP
FROM MATHEMATICS

For most of us, our intuitive notion of psychodynamics has been deeply shaped by Freud's powerful visual imagery of a dynamic unconscious alive with competing and clashing forces, elements fundamental to a psychology of conflict. And though Freud is criticized retrospectively for his reliance on Helmholtzian physics and fluid mechanics, it is difficult to imagine alternative models when describing conflict. Freud's notion of unconscious forces, the idea of a "dynamic" unconscious, relies on something like a linear vector mathematical model. Vectors have both magnitude and direction (e.g., the resultant of going 2 miles north, then 2 miles north, then 3 miles south is 1 mile north) and are helpful for describing forces in tension, as, for example, sailboats tacking against the wind. The concept of "neutralized" psychodynamic forces would be one such vector application. In psychodynamic work, we usually attempt to decipher retrospectively the component forces, or vectors, from the resultant complex compromise formations that we observe clinically. Conflict, defense, and neurotic symptom are all usefully examined within this heuristic model.

However, let us now perform a thought experiment with a hypothetical, and proverbial, camel, adding one straw at a time to our experimental subject's back. If we continue on this path resolutely, common wisdom has it that at some point, a dromedary catastrophe occurs—we have added the straw that breaks the camel's back. For the camel, the broken back is an end state and not merely the sum of the stress of individual straws. *A continuous and increasing stress has eventuated in a sudden and sharp change of state.* The camel's tolerance for the last straw is not best described by linear vectors (see Appendix, Note 1).

One analogous limitation of a linear vectorial model in our clinical work is that we, too, see phenomena that begin as continuous, for example, multiple losses leading to a parallel and increasing depression, but that then become qualitatively different or discontinuous, for example, melancholic or endogenous depression with psychotic features. Our vectors don't add up when it comes to an abrupt and qualitative shift; many of our patients seem to snap under the additional burden of just one more last straw.[2] Here unexpected help arrives from a newer branch of mathematics.

Zeeman (1976), a pioneer in this area of mathematical description, wrote:

> ... the world is full of sudden transformations and unpredictable divergences. .... A mathematical method for dealing with discontinuous and divergent phenomena has only been recently developed. The method ... can be applied with particular effectiveness in those situations where gradually changing forces or motivations lead to abrupt changes in behavior. For this reason the method has been named catastrophe theory. Many events in physics can now be recognized as examples of mathematical catastrophes. Ultimately, however, the most important applications of the theory may be in biology and the social sciences, where discontinuous and divergent phenomena are ubiquitous and where other mathematical techniques have so far proved ineffective. Catastrophe theory could thus provide a mathematical language for the hitherto "inexact sciences" [p. 65].

This is a field, ironically called "catastrophe theory," that is designed to explore last-straw phenomena. At a certain point, with enough continuous stress, a discontinuous phenomenon occurs: a bridge collapses, a bubble bursts (and, indeed, my camel analogy's back will break).

---

[2]And, lest I lose my psychotherapeutic perspective, I am here reminded of Elvin Semrad's comment, "The last straw is always the first straw."

Continuous and Discontinuous States: Some Visual Models

Sashin (1985; Callahan and Sashin, 1987, 1990; Sashin and Callahan, 1990) applied catastrophe theory models to discontinuous states in human experience, most notably to affect response. The catastrophe model is essentially a visual one, a branch of the mathematics of surfaces, or topology. The foundational mathematical formulas themselves are extraordinarily complex, but the beauty of the model lies in its intuitive visual presentation, which permits a descriptive use. Because of its intrinsic visual appeal, it seems appropriate to include here some figures; I hope the reader will bear with this discussion, which will wend its way to the problem of empathizing with alternate states of mind or, in different words, the problem of feeling into another's discontinuities in worldview and self-states.

Two Continuous Models for Anxiety

A continuous model for anxiety is shown in Figure 7.1. As stress increases, there is a parallel increase in anxiety. At some point, the anxiety is of enough intensity that we refer to it as panic.

A more accurate rendering would probably look like that shown in Figure 7.2, with a steeper rise of anxiety as stress mounts.

A Discontinuous Model

Figure 7.3 describes one of many possible discontinuous models. As stress increases, there is a continuous rise in anxiety until a sudden and discontinuous jump to panic occurs.

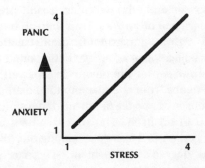

Fig. 7.1. A Continuous Model for Anxiety

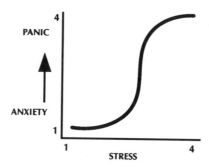

Fig. 7.2. Another Continuous Model for Anxiety

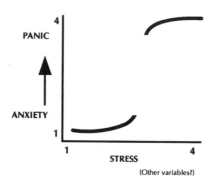

Fig. 7.3. A Discontinuous Model

Catastrophe Models

In Figure 7.4, I adapt, and grossly simplify, Sashin's work. In a certain sense, this model simultaneously combines features of both previous models. There is a continuous curve that describes a "normal" subject not prone to panic disorder and who, with increasing stress, has a gradual and increasing experience of anxiety. And there is a discontinuous segment for someone with an impairment, some structural difficulty (depending on your predilection: e.g., an ego deficit or a neurophysiological abnormality), that predisposes the person to panic attacks, represented by the jump in the figure from one plane to the next.

It is a two-dimensional model (in three-dimensional space), like an elastic sheet folded in on itself. The first two axes are as before. Of particular interest is the third axis, "Z," coming out toward us from the surface and labeled "degree of impairment." This axis is used to describe the relative inability of some people to tolerate feelings, an inability that predisposes them to discontinuous jumps in ego state (Sashin, 1985). We

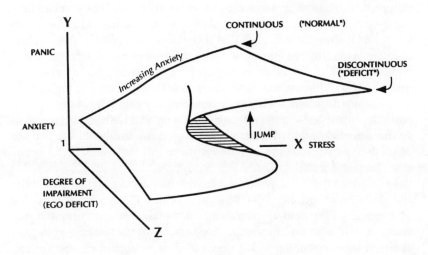

Fig. 7.4. A Catastrophe Model

might conceptually think of this axis in terms of some central dynamics, or—in the true spirit of Pierre Janet and modern ego psychology—in terms of ego deficits. It is a composite axis and in more complex models, Sashin breaks it down further.

Note that a deficit may be mild or severe, that there are degrees of impairment. I think Freud would have appreciated the possibilities of such a model because not only does it have the advantage of describing forces in dynamic tension, but it offers the hope of predicting divergent compromise formations. It should be noted that there are much more sophisticated and differently shaped models that handle more variables, which would be more in keeping with the extraordinary complexity of our clinical work.[3]

SOME IMPLICATIONS

As biologic psychiatry has become more sophisticated, there is a tendency to multiply diagnostic categories in pursuit of the differentiation of dis-

---

[3]See Sashin (1985) for an elaboration of the formal characteristics of this model and its special properties: different states, sudden jumps, hysteresis, inaccessibility, divergence.

crete etiologies that correspond to different medication effects (for example, the increasingly complex categories for anxiety corresponding to differential psychopharmacologic interventions). A dual theory of anxiety alone or even a multiple theory, though, might be misleading, for example, if one draws the inference that there must be a point-to-point correspondence to different etiologies. Given these newer models of discontinuous states, it is not clear to me that such dualistic conclusions are necessarily so: The same etiologic stress in different quantities may lead to dramatically different reactions or qualities of being; we do not have to postulate intrinsically different *beginning* points. Whether this proves to be the actual case with anxiety or not would not invalidate the general point that, as with events in physics, divergent outcomes might occur given the same initial stressors.

Perhaps with mental events the bifurcation occurs farther down the line. Perhaps, as both Nemiah (1984) and Sashin (1985) have suggested, the problem lies in a kind of psychological metabolism, for example, the ability to fantasize and to identify feelings. With particular ego impairments, a short-circuiting might occur leading to abrupt changes in ego affective states. Nemiah points out a conceptual similarity to Freud's notion of the "actual" neuroses. I have no doubt that there are physiological correlates to these psychological abilities, whether we find them in hemisphere lateralization or in neurotransmitter synthesis. As Nemiah indicates, these are different levels of description and discourse.

One point in describing this arcane work is that some of the seeming dichotomies and dilemmas in our field may be more apparent than real: We may be closer to a general synthesis than we yet appreciate. I further believe that, in a qualitative sense, these models can help in the understanding of discontinuous states of experience.

A TOPOLOGY OF POSSIBILITIES: PLANES OF BEING

I will be using the following figures for purely descriptive purposes, to describe anew familiar clinical phenomena. In this sense, the mathematical model is a metaphor, heuristic and pushing to fresh similarities and comparisons. Sashin (1985; Callahan and Sashin, 1987, 1990) uses these models not only in a descriptive sense but also in a predictive sense; that is, the models can derive inherent but not evident features. Moreover, these predictions should be falsifiable and hence possessing the quality of scientific propositions (by Popper's criteria [1968]). This pursuit, however, would be beyond the scope of my intentions here, which are to reexamine that complex problem described earlier: In attempting to empathize, a therapist confronts the dilemma of choosing from among experiential states and even from the possibilities of hitherto only vaguely experienced feelings.

In the case of a conflict, the states may alternate, one to the other. I have sometimes been astonished to witness a person's obvious and re- peated experience of a conflict and to realize only with my commenting on the conflict per se (for example, "You seem to be in conflict") that he or she has been entirely unaware of the idea of conflict itself, that two opposing sets of feelings might exist simultaneously. Previously, the person had only been buffeted about by the competing forces, unaware, shifting from one state to another.

One existential approach is to focus only on the state of mind in the here and now, that which is given and immediate (Havens, 1974). A parallel and powerful analytic approach (Schwaber, 1981, 1983) also emphasizes the subtle affective shifts in the present, in the relationship, now. Such approaches seem to resolve the technical (and theoretical) issue of hidden states by focusing on the "experience near" of the here- and-now of the session. It should be noted that in this respect the "experience near" focus has several points of rationale. One is to avoid imposing "higher level" theoretical constructs on the patient. That is, even though one can never avoid the imposition of points of view and abstrac- tions on the "purity" of the clinical material, one could rank the degrees of abstraction of our theoretical assumptions (Waelder, 1962) and, in this sense, attempt to approximate asymptotically the "real." This would be another way of restating the phenomenological ideal, the successive stripping away of the observer's layers of contribution to perception, revealing the hierarchy. One could draw a parallel to the idea of the hierarchy of defense mechanisms (Semrad, Grinspoon, and Feinberg, 1973, Vaillant, 1977)—that a measure of "health" inheres in the degree to which one's defenses sacrifice reality to maintain a tolerable psycholog- ical state. The point is that one can also attempt to designate the degree to which one's clinical approach more or less obscures what one is trying to observe cleanly.

Another rationale, more from therapeutic than from observational exigencies, is that the "experience near" will always seem more compel- ling to both patient and therapist and hence have greater emotional impact. This is, after all, Freud's genius in making the transference central to analytic treatment—the most real data of all are right there, occurring between patient and therapist, to them both and in the here-and-now. The transference may be a revised edition of an old play, but it is one in which both are actors and are not merely recalling in contemplation.

However, with severe psychopathological states and with mechanisms like splitting (and with the assumption of absent or undeveloped psycho- logical structures), the empathizer's task gets complex and paradoxical:

Does one empathize with the currently experienced state, the alternate hidden (or unavailable or even unexperienced) state, or the conflict itself?[4]

How does this all relate to the experiential level? What is the experience of deficit states? Here we grope about in our language: "emptiness," "fusion," "annihilation," "ego dissolution"—and what does this mean for self-perception and the process of empathy? That is, how does one feel into a state of mind that essentially involves a lack, an absence, a fault line? I will be arguing that one feels not only into a state of mind but also into the *possibility* of a state of mind.

Therapists sometimes approximate this idea when they talk of being an "auxiliary ego" to the patient, of helping the patient to bear his or her affects; that is, the very process of sharing a painful affect can diminish its intensity. This is to say, the mind of another can be entered, shared, even bolstered in its precarious struggle with feelings; we can "share" another's pain and thereby lessen its impact. I submit that these lend-lease auxiliary functions do two things: one is support in the manner of a temporary scaffolding (hence, "supportive" psychotherapy). But the scaffolding also creates the possibility for new structures—this is in part what Kohut (1977) refers to as "transmuting internalizations." The internalization of the therapist, the creating of structures, all begin only as possibilities. The scaffolding is the process of empathy itself.

It is possibilities that we precipitate. We feel into an aspect of the person that does not yet fully exist. Our patients follow us into those potential aspects of themselves: they feel into our feeling into their possibilities for themselves.

In Figure 7.5, state 1 represents a particular way of experiencing, a self-state, an aspect of worldview (for example, one side of splitting), or a feeling state.[5] State 2 would be a disparate, unintegratable, other self-state or aspect of worldview. State 3 is an inaccessible area—a potential area (even an avoided area) but one not yet fully established—such as ego or self-states that are nascent or undeveloped and hence unstable as they are currently constituted. They point the way to possibilities, or areas, that will change if the person develops, for example, affect tolerance. My contention is that this model represents a pictorial (mathematical) notion of possibilities. And that the self is, by its nature, *an entity in process* that

---

[4] And surely, here, one could argue the whole problem of empathy and the "unconscious" itself.

[5] I am mixing several terms and levels of theoretical abstraction that do not fit into a consistent theoretical context. I am doing this so that the reader might here take any of a number of possibilities and work them through, for example, self states in anorexia nervosa (Callahan and Sashin, 1987), or color experience in manic depressive illness, etc.

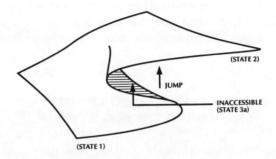

Fig. 7.5. States 1 and 2 and an Inaccessible, Unstable, State, 3a

the therapist envisions as possessing possibilities, potentialities for better or for worse.

See what has happened in our description. At a given time, we empathize with a state of mind (that is, if we are with the patient in the present, now). This state (for example, state 1 on the figure) does not remain stable (as Sashin puts it, it is "stably unstable"). The person will switch into the other state of mind at some point (state 2; there could be, of course, many more states—the dichotomy is for explanatory purposes). Our more distant point of view (not necessarily omniscient) allows us to imagine the multiple states of experience, previous and possible, that are unavailable to the imagination of the other. This density of unawareness is itself an important aspect of experience and frequently contributes to despair, as when one is deeply depressed. If we were to be truly in the other's shoes, we would be unaware of other states (for example, state 2), or dimly aware, or if aware of the state, unable to get to it in experience, and unaware of the middle and unstable position (state 3a). This position is not yet stable—its stability is a possibility that we are in the process of actualizing, working within a small anlage of this state, extending into it, and developing it as we go, like the serendipity of a rivulet carving its own bed (see Appendix, Note 2).

We are not merely extending our experience of the inner world of the other, we are taking the patient into an unrealized area of the patient's own worldview, an aspect that could not be tolerated before. *This new aspect of worldview, belonging to the patient, is paradoxically unfamiliar to the patient. We are into unknown areas of potential self-experience.*

Over time, this area becomes stable—the streambed deepened, reinforcing its own meandering engraving—and a change has occurred (in theoretical terms, an ego structure has been established, a series of transmuting internalizations solidified). Descriptively, the third area (state 3b) has been developed and extended in the figure and is now accessible from either state of being (states 1 and 2), existing as an alternative possibility of experiential state (Fig. 7.6) (see also Appendix, Note 3).

CASE EXAMPLE: INTO THE PAST— SALVAGING THE INNER CHILD[6]

Rather late in life, a man comes to therapy feeling lost about his life's direction. (Years later, I muse that he has lost his sense of his possibilities.) Though technically highly trained and with impeccable credentials, he has never felt at home in his work. His personal life too is in a shambles, his marriage about to fall apart.

About a year into the therapy, he comments on a movie he had just seen, *The Tin Drum*, that left him with disturbing feelings and strong visual images. I ask him about the most vivid images, and he describes the scene in which the little boy's mother is eating fish, "animal-like," as she was trying to induce an abortion. The scene still haunts him.

I wonder about the mother in the movie, a parent and care-giver, who was trying to get rid of, abort, a child—and did this resonate with his experience? No, he says; rather, in fact, he had felt sympathy for the mother, because the pregnancy was the consequence of an affair with a Romanian lover and she had always loved her son. Details of the movie now tumble out: a horse's head filled with eels; the father trying to get the mother to eat eels; the boy hiding in an armoire as the parents argued; the lover sexually stimulating the mother to get her over her distress and sadness—and the little boy observing; the mother then compulsively and disgustingly eating the fish, animal-like, deadened herself and gradually dying. I, too, now recall the movie from my own viewing and remember the horrific scene of eels coming out of the horse's head, an image of decay mixed with phallic sexuality. I comment on that image and how the boy watched his mother deteriorate; was that a point of familiarity in his life?

He recalls an intense visual memory of an ambulance coming to take his mother away, the last time he saw her. He cannot recall any feelings, just his being 4 years old and with this memory like a filmstrip (I *assume* that such feelings must be there; in Figure 7.6, time 1, this would correspond to state 3a). The woman in the movie looked like his mother, with a similar hair color and the "same skull structure." His life, I knew, had

---

[6]This case material also is adapted—and reexplicated—from Margulies (1989).

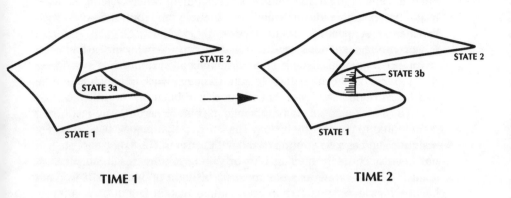

Fig. 7.6. States 1 and 2 and a Now Accessible, Stable State, 3b

changed dramatically after his mother had died; he had been farmed out to relatives who were not prepared or interested in having a child.

I comment that, like the little boy, he too had felt lost and lonely growing up (I am here extending into virtual areas of experience [Fig. 7.6, time 1, state 3a], though this was not evident to me at that clinical moment). He notes quizzically that someone else had once said this very thing to him—in fact, the therapist who had initially evaluated and referred him to me for psychotherapy. (To him, this is a new thought [Fig. 7.6, time 1, state 3a—an unstable state].) Nevertheless, as a boy, he had not experienced these feelings as such. It is curious to him: he understands how another person hearing his story would make that observation (that is, he empathizes with my attempt to empathize with him), but he simply had not felt it (although seeing how *I* would feel it from *his* story, he is about to follow me into his own experience). "When I think about it now, I should have screamed and hollered, but I never did." I ask why he didn't, and he replies that there simply was no awareness of doing such a thing. Not that he felt it was prohibited, it just was not a part of consciousness or even possibility. Nobody ever got angry around him; anger was not part of the language of his boyhood life; it was as if it were a foreign tongue. From my perspective, he was severely neglected after his mother had died, not physically abused, but ignored as irrelevant to the relatives entrusted with his care.

It was not until his adult life that he became capable of feeling deeply angry, and this when his first wife left him. Then he had had a dawning awareness of the experience of rage, that he wanted to hurt her. His sharp

pain at this time convinced him that he should seek help, and this too had
been a new thought for him: his spectrum of angry feeling states—
irritation, anger, sadistic urges, indignation, and outrage—had been
broadened, deepened, "complexified."

Recently, he had observed that for the first time in his life he had been
snapping at people, feeling angry immediately rather than retrospectively. In particular, he described an instance at work in which he felt he
had been treated shabbily, that the boss had been unjust. Injustice had
been a clear part of his upbringing: his referring physician had
commented to me that by history she learned that he had been severely
malnourished as a boy, found dazed in the streets. His foster parents had
not been adequately feeding him or taking care of his basic physical
needs. This too he never spontaneously brought up with me: It was not
harbored as an outrage to him but a simple, distant fact of his history.

The injustice feeling too was never before felt; as a boy, he said, he did
not experience it. More to the point, I later understood, he could not feel
it and not merely because it was repressed or defended against, but
because there was no internal mechanism to structure the complex
feeling. It was not part of his intrapsychic repertoire or worldview.

It was almost as if now, as an adult, he might go back and feel what he,
as a child, could not directly experience. As a child, he had no way to gain
access to the feelings, they remained unelaborated affects. It was not that
for him the memories and affects were *first in consciousness* and then
repressed, or even that they were in unconscious, developed form, and
split off from consciousness. For this man these feelings and memories
remained undeveloped, like a crowded and pale seedling that has never
seen light. Now he has access to a newly developing state of mind. (State
3b [Fig. 7.6, time 2] is accessible to him, and more stable.) We recall Freud
(1915): "all that corresponds in that system [*Ucs.*] to unconscious affects is
a potential beginning which is prevented from developing" (p. 178). These
are planes of existence that begin in possibility, virtual extensions of this
particular person's being—and that actualize and stabilize in the therapeutic dialogue.[7]

It is important to note that creativity is implicit in clinical listening
whether we try to remain neutral or not. The very disjunction of points of

---

[7]Only as this paper was in its final stages did I come across Modell's (1990) *Other Times,
Other Realities*. Drawing on Freud's concept of *Nachträglichkeit*, Modell develops a very
similar notion to the one elaborated here: "The therapist becomes the person with whom
one can reexperience trauma within a new context or experience for the first time what has
been absent in the past. Affects belonging to the past that were never expressed then can
now be recontextualized in current time. This is not just a simple catharsis but an actual
reorganization of memory. It is the process that provides a second chance" (p. 78).

view pushes a continual reappraisal of one's assumptions about oneself (e.g., when the therapist "just" asks a clarifying question—which then creates a reflective awareness in the patient as to why *this* particular question needed to be asked). This is to say, *simply* listening in an empathic dialogue is creative of new thoughts and perspectives as one empathizes with oneself through the medium of the other (Margulies, 1989).[8]

CONCLUSION

Is one function of psychotherapy to go back to do psychological work that could not be supported at an earlier time because of the lack of an internal framework? One can draw an analogy to an adult's rereading of influential childhood books: An older person comes back to the same book in a new context and with changed cognitive and psychological structures, so the understanding must be different because the possibilities that now present themselves are different. In terms of virtuality, one imagines oneself anew, one has an imago of oneself that in its revision is at first virtual and elusive. Affects, too, are felt to be discovered ("dis-covered," meaning uncovered)—but by discovery we really mean birth, elaboration, actualization.

Grief, for example, is already *there* and implicit in the blocked griever before and independent of the empathizer. But the empathizer's empathy with the unexpressed grief creates something new that allows the bearing and hence the elaboration of the affect into a fuller, deeper experience (i.e., an emotion with a larger complex configuration of ideas, memories, affects, self-context, and internal objects). My point here is that the empathizer works with an anlage of something powerful, something *almost* there in its fullness of potential, a seed for experience.

Semrad's straightforward language of the therapeutic process might here be reconsidered (Khantzian, Dalsimer, and Semrad, 1969). The unconscious is kept unconscious because of the person's inability to stay with that part of the self that feels intolerable and is split off. This aspect

---

[8]The decision to attempt to create directly new experience (for example, in the attitude of a "corrective emotional experience") is a different but related, complicated, and controversial matter, relying more heavily on the therapist's assumptions about which planes of being are needed for this individual. One, as it were, prescribes an area of experience which it is hoped the patient will claim as his or her own. There are, of course, a myriad of maneuvers along this spectrum—all fiercely argued in our literature—from admiring the patient to enhance his or her self-esteem to enacting aspects of the transference.

of self is not just split off but is a state of being that is unstable or inaccessible or both. That is, *staying* with the intolerable is not possible.

Semrad's tripartite treatment strategy translates simply:

1. Acknowledging: The therapist and patient enter into and experience the intolerable state of being (Fig. 7.6, time 1, state 3a).

2. Bearing: The therapist helps the patient *stay* (i.e., by sustaining, moving from time 1 to time 2) in a previously inaccessible area or state of mind with the help of the auxiliary strength of the therapist's ego/self.

3. Putting into perspective: The state of mind is held long enough to incorporate it into a changing worldview, the river carves its own bed (Fig. 7.6, time 2, state 3b). The bearing of intolerable affect itself creates the evolving framework to bear affect, stabilizing the state of mind as a new area of experience (see Appendix, Note 4).

It is important to bear in mind that I am here envisioning through metaphors. These mathematical/visual models are for descriptive purposes and are not so much rigorous theoretical derivations (though, as Sashin demonstrated, one could make them that way) as themselves temporary scaffolding to support a way of reexamining therapeutic encounters, elusive psychological states, unstable self-structures, and new and more integrated states of mind. And all until a new heuristic image, metaphor, or analogy extends us into fresh areas.

AFTERWORD

Jerry Sashin had an intense interest in the hidden planes of his models, the unexpected opening up of new folds, and the emergence of unseen possibilities. These nascent planes, constrained by the formal mathematical characteristics of the models, were heuristic, corresponding to variables in the more tangible world of psychodynamics. And so one might approach the models as theoretical guides, searching in the laboratory of the clinical situation for the correspondences.

Is it then that these models create new metaphors that allow us to graze the truth? The models are not in themselves the truth but merely an extension of our consciousness into the universe that unfolds before us as we shape and are shaped by it.

Someone once wrote that new languages create new thoughts. New languages then create the apprehension of possibilities previously hidden from view. And this is, of course, the ultimate value of art and science— our worldview expands, unfolds, and emerges to us in wonder.

We will miss Jerry and his lost possibilities.

REFERENCES

Basch, M. F. (1983), Empathic understanding: A review of the concept and some theoretical considerations. *J. Amer. Psychoanal. Assn.*, 31:101–126.
Callahan, J. & Sashin, J. (1987), Models of affect-response and anorexia nervosa. *Ann. N.Y. Acad. Sci.*, 504:241–259.
_____ _____ (1990), Predictive models in psychoanalysis. *Behav. Sci.*, 35:60–76.
Freud, S. (1915), The unconscious. *Standard Edition*, 14:161–208. London: Hogarth Press, 1957.
Havens, L. L. (1974), The existential use of the self. *Amer J. Psychiat.*, 131:1–10.
_____ (1978a), Explorations in the uses of language in psychotherapy: Simple empathic statements. *Psychiat.*, 41:336–345.
_____ (1978b), Explorations in the uses of language in psychotherapy: Complex empathic statements. *Psychiat.*, 42:40–48.
Horney, K. (1937), *The Neurotic Personality of Our Time*. New York: Norton.
Khantzian, E., Dalsimer, J. & Semrad, E. (1969), The use of interpretation in the psychotherapy of schizophrenia. *Amer. J. Psychother.*, 23:182–197.
Kohut, H. (1977), *The Restoration of the Self*. New York: IUP.
Margulies, A. (1989), *The Empathic Imagination*. New York: Norton.
_____ (1993), Contemplating the mirror of the other: Empathy and self analysis. In: *Self Analysis*, ed. J. Barron. Hillsdale, NJ: The Analytic Press.
Modell, A. (1990), *Other Times, Other Realities*. Cambridge, MA: Harvard University Press.
Nemiah, J. (1984), Anxiety and psychothyamic theory. In: *Psychiatry Update*, Vol. 3, ed. L. Grinspoon. Washington, DC: American Psychiatric Press.
Popper, K. (1968), *The Logic of Scientific Discovery*. New York: Harper & Row.
Proust, M. (1981), *Remembrance of Things Past*, trans. C. K. C. Moncrieff & T. Kilmartin. New York: Random House.
Sashin, J. I. (1985), Affect tolerance: A model of affect-response using catastrophe theory. *J. Soc. Biol. Struct.*, 8:175–200.
_____ & Callahan, J. (1990), A model of affect using dynamical systems. *Annual of Psychoanalysis*, 18:213–231. New York: IUP.
Schwaber, E. (1981), Empathy: A mode of analytic listening. *Psychoanal. Inq.*, 1:357–392.
_____ (1983), Psychoanalytic listening and psychic reality. *Internat. Rev. Psychoanal.*, 10:379–392.
Semrad, E. V., Grinspoon, L. & Feinberg, S. E. (1973), Development of an ego profile scale. *Arch. Gen. Psychiat.*, 38:70–77.
_____ (1977), *Adaptation to Life*. Boston: Little, Brown.
Vaillant, G. (1977), *Adaptation to Life*. Boston: Little, Brown.
Waelder, R. (1962), Psychoanalysis, scientific method, and philosophy. *J. Amer. Psychoanal. Assn.*, 10:617–637.
Zeeman, E. (1976), Catastrophe theory. *Sci. Amer.*, 234:65–83.

APPENDIX

Note 1.

Jerome Sashin (personal communication) clarified: A linear vector model of defense versus drive and its effect on behavior (with the formula $B = Dr - Def$; where B = behavior, Dr = drive, and Def = defense) might look like Fig. App. 1.

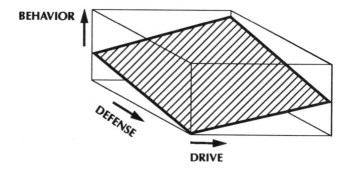

Fig. App. 1. A Linear Vector Model of Defense

A nonlinear model (with the formula $B^3 = Dr - B \times Def$) might appear as Fig. App. 2.

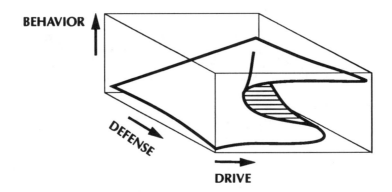

Fig. App. 2. A Nonlinear Model of Defense

Both are vector models of forces interacting. It should be noted that the nonlinear formula has the term B on both sides of the equation. That is, there is a recursive property of feedback of the terms upon themselves: B is a function of itself and is in part determined by its previous value. This circularity is a fundamental feature of nonlinear systems and, to be sure, of such processes as empathy, self-reflection, social interaction.

Note 2.

As Sashin put it, "The possibility (*any* possibility) always exists, the position is however unstable. To stabilize it, we expand and develop it by enlarging the basins of attraction. We go from a hill to a valley (Fig. App. 3)."

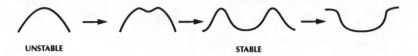

UNSTABLE   STABLE

Fig. App. 3.   The Stabilization of a Position

Note 3.

Sashin elaborates, "You must now expand to the butterfly [a more complex catastrophe model] to picture this, the cusp [our simpler, instructive model] does not allow for these possibilities (Fig. App. 4). State 3 is now a stable state accessible from 1 or 2."

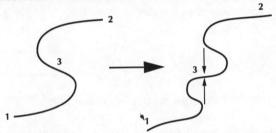

Fig. App. 4.   State 3 Becoming a Stable State Accessible from State 1 or 2

Note 4.

Sashin has provided some further explanation here that is invaluable: "Stable and inaccessible should not be confused; they are different properties and can be represented in various ways. For example, two-dimensional pictures can help us visualize an unstable state 3 becoming stable" (as in the previous Fig. App. 4). "Nevertheless such a state may also be inaccessible, though still stable" (Fig. App. 5 and Fig. App. 6).

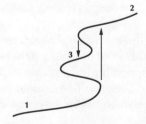

Fig. App. 5.   Inaccessible from State 1

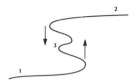

Fig. App. 6.   Stable but Inaccessible from Either State 1 or 2

Sashin recommended another pictorial approach, the metaphor of "basins of attraction," that is, "sinks in the psychological landscape." "To be empathic requires an awareness of possibilities. Seeing two disjoint extreme states (1 and 2) may seem to be a situation of 2 separate sinks" (Fig. App. 7. Especially note the discontinuities):

Fig. App. 7.   Disjoint Extreme States

"In fact these are possibilities—initially very slight, very unstable but nevertheless there. By focusing on them, they can be enlarged and made stable and accessible (Fig. App. 8).

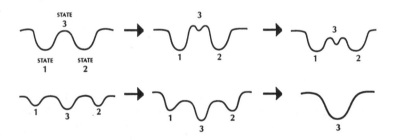

Fig. App. 8.   A Possibility Becoming Stable and Accessible

"When faced with a situation of disjoint extremes, . . . there are at least three choices: (a) a true absence of feeling in between (the 'true alexithymic'); (b) an unstable, inaccessible but possible state in between; (c) a stable but inaccessible state in between (the 'classic psychoanalytic' attitude). The usual debate is between those favoring choice (a) versus those favoring choice (c)."

In this chapter, I am, of course, emphasizing (b).

Chapter 8

AFFECT IN THE ELDERLY
Do Older People Feel Differently?

Alexander C. Morgan

The question contained in the chapter title actually comprises several questions. The first and obvious one is whether older persons have a different way of handling emotion: do we handle affect differently as we get older? This chapter demonstrates how older people experience emotions similarly to the ways they did as younger people.

More versions of the title question are: Do old people feel different *to* others? Do people working with elderly persons experience them differently from the ways they experience people of other ages? The feelings of therapists about their patients are a vital part of the therapeutic interchange. It applies just as much to our work with older persons because our countertransference feelings toward them are as central to their ability to change in therapy as is their own capacity for emotional experience.

Another way of hearing this question about the way older people feel constitutes the main focus of this chapter; namely, can older people change their capacity for affective experience, and if they can, *how* do they do it? Studies about the psychotherapy of older persons show that older people can and do go through changes in their way of experiencing emotions (Colarusso and Nemiroff, 1981; Erikson, Erikson, and Kivnick, 1986; Nemiroff and Colarusso, 1985). The important questions are: How can we explain the way the affects of older persons change? And how do they come to feel different? These are admittedly somewhat altered versions of the original question. The chapter will use some of the contributions of research on affects in infancy to address the question of how older persons undergo changes in their emotions in psychotherapy. Following a summary of what is known about affect and aging, together with an explication of certain pertinent aspects of research on affect in infants, the chapter focuses on the case of a woman in her 80s who during a course of psychotherapy substantially changed her way of dealing with her emotions. Then the findings of infant affect research are used to explore how these changes in her affect may have occurred.

It is certainly a long leap from infancy to the ninth decade, but bringing a developmental point of view to therapy is useful regardless of the age of the patient. Most of my work as an analyst, therapist, and consultant has been in connection with people in early and middle adulthood, and the principles useful with those in that age group are likewise useful with older persons. What we are learning about infant–mother interaction seems applicable to the therapy relationship regardless of the age of the patient, and this chapter deals with affective aspects of that interaction.

STUDIES ON EMOTIONS IN THE ELDERLY

Relative to the immense amount of data on physiologic and cognitive changes with aging that might impact on affect in the elderly, there is in fact meager research on aging and affect itself (Birren and Schaie, 1990; Schulz, 1985; Stevens-Long, 1990). Some confirm the popular notion that aging is associated with a rigidification and a dampening of feeling and behavior. Such data show that we become more cautious with increasing age, implying greater anxiety. This viewpoint is at variance with the experience of many who work with older persons (Erikson et al., 1986) and who contend that increasing age permits a greater ability to be reflective and somewhat calmer about life's vicissitudes and lends a greater potential for wisdom. This mellowing and greater degree of tolerance seem to indicate that older persons also have a greater capacity for emotion. However, both of these contrasting views of the emotions of older people are drawn from cross-sectional observations, and data based on more sophisticated and longitudinal birth cohort studies show little actual demonstrable change with advancing age itself (Field, 1991; Field and Millsap, 1991). For instance, in a study on various measures of flexibility (Schaie and Willis, 1991), there was no significant change in mental flexibility with advancing age if a birth cohort (everyone born around the same time) was followed over time. There were differences only if the comparison of flexibility was in a cross-sectional fashion; meaning, at a given time, say 1990, the older subjects performed less well on flexibility tests than did younger subjects. If the testing is examined over time, however, each group changed little. For example, the 80-year-olds in 1990 (born in 1910) were little different from what they were in 1980 or 1970, and they were always less flexible than the 70-year-olds (born in 1920) regardless of the year of the testing. In general, most other longitudinal studies of aging reinforce this finding of personality stability over time, and they contradict the stereotypic and negative views of increasing rigidity with advancing age (Field, 1991). Although these studies do not directly address affect and aging, they imply that the dynamics of emotion in older persons are similar to the way the persons dealt with emotion at earlier points in their life.

INFANT RESEARCH AND AFFECT THEORY

It is important to say that a number of areas of infant research could be applied to work with older persons. One could look at attachment theory that is based on work with infant–mother interactions, at studies of the infant's development of the ability for self-regulation of the changes of its own different states, or perhaps at the way the infant is involved in an intersystemic manner with its care-givers that shapes their behavior as much as the infant is shaped by them. Research on infancy is a rich area for further application to the way we work with adults, but the purpose of this chapter is to focus on the application of affect theory.

Tomkins (1962, 1963, 1981) was a central force in trying to describe what actually is observed with affect in infants, and Demos (1989) has amplified Tompkin's work and made further contributions to our understanding of affective development. Ainsworth et al. (1978), Barrett and Campos (1987), Emde (1985, 1988a, 1988b, 1991), Emde and Easterbrooks (1985), Izard and Malatesta (1987), Malatesta (1981), Sroufe (1988), Stern (1985, 1988), Tronick, Chon, and Shea (1986), Zeanah et al. (1989), and numerous others have also been studying infants and affect, particularly the interactional consequences of babies' expression of emotion and affective competence. With affect defined as the combination of physiologic, behavioral, and, by inference, subjective states that are associated together as responses to the environment, Tomkins wrote of discrete affects that are innate to the human organism, (in a sense being "hardwired" into the newborn). Tomkins described observing nine primary affective responses. Listed in both their moderate and intense forms (e.g., interest–excitement) and beginning with positive affects and moving to negative ones, the nine primary affects are interest–excitement, enjoyment–joy, surprise–startle, distress–anguish, fear–terror, anger–rage, shame–humiliation, contempt, and disgust. Ekman, Friesen, and Ellsworth (1972) and Izard (1971) have separately confirmed the presence of these specific affects in other cultures with the use of similar observational techniques.

What is important is less whether these are the exact affects present in newborns but rather the way the infant organizes and is organized by these affects. Affect in general then is seen as an amplifier to experience and therefore a motivator of behavior, and the specific affects are organized in a sequence that along with other affective sequences forms a script of affect and behavior. For instance, one can imagine a mother entering a room in which her baby has been sitting alone. For purposes of demonstration, one can assume that, in the past, reunions with her mother have been associated with the baby's affect of interest being superseded by joyous affect and then with Mother's picking the baby up and the baby's affect shifting to pleasant excitement. What will now be witnessed as we watch mother and baby is an affect and behavior script. The baby will respond with the affects of interest, joy, and excitement and with the behavior of extending its arms to be picked up. The first affect was interest, followed by joy, followed by excitement—all positive affects. Demos (1989) and Demos and Kaplan (1986) have shown the importance of the direction of these sequences, namely toward either positive or negative affects, with the direction's being related to the establishment of positive or negative self-esteem. Leaving aside the issue of self-esteem and focusing on the affective sequence itself with this baby, the example above clearly led to a positive affect: excitement. However, what would one see if, following the baby's interest and then joy, the mother ignored the child? Then the next affect in the sequence would be a negative one such as shame. If this negatively aimed sequence were repeated enough times, there would be a persistence of the sequences in such a way that affects of excitement would infrequently be seen in that baby, and instead, feelings of shame would predominate whenever the baby felt joy.

RELATIONSHIP OF INFANT AFFECT SEQUENCE
TO AFFECTS IN OLDER PERSONS

The foregoing affect sequences persist and become more and more reinforced with continued development. The way affect is managed in the early years becomes part of the continuity via which later continuous development unfolds. Thus in adults, including the elderly, one can see the way people experience their feelings as being connected to these early sequences of affects. To continue with the rather simplified examples given earlier, when that first baby is an adult, one could expect to see interest and joy being followed by excitement and a continuation of exploration of the world. With the second baby, however, interest and joy would be followed by shame and possibly withdrawal from the world of people. Obviously, the full picture of infant affect development and its relationship to adult affect is vastly more complicated than that, but it is hoped these ideas can be used as a model to explain the way older people can undergo a change in the way their affects are experienced.

CLINICAL MATERIAL

History

In order to demonstrate the way an older person can change his or her experience of affect, the case of an 80-year-old woman, Mrs. N, follows. Our work together was the first time she had had any contact with psychotherapy. She had always been hesitant to give much weight to the importance of feelings in her life. In her six years of therapy, she underwent considerable change in her experience of affect, particularly her anger.

Mrs. N and I met for two courses of therapy, the first for 18 months and then, after a break of 4 months, a second period of more than 4 years, most of which consisted of fairly regular visits every two weeks. Mrs. N had been a widow of 35 years and was referred by the physician husband of her daughter and only child for evaluation of how much of her bowel complaints were of psychological origin. She was agreeable to seeing me, though she felt she had no problems with her feelings and had never considered seeing a psychiatrist. She recurrently questioned what good talking with me would do, although at the same time she said she enjoyed coming to the sessions. She was of moderate height with thin white hair; she presented with a polite graciousness that also had a homespun quality to it; and she made frequent references to her rural interests, such as whittling, hooking rugs, or watching the leaves turn. She let it be clearly seen that she considered herself a New England Yankee country girl who felt virtue lay in the simple life of the farm and the woods.

She had grown up on a farm in Vermont. Her mother died when she was 2. She denied any feeling that she ever had a mother, saying instead she had been reared by her father and her older brother and sister. The hardships she suffered through her life are difficult to portray adequately by a simple recounting, because after her mother's death, she apparently suffered a new emotional trauma every year or so. Prior to her mother's death, she was already seen as independent, a trait that persisted throughout her development. After severe economic hardships, her father died of pellagra when she was 12, but Mrs. N said she had already been taking care of herself by then so she didn't remember feeling too bad. After spending her teenage years with some dour relatives and in a boarding school, she moved near her older, married sister. Her brother had abandoned his family some years earlier.

At age 21, Mrs. N married Milton, an older man with a domineering mother. They had a son, Teddy. However, Teddy died at age 1 of fulminating diarrhea. Because the doctors had reassured Mrs. N there was no need to stay at the hospital to care for him, she was sad and felt resentful toward the doctors. However, she never really got angry at them. A couple of years later, she and Milton had a daughter, Sally, who as a toddler also became quite sick and was hospitalized at one point. However, this time Mrs. N "saved" Sally by nursing her herself in the hospital in opposition to doctor's orders to go home. Again, this was all accomplished pleasantly, without anger.

Mrs. N spent most of her life working, first in homemade craft sales, which were lucrative enough to be useful during the economic depression, and later in clerical work in industry. She did not have a particularly close relationship with either Milton or Sally and got most of her pleasure from a sense of being responsible. Her husband died when she was 44, and she denies having much grief, instead feeling "You just had to do what you had to do." Sally was in college by then, and Mrs. N began a series of jobs that resulted in her moving around a lot on her own, mostly in small towns in rural New England. She enjoyed her life a great deal during this time, at times doing unusual and somewhat idiosyncratically rebellious things, such as arranging an adoption between two of her Welcome Wagon clients, a step that was beyond what her supervisors would have approved of. In her early 50s she experienced some sexual freedom that she had never before felt. When this relationship with Bill broke up, however, she reported that she had few feelings about it except that she claimed she had never thought there was much chance of the relationship's success. During her late 50s Mrs. N lived in a trailer on a wooded lot outside the small Vermont town where she worked, and at 62 she retired to a cottage she built on that property, again greatly enjoying the solitude. However, in her 70s the diarrhea and constipation that had bothered her all her life worsened dramatically, and that, combined with declining vision and back problems, resulted in her moving at age 78 into a housing unit for the elderly near Sally. She had extensive medical evaluations through the connections of her very successful physician son-in-law, Kenny, of whom she was both extremely fond and immensely proud. However, no adequate treatment could be found, and the only diagnosis was irritable bowel syndrome. At times she would even lose control of her bowels, and it was after several years of these medical evaluations that she began psychotherapy.

Course of the Psychotherapy

For the purposes of this discussion, the psychotherapy can be divided into three phases: the first, about a year and a half long, focused first on the somatic concerns and later Sally's worries about her mother's lack of involvement in activities; the second phase started four months after the termination of the first, was about two years long, and dealt with Mrs. N's feelings about the surprise collapse of her daughter's marriage and with the new experience for Mrs. N of feeling sadness and rage at her son-in-law; the third phase flowed out of the second without hiatus, lasted about three years, and addressed her generally increased attention to her emotions both currently and in the past.

Somatic Concerns and Lack of Involvement in Activities

In the first part of her treatment, when Mrs. N would talk about her bowel complaints, she would subtly ridicule her doctors for acting so important but not really knowing what her problem was. She denied feeling angry, saying she just wished they would admit they might not be able to give her some definitive cure. As we explored that wish and her difficulty in addressing what she wanted from her doctors, she eventually was able to assert herself and get some admission from them that not much more could be done for her other than intermittent symptomatic relief. At the same time, she began to pursue alternative health methods such as massage, yoga, meditation, and acupuncture, all of which she had already had some interest in and which she now found more helpful than any of her previous treatments.

It became clear the bowel symptoms were at least somewhat connected to a debate between Sally and Mrs. N about the extent of Mrs. N's involvement in activities at the elderly living site. Mrs. N used her symptoms as a reason she could not go out to teas, aquarium trips, and the like. She felt pressured by Sally to be more "social," but she never felt any irritation about it. As Mrs. N and I talked about her life, we discussed the friends she had had during her life, and although she had always been friendly with many people, she talked with feelings of both embarrassment and proud self-reliance that she had always preferred being alone. She felt she had always been on her own because she felt she "had never had a mother."

This led to my learning that Mrs. N. had a collection of her mother's letters to her own mother—Mrs. N's grandmother—and that one of Mrs. N's granddaughters had compiled them on an audiotape for Mrs. N, whose vision was too poor to decipher them. Thinking that certainly here lay a way into Mrs. N's emotional world, I suggested that she and I look them over. I myself found the letters both emotionally involving and fascinating for insights into her mother and her, but Mrs. N seemed to find them only mildly interesting and not very affectively involving. She did feel some pride that the letters gave evidence of her lifelong independence, with descriptions of her at 18 months as being a "trickster," and she maintained that throughout the difficulties of her life, she had just never let herself get upset. Eventually it became clear that in her current life, Mrs. N simply preferred a solitary life to the life her daughter thought would be good for her. She simply was not a "mixer," and after some review of this in the treatment, she brought herself to explain it to Sally, who was able to accept the accuracy of her mother's self-appraisal and stop pushing her.

Over time, Mrs. N's bowel symptoms had lessened somewhat, and she began to talk about ending our visits. I felt she had always kept me at something of a distance, often questioning what good talking with me did, but with her symptoms' being better, I agreed we had done the work for which she had come to see me. We terminated over a ten-week period that at the end did include some tears of gratitude along with her recurring comments that questioned how therapy helps anyone.

Grief for the Sudden Collapse of Her Daughter's Marriage

The second part of the treatment, Mrs. N's grief over the collapse of Sally's marriage, began four months after her previous visit. Mrs. N herself called me saying that she wanted to talk with me about her distress over learning that her much revered physician son-in-law, Kenny, wanted to divorce Sally in order to pursue a relationship with another woman. The next two years of treatment revolved around the emotional changes that this brought into Mrs. N's life. She was still very much the self-reliant woman, but she was open in her willingness to use me to help her with her feelings about Kenny. Her pain over Sally and Kenny was immense. She had believed Kenny to be as dedicated to her as he was to her daughter, and she was crushed that he could be so disloyal. Even though he had come to be a kind of ombudsman for her in the medical world and she had relied on him for advice as well as services, such as special salves, she spurned any attempts he made to maintain friendly contact with her.

Our work consisted of her talking about her anger at Kenny and her disquieting surprise that she could feel such hateful resentment toward him. These emotions made her feel bad about herself, and for several months her sleep and daily life were disturbed by thoughts about Kenny. Soon the involvement in psychotherapy did become adequate to help her distress, and much of the content of the therapy consisted of a fairly common type of grief work, except that Mrs N seemed to have little grief over her previous losses. She would recount the earlier importance of Kenny to her and her sense of betrayal at his turning away from Sally and, consequently, as far as she was concerned, away from her.

Mrs. N would find herself fantasizing about horrid fates for Kenny and then feel terrible, saying that she thought she had never hated anyone in her life and that such hatred toward Kenny meant she was a despicable person herself. She discovered, however, that she also enjoyed expressing her fury at Kenny. She composed a letter of complaints to Kenny, showing me several drafts of it. Each version varied only slightly in the amount of venom it contained, but she enjoyed deciding how many of the denigrating comments to take out or leave in. Her thoughts would turn to the doctors who had cared for her son and whom she blamed so severely but whom she had never confronted. She became aware that in fact there had been a large number of persons toward whom she had felt hatred. But because she had never previously felt she could express such rage, much of the therapy revolved around her beginning to permit herself to verbalize the resentment felt toward Kenny and other disappointing figures in her life. She actually arranged a fairly sadistic confrontation with Kenny in which she invited him to bring her the last jar of salve he was to get for her and upon his arrival presented him with the letter she had written.

There was certainly reality in Kenny's abandonment of her, but she also devalued him, making his loss more tolerable. Because she seemed comfortable with the extent of her fury, I chose to stay with that affect and did not interpret the narcissistically defensive aspects of her denigration of Kenny. Kenny was also an object of anger displaced from other persons who had disappointed her, including her own husband. Most notable was the fact that despite her resentment toward Kenny, she was also able to experience him as having been "another Teddy," the son she had lost 60 years previously. To her puzzlement, she would cry about losing Teddy as she "had never done before" and be angry at the doctors for failing to save him. With the emergence of some of this sad affect there was a gradual shifting of the therapy away from a focus on Kenny to some exploration about her feelings and her own view about herself.

*Introspection and Recovery of Memories Regarding Past
and Current Emotions*

After about two years, the third phase of Mrs. N's treatment, involving her greater attention to her current and past emotional states, was heralded by her telling a dream in which she was wandering in some woods, trying to find her way back home. She felt lost but not scared so much as puzzled about how to find the right path. There were other people walking around who did not seem lost but who also did not respond to her questions about her path home. The woods felt pleasant, but it was distressing to feel it was time to go home but to find no path. It was not exactly her home that she was seeking but more somewhere "back where I was supposed to be." I asked her about where she was supposed to be, and her continued associations were to her "life having been a search" and to a sense of never having "found herself."

In the three years after that dream, Mrs. N and I paid increasing attention to her own view of herself and her emotions. Six months later, she had a dream about being in a female psychiatrist's office and being frustrated by failing to get the appointment she had come for. This reminded her about a feeling of anger at her female internist and about the way she feels doctors generally disappoint her. In fact, throughout her life she has felt the same way toward people in general; she likes them but finds them frustrating. She added that only her acupuncturist and I are excluded from this overall list of frustrating people. She then thought of the relief she felt when she first came to see me and got "permission" to keep to herself in her apartment. Eventually we were able to work on the transference implications of that dream to the extent that she could acknowledge a sense of unfairness about my changing one of her appointments. It wasn't a feeling of fully expressed anger, but there *was* some irritation she was able to experience. In general, my attempts at interpretation of transference implications netted little, whether it related to angry feelings or libidinal ones. There were clearly both, including at a later point some erotic elements in her talk of her memories, for instance, when she talked about her lover, Bill.

In the time following this second dream, she talked of feeling "surer of myself as a person." She also began to explore in therapy as well in her substantial readings (via books on tape) the literature of body–mind problems, such as Benson's *Relaxation Response* (1975). Through this process, she wondered whether some of her somatic symptoms were due to her having, as she put it, "blocked out the tension," by which she meant the emotional discomfort, that would have been natural for her to feel during the "tough times" of her life.

For a while there was an intellectualized manner to her looking back on these times. However, after some discussion about her concern that she had no "identity," a fact she connected to having been so independent, she did begin to relate a variety of memories in a way that was new for her, namely, with more feeling. She had previously seen her losses in life as not particularly out of the ordinary and certainly not cause for much feeling. She said it was as if she could bring herself to admire herself but not necessarily to like herself. She had felt that in the face of the losses, she had simply been doing what she had had to do to get by. For the first time now, she began to talk of her memories with the sense that she had suffered without much acknowledgment of it by herself or others.

The first memories she began speaking of in this new way were those of the unhappy days with her husband, Milton. She had always told of them as being unhappy, but she was now saying that she ought to have been angry at him. She gave details about how distant he was and how she now saw that his habit of naps after supper were part of a pattern by which he avoided having sex with her. She now regarded this as a deprivation, having had freer sexual experiences in the years after Milton's death. She felt that as a young married woman, she had known nothing about sex because she grew up "almost as an orphan," again a painful thought that felt new to her. She summed up this more sympathetic view of herself by saying, "I guess I really was a po' little critter back then but didn't know it."

Other stories came out in this new way, with feelings of anger that she had suffered more than she had realized at the time. She described the pain and fury at the doctors at the time of Teddy's death, before which she had accepted their reassurances and gone home from her nursing him only to hear he died a few hours later. She also recounted the ambiguity and uncertainty in her relationship with her lover, Bill, whom she now felt had not been fair to her. She had told these stories before but without much feeling, but she now said she could feel sorry for herself in having had to go through such ordeals.

In one session during her 86th year, she told me the following in a way that was so impelling that I immediately wrote it down. She said, "You know, I didn't know I had emotions before. Emotions were juvenile, childish, but now I think feeling what I've been through makes me somehow more peaceful about myself, almost serene at times. I compare me now and me then, 15 years old, or even 40 years old, and I feel more put together now." "How does it work that way?" I asked. "Well, I think they [the feelings] were in there, but I didn't know it. You know, for example, there was that business with Bill. I never felt the sexual fun with Milton, but it must have been there because I felt all those feelings with Bill. I think it has been that way with a lot of things—I didn't have feelings, but now I do."

LATE-LIFE AFFECTIVE CHANGE
AND THE MODEL OF AFFECT SEQUENCES

Returning now to the question posed at the beginning of the chapter, what permitted this woman to feel so different? There are a number of possible theoretical vantage points from which to explain such change. It could be said that in the course of the therapy, Mrs. N underwent a regression in her ego defenses that permitted a reorganization of these defenses so as to permit more access to her affect. From the point of self psychology, the changes could be described as being due to an internalization of some of the selfobject functions for her affect management that were part of a selfobject transference with me. Other theoretical perspectives might likewise describe the process of the treatment using still other terminology. However, affect theory that is based on infant research seems the most data-based and sensible way of describing what went on with Mrs. N.

Remembering the data on affect sequences in studies on infants reviewed earlier in this chapter, one can say with a fair degree of confidence that Mrs. N had sequences of affects that led both to a dampening of affective expression in general and to negative affects in particular. For the purposes of this chapter, the dampening of her affective expression will be left aside, and the focus will be on the negative affects themselves and the way they underwent change. For instance, in a simple example, one can imagine Mrs. N as a child having an affective sequence of surprise over a loss superseded by angry feelings that were then followed by shame and withdrawal when the important people around her failed to tolerate her anger.

What permitted her to change in her ninth decade? I think there was a combination of first a trauma—the break between Kenny and Sally—which caused a great upwelling of affect, including the rekindling of prior unacknowledged feelings over her losses. Second, because of her earlier connection with me, which she had used to assert her wish to live her life in her usual solitary way, she now had a relationship in which she could try out a new sequence of affects, both in reality and in the transference. In fact, I felt particularly involved with her after that first year-and-a-half segment of her treatment because somehow I was quite taken by the resilience and courage I heard contained within the stories she told me. I was impressed by the ways she had used the experience of her increasing years to broaden and deepen her responses to her life, one demonstration of which was the fact that in her 80s she agreed to see a psychotherapist for the first time. It was clear that she found me to be someone with whom she could share her affective experience, and that was a different response from ones she had had when her affective sequences were laid down early in her development. Instead of the old sequence of surprise over the loss followed by anger and followed by shame, a new sequence was developed in which the anger was followed by a kind of enjoyment. She very much relished her fury at Kenny, and although there was a sadistic element in her enjoyment of letting Kenny have it, her overall experience following her anger was positive. It was in the repetitive reworking of this sequence of her feelings in the therapy and of her reminiscences about her past that a new way of experiencing her affect evolved. From the case material, it is clear that Mrs. N's affects other than anger also underwent change, and I believe the process of change in those affects was similar to what I have outlined about her anger.

CONCLUSION

As a way of summarizing, we should return to the questions put forth at the beginning of this chapter. First, the research data and Mrs. N's story both indicate that older persons do not really experience their feelings differently from those in other age groups. Second, although the role of countertransference feeling about older patients was not directly addressed, it should be clear by implication from Mrs. N's case that, if therapists can remain open-minded about an older person's having feelings as does a person of any other age, one can witness very dramatic changes in that person. With Mrs. N, despite her distancing stance, I found myself very involved with her story and her current experiences, and I am certain that that involvement lent a particularly positive tone to the interaction between us and consequently had a strong influence on the course of the therapy. Third, the findings of infant research—in this case, the work in the area of affect sequences—are applicable to the treatment of adults as well and are an extremely useful way of explaining how our patients, including our older ones, can change their feelings. Psychotherapists are only now beginning to make use of research on infants in work with adults, and it is hoped that the results of the leap taken in this chapter, from age 1 to age 91, will remain a convincing demonstration of the benefits that lie ahead in trying to make the jump that clinicians are always trying to make, back and forth, between what is seen in the nursery and what is seen in psychotherapy.

REFERENCES

Ainsworth, M. D. S., Blehar, M., Waters, E. & Wall, S. (1978), *Patterns of Attachment*. Hillsdale, NJ: Lawrence Erlbaum Associates.

Barrett, K. C. & Campos, J. J. (1987), Perspectives on emotional development II. In: *Handbook of Infant Development*, ed. J. D. Osofsky. New York: Academic Press.

Benson, H. (1975), *The Relaxation Response*. New York: Morrow Press.

Birren, J. E. & Schaie, K. W., eds. (1990), *Handbook of the Psychology of Aging* (3rd ed.). San Diego, CA: Academic Press.

Colarusso, C. A. & Nemiroff, R. A. (1981), *Adult Development*. New York: Plenum Press.

Demos, V. (1989), A prospective constructionist view of development. *Annual of Psychoanalysis*, 17:287–308. New York: IUP.

_____ & Kaplan, S. (1986), Motivation and affect reconsidered: Affect biographies of two infants. *Psychoanal. Contemp. Thought*, 9:147–221.

Ekman, P., Friesen, W. V. & Ellsworth, P. (1972), *Emotion in the Human Face*. New York: Pergamon Press.

Emde, R. N. (1985), The affective self: Continuities and transformation from infancy. In: *Frontiers of Infant Psychiatry, Vol. 2*, ed. J. Call, E. Galenson & R. Stimston. New York: Basic Books.

_____ (1988a), Development terminable and interminable I. *Internat. J. Psycho-Anal.*, 69:23–42.

_____ (1988b), Development terminable and interminable II. *Internat. J. Psycho-Anal.*, 69:283–296.

_____ (1991), Positive emotions for psychoanalytic theory: Surprises from infancy research and new directions. *J. Amer. Psychoanal. Assn.*, 39–44 (suppl.):5–44.

_____ & Easterbrooks, M. A. (1985), Assessing emotional availability in early development. In: *Early Identification of Children at Risk*, ed. W. K. Frankenberg, R. N. Emde & J. W. S. Sullivan. New York: Plenum Press.

Erikson, E. H., Erikson, J. M. & Kivnick, H. Q. (1986), *Vital Involvement in Old Age*. New York: Norton.

Field, D. (1991), Continuity and change in personality in old age. *J. Gerontol.*, 46:299–308.

_____ & Millsap, R. E. (1991), Personality in advanced old age. *J. Gerontol.*, 46:271–274.

Izard, C. (1971), *The Face of Emotions*. New York: Appleton-Century-Crofts.

_____ & Malatesta, C. Z. (1987), *Perspectives on Emotional Development I*. New York: Wiley.

Malatesta, C. Z. (1981), Infant emotion and the vocal affect lexicon. *Motivat. Emot.*, 5:1–23.

Nemiroff, R. A. & Colarusso, C. A. (1985), *The Race Against Time*. New York: Plenum Press.

Schaie, K. W. & Willis, S. L. (1991), Adult personality and psychomotor performance: Cross-sectional and longitudinal analyses. *J. Gerontol.*, 45:275–284.

Schulz, R. (1985), Emotion and affect. In: *Handbook of Psychology of Aging* (2nd ed.), ed. J. E. Birren & J. W. Schaie. New York: Reinhold, pp. 531–543.

Sroufe, L. A. (1988), The role of infant-caregiver attachment in development. In: *Clinical Aspects of Attachment*, ed. J. Belsky & T. Nesworski. Hillsdale, NJ: Lawrence Erlbaum Associates.

Stern, D. N. (1985), *The Interpersonal World of the Infant*. New York: Basic Books.

_____ (1988), Affect in the context of the infant's lived experience. *Internat. J. Psycho-Anal.*, 69:233–238.

Stevens-Long, J. (1990), Adult development: Theories past and future. In: *New Dimensions in Adult Development*, ed. R. A. Nemiroff & C. A. Colarusso. New York: Basic Books, pp. 125–170.

Tomkins, S. (1962), *Affect, Imagery, Consciousness, Vol. I*. New York: Springer.

_____ (1963), *Affect, Imagery, Consciousness, Vol. II*. New York: Springer.

_____ (1981), The quest for primary motives: Biography and autobiography on an idea. *J. Personal. Soc. Psychol.*, 41:306–329.

Tronick, E. Z., Chon, J. E. & Shea, E. (1986), The transfer of affect between mothers and infants. In: *Affective Development in Infancy*, ed. M. Yogman & T. B. Brazelton. Norwood, NJ: Ablex.

Zeanah, C., Anders, T., Seifer, R. & Stern, D. (1989), Implication of research on infant development for psychodynamic theory and practice. *J. Amer. Acad. Child Adol. Psychiat.*, 28:657–668.

Part III

TRAUMA, ADDICTION, AND PSYCHOSOMATICS

This section explores some of the common clinical manifestations of developmental deficits in the somatic-cognitive integration of affect experience, affect tolerance, affect verbalization, and affect defense. Failure to master these developmental tasks is associated with psychological trauma, addiction, and psychosomatic conditions, which clinical conditions constitute the substance of this section.

Chapter 1 of this book described how trauma can result in developmental arrest or regression along the line of affective development. Such regressive swings caused by psychological traumatization result not only in disruption in affective development with respect to affective defenses, verbalization, and tolerance but sometimes also in the normal capacity for affective experience. Severely traumatized individuals develop relatively enduring pathological conditions with respect to affect and associated selfobject representations. Some of the chapters in this section explore these themes in more detail.

Bessel van der Kolk, in "Biological Considerations About Emotions, Trauma, Memory, and the Brain" looks more carefully at the psychobiology of trauma, specifically at the enduring biological effects resulting from the intense emotional stimulation that accompanies psychological trauma. Drawing on the pioneering work of Pierre Janet about 100 years ago, van der Kolk discusses Janet's views that the excessive emotional stimuli accompanying trauma (what Janet called "vehement emotions") interfere with normal memory storage and result in a variety of specific posttraumatic stress symptoms. Intrusive reexperiencing, generalized numbing of responsiveness, and a spectrum of developmental and behavioral manifestations represent the typical long-term results of psychological traumatization. Van der Kolk asserts that these excessive emotional states are often accompanied by intense physiological arousal. According to van der Kolk, such intense autonomic arousal is essential to understanding the effects of trauma. Van der Kolk reviews the relevant neurobiological evidence, drawn from both animal and human studies, to construct a model that explains how intense stress arousal can produce a range of trauma symptoms. Intense autonomic stimulation is registered in the amygdala, which assigns emotional significance to emotional stimuli. Excessive emotional stimulation in turn interferes with normal conscious memory storage by the hippocampus, and memories of the excessively emotional event or trauma are laid down in an alternate memory system, usually in the form of visual or bodily memories of the trauma. Under conditions of similar arousal, these trauma memories and associated affects can return in the form of intrusive reexperiencing. Repeated or sustained arousal can result in a withdrawal state. Motivation to avoid this withdrawal can result in a pattern of sensation-seeking behavior and addiction to trauma. Repeated or sustained arousal can also result in opiate release. Thus, arousal contributes to both the intrusive reexperiencing and the generalized numbing of responsiveness, which are the two poles of posttraumatic adjustment.

Sarah Haley, in "I Feel a Little Sad: The Application of Object Relations Theory to the Hypnotherapy of Posttraumatic Stress Disorder in Vietnam Veterans," addresses the effects of trauma on the development of both affect, self-representation, and object representations. Focusing specifically on war traumatization, notably on the effects of the Vietnam war on veterans, Haley demonstrates how war traumatization can result in pervasive developmental disruptions, especially in veterans in late adolescence. She discusses in some length the case of David, a 32-year-old combat veteran who served in Vietnam when he was 20 and who subsequently suffered from 12 years of debilitating symptoms prior to treatment. A unique aspect of the case is David's participation in Operation Phoenix, a counterinsurgency program in which David committed systematic atrocities. Haley shows how David's participation in Operation Phoenix resulted in arrested superego development, ego passivity, and pervasive affective numbing. Under hypnotherapy, David was able to progress along a developmental continuum to relative autonomy from archaic superego demands, to increased ego activity, and to the rediscovery of his capacity to experience feelings.

Edward Khantzian, in "Affects in Addictive Suffering: A Clinical Perspective," addresses the issue of affect development and substance abuse. Khantzian views substance abuse from a biological, social-cultural, and developmental perspective, but his work places heavy emphasis on a developmental understanding of alcoholism and substance abuse. Khantzian sees alcoholism and substance abuse as arising from developmental deficits in affective regulation, especially with respect to affect tolerance, affect verbalization, and affect defense. These are also associated with disturbances along the line of self-representational and object representational development, especially with respect to nuturance and comfort. Khantzian reviews substance abuse as an adaptive means or a "solution" to the problem of regulating affective states. Moreover, according to Khantzian, the interaction between the specific deficit in affective development and the pharmacological properties of a given substance determine the preferential selection of a substance by a given addict. Khantzian shows how analgesic, sedative-hypnotic, and stimulant drugs are preferentially selected by different addicts according to affective developmental deficits that are manifest. He further explains how the negative and painful consequences of substance abuse can also serve an adaptive function in regulating or controlling affects that are vague, confusing, and otherwise unmanageable.

Daniel Brown, in "Stress and Emotion: Implications for Illness Development and Wellness" reviews how illness development is also related to the developmental failures in the midrange along the continuum of affective development—from affect experience through affect defense and especially in respect to affect tolerance and affect verbalization. He briefly reviews the extensive research on stress and illness development to demonstrate how stress can contribute to illness development along two pathways: through disregulation of the autonomic nervous system and through the disregulation of the immune system. Then he reviews the research relevant to affect and illness development. Drawing largely on a few selected, well-designed prospective studies, Brown shows how the development of cancer and heart disease is significantly correlated with a personality style of suppressing the expression of affect, when all other risk factors are controlled. In developmental terms, there is a growing body of evidence to suggest that developmental failures in affect tolerance, affect verbalization, and affect defense are not healthy and may predispose the individual to disregulation of the autonomic or immune system or both and therefore to serious illness.

Chapter 9

BIOLOGICAL CONSIDERATIONS ABOUT EMOTIONS, TRAUMA, MEMORY, AND THE BRAIN

Bessel A. van der Kolk

The rapidly converging knowledge in psychology and the neurosciences makes it increasingly untenable to make a clear distinction between mental problems that are "really due to a chemical imbalance" and others that are "really all in the head." The fact is, of course, that all mental representation necessarily is processed on a biological level. The symptoms of posttraumatic stress disorder (PTSD), which have long been understood to have a clear psychobiological foundation, were first called a "physioneurosis" by Kardiner (1941). The availability of animal models of inescapable shock and the understanding of the biological effects of disruptions of attachment in nonhuman primates make psychological trauma a particularly promising area to explore the interface between mind and body.

Over a century ago, Pierre Janet (1889) first proposed that what makes experiences traumatic are the "vehement emotions" that accompany them. In line with current knowledge of psychobiology, he claimed that overwhelming affects interfere with proper information processing on a symbolic, linguistic level, which results in the characteristic posttraumatic memory disturbances (van der Kolk, Roth, and Pelcovitz, 1992). Extreme emotions, according to Janet, cause memories to be split off from conscious awareness and to be stored, instead, as visual images or bodily sensations. Fragments of these "visceral" memories return later as physiological reactions, emotional states, nightmares, flashbacks, or behavioral reenactments (van der Kolk and van der Hart, 1989).

Janet looked for a biological explanation for this reaction to trauma, asserting that the initial emotions were accompanied by physiological hyperarousal, which set up (by conditioning) continued emergency reactions to subsequent stresses. He claimed that as long as the experience could not be appropriately integrated within the totality of a person's experience and as long as it remained dissociated, it would continue to ("subconsciously") exert influence on how one reacts to subsequent events. Clearly, fear needs to be tamed before proper integration of experience can occur: excessive emotions interfere with proper cognitive appraisal and with appropriate action. Experiences that overwhelm people's coping mechanisms set the stage for further excessive emotional reactions to subsequent stressors. These intense affects will continue to be accompanied by inordinate physical (motoric or visceral) responses, usually without much awareness that such reactions to current experiences once were appropriate to earlier experiences, but now are no longer relevant. As Krystal (1978) pointed out, after traumatization, affects loose their function as signals and come to interfere with effective functioning.

Kardiner (1941), who first systematically defined posttraumatic stress for American audiences, noted that people who are unable to overcome traumatic experiences continue to live in the emotional environment of the traumatic event, with enduring vigilance for and sensitivity to environmental threat. He suggested that the startle reaction probably was a conditioned reflex and considered it to be the central element of the posttraumatic stress reaction, relating it to the development of affect disregulation and psychosomatic symptoms in these patients. He claimed, "This is present on the battlefield and during the entire process of organization; it outlives every intermediary accommodative device, and persists in the chronic forms. The traumatic syndrome is ever present and unchanged." Contemporary studies, generally unaware of this earlier research, have continued to scientifically test the conceptions, and they confirm that the stress hormones of traumatized people continue to react to minor stimuli as emergencies (van der Kolk and Saporta, 1991). Recent and as yet unpublished studies by Shalev's, Pitman's and my research group have all shown that traumatized people do not habituate to startle. Normal people are able to dampen repeated presentations of loud noises, but traumatized individuals do not habituate: their central nervous system (CNS) is unable both to make the accommodation that such a stimulus is not threatening and to block it out to attend to other cues. For such persons, even familiar stimuli continue to be perceived, on a physiological level, as potential threats. The neocortex is eminently equipped to provide rationalizations to justify such inordinate responses to current stimuli. Traumatized persons thereby lose track of the fact that their responses are rooted in past experience rather than current exigencies.

SYMPTOMATOLOGY OF POSTTRAUMATIC STRESS

Starting with Kardiner (1941) and Lindemann (1944), a vast literature on combat trauma, crimes, rape, kidnapping, natural disasters, accidents, and imprisonment has shown that the basic nature of the trauma response is biphasic. Hyperalertness, hyperreactivity to stimuli, and traumatic reexperiencing alternate or coexist with psychic numbing and anhedonia. This response to trauma is so consistent across traumatic stimuli that it is safe to say that the CNS seems to react to any overwhelming, threatening, and uncontrollable experience in quite a predictable pattern. Regardless of the circumstances, traumatized people are prone to react emotionally to current stimuli that are (unconsciously) reminiscent of the trauma with responses that were appropriate to the original stimulus but that lack current adaptive value. A conditioned emotional response takes place, in which they react with affects that belong to past events rather than to current experience. Like the bell for Pavlov's dogs, any number of elements that started off as neutral stimuli for traumatized people but that (unconsciously) became associated with the trauma may become conditioned to signify threat. Thus, a large number of trauma-associated stimuli may trigger intrusive memories of the trauma. Over time, all traumatized people seem both to develop a poor tolerance for arousal and to respond to stress in an all-or-nothing way (van der Kolk et al., 1992). The loss of neuromodulation that is so central in PTSD (van der Kolk et al., 1992) seems to be at the core of Krystal's (1978) observation that in traumatized people, affects have lost their function as signals. As a result, they tend to go immediately from stimulus to response without being able to make the intervening psychological assessment of the meaning of their emotions. This in turn makes them prone to freeze or, alternatively, to overreact and intimidate others in response to minor provocations (van der Kolk and Ducey, 1989). Their intense, unmodulated emotions interfere with psychotherapy by preventing remembering and working through painful memories. Instead they re-create extremely stressful interpersonal relations. In response to excessive reactivity to environmental stimuli, both body and mind attempt to block out external stimuli. This results in the characteristic numbing response of PTSD.

Somatic Arousal and Intrusive Reexperiencing

Kardiner (1941) pointed out that the mind is better able than the body to block out conditioned stimuli: while people with PTSD tend to deal with their environment by *affective* constriction, their *bodies* continue to react to certain stimuli as if there were a continuing threat of annihilation. The past decade has seen important advances that clarify the link between psychological states and their accompanying biological abnormalities. Many contemporary investigators have found that traumatized individuals respond to stimuli reminiscent of the original trauma with significant conditioned autonomic reactions, as measured by heart rate, blood pressure and electromyogram (Blanchard et al., 1986; Dobbs and Wilson, 1960; Kolb and Mutalipassi, 1982; Malloy, Fairbank, and Keane, 1983; Pitman et al., 1987). Confirming and expanding on the James-Lange theory of emotions, contemporary researchers (Rainey et al., 1987; Southwick, in press) have shown that autonomic arousal precipitates either panic attacks or flashbacks (exact reliving experiences) of earlier trauma in most subjects with PTSD.

Numbing of Responsiveness

Numbing of responsiveness may be registered as depression, anhedonia, psychosomatic reactions, or dissociative states. In contrast to phasic intrusive PTSD symptoms, numbing is tonic and part of patients' baseline functioning. It interferes with the ability to explore, remember, and integrate experience, and it undermines the capacity to fantasize and symbolize, which are essential for finding new meaning. Contemporary studies have linked numbing to alterations in both noradrenergic and endogenous opiate functioning (van der Kolk and Saporta, 1991).

DEVELOPMENTAL LEVEL INFLUENCES THE
PSYCHOBIOLOGICAL EFFECTS OF TRAUMA

Most studies on PTSD have been done on adults, particularly war veterans, but in recent years, a small prospective literature has emerged that calls attention to the differential effects of trauma at various age levels. Anxiety disorders, chronic hyperarousal, and reenactments have been described with some regularity in acutely traumatized children (Bowlby, 1973; Pynoos and Eth, 1975; Stoddard, Norman, and Murphy, 1989; Terr, 1991). In addition to the reactions to the discrete, onetime traumatic incidents documented in these studies, intrafamilial abuse is increasingly recognized as producing complex posttraumatic syndromes. This recognition opens up the boundaries between the current concept of PTSD and what we have provisionally called "the trauma spectrum" (Herman, Perry, and van der Kolk, 1989; van der Kolk, 1988). A whole range of neurobiological abnormalities is beginning to be identified along this spectrum: prospective studies by Putnam (unpublished data) show major neuroendocrine disturbances in sexually abused girls compared with normals. Psychiatric patients who engage in self-injurious behavior and who appear to achieve a desired internal state change in response to self-harm invariably seem to have a history of severe childhood trauma. Their behavior has been associated with abnormalities of the endogenous opiate, serotonin, and catecholamine systems (Bach-y-Rita 1974; van der Kolk et al., 1991). Research in the past decade has shown that many children who have been victims of intrafamilial abuse have chronic problems with affect modulation, ranging from extremes in hyperreactivity to psychic numbing (Cicchetti and Carlson, 1989; Green, 1980).

The biological effects of developmental trauma have been best studied in young nonhuman primates, which in many ways resemble young human beings. Forty years of primate research has firmly established that early disruption of the social attachment bond reduces the long-term capacity to cope with subsequent social disruptions and to modulate physiological arousal. Young primates with disrupted early attachments seem to lack the essential synchrony with peers to form comfortable partners in social hierarchies, play, grooming, or sex. These behavioral abnormalities have been well correlated with neurochemical disregulation, including the magnitude of the catecholamine response, the duration and extent of the cortisol response, and a number of other biological systems, such as the serotonin and endogenous opiate systems (Kraemer, Ebert, and Lake, 1984; Reite and Field, 1985). In these animals, even mildly stressful stimuli provoke excessive emotional and behavioral responses that appear to be rooted in neurochemical abnormalities.

AFFECT AND MEMORY

One hundred years ago, Pierre Janet (1889) suggested that the basic functions of the memory system are the storage and categorization of incoming sensations into a matrix for proper integration of subsequent internal and external stimuli. A century later, the neurobiologist Gerald Edelman (1987) proposed that the basic function of the CNS is to "carry on adaptive perceptual categorization in an unlabeled world . . . that cannot be prefigured for an organism" (p. 7). Edelman goes on to say that after birth, categorization is the most fundamental of mental activities. "With sufficient experience, the brain comes to contain a model of the world" (Calvin, 1990, p. 261). It is now widely accepted that memory is an active and constructive process and that remembering depends on existing mental schemas, "an active organization of past reactions or of past experiences which must always be operating in any well-adapted organic response" (Bartlett, 1932, p. 201). Mandler (1979) asserted that

> a schema is formed on the basis of past experience with objects, scenes, or events and consist of a set of (usually unconscious) expectations about what things look like and/or the order in which they occur. The parts, or units, of a schema consist of a set of variables, or slots, which can be filled or instantiated in any given instance by values that have greater or lesser degrees of probability of occurrence attached to them [p. 263].

In other words, preexisting schemes determine to what extent new information is absorbed and integrated.

The particular emotional state in which people find themselves at the time an event takes place will affect what prior meaning schemes are activated and will determine into what preexisting patterns new sensory information is integrated. In general, once a particular event or bit of information becomes integrated in a larger scheme it will no longer be accessible as an individual entity, but because it has become attached to previous meaning schemes, the memory will be distorted both by prior experience and by the emotional state prevailing at the time the memory is laid down.

Memories generally are malleable by reworking and recategorization, unless they somehow are frozen into the mind. One particular aspect of traumatic memories is that they are fixed in the mind and are not altered by the passage of time or the intervention of subsequent experience. The power of these overwhelming memories has always been a central preoccupation of students of the mind. Four generations ago, Pierre Janet noted that, "All the famous moralists of olden days drew attention to the way in which certain happenings would leave indelible and distressing memories—memories to which the sufferer was continually returning, and by which he was tormented by day and by night" (Janet, 1919, p. 589). One of the hallmarks of PTSD is the intrusive reexperiencing of elements of the trauma in nightmares, flashbacks, or somatic reactions. Intrusive recollections of traumatic memories are the hallmark of PTSD; in our studies on posttraumatic nightmares, traumatic scenes were reexperienced at night over and over again without modification (van der Kolk et al., 1984). Rorschach tests administered to trauma victims demonstrated an unmodified reliving of traumatic episodes of ten, twenty, or thirty years ago (van der Kolk and Ducey, 1989). So how does memory occasionally escape integration and instead get "fixed" to resist further change? Today's knowledge of neurobiology allows us to speculate about underlying biological mechanisms.

One way in which fixation of memory occurs is by myelinization: developmentally, the brain is extremely plastic until axons are myelinized, which occurs in different parts of the brain at different ages but which is complete by the end of puberty. Modern research (Jacobs and Nadel, 1985; Schachter, 1990) indicates that infantile amnesia is the result of lack of myelinization of the hippocampus. However, even after the hippocampus is myelinized, the hippocampal localization system, which allows memories to be placed in their proper context in time and place, remains vulnerable to disruption by intense emotional states: the emotional experience is remembered, but the precise context is lost (van der Kolk and van der Hart, 1991). Traumatic memories can be "fixed" and left unintegrated by intense emotional activation at the time of the event and by the lack of opportunity to do anything about it. Janet (1889, 1909) described that the combination of intense arousal ("vehement emotions") and paralysis of action in response to threat interfere with proper information processing and appropriate adaptation. The inability to act appropriately to threat leads to both hypermnesia and amnesia about the event.

Autonomic arousal is mediated by the locus coeruleus (LC), which functions as the "alarm bell" of the CNS. The LC goes off, if it functions properly, under situations of threat only. In traumatized people, however, it is liable to get activated by any number of conditioned stimuli. When activated, it secretes noradrenaline or after prolonged or severe stimulation, endogenous opiates. These, in turn, dampen perception of pain—physical as well as psychological. It is likely that in humans, just like in animals, long-term potentiation of neuronal connections made during intense autonomic hyperarousal is at the core of the repetitive, fixed, intrusive reliving of traumatic memories when people later find themselves in a state which resembling the original one. The states of physiologic arousal, activation of neurotransmitter systems, and access to particular memory tracks all seem to be interconnected (van der Kolk and Saporta, 1991, van der Kolk and van der Hart, 1991).

In traumatized people, visual and motoric reliving experiences, nightmares, flashbacks, and reenactments seem to be preceded by physiological arousal. There is growing evidence (Rainey et al., 1987; Southwick, in press; Squire and Zola-Morgan, 1991) that autonomic arousal causes preferential access to memories that were originally laid down under conditions of similar arousal. This is known as state-dependent learning. During states of intense autonomic arousal, memories are laid down in ways that powerfully influence later interpretations of experience. This phenomenon has been attributed to massive noradrenergic activity at the time of the stress. The activation of long-term augmented memory tracts by autonomic arousal may explain why current stress is experienced as a return of the trauma. Thus, in humans, state-dependent emotions and learning seem to be closely intertwined, just as they are in other animal species: the retrieval of memories and trauma-related states is to a large degree dependent on the context in which the remembering occurs (i.e., it is dependent on the emotional state of the object) (Bower 1981; Putnam, 1989). The more the contextual stimuli resemble conditions prevailing at the time of the original storage, the more memory retrieval is likely. Conversely, the more often people find themselves in emotional states resembling the traumatic one, the more they will "remember" the trauma. Traumatized people continue to experience extremes of hyperarousal and numbing, which makes them vulnerable to continue to reexperience traumatic memories in proportion to their disordered state of arousal. This underscores the importance of autonomic stabilization in people with trauma histories. Without such stabilization, they continue to react to a variety of stimuli with affective responses that were appropriate to a previous traumatic event but that currently merely serve to disorganize them.

TRAUMA AND THE LIMBIC SYSTEM

The limbic system is the (unconscious) part of the brain that guides the emotions that stimulate the behavior necessary for self-preservation and survival of the species. It is responsible for such complex behaviors as attachment seeking, nurturing of self and others, mating, care giving of the young, hierarchy dominance, and territoriality. In lower animals, removing the neocortex while leaving the limbic system intact results in few easily observable behavioral changes: they go on with their self-preservational and reproductive life, including proper care of the young (MacLean, 1985). During both waking and sleeping states, signals from the sensory organs continuously travel to the limbic system, where they are scanned for their significance before being passed on to the conscious brain (the neocortex) for further attention. Experiments with two critical areas of the limbic system have shown that damage to the hippocampus causes major memory impairment.

The Amygdala

The amygdala is a component of the limbic system that assigns emotional significance to incoming stimuli. Electrical probes in the amygdala of monkeys show varying degrees of electrical discharge, depending on the significance of various incoming stimuli (Kling and Steklis, 1976): the amygdala attaches affect to objectively neutral stimuli. Partial or complete ablation of the amygdala causes monkeys to be less fearful and more willing to interact with novel stimuli (Squire and Zola-Morgan, 1991). The amygdala uniquely integrates complex information about the external world and emotional states. Moreover, in humans, this integration may be extended to include internal representations of the external world in the form of memory images with emotional experiences associated with those memories. Thus, of all brain areas, the amygdala is most clearly related to affective states. Roughly speaking, it assigns free-floating feelings of significance, truth, and meaning to experience (MacLean, 1985) which the neocortex (consciousness) then further elaborates and associates with larger schemes.

The Septohippocampal System

The septohippocampal system, anatomically next to the amygdala, plays an important role in the evaluation, categorization, and storage of incoming stimuli. It evaluates the meaning of incoming stimuli by comparing them with previously stored information and determines whether they are associated with reward, punishment, novelty, or nonreward. The hippocampus thus is thought to be the evaluation center involved in behavioral inhibition, obsessional thinking, inhibition of exploratory behavior, scanning, and construction of a spatial map (O'Keefe and Nadel, 1978). It performs that most essential of mental activities, the categorization of experience in the light of previously acquired knowledge. After the septohippocampal system categorizes incoming stimuli, it disengages from active control of behavior. Unless incoming information is endowed with particular significance, such as threat, novelty, or reward, it is not passed on to conscious mental processing: most processing of experience is done outside of awareness (Schachter, 1990).

The hippocampus is essential for proper memory function: if experience is to be translated into stable long-term memory, then the hippocampus must be engaged at the time of learning. The hippocampus may serve as a device for forming conjunctions between ordinarily unrelated events or stimulus features, which are processed and represented by distinct cortical sites (Ademec and Stark-Ademec, 1987). In this sense, the hippocampal system is a storage site for a simple memory, a summary sketch, or an index.

The hippocampal connections with the neocortex are the main communication routes between the neocortex and the limbic system and thus presumably between conscious and unconscious mental experience. Therefore, for conscious experience to effect changes in the limbic system, it needs to take the pathways necessary for recategorization of experience by means of the septohippocampal system.

A variety of external and internal stimuli affect hippocampal functioning: stress-induced corticosterone production decreases activity of the hippocampus (Pfaff, Silva, and Weiss, 1971), affecting the interpretation of incoming stimuli in the direction of emergency or fight/flight responses. The neurotransmitter serotonin plays a crucial role in the capacity of the septohippocampal system to activate inhibitory pathways that prevent initiation of emergency responses until it is clear that they will be of use. Decreased septohippocampal functioning due to of low levels of serotonin may account for increased aggression in response to stress and for hyperreactivity to external stimuli (Sheard and Davis, 1976). Serotonin reuptake blockers reverse the inhibition of behavior caused by previous punishment (Cook and Sepinwall, 1975). In our laboratory, we have shown that the serotonin reuptake blocker fluoxetine has a remarkable capacity to decrease psychic numbing in people with PTSD. On the Rorschach, percepts that previously were dominated by traumatic material were, after treatment with serotonin-enhancing agents, reinterpreted as nonthreatening stimuli (van der Kolk et al., unpublished data). Hence, alterations of relative serotonin levels in the limbic system may produce dramatic changes in subjective perceptions of reality in the direction of threat or safety.

Interactions Between the Amygdala and the Hippocampus

High-level stimulation of the amygdala (the equivalent of intense affective experience) interferes with hippocampal functioning: intense affect inhibits proper evaluation and categorization of experience. Behavioral disposition toward defensiveness and aggression (some aspects of character) is encoded in the pattern of distribution of how neural information flows through a variety of limbic circuits. Both nature and nurture greatly affect these traits: animals can be selectively bred for aggression or defensiveness, and in many animal species, early experience can permanently and predictably affect relative tendencies to attack or withdraw. Early differences in defensive responses are the behavioral signature of early differences in this neurodevelopmental process (Ademec, 1991).

LONG-TERM EMOTIONAL CHANGES FOLLOWING TRAUMATIC STRESS

The hippocampus, as we have seen, records in memory the spatial and temporal dimensions of experience. It does not fully mature till the third or fourth year of life. In contrast, the system that subserves the experience of the quality (feel and sound) of things (roughly located in the amygdala) matures much earlier (O'Keefe and Nadel, 1978). Thus in the first few years of life, only the quality of events, but not their context can be remembered. As the CNS matures, memory storage shifts from primarily sensorimotor (motoric action), to perceptual representations (iconic), to symbolic and linguistic modes of organization of mental experience. Even after that, the hippocampal localization system remains vulnerable to disruption: severe or prolonged stress can suppress hippocampal functioning (Gray, 1982; Nadel and Zola Morgan, 1984; Sapolsky, Krey, and McEwen, 1984), 1982), creating memory storage outside of the hippocampal memory system, a hypothesized system dominated by affective experience, with little capacity for categorization and placement in space and time. Even adults who are exposed to a traumatic situation experience "speechless terror." The totality of the experience cannot be integrated on a symbolic, linguistic level. Failure to arrange the memory in words and symbols leaves it to be organized on a somatosensory or iconic level—as somatic sensations, behavioral reenactments, nightmares, and flashbacks. As Piaget (1962) pointed out, "It is precisely because there is no immediate accommodation that there is complete dissociation of the inner activity from the external world. As the external world is solely represented by images, it is assimilated without resistance (i.e., unattached to other memories) to the unconscious ego." The memories therefore cannot be easily translated into the symbolic language necessary for linguistic retrieval. This results in amnesia for the specific context of traumatic experiences (based in the hippocampus) but not the feelings associated with them (based in the amygdala) (Ademec, 1991; Sapolsky et al., 1984). The memory is reexperienced as a behavioral state, a somatic sensation, or a visual image instead.

In animals, high-level stimulation of the amygdala (the equivalent of intense affective experience) has been shown to interfere with hippocampal functioning. Translating this from a neurobiological to a psychological level, this means that intense affect inhibits proper evaluation and categorization of experience. What makes an experience traumatic, on the neurobiological level, is that incoming experience is evaluated by the amygdala as being of great emotional significance, without the chance for proper categorization of the experience by the septohippocampal system. Thus, under conditions of threat, the hippocampus shuts down its categorization function, preventing the incoming stimuli from being integrated with previously acquired knowledge. The experience is not stored in conscious, "explicit" memory and instead is laid down in alternative memory store, which Jacobs and Nadel (1985) have called the "taxon" system: the emotions and visceral reactions related to past experiences are remembered, but they are not clearly recalled as being derivative of an experience that belongs to a different time and space. When evoked, they are affectively experienced as a contemporary terror, or physical sensation, without clear recognition that they are memories of a past event rather than a current threat that is responsible for the current state of body and mind. These acute, unmodified reliving experiences (in the form of flashbacks, panic reactions, and nightmares) then become new traumatogen stimuli, sensitizing the organism to react even more strongly to reminders of past trauma. In other words, the reminders of trauma seem to become more and more affectively charged over time. The task of therapy with people who have stored terrifying information on a visceral level is to help them remember the fragments stored in the taxon system and recategorize them in the ways that ordinary memories are stored, by attaching context and meaning.

In animals, the sensitization that occurs when they are repeatedly exposed to stressful stimuli is called kindling. In this model, ever smaller stimuli are required to elicit the same, or larger (electrical or emotional), discharges. Using kindling models, Ledoux, Romansky, and Xagoris (1989) and Ademec (1991) have shown that, following increasing responsiveness of the amygdala and the hippocampus to small electrical stimuli are a lasting increase in behavioral defensiveness and a lasting decrease in predatory aggressiveness. In reaction to stimulation of the amygdala (equivalent to emotional arousal), animals whose temperament and prior experience disposed them to be insensitive to threat and prone to attack tended to have increased activation of the amygdaloid-hippocampal neuronal circuits, which facilitates attack, whereas in highly defensive animals, different pathways were activated, causing further behavioral inhibition (Adamec and Stark-Adamec, 1986, 1987). Both nature and nurture greatly affect these traits: animals can be selectively bred for aggression or defensiveness, while early experience can permanently and predictably affect relative tendencies to attack or withdraw in many animal species (Adamec, 1991; Adamec and Stark-Adamec, 1987).

Thus, early experience affects how organisms react to trauma and to subsequent stress: early exposure to threat renders particular hippocampal cells more sensitive to subsequent excitatory input, which permanently lowers their firing threshold. Behavioral disposition toward defensiveness and aggression (comparable to aspects of people's character) is encoded in the pattern of distribution of neural information flow through a variety of limbic circuits. In (temperamentally) defensive animals who previously have received strong electrical stimulation of the amygdala subsequent excitatory stimuli cannot drive the hippocampal cells necessary for attack, which is the normal response in animals that have not previously received such amygdala stimulation. The opposite occurs in (temperamentally) uninhibited animals. Earlier stimulation of the amygdala stimulates a more intense attack response as a reaction to appropriate stimulation. If the situation is analogous in people, then trauma will activate aggression in those with a previous dispositions in that direction, and comparable affects will make people who temperamentally are more shy, anxious, and clinging more inhibited.

THE "RETURN OF THE REPRESSED" IN SITUATIONS OF THREAT

Under ordinary conditions, most previously traumatized individuals can adjust psychologically and socially. Studies have shown this to be true of rape victims (Kilpatrick et al., 1985a; Kilpatrick, Veronen, and Best, 1985b), battered women (Hilberman and Munson, 1978), and victims of child abuse (Green, 1980). Nonhuman primates subjected to extended periods of isolation may later become reasonably well integrated socially. However, these people and animals do not respond to stress in the same ways as their nontraumatized peers. This has best been observed in nonhuman primates. Studies in the Wisconsin primate laboratory have shown that even after an initial good social adjustment, heightened emotional or physical arousal causes an increase in stereotyped activity as well as inappropriate social behavior in the form of either withdrawal or aggression (Kraemer et al., 1984). Animals with a history of trauma also have much more intense catecholamine responses to stress, as well as a blunted cortisol response (Coe, Weiner, and Rosenberg, 1985). Even monkeys that recover in other respects tend to respond inappropriately to sexual arousal, and they misperceive social cues when threatened by a dominant animal (Novack and Harlow, 1979).

Stress causes a return to earlier behavior patterns throughout the animal kingdom. In experiments in mice, Mitchell, Osborne, and O'Boyle (1985) found that arousal state determines how an animal reacts to stimuli. In a state of low arousal, animals tend to be curious and to seek novelty. During high arousal, they are frightened, avoid novelty, and perseverate in familiar behavior regardless of the outcome. Under ordinary circumstances, an animal chooses the most pleasant of two alternatives. When hyperaroused, it seeks the familiar, regardless of the intrinsic rewards. Thus, shocked animals returned to the box in which they were originally shocked, in preference to less familiar locations not associated with punishment. Punished animals actually increased their exposure to shock as the trials continued. Mitchell concluded that this perseveration is nonassociative; that is, uncoupled from the usual reward systems, animals seek optimal levels of arousal (Sheldon, 1969), which mediates patterns of alternation and perseveration. Because novel stimuli cause arousal, an animal in a state of high arousal avoids even mildly novel stimuli even if it reduced exposure to pain.

THE COSTS OF PLEASURE AND THE BENEFITS OF PAIN

Solomon (1980) has proposed the existence of an "opponent process theory of acquired motivation" to explain how people can learn to enjoy stimuli that initially provoked intense negative affects. He pointed out that frequent exposure to stimuli, both pleasant or unpleasant, may lead to habituation—a gradual decrease in the emotional response to that stimulus. At the same time that habituation occurs, people experience withdrawal or abstinence states when the initially frightening stimulus is withdrawn. The feelings that accompany this withdrawal state can take on a powerful life of their own and may become effective sources of motivation. In drug addiction, for example, the motivation changes from "getting high" (pleasure) to controlling a highly aversive withdrawal state. In contrast to drug taking, which initially is pleasant, many initially aversive stimuli, such as sauna bathing, marathon running, and parachute jumping, may also be eventually perceived as highly rewarding by people who have repeatedly exposed themselves to these frightening or painful situations. Parachute jumpers, sauna bathers, and marathon runners all feel exhilaration and a sense of well-being in their initially aversive activities. These new sources of pleasure become independent of the fear that was necessary to produce them in the first place. Solomon concludes that certain behaviors can become highly pleasurable: ". . . if they are derived from aversive processes they can provide a relatively enduring source of positive hedonic tone following the removal of the aversive reinforcer."

Solomon and colleagues have applied these observations to imprinting and social attachment. Their research showed that young animals responded with increasing distress to repeated separations (Hoffman and Ratner, 1973). Habituation did not occur, and attachment in fact increased, provided that the imprinting object was presented at fairly regular intervals. In similar experiments with non-human primates, it was found that the protest phase abates over time, but separation continues to be followed by despair, regardless of the number of trials. Animals earlier exposed to repeated separations are more vulnerable to increased distress upon later separations: "Repeated exposures to the imprinting object took less time and fewer exposures than did the original exposures." Solomon and coworkers established experimentally that animals and people become habituated to the original stimulus, whether it is morphine, parachute jumping, or marathon running, but the withdrawal syndromes that follow a large number of arousing events retain their integrity over time, and they recur when the original stimuli are reintroduced (Solomon, 1980). Thus, the positive reinforcer loses some of its power, but the negative reinforcer gains power and lasts longer: parachute jumpers continue to feel exhilarated after jumping, even when they feel less fear beforehand. Solomon hypothesized that endorphins are secreted in response to certain environmental stresses and play a role in the opponent process. We have found some evidence that supports this view (van der Kolk and van der Hart, 1989; Pitman et al., 1990).

TRAUMA AND THE ENDOGENOUS OPIATE SYSTEM

The numbing in responsiveness in PTSD has historically been conceptualized only in psychological terms, as a defense against reliving memories of the trauma, but recent research has opened up new understandings of the complex biology of this aspect of PTSD. Stimulation-induced analgesia (SIA) has been described in experimental animals following a variety of inescapable stressors such as electric shock, fighting, starvation, and cold water swim (Kelley, 1982). In these severely stressed animals, opiate withdrawal symptoms can be produced equally by termination of the stressful stimulus or by naloxone injections. Thus, severe, chronic stress in animals results in a physiological state that resembles dependence on high levels of exogenous opiates (Maier and Seligman, 1984; Terman et al., 1984).

Encouraged by the finding that fear activates the secretion of endogenous opiate peptides (Bolles and Fanselow, 1980) and that SIA can become conditioned to subsequent stressors and to previously neutral events associated with the noxious stimulus, we confirmed the hypothesis that in people with PTSD, reexposure to a stimulus resembling the original trauma causes the secretion of endogenous opiates, which appears to account for emotional blunting, and possibly the dissociation, that people experience when they are presented with a recurrent traumatic stimulus (van der Kolk and van der Hart, 1989; Pitman et al., 1990). These early findings may represent a clue to the biological basis of why it is that people who experience overwhelming emotions may deal with them by numbing and dissociation.

PAIN, NUMBING, AND RECOVERY

When young animals are isolated, and older ones attacked, they respond initially with aggression (hyperarousal–fight–protest), and if that is ineffective, with withdrawal (numbing–flight–despair). Fear-induced attack or protest patterns serve to attract protection for the young and to prevent or counteract the predator's activity in mature animals. During external attacks, pain inhibition is a useful defensive capacity, because paying attention to pain would interfere with effective action to counteract attack (Siegfried, Frischnecht, and Nuñez, 1990). During aggressive encounters, responses to pain would compromise the effectiveness of defensive reactions: grooming or the licking of wounds would attract the opponent and stimulate further attack. Thus defensive and pain-motivated behaviors are mutually inhibitory. In nature, organisms are provided with Stress Induced Analgesia (SIA), which allows them to feel little pain while engaged in defensive activities. We have been able to demonstrate that in human beings, opiate-mediated SIA occurs in response to traumatic stimuli as well (Pitman et al., 1990; van der Kolk et al., 1989). We concluded that Beecher (1956) was right when, after observing that wounded soldiers required less morphine, he speculated that "strong emotions can block pain" because of the release of endogenous opiates. After prolonged exposure to stress, animals show increasing activation of endogenous opiate substances, which produce an overall reduction of activity, leading to immobility and delay of panic escape. This behavioral inhibition eliminates cues that might otherwise provoke further attack. It is likely that dissociative reactions in people are part of this same complex of opiate-mediated behaviors, which occur after prolonged exposure to severe uncontrollable stress. In animals, memory is impaired when the situation can no longer be affected by activity. Both the freeze response and panic interfere with effective memory processing. These responses seem to be terminal defensive ways of allowing organisms to not "consciously experience" or to not remember situations of overwhelming stress (and which hence keep them from learning from experience). As long as animals remain analgesic, they do not engage in recuperative behaviors. In contrast, when pain starts being actively experienced, animals cease fighting or freezing, and they turn their attention to providing themselves with recuperative maneuvers directed at the locus of injury and the healing of wounds, such as licking and grooming (Siegfried et al., 1990). Thus, the pain motivational system activates self-care behavior, which includes suitable places to rest the body. Increasing pain tends to shift behaviors from defense to recuperation.

CONCLUSIONS

The languages we use to speak about the functions of the brain and the functions of the mind may often seem untranslatable and mutually exclusive. However, the issues of how the past is processed and how it continues to affect current emotions, perceptions, and behaviors force us to attempt to be bilingual, lest we become lost in provincial conceptualizations and partial understandings about the meanings of suffering and healing. The remarkable new insights into how emotions affect memory and how mental schemes (and neuronal organizations) determine perceptions can help us begin to understand both the development of self-systems and the fragmented compulsions to repeat and reenact. Fear needs to be tamed so that people are able to think and be conscious of current needs. This bodily response of fear can be mitigated by safety of attachments, by security-of-meaning schemes, and by a body whose reactions to environmental stress can be predicted and controlled. One of the great mysteries of the processing of traumatic experience is that, while the trauma is being experienced as speechless terror, the body continues to keep score and react to conditional stimuli as a return of the trauma. When the mind is able to create symbolic representations of these past experiences, however, there often seems to be a taming of terror, a desomatization of experience. The need to be able to, probably literally, endure pain in order to attend to recuperation is obvious from animal research. The implications for the psychotherapy of severely traumatized, numbed human beings is also obvious. As Charles Ducey and I found in the Rorschach in Vietnam veterans (van der Kolk and Ducey, 1989), patients were unresponsive to outside influences (for good or evil) as long as they remained in a state of psychic numbing. When pain returned, and intrusions were reexperienced in the emotional life of these patients, they tended to feel easily overwhelmed, but at the same time, they became available to attempt improved self-care. The task of therapist and researchers alike continues to be to understand what memories are related to what affects, when to explore affects in order to allow conscious remembrance of past horrors, and when to focus on recuperative behavior.

REFERENCES

Ademec, R. E. (1991), The role of the temporal lobe in feline aggression and defense. *Psycholog. Rec.*, 41:233–253.
_____ & Stark-Ademec, C. (1986), Limbic traces and interictal behavior. *Internat. J. Neurology*, 20:117–126.

_____ & Stark-Adamec, C. (1987), Behavioral inhibition and anxiety. In: *Perspectives on Behavioral Inhibition*, ed. J. S. Reznick. Chicago: University of Chicago Press.

Bach-y-Rita, G. (1974), Habitual violence and self-mutilation. *Amer. J. Psychiat.*, 131:1018–1020.

Bartlett, F. C. (1932), *Remembering*. London: Cambridge University Press.

Beecher, H. K. (1956). Relationship of significance of wound to the pain experienced. *J. Amer. Med. Assoc.*, 161:1609–13.

Blanchard, B. E., Kolb, L. C., Gerardi, R. J., Ryan, P. & Pallmeyer, T. P. (1986), Cardiac response to relevant stimuli as an adjunctive tool for diagnosing post-traumatic stress disorder in Vietnam veterans. *Behav. Ther.*, 17:592–606.

Bolles, R. C. & Fanselow, M. S. (1980), A perceptual-recuperative model of fear and pain. *Behav. Brain Sci.*, 3:291–323.

Bower, M. (1981), Mood and memory. *Amer. Psychol.*, 36:129–148.

Bowlby, J. (1973), *Attachment and Loss. Vol 2.* New York: Basic Books.

Calvin, W. H. (1990), *The Cerebral Symphony*. New York: Bantam.

Cicchetti, D. & Carlson, V. (1989). *Child Maltreatment*. London: Cambridge University Press.

Coe, C. L., Weiner, S. & Rosenberg, L. T. (1985), Endocrine and immune responses to separation and maternal loss in non-human primates. In: *The Psychobiology of Attachment and Separation*, ed. M. Reite & T. Fields. Orlando, FL: Academic Press, pp. 163–197.

Cook, L. & Sepinwall, J. (1975), Behavioral analysis of the effect and mechanism of action of the benzodiazepines. In: *Mechanisms of Action of the Benzodiazepines*, ed. E. Costa & P. Greengard. New York: Raven Press, pp. 1–28.

Dobbs, D. & Wilson, W. P. (1960), Observations on the persistence of traumatic war neurosis. *J. Nerv. Ment. Dis.*, 21:40–46.

Edelman, G. M. (1987), Neural Darwinism. New York: Basic Books.

Gray, J. (1982), *The Neuropsychology of Anxiety*. London: Oxford University Press.

Green, A. H. (1980), *Child Maltreatment*. New York: Aronson.

Herman, J. L., Perry, J. C. & van der Kolk, B. A. (1989), Childhood trauma in borderline personality disorder. *Amer. J. Psychiat.*, 146:390–395.

Hilberman, E. & Munson, M. (1978). Sixty battered women. *Victimol.*, 2:460–471.

Hoffman, H. S. & Ratner, A. M. (1973). A reinforcement model of imprinting: Implications for socialization in monkeys and men. *Psychol. Rev.*, 80: 527–544.

Jacobs, W. J. & Nadel, L. (1985), Stress-induced recovery of fears and phobias. *Psycholog. Rev.*, 92:512–531.

Janet, P. (1889), *L'Automatisme psychologique*. Paris: Alcan.

_____ (1909), *Les Neuroses*. Paris: Flammarion.

_____ (1919), *Les Medications psychologiques* (3 vols.). Paris: Flex Alcan.

Kardiner, A. (1941), The traumatic neurosis of war. *Psychosomatic Medical Monograph*. New York: Paul Hoeber.

Kelley, D. D. (1982), The role of endorphins in stress-induced analgesia. *Ann. N.Y. Acad. Sci.*, 398:260–271.

Kilpatrick, D. G., Best, C. L., Veronen, L. J., Amick, A. E., & Villeponteaux, L. A. (1985a), Mental health correlates of criminal victimization. *Consult. Clin. Psychol.*, 53:866–873.

_____ Veronen, L. J. & Best, C. L. (1985b), Factors predicting psychological distress in rape victims. In: *Trauma and Its Wake, Vol. 1*, ed. C. Figley. New York: Brunner/Mazel, pp. 113–141.

Kling, A. & Steklis, H. D. (1976). A neural substrate for affiliative behavior in non-human primates. *Brain Behav. Evol.*, 13:216–238.

Kolb, L. C. & Mutalipassi, L. R. (1982), The conditioned emotional response. *Psychiat. Ann.*, 12:979–987.

Kraemer, G. W., Ebert, M. H., Lake, C. R., et. al. (1984), Cerebrospinal fluid measures of neurotransmitter changes associated with pharmacological alteration of the despair response to social separation in rhesus monkeys. *Psychiat. Res.*, 11:303–315.

Krystal, H. (1978), Trauma and affects. *The Psychoanalytic Study of the Child*, 33:81–116. New Haven, CT: Yale University Press.

Ledoux, J. E., Romansky, L. & Xagoris, A. (1989), The indelibility of subcortical emotional networks. *J. Cogn. Neurosci.*, 1:238–243.

Lindemann, E. (1944), The symptomatology and management of acute grief. *Amer. J. Psychiat.*, 101:141–148.

MacLean, P. D. (1985). Brain evolution relating to family, play, and the separation call. *Arch. Gen. Psychiat.*, 42:505–517.

Maier, S. F. & Seligman, M. E. P. (1976). Learned helplessness: Theory and evidence. *J. Exp. Psychol. (Gen.)*, 105:3–46.

Malloy, P. F., Fairbank, J. A. & Keane, T. M. (1983), Validation of a multimethod assessment of post traumatic stress disorders in Vietnam veterans. *J. Consult. Clin. Psycholog.*, 51:4–21.

Mandler, J. M. (1979), Categorical and schematic organization of memory. In: *Memory Organization and Structure*, ed. C. R. Puff. New York: Academic Press.

Mitchell, D., Osborne, E. W. & O'Boyle, M. W. (1985), Habituation under stress. *Behav. Neurolg. Biol.*, 43:212–217.

Nadel, L. & Zola-Morgan, S. (1984), Infantile amnesia: A neurobiological perspective. In: *Infant Memory*, ed. M. Moskovitz. New York: Plenum Press.

Novack, M. A. & Harlow, H. F. (1979), Social recovery of monkeys isolated for the first year of life. *Dev. Psychol.*, 15:50–61.

O'Keefe, J. & Nadel, L. (1978), *The Hippocampus as a Cognitive Map*. Oxford: Clarendon Press.

Pfaff, D. W., Silva, M. T. & Weiss, J. M. (1971), Telemetered recording of hormone effects on hippocampal nerves. *Science*, 172:394–395.

Piaget, J. (1962), *Dreams, Play, and Imitation in Childhood*. New York: Norton.

Pitman, R. K., Orr, S. P., Forguw, D. F., de Jong, J. & Clairborn, J. M. (1987), Psychophysiologic assessment of post traumatic stress disorder imagery in Vietnam combat veterans. *Arch. Gen. Psychiat.*, 44:970–975.

——— van der Kolk, B. A., Orr, S. P. & Greenberg, M. S. (1990), Naloxone reversible stress induced analgesia in post traumatic stress disorder. *Arch. Gen. Psychiat.*, 47:541–547.

Putnam, F. W. (1989), *Diagnosis and Treatment of Multiple Personality Disorder*. New York: Guilford.

Pynoos, R. S. & Eth, S. (1985), Developmental perspective on psychic trauma in childhood. In: *Trauma and Its Wake: The Study and Treatment of Post-Traumatic Stress Disorder*, Vol. 1, ed. C. R. Figley. New York: Brunner/Mazel, pp. 36–52.

Rainey, J. M., Aleem, A., Ortiz, a., Yaragani, V., Pohl, R. & Berchow, R. (1987), Laboratory procedure for the inducement of flashbacks. *Amer. J. Psychiat.*, 144:1317–1319.

Reite, M. & Field, T., eds. (1985), *The Psychobiology of Attachment and Separation*. Orlando, FL: Academic Press.

Sapolsky, R., Krey, L. & McEwen, B. S. (1984), Stress down-regulates corticosterone receptors in a site specific manner in the brain. *Endocrinology*, 114:287–292.

Schachter, D. L. (1990). Toward a cognitive neuropsychology of awareness: Implicit knowledge and anosognosia. *J. Clin. Exp. Neuropsychol.*, 12:155–178.

Sheard, M. H. & Davis, M. (1976), Shock elicited fighting in rats. *Brain Res.*, 111:287–292.

Sheldon, A. B. (1969), Preferences for familiar vs. novel stimuli as a function of the familiarity of the environment. *J. Comp. Physiolog. Psychol.*, 67:516–521.

Siegfried, B., Frischnecht, H. R. & Nuñez, R. (1990), An ethological model for the study of activation and interaction of pain, memory and defensive systems in the attacked mouse. *Neurosci. Behav. Rev.*, 14:481–490.

Solomon, R. (1980), The opponent process of acquired motivation. *Amer. Psycholog.*, 27:35–49.

Southwick, S. (in press), Flashbacks in PTSD. *Arch. Gen. Psychiat.*

Squire, L. R. & Zola-Morgan, S. (1991), The medial temporal lobe memory system. *Science*, 253:1380–1386.

Stoddard, F. J., Norman, D. K. & Murphy, J. M. (1989), A diagnostic outcome study of children and adolescents with severe burns. *J. Trauma*, 29:471–477.

Terman, G. W., Shavit, Y., Lewis, J. W., Cannon, J. T. & Liebeskind, J. C. (1984), Intrinsic mechanisms of pain inhibition. *Science*, 26:1270–1277.

Terr, L. (1991), Childhood traumas. *Amer. J. Psychiat.*, 148:10–20.

van der Kolk, B. A. (1988), The trauma spectrum. *J. Traumat. Stress*, 1:273–325.

_____ Blitz, R., Burr, W. & Hartmann, E. (1984), Nightmares and trauma. *Amer. J. Psychiat.*, 141:187–190.

_____ & Ducey, C. R. (1989). The psychological processing of traumatic experience: Rorschach patterns in PTSD. *J. Traumat. Stress*, 2:259–274.

_____ & Saporta, J. (1991), The biological response to psychic trauma. *Anxiety Res.*, 4:199–212.

_____ & van der Hart, O. (1989), Pierre Janet and the breakdown of adaption in psychological trauma. *Amer. J. Psychiat.*, 146:1530–1540.

_____ _____ (1991), The intrusive past. *Imago*, 48:425–454.

Chapter 10

I FEEL A LITTLE SAD

The Application of Object Relations Theory to the Hypnotherapy of Posttraumatic Stress Disorders in Vietnam Veterans

Sarah Haley

> And somewhere lions still roam, all unaware in being magnificent, of any weakness.
>
> —Rainer Maria Rilke

The utilization of hypnosis in the treatment of posttraumatic stress disorders (PTSD) fosters the integration of memories and their split-off affects, and it enhances the strength of the transference and the real relationship in Vietnam veterans' efforts to make meaning of the traumatic events in their life. The integration of memories and their affects, as contrasted with abreaction or catharsis, is the goal of the treatment of PTSD (Brende and Benedict, 1980; Brown and Fromm, 1986).

The traumatized veteran is bombarded by the cyclical phases of the stress response recovery process as described by Horowitz (1974, 1976), consisting of alternating stages of denial/numbing and intrusive repetition of images, memories, and/or feeling about the traumatic event. PTSD represents an inability to successfully work through the traumatic experience via a gradual "dosing" of the painful memories and the associated affects (Fig. 10.1.). The DSM III-R defines PTSD as consisting of four criteria: (1) existence of a recognizable stressor that would evoke significant symptoms of distress in almost everyone; (2) persistent reexperiencing of the trauma with intrusive recollections, recurrent dreams, or a sudden feeling that the event was reoccurring; (3) persistent avoidance of

STRESS
RESPONSE
STATES

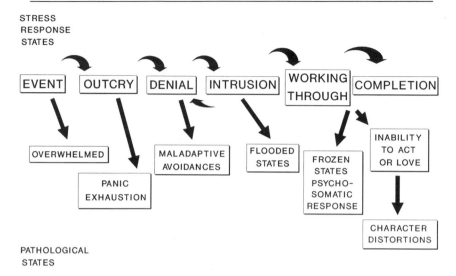

Fig. 10.1. Stress Recovery Process (from Horowitz, 1976). Reprinted with permission of the publisher.

stimuli associated with the trauma and a sense of isolation from others, characterized by a generalized numbing of responsiveness or loss of interest in activities, a feeling of detachment, or a constricted affect; and (4) persistent symptoms of increased arousal indicated by hyperalertness, sleep disturbance, survivor guilt, concentration or memory impairment, avoidance of activities that stimulate recollections of the traumatic event, or intensification of symptoms by exposure to such activities.

The postcombat stress disorders of Vietnam veterans are most readily diagnosed during the intrusive reexperiencing phase: insomnia, night-mares, day imaging, startle responses, hypervigilance, explosive aggressive reactions, and dissociative episodes, referred to as flashbacks (Neff, 1975). The disorder often goes undetected during the denial/numbing phase. As van der Kolk (1984) has noted, when controls predominate and intrusive events are warded off, emotional constriction, chronic passivity, and a vague sense of victimization may be the only sequelae of the trauma, usually missed by the diagnostician who is not alert to the possibility (Laufer, Brett, and Gallops, 1984; Parson, 1984).

In previous research (Haley, 1985), I argued the insufficiency of earlier psychoanalytic theories to fully appreciate the deforming impact of catastrophic stress, particularly combat, on psychic structures. The expanded conceptual framework available to clinicians today draws on our greater understanding of the psychology and physiology of stress response syndromes (Grinker and Spiegel, 1945; Horowitz, 1976; Kardiner, 1941; Kolb and Mutalipassi, 1982; van der Kolk, 1984), object relations theory (Kernberg, 1976; Parson, 1984), issues of narcissism (Fox, 1974; Kohut, 1972, 1977), separation-individuation (Bowlby, 1973; Mahler, 1968), the concept of ego activity–ego passivity (Fromm, 1972; Rapaport, 1967), and affective development (Krystal, 1977). The long-term effects of war traumatization may become manifest less in terms of posttraumatic or dissociative symptoms and more in terms of pervasive developmental disruptions. War traumatization can result in severe disturbances in the areas of object representations, affective expression (Krystal, 1977), and self-pathology— what Parson (1984) has called fluid character pathology. Because the majority of Vietnam veterans served in combat during late adolescence, it is crucial for clinicians to become knowledgeable about adolescent psychology (Blos, 1962) and to attempt to assess the impact of combat (killing, fear of dying, loss of buddies, atrocities) on the ego and, in particular, on the superego and the ego ideal, which are still fluid, venerable adolescent psychic structures (DeFazio and Pascucci, 1984; Shatan, 1978; van der Kolk, 1985). In the work "Some of My Best Friends Are Dead" (Haley, 1985), I offered a conceptual framework regarding one aspect of combat stress, namely, the loss of a soldier's buddy—his sustaining transitional object— as a potential precipitant to the unleashing of sadistic impulses and actions in the surviving soldier. In this chapter, I present the impact on the combatant of not only the loss of transitional objects but also the loss of faith in his traditional authority figures and the concomitant vulnerability to regression, seduction, or both by archaic superego role models.

The chapter also treats the psychic numbing that is characteristic of traumatized patients in general (Krystal, 1968) and of Vietnam veterans in particular (Lifton, 1973; Parson, 1984). Such pervasive affective numbing is the usual outcome of exposure to abusive violence (Laufer et al., 1984), to killing (Brende and McCann, 1984), and especially to participation in atrocity (Haley, 1974; Parson, 1984). Such individuals show severe impairments in their capacity to feel and to tolerate and express feelings. A case history is presented that demonstrates the impact on one man of his participation in the CIA's Operation Phoenix. Hypnotherapy enabled this veteran, who had long somatized his psychic pain, to begin to integrate the memories with their long split-off affects. Crucial to this integration, the veteran used the therapist as a model of renewed and strengthened ego ideals to risk telling his father about his participation in Phoenix and its impact on his life.

Because of the ambiguous nature of the Vietnam war, one of the most damaging effects of the stress of combat on soldiers was the stripping away of their adolescent illusions and the tarnishing of their ego ideals. The deforming of psychic structures under stress, especially superego regressions to identification with the aggressor, has occurred in all wars. Such regressions and the taking on of the group superego permitted preservation of psychic integrity in the face of catastrophe (Shatan, 1973, 1977, 1978; van der Kolk, 1985). Returning from combat, the veteran was expected to forge a realignment of psychic structures with the ego once again predominant in the management of affects and instincts. Vietnam veterans, however, are associated in the public imagination with My Lai and the loss of "their" war and have had few societal sanctions or reentry rituals to aid them in this realignment, which is most crucial in the reinstatement of a viable ego ideal (Borus, 1973, 1976; Brende and Parson, 1985; Lifton, 1973).

Research consistently bears out the clinical impression that the severity of postcombat stress is directly related to age (Wilson, Smith, and Johnson, 1985), amount of combat (DeFazio, Rustin, and Diamond, 1975; Laufer et al., 1984; Strayer and Ellenhorn, 1975), and exposure to abusive violence (Laufer et al., 1984). Regardless of premorbid personality, the younger the combatant and the more intense, prolonged, and savage the combat, the greater the incidence, severity, and chronicity of PTSD in Vietnam veterans. The younger combatants "buddy'd up" to hold back annihilation anxiety (Fox, 1974). The older noncoms and officers looked to each other for support and affirmation of their value and shared purpose. They too were subject to psychic regression, but many stopped short of ego disintegration by fusion with a regressed, archaic superego role model that held out the promise of containment by restoring to the soldier a sense of control over his fate and his state of mind. If trauma can be defined as the experience of being made into an object (Krystal, 1968) and if even being a "lean green fighting machine" cannot spare one from the fates, then surely merger with a group that purports to have special power and special license offers to the venerable combatant only the time-limited illusion that he is the subject of his universe once again. The very terms "CIA," "special forces," "commandos," "guerrillas," and "secret agent" imply knowledge and strength not available to every combatant.

As contrasted with the atrocities of My Lai, the taking on of a new, albeit more archaic, superego role model led many combatants into "sanctioned atrocities." Numerous counterinsurgency techniques and programs were instituted during the Vietnam war, and young combatants and officers were frequently assigned, detained, or seduced at moments of venerability into counterinsurgency work for the CIA. The best known and most infamous of these programs was Operation Phoenix. Conceived in 1967 by the CIA, Operation Phoenix was an attempt to deny the Viet Cong access to the rural administrators, an apparatus on which they relied for recruits, food, money, and asylum. The CIA claimed that during the three years of the program, they eliminated some 60,000 authentic Viet Cong agents. This figure was confirmed after the war by senior North Vietnamese and Viet Cong officials. MacPherson (1984) discusses the impact of Operation Phoenix on the lives of two men who refused to train or participate and on one man whose involvement initially stemmed from a sense of duty. The following examples set the moral parameters that confronted some combatants.

> Although the U.S. Government officially protested that Phoenix was not an assassination program, the highly secret and unconventional operation nonetheless was marked by indiscriminate anti-vc terror.
>   Some of this came to light when Francis T. Reitemeyer and Michael J. Cohn, two Army Lieutenants assigned to the Phoenix program, received honorable discharges after convincing a federal judge they were legitimate conscientious objectors although in the service. . . . They reported that their instructors informed them they might be required to maintain a small bill "Kill quota" of fifty Viet Cong a month. The Army unsuccessfully fought their honorable discharge and denied such nefarious activities. . . . However, in congressional testimony, two former U. S. military intelligence agents testified that Vietnamese were indiscriminately rounded up, tortured and murdered by Americans in the effort to eliminate Viet Cong cadres [p. 255].

Later, MacPherson recounts the story of a former Phoenix operative whose girlfriend rejected him when he told her about it.

> You finally let down the barrier, after all these years. The first person you tell backs off. . . . You had to kill on a personal basis and yet you had to be unpersonal to the fact you're doing something against your moral upbringing and you justify and rationalize. . . . At the time, you didn't question. I thought I was doing something right. We actually thought it was something to help the war effort—but you can't help but blame yourself now [p. 254].

CASE REPORT

At the time of his referral to me in 1982, David was a 32-year-old, unmarried combat veteran who was 70% service-connected disabled from PTSD and multiple gunshot wounds. He exhibited an avoidant life-style: he lived alone, he had no close friends, and his relationships with women were superficial and transient. Despite two years of college prior to the service, he was employed in a job in which he worked mostly with animals. Unlike a schizoid personality, he wished for closeness with others but felt constrained to remain apart. Only as I came to know him better could I appreciate the degree of ego constriction that rendered him quite phobic. He felt "OK" traveling between his apartment and his job, the VA, and his parents' home. He rarely went out at night. Like many other Vietnam veterans, whether realistically or not, he feared reprisals from the Vietnamese government by way of Vietnamese refugees in America whose relatives had been victims of operations such as Phoenix. These veterans often avoid neighborhoods where Vietnamese live so as not to suffer severe startle response, hypervigilance, or frankly paranoid ideation when unexpectedly confronted with a Vietnamese, Cambodian, or Laotian. David's ego strengths included intelligence, humor, and a capacity for concern.

Clinically he presented with a 12-year history of rumination about three near-death experiences in Vietnam in addition to insomnia and combat nightmares, startle response, hypervigilance, day imaging, and severe somatization of his combat sustained injuries. During the years since discharge, he had been followed at various VA medical centers, where his physical symptoms were exhaustively worked up. He suffered from severe headaches but resisted accepting the negative neurological findings. He had degenerative arthritis of the knees and ankles and accompanying psoriasis related to the gunshot wounds. He also resisted the idea that his state of mind could influence the severity of his pain, although he often observed that the pain was worse in the summer and on the anniversary of his injuries. His anxiety and ruminations were treated over the years with medication and one trial of classical psychoanalytic therapy focusing on an early, genetic reconstruction of symptomatology.

One event stands out in David's history since 1970 but was heretofore never explored in treatment. In 1975, David was arrested for forging bad checks. He received a suspended sentence because he had no prior criminal record and because he was a highly decorated disabled veteran. He had no explanation for his actions but the issue caused such a strain on his relationship with his family that he relocated to the Boston area. Prior to his referral to me, he had been in a combat group led by a Vietnam veteran. It was the first corrective, ego-supportive, ego-ideal-enhancing experience since his return from Vietnam in 1970. Sadly, when I reviewed his voluminous medical record and when I first met him, I was not surprised to find that a combat history had never been elicited, nor had David volunteered anything more than his obsessive rumination about his near-death experiences.

David came from a middle-class background, and his parents had high expectations for his academic and athletic excellence. His father was a World War II combat veteran, and an uncle had been with the Office of Strategic Services (OSS) in North Africa. His mother and other women in the family were "nervous" and "needed to be sheltered." By his sopho-more year in college in 1969, he felt suffocated and saw his life laid out for him: marriage to his high school girlfriend and carrying on his father's business. Despite the family's protestations, he entered the Marine Corps. David's father obtained a post office box so that David could write about his experiences to his father without "upsetting" his mother

Military History

At age 20, David was two years older and better educated than most recruits, and he was selected for advanced technical training in reconnaissance. He was sent to Vietnam in 1970 and was attached both as an adviser to a unit of the Army of the Republic of Vietnam (ARVN) (South Vietnam) and as a naval gunship spotter. During his first five months of combat, he made a number of friends and lost several to death or injury. As the losses mounted, he distanced himself from his peers. He remembers feeling "frightened and invincible at the same time." In his fifth month, he met Lin, a woman who worked at his base camp and who had a 2-year-old child by an American. He spent all his spare time with Lin and took his R&R (vacation) in Vietnam with Lin and her child. Then, in his sixth month, he suffered three near-death experiences and was awarded two Purple Hearts. In the first experience, he was one of four American advisers attached to an ARVN company in the Mekong Delta. "We were bait; they wanted to test the Viet Cong strength." They were surrounded and attacked during the night. David woke to the pain of shrapnel entering his feet and legs. The fighting became hand-to-hand with knives and lasted until dawn. The number of casualties on both sides "was staggering; I'll never forget it, bodies everywhere, only six of us made it. Before we got there, they told us that 3,000 French soldiers had been sent here in the 50s and they never found a trace of them."

David's injuries were treated and he was assigned as a driver for a visiting general. They were ambushed and the jeep overturned on them. David sustained flesh wounds and his second Purple Heart. Within days of this second injury, however, he was assigned to a light reconnaissance plane as a spotter. "I felt split in two; part of me said, 'Hey, I'm still recovering from GSW [gunshot wounds]," and the other part said, 'I want to go up.' " On one mission, the pilot was shot through the shoulder, and a bullet grazed David's forehead, ripping his helmet off. The pilot lost control of the plane, and David, stunned, remembers the "ground racing up to us." The pilot regained control and they were able to return and land safely. The cries of pain, confusion, and reassurance from ground control were recorded on cockpit tape, a copy of which David still has.

Upon deplaning, David was asked by his commanding officer (CO) if he "thought my head injury was bad enough for me to be flown the 100 miles to Cam Ranh Bay for treatment." I felt torn: this injury would get me my third Purple Heart and I would be legally exempt from combat; however, my CO was inviting me not to treat or report it but to be a tough marine: "Just a flesh wound Sarge," à la John Wayne.

With a resentment and a sense of "being used" that would come into awareness only many years later, David refused treatment and was put on light duty for two weeks.

During this period, he began to spend evenings playing cards with a number of "civilians" also at the same base camp. "They were a law unto themselves; we all knew they were CIA." One night they suggested, "Why don't you come along on one of our missions?" For the next two months, David participated in night time raids, interrogations, and assassinations in suspected Viet Cong villages. He experienced himself as "wild and out of control." On returning from a mission one morning, weary and blood splattered, David was approached by his CO, who said, "I have no authority over you; I know what you're doing and I just want you to think about it."

That day, David ceased his involvement in Operation Phoenix, resuming his regular combat assignment for the remainder of his tour in Vietnam. The farewell with Lin was painful, and he wrote to her until 1975, when the war ended. While in Vietnam, he wrote to his father about everything except Operation Phoenix.

David's description of his airport welcome-home captures the family dynamics: his mother exclaiming about his Purple Hearts and other medals because "you didn't say you were near the combat," and his father winking knowingly.

DISCUSSION

Stress, Ego Passivity and Ego Activity

Fromm (1972) states, "Hypnosis is viewed by most layman as a state in which the patient surrenders his autonomy and passively follows the commands of an external figure, the hypnotist. Many hypnotherapists believe this to be true for authoritarian hypnosis, but not for permissive hypnosis" (p. 238). Stolar and Fromm (1974) propose a model relating the dynamically passive ego and the dynamically active ego with the superego. The ego is active, or autonomous, when one can make a choice or act with "free will"; it is passive, or lacks autonomy, when a one is overwhelmed either by one's instinctual demands or by demands coming from the environment. Figure 10.2 illustrates David's progression from ego passivity and loss of autonomy, to archaic superego demands, to ego activity and relative autonomy from superego demands. Survivors of catastrophic stress are defined to have suffered a "psychologically trau-

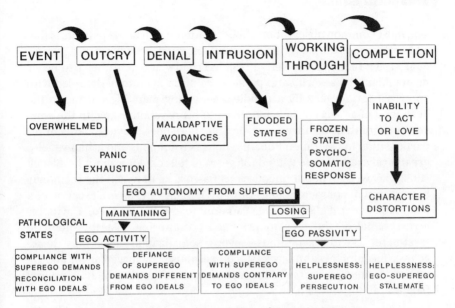

Fig. 10.2. Recovery, Ego Activity, and Superego Autonomy

matic event that is generally outside the range of usual human experience" (American Psychiatric Association, 1987), and as with veterans, recovery is more difficult if the stressor is of human design.

Morrier (1984) has applied this model to his work with Vietnam veterans, and I have extended its application to stress recovery and the hypnotherapy of PTSD. It has been useful for me to conceptualize stress response recovery as ego active, and stress disorders and manifestations of varying degrees as ego passivity in integrating the traumatic event. Figure 10.2 is a schematic representation of this conceptualization, with the understanding that psychological health and disorder are never clear cut but usually overlap. As therapists, however, we have been particularly concerned with the pervasiveness of a seeming trade-off toward passivity in our Vietnam veteran population in order to counter fears of their past and potential aggressiveness. With few societal ego supports and an impoverished ego ideal, the regressed superego stands virtually unopposed. For many veterans, activity, initiation, assertion, aggression, and murder have clearly become and remain fused in a dynamic continuum, for although Vietnam veterans have been characterized in the public and clinical media as having explosive aggressive reactions, Morrier (1984) has noted that these episodes are often punctuation marks in a more stultifying passivity.

Treatment Issues

The most common observation about treatment of trauma patients is that a history of the trauma is rarely elicited, pursued, or volunteered (Laufer et al., 1984; Lindy, 1988; Neff, 1975). In David's case, a history had never been taken. The severity and persistence of his symptoms, coupled with an arrest for forgery by a middle-class young man, alerted me to the likelihood of a "secret." Five months into his psychotherapy, in the anniversary month of his three near-death experiences, David told me of his participation in Operation Phoenix. He was tremulous and ashen yet also greatly relieved. "I have waited for years to tell someone about it." Blanck (1982) has written about unconscious flashbacks in which the seemingly bizarre, out-of-character behavior of a Vietnam veteran is a creation of a traumatic event if the observer can only follow the lead. For David, his arrest signaled "the life I'm leading is counterfeit." At this point in treatment, David's symptoms—severe somatization (especially headaches), insomnia, nightmares, startle response, hypervigilance, and diminished interpersonal relationships—were intense, but he had "no real feelings" about Vietnam.

Hypnotherapy

I have treated Vietnam veterans since 1969 and have written about the potential for a negative countertransference reaction by the therapist, particularly to "the patient who reports atrocities" (Haley, 1974). I was invited to participate in a symposium (American Psychological Association, Chicago, 1979) on Vietnam veterans, moderated by David Spiegel, M.D. I was encouraged by his work that enlarged and deepened my own clinical skills to include hypnosis in the treatment of this most misunderstood and inadequately cared for patient population. To quote Spiegel (1981):

> Plato defined courage as knowing when to be afraid; this problem haunts many individuals with post traumatic stress disorders and becomes one of the challenges in psychotherapy. Their treatment involves helping return to them a sense of control over their lives that was wrested from them by the traumatic event. Hypnosis, often viewed as depriving patients of control, can be a useful tool for enhancing a patient's sense of control over his state of mind while integrating traumatic experiences [p. 33].

Hypnosis and self-hypnosis were presented to David "as a self-controlled activity, with the therapist serving as a commentator and advisor" (Brown and Fromm, 1986; Fass and Brown, 1990; Spiegel, 1981). Hypnosis, it is suggested to the veteran, is simply a state of focused attention accessible to virtually anyone after becoming familiar with the technique. Repeatedly stressed is that ultimate control rests in the person being hypnotized. This calls for relatively nondirective approaches, which tend to follow the individual and which use less potentially confrontive techniques, such as metaphor (Silver and Kelly, 1985). David knew that I too was a "beginner" at hypnosis, and an atmosphere of candor, helpfulness, and at times playfulness characterized the hypnotherapy. For example, our very first attempt at a closed-eye induction was unsuccessful until David informed me that "it's like I'm on guard duty and you're telling me to close my eyes. The VC are out there!" I suggested that he think of a safe place and open his eyes; then he would become progressively more relaxed. After some minutes, he began to cry and came spontaneously out of trance, saying, "I saw Lin." He had seen Lin and her child in her home, a place he had frequently visited and where he felt safe and accepted by her family. However, the immensity of her importance to him had heretofore never been realized.

For trauma patients, just the induction itself can bring them to the trauma. It is not the depth of trance but the material that one has access to that is frightening. Trauma patients defend against the altered state, so that controls, delays, stops, and feedback signals must be built in. The use of an imaginary television was introduced, which utilized a split screen or different channels (Brown and Fromm, 1986; Parson, 1984; Spiegel, 1981) for the "dosing" of memories and their associated affects. The patient imagines a program about feeling especially relaxed and safe and then another program about some aspect of the trauma. By imagining the safe scenes and the trauma scenes on a split screen or by switching back and forth between scenes, the patient is able to explore the trauma concurrent with feeling safe and in control. David also was taught both self-hypnosis and progressive relaxation for symptom relief, for example, from insomnia, but most importantly for increasing mastery over his state of mind. In trance, it was suggested to him that he would have a dream that would not disturb his sleep, that he would remember at our next meeting, and that the dream would aid us in our work together.

The potential for a negative countertransference reaction by the therapist when confronted with the deep pain of the survivor of catastrophic events is well documented (Haley, 1974, 1985; Lindy, 1988; Shapiro, 1984) but still poorly integrated into our training and practice. For Vietnam veterans, the therapist is a representative of the larger society that did not offer sanction and reentry rituals but a "dysreception" (Figley, 1978). As Payne (1978) has stated:

> When the veteran, or any of us, has committed acts which violently conflict with his values, which he regards as atrocities, he is indeed alienated from the internal representatives of his first-loved objects, whose values he has

violated, and is deprived of the protective shield which the relationship confers. The vulnerability to guilt is of course increased when he leaves the group which supported his acts, and is once more dependent on the group which shares the values that he violated. The necessity for the therapist, therefore, to be able genuinely to empathize with and tolerate the experiences of the veteran who has committed atrocities, allows for the restoration of the protective relationship (real or internalized) which was ruptured, making dissociation necessary. It is this which permits the toleration of previously intolerable affects, the removal of repression and the assimilation of previously unacceptable experiences [p. 30].

Three months after his disclosure about Phoenix, David attempted to tell his father but "couldn't get the words out." His urge to speak of this atrocious event is akin, as Brown (personal communication, 1983) has noted, to the incest survivor's impulse to "spill the beans" after the incest has been revealed. As I have done with other veterans at times of transition, we invited David's father to join us in an interview. David told his father about Phoenix. His father, a distinguished-looking businessman, was supportive and reminded David that he had warned him to rely on his COs for guidelines about "who's the enemy." The Cally trial had deeply disturbed the father, and he felt fear for his son. In advanced infantry training, David had asked his CO, "What do we do about civilians?" and was told, "Use your best judgment." David's father commented that he and his brother (OSS in North Africa) "were heroes after WW II. Lots of stuff like My Lai and Phoenix happened in WW II, but no one talks about it. We got medals; guys like David got spit upon."

This meeting strengthened David's cognitive, narcissistic, and ego defenses and cemented the therapeutic alliance, which worked to foster renewed ego ideals as a counterforce to a superego regressed to an archaic level during combat. "Super ego standards are relatively archaic and inflexible. . . . In the adult they rarely serve adaptation or the needs of the other psychic institutions" (Stolar and Fromm, 1974).

Following is a series of "hypnotherapy vignettes" with comments from David's treatment in the year after the meeting with his father.

> 1. David reported a hypnotic dream in which he was on the plane coming home from Vietnam, and "a little ghost I've named Casper was flying alongside the plane. He was smiling, and at the airport he took my hand and led me to my parents. Then he said he had to go back to Vietnam and bring others back home."

Children who have had a major illness may develop a double of the self or an imaginary playmate for comfort and protection. Combatants regress to transitional, fused "bonding" relationships (Fox, 1974) which are always at high risk. After months of losing friends, David stayed more and more to himself, turning to Lin and his officers for maternal/paternal succor. "Casper is a protector; he saves people." David was internalizing that he is valued and is bracing himself to deal with the disillusionment and terror he has long somatized.

> 2. In trance, David visualized a news broadcast on TV. Gradually, he "turned up the volume" and "they were reporting on wars and CIA stuff in Latin America." As he reported he was beginning to feel tense, I suggested he was in control of the "volume" and that he lower or raise the "sound." He did this for a few minutes until he felt comfortable and told me more of the newscast. Then he said, "I've just turned the TV off. I'm going to my bedroom. I'm lying on my bed with my arm over my eyes and doing the waves [of relaxation], cause I want to take a nap. That's enough for today."

The patient's memories are secondary process, whereas imagery is primary process. David has increasing access to imagery and to mechanisms to titrate his affective response associated with the imagery. In contrast to the crippling regression and somatization since Vietnam, he can now choose to *suppress* some painful material, and he has already taken up self-hypnosis as a coping device.

> 3. During trance, David used a TV with a channel each for pleasant material and problem material. At the end of one session, he said while still in trance, "You always have me start with the pleasant memories, which then leaves me with the sad memories at the end. Let's reverse the order. I want to leave feeling in better control."

Still unable to "feel" sad out of trance, David continued somatization and incessant medical workups. During the next year, however, David had moved into a house with three roommates. He came to his hour one day looking distraught and disheveled. The mother of his roommate John had been killed by a drunken driver that morning. David had taken the call and driven John to the airport. He took care of business for John and was in contact with John's family throughout the day.

David was writhing in his chair: rubbing his head, knees, and ankles and grimacing in pain. "She was killed by a drunken kid with no license. I feel so terrible; my head is killing me. John might have to relocate to California, and I'll never see him again. And my knees and ankles are pounding. *And I feel a little sad.* And I've got to take a pain med [swallows a pill], and you may need to put me in a hospital."

David had never revealed his closeness to John because, like in Vietnam, it put him at risk for another loss. He identified with John's loss, but he also identified "that an out-of-control kid killed an innocent civilian, just like in Phoenix." That he "felt a little sad" was a major accomplishment for him. But I know he feared acknowledging any gains for fear I would "send him along."

> 4. Three days later, during an age regression to Vietnam, David saw himself in combat. He was pale, sweaty, and tremulous. "We're in a fire fight; there's stuff coming from everywhere." I suggested to him that as a good soldier, he knew how to protect himself and his men. I asked, "What do you need to your rear?" He responded, "There's artillery there—they're really pounding them." I said, "And to your right? What do you see?" He said, "Three guy's— one with a sixty [machine gun]. I feel a lot better now." I continued, "And to your left?" And he said, "It's a fire fight, but I'm safe on three sides." Then I asked, "And how do you feel?" After some hesitation, he said, "I feel excited. Real excited. I went from dead scared to secure on all three sides to excited."

Psychic regression to eroticized anal sadism, which is pleasurable albeit guilt provoking, during combat is one of the more damaging influences on the combatant's self-esteem. Physiologically intense stress brings its own endorphin anesthesia and "high," and combat is remembered as "the time I felt most alive."

In April 1984, the *Boston Globe* wrote in an editorial

> There is the moral dilemma of hiring murderers to kill other murderers—or to kill anyone defined as an enemy. The CIA's Phoenix Program in South Vietnam, a conscious effort to assassinate the political cadres that made up the "infrastructure" of the Vietcong, caused many Americans to think of their government as a branch of Murder Incorporated.

David responded, "We were not Murder Incorporated. But I know it still goes on. You can't stop the [CIA]." On May 1, David talked of his feelings about the "Four Dead in Ohio" (Kent State killings, 5/1/70). As in all psychotherapies but especially with trauma patients, one must be alert to the impact of anniversaries. For Vietnam veterans the Christmas holidays, the Kent State shootings, and April 25, 1975, which marked the fall of South Vietnam, are charged associations. On May 2, David reported the following dreams.

> 5. "There are these men telling me they need my help. Someone has to be assassinated. He's a threat to world peace. I know they're the CIA. They kept at me and said I'm the only one who can do it and I agree. It's Qaddafi.
> "In the next dream, I'm on a roof with a rifle, and when the man comes out of the door across the street, I'm to kill him. But just as the door starts to open, soldiers come onto the street and see me. They start to run toward me and I wake up."

David said that the first dream meant that when he was 20 years old, disillusioned and scared, the CIA could talk him into an operation like Phoenix. But today it "would have to be pretty big to save the world. I'm not a murderer" (referring to the Boston Globe article). I added that the second dream suggested that he was of two minds about killing under any circumstances, as the soldiers who come to chase him away represent one aspect of his own ambivalence.

In the following weeks, David began "noticing all kinds of things I think were always there." He "saw" a program and "read" an article on stress and physical pain. He started reading more about Vietnam and began "hanging around" the U.S. printing office reading official reports of the war. I had been on a vacation, and he reported, "My head was killing me. Then I thought, maybe I'm angry with you for being away. So I went on vacation myself. I know a beach that looks like the South China Sea and I listened to the waves and thought of Lin and slept for eight hours." During the next hour, he told me that he "looked up something kind of impor-tant." Some months after his airplane was fired on, a copilot in a similar low-flying reconnaissance plane was killed. He was awarded posthu-mously a Medal of Honor. "It could have been me. I didn't even get a Band-Aid. I was up in a plane the next day. I should have gotten my third Purple Heart and been sent home." After a pause, he described the next crucial experience as if the facts, long remembered, now *meant* some-thing.

6. "The CO said, 'Do you think you need to get it looked at? It's 100 miles to the hospital.' My head was pounding and there was blood everywhere. I wanted my third heart and out of there. But I also wanted to be there—the people, the excitement. He was leaving the decision to me; I wanted him to make it. I know he didn't want to lose me, but I felt used, like a piece of meat. You don't let a kid decide if he's too sick to go to school or not! But I wanted to please him so I said I'd be OK. I think my headaches are my anger at him. After that is when I got into Phoenix."

CONCLUSION

The process of recovery for Vietnam veterans like David is as follows: integration of split-off parts of the self (Parson, 1984), especially the killer-self introject (Brende and McCann, 1984); fostering of superego development (van der Kolk, 1985); and facilitation of affective develop-ment (Brown and Fromm, 1986). Through the course of hypnotherapeutic treatment, David was able to shift his ego orientation from ego passivity, together with the associated sense of being overwhelmed by massive traumatization, to ego activity, through which he gained an increasing sense of mastery over his internal and external life (Fromm, 1972). Figure 10.2 shows the progression of recovery from severe character pathology and ego passivity to an active ego working through and integrating the memories, feelings, and selfobject representations associated with the war traumatization and atrocity.

Through the course of the hypnotherapy, David gradually rediscovered the capacity to feel. An important goal of the treatment was "affective revival" (Parson, 1984, p. 44). Egendorf (1978, p. 245) has described the task of treatment with Vietnam veterans as helping them "acquire or re-learn the capacity to feel." After years of treatment in the context of a stable, containing therapeutic relationship, this patient was able to say, "I feel a little sad."

REFERENCES

American Psychiatric Association (1987), *Diagnostic and Statistical Manual of Mental Disorders*, 3rd ed.-rev. Washington, DC: American Psychiatric Association.

Blanck, A. S. (1982), Apocalypse terminable and interminable: Operation outreach for Vietnam veterans. *Hosp. Commun. Psychiat.*, 33:913–918.

Blos, P. (1962), *On Adolescence*. New York: Free Press.

Borus, J. F. (1973), Re-entry I. *Arch. Gen. Psychiat.*, 28:501–506.

_____ (1976), The re-entry transition of the Vietnam veteran. In: *The Social Psychology of Military Service*, ed. N. L. Goldman & D. R. Segal. Beverly Hills, CA: Sage, pp. 27–44.

Bowlby, J. (1973), *Attachment and Loss. Vol 2.* New York: Basic Books.

Brende, J. O. & Benedict, B. D. (1980), The Vietnam combat delayed stress syndrome. *Amer. J. Clin. Hypn.*, 23:34–40.

_____ & McCann, I. L. (1984), Regressive experiences in Vietnam veterans. *J. Contemp. Psychother.*, 14:57–75.

Brown, D. & Fromm, E. (1986), *Hypnotherapy and Hypnoanalysis*. Hillsdale, NJ: Lawrence Erlbaum Associates.

DeFazio, V. J. & Pascucci, N. J. (1984), Return to Ithaca: A perspective on marriage and love in post-traumatic stress disorder. *J. Contemp. Psychother.*, 14:76–89.

_____ Rustin, S. & Diamond, A. (1975), Symptom development in Vietnam era veterans. *Amer. J. Orthopsychiat.*, 45:158–163.

Egendorf, A. (1978), Psychotherapy with Vietnam veterans. In: *Stress Disorders Among Vietnam Veterans*, ed. C. R. Figley. New York: Brunner/Mazel, pp. 231–253.

Fass, M. & Brown, D. (1990), *Creative Mastery in Hypnosis and Hypnoanalysis*. Hillsdale, NJ: Lawrence Erlbaum Associates.

Figley, C. R., ed. (1978), *Stress Disorders Among Vietnam Veterans*. New York: Brunner/Mazel.

Fox, R. P. (1974), Narcissistic rage and the problem of combat aggression. *Arch. Gen. Psychiat.*, 31:807–811.

Fromm, E. (1972), Ego activity and ego passivity in hypnosis. *Internat. J. Clin. Exp. Hypn.*, 20:238–251.

Grinker, R. R. & Spiegel, J. P. (1945), *Men Under Stress*. Philadelphia: Blakeston.

Haley, S. (1974), When patients report atrocities. *Arch. Gen. Psychiat.*, 30:191–196.

_____ (1985), Some of my best friends are dead: Treatment of PTSD patient and his family. In: *Post-Traumatic Stress Disorder and the War Veteran Patient*, ed. W. E. Kelly. New York: Brunner/Mazel, pp. 54–70.

Horowitz, M. J. (1974), Stress response syndromes: Character style and dynamic psychotherapy. *Arch. Gen. Psychiat.*, 31:768–781.

_____ (1976), *Stress Response Syndromes*. New York: Aronson.

Kardiner, A. (1941), The traumatic neurosis of war. *Psychosom. Med. Monograph.* New York: Paul Hoeber.

Kernberg, O. (1976), *Object Relations Theory and Clinical Psychoanalysis*. New York: Aronson.

Kohut, H. (1971), *The Analysis of Self*. New York: IUP.

Kohut, H. (1977), *The Restoration of the Self*. New York: IUP.

Kolb, L. C. & Mutalipassi, L. R. (1982), The conditioned emotional response: A subclass of the chronic and delayed post-traumatic stress disorder. *Psychiatric Ann.*, 12:979–987.

Krystal, H., ed. (1968), *Massive Psychic Trauma*. New York: IUP.

_____ (1977), Aspects of affect theory. *Bull. Menn. Clin.*, 41:1–26.

Laufer, R., Brett, E. & Gallops, M. S. (1984), Post-traumatic stress disorder reconsidered: PTSD among Vietnam veterans. In: *Post-Traumatic Stress Disorders*, ed. B. A. van der Kolk. Washington, DC: American Psychiatric Press, pp. 60–79.

Lifton, R. (1973), *Home from the War*. New York: Simon and Schuster.

Lindy, J. D. (1988), *Vietnam Casebook*. New York: Brunner/Mazel.

MacPherson, M. (1984), *Long Time Passing* New York: Doubleday.

Mahler, M. (1968), *On Human Symbiosis and the Vicissitudes of Individuation*. New York: IUP.

Morrier, E. (1984), Passivity as a sequel to combat trauma. *J. Comtemp. Psychother.*, 14:99–113.

Neff, L. (1975), Traumatic neurosis: A syndrome seen in Vietnam war veterans. Paper presented at the American Orthopsychiatric Association, annual meeting, Atlanta, Georgia, March, 1976.

Parson, E. R. (1984), The reparation of the self: Clinical and theoretical dimensions in the treatment of Vietnam combat veterans. *J. Contemp. Psychother.*, 14:4–56.

Payne, E. (1978), Psychic trauma revisited. Unpublished manuscript.

Rapaport, D. (1967), Some metapsychological considerations concerning activity and passivity. In: *The Collected Papers of David Rapaport*, ed. M. M. Gill. New York: Basic Books, pp. 530–568.

Shapiro, R. B. (1984), Transference, countertransference and the Vietnam veteran. In: *Psychotherapy of the Combat Veteran*, ed. H. J. Schwartz. New York: Spectrum Medical and Scientific Books, pp. 85–101.

Shatan, C. F. (1973), The grief of soldiers—Vietnam combat veteran's self help movement. *Amer. J. Orthopsychiat.*, 43:640–653.

_____ (1977), Bogus manhood, bogus honor: Surrender and transfiguration in the U.S. Marine Corps. *Psychoanal. Rev.*, 25:325–349.

_____ (1978), Stress disorders among Vietnam veterans. In: *Stress Disorders Among Vietnam Veterans: Theory, Research and Treatment*, ed. C. R. Figley. New York: Brunner/Mazel, pp. 43–55.

Silver, S. M. & Kelly, W. E. (1985), Hypnotherapy of post-traumatic stress disorder in combat veterans from WWII and Vietnam. In: *Post-Traumatic Stress Disorder and the War Veteran Patient*, ed. W. E. Kelly. New York: Brunner/Mazel, pp. 211–233.

Spiegel, D. (1981), Vietnam grief work using hypnosis. *Amer. J. Clin. Hypn.*, 24:33–40.

Stolar, D. & Fromm, E. (1974), Activity and passivity of the ego in relation to the superego. *Internat. Rev. Psychoanal.*, 1:297–311.

Strayer, R. & Ellenhorn, L. (1975), Vietnam veterans: A study exploring adjustment patterns and attitudes. *J. Social Issues*, 31:81–93.

Van der Kolk, B. A., ed. (1984), *Post-Traumatic Stress Disorder: Psychological and Biological Sequelae.* Washington, DC: American Psychiatric Press.

———— (1985), Inescapable shock, neurotransmitters and addiction. *Biolog. Psychiat.,* 20:314–325.

Wilson, J. P., Smith, W. &. Johnson, S. K. (1985), A comparative analysis of PTSD among various survivor groups. In: *Trauma and Its Wake: The Study and Treatment of Post-Traumatic Stress Disorder,* ed. C. R. Figley. New York: Brunner/Mazel, pp. 142–172.

Chapter 11

AFFECTS AND ADDICTIVE SUFFERING
A Clinical Perspective

Edward J. Khantzian

Substance abusers have a penchant for adopting the use of addictive substances and behaviors as a means to control or regulate painful and confusing affect states that they are otherwise unable to achieve on their own. Despite this, however, other factors such as biological and sociocultural ones need to be considered as well for an understanding of the evolution of addictive problems.

The acceptance and legitimate use of alcohol in our society demonstrates that misuse of and dysfunctional dependence on substances are not invariable or inevitable consequences. As is repeatedly emphasized in this chapter, distress and suffering are constant antecedents and sequelae of addictive behavior. Nevertheless, clinical perspectives, literary and scholarly studies, and media accounts also make it abundantly clear that our capacity to endure and transform human psychological suffering without resorting to substance is significantly influenced by the way small-group and large-group experiences in our culture, starting with family, succeed or fail to sustain our need for comfort, protection, and contact.

Excessive and maladaptive use of drugs and alcohol becomes an alternative when the structure and support provided by our social institutions and peer relations deteriorate or are unable to meet our needs. It is likely that the pervasive drug problems in our society over the past four decades are related to and have paralleled corresponding extraordinary societal developments and disruptions. The 1960s was the decade of assassinations, the Vietnam war, and the advent of widespread, heavy marijuana use; with the 1970s, we ushered in the Watergate scandals, the dislodging of a president, and the heroin epidemic; the 1980s brought global transformations in government, more grand-scale corruption in political and business arenas, and the staggering problems of cocaine dependence, including its more menacing version, "crack" cocaine, which has brought us into the 1990s with only slight abatement in the use of any of these drugs. We need consider only a few examples of the consequences of such breakdowns in society: take the plight of the homeless, mentally ill who we know have major problems with drugs and alcohol, or reflect on the added threat of cocaine turf wars in inner-city neighborhoods that are already overwhelmed, or look at the constant display in the media of public figures and leaders who are unable to govern either themselves or those for whom they are responsible. It is little wonder that the loss of sanctuary, safety, and confidence in so many quarters of our society leaves us prone to seek and temporarily find such sanctuary in drug or alcohol solutions and related addicted behaviors.

This chapter focuses on the psychological underpinnings of addictive process and vulnerability and how one's incapacity to sustain, identity, or control painful affects is at the heart of addictive disorders, including certain forms of compulsive activities and behaviors not involving substances but that have in common many of these incapacities.

ADDICTIVE PROCESS AND EXPERIENCE

"Addiction" has traditionally referred to the habitual use of psychoactive substances and has been linked to physiological mechanisms involving physical tolerance (i.e., the need for more and more substance to obtain the same effect) and dependence (i.e., physiological withdrawal symptoms if substance is abruptly discontinued). These mechanisms were worked out three and four decades ago based on research at the Federal Hospital/Prison system with individuals who had become dependent on opiates and sedative-hypnotics (Ewing and Bakewell, 1967; Wikler, 1968), and before widespread use and misuse of stimulants and marijuana, drugs that do not so neatly or simply meet the physiologic criteria of addiction.

Starting with the heroin epidemic of the 1960s and 1970s, the widespread use of marijuana and stimulants (especially cocaine) during the 1970s and 1980s, and a corresponding acceptance of alcoholism as a disease, there has been growing awareness and concern among citizens,

clinicians, and social scientists about human "addictive" vulnerability in
addition to a search for explanations and solutions. Not without significance, three major or main neurotransmitter systems—catecholamines,
endorphins, and γ-aminobutyric acid—have been identified during this
time. Although much evidence shows that these neurotransmitters are
important in the regulation and expression of emotion, it remains to be
learned how emotions and the neurotransmitter systems affect each
other. Computer and technological breakthroughs have combined to
delineate and document more precisely the genetic and biological underpinnings of addictions, but at the same time there is still interest in
understanding addictions' psychological basis. In addition, burgeoning
interest has arisen in a range of behaviors or activity characterized as
"addictive" in nature, including compulsive or habitual behaviors such as
gambling, bulimia/anorexia, compulsive running, violence, risk taking,
and even sexuality. These behavioral excesses share with the addictions
an inordinate mental preoccupation with the behavior or activity, an
excessive desire or need to pursue it, a seeming inability to control it, and
a persistent, repeated reversion to it despite deleterious consequences.
Like the addictions, they also seem to be associated with short-term
comfort, pleasure, and gratification, but invariably also with short- and
long-term deleterious and destructive consequences, often entailing
much suffering.

This chapter describes the centrality of affect experience in the
addictive process and how addicts suffer in extremes, their feelings being
either intense, unbearable, and overwhelming or diffuse, confusing, or
absent. Most of all, addicts suffer because their feelings are out of
their control, and they believe a drug or alcohol "solution" to this state
of affairs provides relief even at the same time as it perpetuates their
suffering.

Many of the addicts' difficulties can be accounted for by examining
addicts' disturbances in psychological (ego) structures and selfobject relationships. The recent clarification of affect deficits in addicts as well as
other special populations and the contemporary object-relations view of
the repetition compulsion are helpful in explaining how attachment to
addictive substances and related behaviors become so compelling.

Alcoholism and drug addiction are primary here, but the chapter also
explores clinical examples involving some of the other "addictive" behaviors and patterns because they contribute to a more comprehensive,
composite understanding of the addiction process. Such understanding is
not always best articulated by or garnered from any one individual
suffering with an addictive disorder, given the not infrequent no-
words-for-feelings problems they exhibit.

SELF-MEDICATION FACTORS

General

Because of the growing drug epidemic of the 1960s and 1970s, especially the growing heroin problem, many government-funded programs began to proliferate. At the same time, private practitioners were seeing an increasing number of adolescent and young adult patients with drug abuse problems. Thus, an increasing number of clinicians, many with psychoanalytic training or interest, began publishing clinical and theoretical findings that indicated a surprising degree of consensus about substance abusers' psychological vulnerabilities. Most reports stressed developmental disturbances and problems in adaptation in which dependence on drugs appeared to be associated with painful affect states and coexisting psychiatric conditions (Khantzian and Treece, 1977).

Although most substance abusers had experimented with all of the classes of drugs (analgesic opiates, sedative-hypnotics, stimulants, and hallucinogens), it was a striking finding, based on their drug histories and self-reports, that a majority of patients demonstrated preference for a particular class of drugs. Such special attachment to a class of drugs, variously referred to as a "drug of choice," the "preferential use of drugs," and the "self-selection" process (Khantzian, 1975; Milkman and Frosch, 1973; Weider and Kaplan, 1969), suggested that the specific psychotropic effects of the different classes of drugs interacted with particular painful affect states to make them compelling.

More recently, clinical observations and psychodynamic formulations, complemented by diagnostic studies, have generated empirical findings and a theoretical understanding that a self-medication factor is involved for many individuals who become dependent on substances (Khantzian, 1974, 1975, 1985; Krystal and Raskin, 1970; Milkman and Frosch, 1973; Weider and Kaplan, 1969). In contrast to some of the patients mentioned in this chapter whose dysphoria is distressing because affects are so diffuse and confusing, in the instances when self-medication motives predominate, patients describe more precisely identifiable painful feeling states that were relieved by drug effects. Although many patients suggest that the self-medication motive is a constant determinant in their drug use, the histories of these patients and others suggest that over time the emotional states associated with drug-use determinance are highly variable and might involve either vaguely experienced dysphoria or, for that matter, the absence of feeling, or even euphoria. These latter possibilities do not invalidate the self-medication hypothesis. Rather, the variability of affect states associated with drug use suggests several possibilities, including relief of dysphoria associated with identifiable painful affects, perpetuation of dysphoria, and, perhaps foremost, the attempt to control dysphoria. This section concerns the relief of particular dysphoric affect states associated with the action of the main drugs of abuse.

Analgesic-Opiates

The general pain–relieving qualities of analgesic opiates are well known. Their tranquilizing, or ataractic, and psychotropic properties in the relief of emotional distress have also been described (Chein et al., 1964; Jaffe, 1970). Such properties of addictive drugs in general were described by earlier psychoanalytic investigators (Fenichel, 1945; Rado, 1933; Savit, 1954) but prior to the advent of modern psychopharmacology. Thus, most investigators did not distinguish between the classes of drugs and did not appreciate the different action of each class of drugs (Khantzian, 1974, 1985). More recently, clinical observations of opiate-dependent individuals have suggested that the containing-muting action of opiates is used to avoid or reduce adolescent turmoil associated with anxiety, depression, and somatic distress (Weider and Kaplan, 1969); to gain a sense of calm; to foster a preference for withdrawal and isolation (Milkman and Frosch, 1973); or to counter feelings of hurt, shame, loneliness, and rage (Wurmser, 1974).

Beyond the general muting and dampening effects of opiates, my own observations and work have noted the specific antirage, antiviolence action of this class of drugs, and I have proposed that such action constitutes the principal and compelling reason for its appeal to certain individuals. Based on evaluation of more than 200 narcotic addicts, I have described in a series of reports the special lifelong relationship and experiences that opiate addicts have had with extreme aggression, violence, and sadistic behavior in their home and surrounding environments (Khantzian, 1972, 1974, 1978, 1979, 1982). Although in their childhood and adolescence, these addicts had been more often than not victims of these harsh environments, they themselves invariably and eventually became perpetrators of physical abuse, violence, brutality, and sadistic behaviors. In evaluating them, I discovered how distressed they were with the aggressive and rageful affects behind their violent behaviors, consistently describing a calming and subduing effect on these emotions when they used opiates. I proposed that such individuals found opiates compelling because the antiaggression action of opiates muted uncontrolled rage. Opiates thereby counter the threat of both internal psychological disorganization and external counteraggression from others, a not unusual reaction in people who wrestle with rage and violent impulses (Khantzian, 1985).

Sedative-Hypnotics (including alcohol)

In contrast to the muting and containing action of opiates, sedative-hypnotic drugs (including alcohol) have the opposite—a disinhibiting or releasing— effect on emotions. Fenichel (1945) quotes an unknown source—"The superego is that part of the mind that is soluble in alcohol"—to capture the appeal of sedative-hypnotics. It is probably on this basis that alcohol has such universal appeal in Western cultures as a "social lubricant" whose disinhibiting action might explain its appeal for some tense, neurotically inhibited individuals. In my experience, however, the majority of individuals who have become and remained dependent on alcohol or sedatives have struggled with more severe inhibitions and restrictive personality structures involving rigid and unstable defenses against narcissistic longings and aggressive impulses. Krystal and Raskin (1970) have reported that these drugs appeal to individuals whose use the exaggerated defenses of denial and splitting in the service of "walling off" aggressive and loving feelings in relation to self and others. Such patients do not tolerate ambivalence and thus prefer the short-acting drugs in order to both experience and express such feeling briefly and, therefore, "safely."

In a consultation, Jeff, a 28-year-old salesman, claimed that alcohol helped to break through the "wall" of his overriding sense of social and emotional restriction which he dated back to childhood. He characterized his mother as "cold and punitive" and described the pervasive attitude as he grew up that children "should be seen and not heard"; self-expression was either discouraged or not allowed. He confirmed his therapist's impression that alcohol and Valium® helped to undo repression of his feelings and self-expression when he described how "engaging and gregarious" he was when under the influence of alcohol or Valium, without which he was avoidant and socially isolated. Unfortunately, he sometimes overshot the mark with alcohol by becoming excited, aggressive, and impulsive, and interestingly, he relied on his girlfriend to control these reactions and help him avoid harm and embarrassment.

Stimulants

The energizing and activating properties of the stimulants have been well described (Ellinwood, 1967; Gawin and Ellinwood, 1988). The short-term effects on mood elevation, energy, sense of power, improved performance, and reduction in appetite have tended, especially in the case of cocaine, to make these drugs glamorous and appealing in certain sectors of society, especially among affluent, "fast-lane" people, performers, and athletes. Once again, however, the reasons why certain individuals become and remain dependent on these drugs go beyond the drugs' super-ficial glamour and appeal. My own work has stressed that the energizing properties of stimulants become compelling for certain individuals be-cause they help them to counter the fatigue and depletion states associ-ated with depression (Khantzian, 1975). Furthermore, the activating prop-erties of these drugs, currently most often seen with cocaine, help chronically depressed individuals (often subclinical or atypical in nature) to overcome their anergia, to relate better to others ("speed talk"), and to complete tasks, thus providing a temporary sense of well-being and a boost in self-esteem (Khantzian, 1985; Khantzian and Khantzian, 1984). In other instances, amphetamine or cocaine users take advantage of the stimulating properties of these drugs as augmenters for a hypomanic, self-sufficient life-style (Khantzian, 1979); for others still, who are hyper-active and restless, these drugs paradoxically calm (Khantzian, 1985; Khantzian and Khantzian, 1984).

Along similar lines, other researchers report that stimulants have appeal because they either produce increased feelings of self-assertiveness, self-esteem, and frustration tolerance (Weider and Kaplan, 1969) or help to relieve or eliminate feelings of boredom and emptiness (Wurmser, 1974) and to facilitate active confrontation of one's environ-ment (Milkman and Frosch, 1973).

Self-medication motives may govern dependence on substances, but it may also be that for these same individuals and others, the motives for drug use are more complex and not so clear, especially when the practice perpetuates their suffering or makes it worse. Perhaps the main motive is the attempt to control suffering, regardless of whether the result is to increase or decrease suffering.

THE CONTROL OF SUFFERING

Disturbances in affect development and affect defense lie at the core of addictive vulnerabilities and appear to have originated in early life expe-riences with important care-givers. In the context of disturbed or dys-functional object relations, affect deficits conspire to produce at least a two-fold feeling (or affect) problem in the lives of these individuals: On one hand, affects may be diffuse, nameless, or absent; on the other, they may be intense and overwhelming. In either extreme, for such individu-als, feeling life constantly threatens to be beyond their control.

Appreciating that affects have a "normal" developmental line and that they may be subject to developmental arrest or regression provides a basis for appreciation of some of the peculiar and atypical ways special populations such as addicts and psychosomatic and character-disordered individuals experience and express their emotions. These patients also experience and perpetuate a great deal of emotional pain and suffering in self and others in their special adaptations and their attempts to relieve their suffering. To the extent that they seem to author and stubbornly hold onto their pain, they are often accused of being masochistic. To the extent that their adaptation inflicts or produces suffering for others (consider the painful lot of the spouse of a chronic somatizer, addict, or character-disordered person), we describe them as being sadistic.

Many of these problems are self-perpetuating, and the "repetition compulsion" is often invoked to explain what appear to be sadomasochistic motives on the part of these patients. Unfortunately, when used in this way (so often pejoratively), drive psychology is employed, which places undue emphasis on pleasure and on aggressive instincts. Popular and theoretical explanations too often suggest that the repetitious pain and suffering that addicts sustain and inflict on others represent an attempt to expiate and resolve guilt associated with aggression, which is inverted and directed at the self.

In the opinion of some (Gedo, 1979; Greenberg and Mitchell, 1983), Freud (1920) was ultimately misguided when he invoked a "death instinct" to explain the repetition compulsion. In any case, his observations and formulations about turning passive unpleasure into active mastery and the defensive aspects of children's play are more germane to understanding the experience with and perpetuation of suffering observed in addictive phenomena. Freud's ideas served as an early model to explain repetition compulsion on the basis of object relations and structural factors.

Fairbairn (1944) proposed that libido was object seeking, not pleasure seeking, in life and that the main striving of the child is not toward pleasure but toward contact. More contemporary theorists have linked certain patients' painful attachments to earliest object ties, which more often coalesce around affective elements versus cognitive ones (Valenstein, 1973). These early experiences are not "encoded in words" (Gedo, 1986, p. 206), but they express themselves without conscious memories in perceptual-action-affect responses (Gedo, 1986; Lichtenberg, 1983), and they control one's traumatic pain by "inoculating oneself with repeated small doses" (Modell, 1984, p. 34). To this extent, as Fairbairn suggests, individuals maintain an "obstinate attachment" to some of the most unsatisfactory and ungratifying aspects of their relationship with their parents, hoping to work out a more satisfactory contact. Later in life, these "allegiances" are borne out in painful, self-defeating attachments and relationships (Fairbairn, 1944; Greenberg and Mitchell, 1983).

The problems and pitfalls of reductionism and reconstruction make it difficult to conclusively attribute the dynamics of addictive process to these early factors alone. Nevertheless, an integrative approach may consider how affect experience interacts with "core relationship themes/ pattern" in psychotherapy (Luborsky, 1984). Affect experience plays itself out meaningfully in the treatment relationship with the therapist and begins to provide a basis for observing and explaining how affects coalesce around early object experience and make feeling life so confusing, unbearable, and out of control. The following summary of a treatment hour provides an example of how a patient and therapist can discover together a validity to such formulations and the formulations' not entirely speculative nature.

Mary Ann, a 45-year-old physician recovering from narcotic dependence and benzodiazepine abuse typifies addicts' dread of distress. She also amplifies on the nature of drug-induced "euphoria" and hints at how the origins of such problems derive from early, troubled object relations. She was anticipating vulvar and vaginal laser surgery for dysplasia and was very anxious, reporting this during the hour. She added that perhaps she was "getting anxious about getting anxious"—referring to the "smile reaction" she gets and remembers "deep in [her] brain" that follows a dose of narcotics (which she would need for surgery), the "smile reaction that almost invariably leads to readdiction."

For part of the hour, we discussed practical aspects of what pain medication she might have during and after the surgery, focusing on the advantages of methadone ("I don't get that smile") versus the protracted withdrawal from it, which represents a disadvantage, a not insignificant problem given her intolerance of the painful feelings that she (and other addicts) often experiences as "deadly."

At a certain point, she shifted the focus of her concerns from the practical to the deeper dread of relapse and its psychological significance for her. She told me a story that had evolved over the past week as an example of what her worry and vulnerability were about. She had attended a promotional reception sponsored by her fiancé's company, at which she had violated her usual commitment to total abstinence by accepting a glass of wine. She referred to "the warmth and the glow" she experienced from the wine as familiar and enjoyable. She did not think of it again until two days later when she uncharacteristically thought of ordering a glass of wine with dinner. Immediately, she realized that she was in danger because of the false security she derived from having had just a single glass of wine two days previously, but she also realized danger by subliminally remembering the warm glow she had experienced when she last drank. Thus, recognizing her vulnerability, she decided not to order the glass of wine.

Later in the hour, I underscored how much she was improving in her self-care, making use of her awareness of the danger signs, even though subtle, to guide her behavior. More important, however, she was able to derive deeper understanding of her vulnerabilities when I speculated aloud with her about how important it might be to understand the feeling state she described as a "glow." I told her I had an image of the alcohol's stimulating the release of an internal opiate ligand (a molecule) and settling into a receptor site in a soothing and comforting way, the way it happens naturally, for example, when there is the right fit between a small child and its mother—a fit she had previously suggested to me had always been a poor and uncomfortable one between her and her mother. I pointed at the Kathe Kollowitz print of mother and child over my shoulder, indicating the "right fit" might be something like the ideal portrayed in the print.

Mary Ann responded to my speculation by recalling that the only time she had had a glass of wine recently was about six weeks before at a similar reception and that, feeling a similar "glow" from wine, she had experienced a playful and warm attraction to her fiancé's boss. However, when that man joined them recently for dinner and she was sober, she in fact responded indifferently, if not negatively, wondering what the appeal had been about, but now realizing it had probably been a result of the alcohol glow. She said, "It means when I'm not under the influence of that glow, I'm not happy, and all those years I've been on a search, yearning for the glow." She supposed that a memory of the "glow" had been implanted sometime in the past, before she had became addicted, from "a shot of Demerol® or a drink somewhere back then." She emphasized how such a "memory" stays with a person, citing as an example a recovering alcoholic colleague who could still remember the first and special alcohol "high" he had experienced 18 years before.

She added that she experienced a "high" once she could relieve physical pain with an opiate drug. I suggested that this was not universally true and that I had come to learn from patients that it more often occurred in people who could not soothe, calm, or comfort themselves when distressed physically or emotionally. I again suggested that the self-soothing capacity or the lack of it might derive from an early time in life when maybe her mother could not adequately soothe or comfort her. At this point and as the end of the hour approached, she animatedly lent credence to this possibility by adding, "Whenever we kids had pain or discomfort, Mother didn't know how to deal with it; she either gave us a medicine or took us to the doctor. She certainly wasn't like Tom [Mary Ann's fiancé], who [within the past] week took care of my headache by applying a cool wet towel to my forehead and rubbing my back."

When addicts such as Mary Ann speak of the "high" they achieve with drug effects, such statements serve as markers for disturbed early object relations around needs for nurturance and comfort (Woolcott, 1980).

Unfortunately, the affective correlates of these needs are often inadequately elaborated in memories or symbols and as Gedo (1986) and Lichtenberg (1983) suggest, are played out as perceptual-affect-action patterns. Although neither Gedo or Lichtenberg has considered addictive phenomena, the two have applied these observations to personality disturbances and they likely apply as well to addictions.

As indicated earlier, there are degrees of differentiation and specificity in the affect experience of addicted individuals. To the extent that addicts are able to be aware of and suffer with particular painful feelings such as rage or depression, they probably primarily need to "self-medicate" their suffering. To the extent that feelings are distressingly vague, confusing, or diffuse, they might adopt or use the painful effects and aftereffects of drugs as substituted suffering to counter their confusion. In reality, there are admixtures of painful states and confusion, in determine drug use or related behaviors. In either instance, as my patients and I have discovered, feelings threaten to be out of control and overwhelming. Such individuals succeed in coping with this threat by adopting addictive solutions with admixtures of pain and relief of pain. The main adaptational value, however, is that they substitute dysphoria and a relationship with suffering they do not understand or control for one's they do understand and control.

AFFECT DEVELOPMENT AND BORDERLANDS
OF ADDICTION

As Brown (this volume) indicates, the way individuals experience, tolerate, and express affects develops along certain lines. There is evidence that the caretaking environment significantly influences how and whether affect development adheres to a more or less normal line or whether pathological distortions or deficits in affects occur. Krystal (1982, 1988; Krystal and Raskin, 1970) has observed striking similarities in the way patients who have suffered major psychological trauma, psychosomatic problems, or substance dependence process emotions. As some of the case vignettes in this section also suggest, these same deficits and distortions are also present in compulsive behaviors not associated with substance usage. Krystal traces the origins of these problems, along theoretical lines, to disturbances in affect development or regression in affect experience as a consequence of major trauma. Krystal has adopted the term "alexithymia" (Nemiah, 1970, Sifneos 1967) to underscore the inability of certain patients to verbalize their feelings. Krystal has also proposed that affects are undifferentiated and that separate feelings such as anxiety and depression do not appear and more often are somatized.

He accounts for such disabilities by tracing how affects develop out of a common undifferentiated matrix; evolve through differentiation, desomatization, and verbalization; and allow feelings to be used as signals and guides in adapting to internal life and external reality (Krystal and Raskin, 1970). The work of Krystal (1982), Greenspan (1977), Wurmser (1974), McDougall (1984), Marty and De M'Uzan (1963), and Brown (this volume) shares in common a consideration of developmental factors and influences in explaining some of the vague, confusing, and painfully intense qualities in affect experience. These authors explore how addictive solutions represent a countermeasure to core disturbances in affect experience and affect defense. Although not specifically concerned with addictive phenomena, recent clinical and theoretical observations about infant development provide additional bases to understand that affects are hard to tolerate not only because they may be intense and painful but also because they may be diffuse, nameless, and elusive (Sashin, 1985; Gedo, 1986; Lichtenberg, 1983; Stern, 1985; Lane and Schwartz, 1987).

The observations of the developmentalists about manifestations of abnormality in newborns, infants, and young children (Brown, this volume), parallel those made with individuals who experience addictive disorders. This is most striking in the realm of affect experience. Although it is difficult to precisely trace addicts' aberrant affect responses in infancy or to reconstruct when or how they occur in childhood, our clinical experience suggests that addictive behaviors give meaning to and organize dysphoric states deriving from early periods of development.

In the following case, an eating-disordered patient revealed in therapy the early origins of her difficulties in her interactions with her parents. Accounts such as this indicate parents' pervasive and recurrent insensitivity to their intolerance of emotions, also an important factor in addictive disorders and behaviors.

Jane, an obese 38-year-old accountant, complained that her family "didn't do feelings at all," describing how as a child any expression of upset or unhappiness, unless linked to a very specific event would be met by a barrage of Mother's impatient comments: "Why should you be upset? You have everything you want. . . ." Then Jane might be offered a "hot cake" or muffin in her very food oriented home. Through therapy, Jane has come to realize that her almost continuous crying during treatment sessions represented a lifetime reservoir of sadness and yearning never acknowledged or appreciated by her parents, which she had learned to keep back by being "totally self-sufficient." Although not as fragmented or extreme as some patients (cf. "Pat," described later), Jane has had a penchant for talking in extensive detail and usually in a clipped rapid manner, often finding great difficulty in linking feelings to events. It took nearly two years of once-weekly psychotherapy to break through her shame (a reactive and protective affect common in addicts—Wurmser, 1987) and to even begin to describe any details about or find words for the feelings associated with her overeating. She said, "I get frustrated, overwhelmed, and uncomfortable and then I begin to eat. At first I feel soothed, but then I'm back to feeling frustrated. Instead of a feeling I can't identify, I have a new focus—on being angry or upset with myself—but I can understand it." Ironically, these clarifications came to light during a session when she anticipated great relief at the imminent completion of an intense graduate study program. Her associations about what happens when she eats had followed my pointing out that some of the current distress she experienced seemed to develop at a time of change and reprieve. She further elaborated that she ate whether she was feeling "good, bad, down, confused, or overwhelmed." She said, "I 'treat' myself with food—as in 'treatment'—the concept caught hold of me this week, even if I'm having fun or not having fun, I treat myself with food." She ended this session by clarifying that her weight had jumped several increments, each associated with "major change," such as her divorce ten years ago, a corporate crisis, and the return to graduate studies.

The previous section on the self-medication hypothesis elaborated on how certain individuals adopt the use of drugs because they discover that different drugs have specific actions on affect states that they experience as intense and unbearable. Many of these are the result of deficits or defects in ego structures, causing individuals to suffer with painful feelings of rage, tension/anxiety, or depression and anergia. Although patients such as Jane do not escape these feelings, their impulses toward certain behaviors, including addictive ones, are determined more by an inability to feel or by a confusion about feelings than by any particular painful feeling. Greenspan (1977) has made similar observations about substance abusers, linking such inability to feel and the use of substances to disturbances in developmental lines proposed by Mahler (1968). He proposes that the "highs" or the "lows" are acceptable substitutes for the absence of feelings.

Patients may or may not resort to drugs, but the common themes of drivenness, suffering, and dangerous pursuits govern their addictive attachments and behaviors. A physician was referred for debilitating anxiety, which manifested itself primarily somatically. He was seeking temporary disability benefits to escape an intolerable job; he hated his supervisors and coworkers and felt their reciprocal dislike and lack of respect. Exploration of his difficulties suggested that his symptoms of diarrhea and back pain together with the struggle against his peers and supervisors were expressions and externalizations of a much deadlier and more menacing sense of emptiness, which dated back to childhood. He complained of feeling "stuck and unable to make progress' and described a pervasive, rather constant inner mood of being "in a cloud—my mind is unclear and I'm in a daze and restless." He was prone to "bury problems in activity." He said, "I'm going as fast as I can; I'm constantly on the go—very busy; otherwise, I start to think about things. I feel worthless. I feel like everything would stop—I would die. I would stop functioning and go to sleep forever." In discussing him with his referring therapist, I learned that through much of his adult life,this patient would periodically race his motorcycle at speeds of 90–100 mph (he called it "red-lining") as a way to feel alive at times of distress but didn't realize "what he was doing until it was over"; his therapist was surprised that he was "not into drugs." Another physician, who did have problems with drugs, gave a similar explanation of how a dangerous and painful behavior can serve adaptively. He was confronted by me with the observation that his drug of choice, an intravenous stimulant, was apt to be harsh if not disorganizing because it could produce threatening violent and paranoid states. He said, "I (at least) know why I feel bad—and when I'm going to control it—maybe it's feeling, instead of not feeling."

ADDICTION AS METAPHOR—THE CASE OF PAT

Pat, although not an addict, provides evidence that core issues of affect deficits and intolerance can painfully weave their way through a person's entire life and behaviorally and symptomatically resemble many of the repetitions and self-defeating qualities of addictive disorders. During our work together, both the patient and I began to better understand her distress by adopting an addictive paradigm to understand her extreme distress and suffering.

One of Pat's poems demonstrates the quality and intensity of the distress that governed so much of her inner life and her behavior.

As a Child . . .

Here I was shrieking in
the wilderness
Why didn't anybody
hear.
No one picked up the
terror
nobody saved me from
me.
No one wanted to hear
or see
or believe
life wasn't perfect.

The dot to dots
didn't connect.
Once in a while
I didn't even
bother with defenses
the gates were down
the goats and cattle run
away.
no fence posts
no barbed wire
no comfort.
Just the great Morassa Swamp
sucking me down
pulling me away.
Build up the heat
so only cold gets through
to comfort
to condone
the hell inside of me
the key to it all is
comfort
the word turns
my insides out
crashes waves down
upon my head
sweeps me away.
drowns me.
I deserve suffering
and death.

The clinician is often served well by the artist in depicting the human problems encountered in clinical practice. It is even better when the artist is a patient. In Pat's case, the foregoing was one of many poems the patient offered to me during 12 years of treatment as a means of conveying her internal distress, which, invariably for her, was more difficult, if not impossible, to do by the spoken word. Pat was not an addict, but she could have been. Her attachment to action and activity in her vocational, avocational, and civic commitments had "addictive" qualities. At the same time, these activities produced a painful sense of overextension and absorption at the expense of her own well-being and self-care and to the avoidance of other responsibilities.

As with addicts, her feelings have been an extraordinary source of "terror" and threat, as well as a source of bewilderment and confusion. Over the course of treatment, she has remained consistently at a loss to identify or convey her distress in the spoken word but has been able to describe some aspects of it, often concretely and dramatically, through her poetry, which, over the years has tended to be more feelingful. As indicated in her poem "As a Child" however, she struggles to find language to express her emotions, and her inability to find comfort remains intense and extreme. When I was attempting to convey what I thought she was saying and that I was interested in using her poem in my writing, she consented, completing my explanation before I did by saying, "It is called addictive suffering."

Our understanding of both her dilemma and her poem "As a Child" probably evolved out of a discussion several months before. During that therapy hour, she had helped to schematize some of the core qualities of her suffering, which felt overwhelming and unbearable as a consequence of her feeling too much or too little, a not infrequent observation among people who suffer with substance dependencies (Khantzian, 1990).

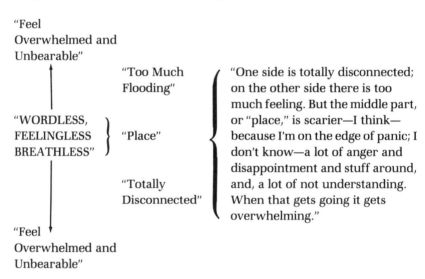

"Feel
Overwhelmed and
Unbearable"

                          "Too Much   "One side is totally disconnected;
                          Flooding"   on the other side there is too
                                               much feeling. But the middle part,
"WORDLESS,   or "place," is scarier—I think—
FEELINGLESS   "Place"   because I'm on the edge of panic; I
BREATHLESS"   don't know—a lot of anger and
                                               disappointment and stuff around,
                          "Totally   and, a lot of not understanding.
                          Disconnected"   When that gets going it gets
                                               overwhelming."

"Feel
Overwhelmed and
Unbearable"

This patient's poem and her schema for describing her emotions are extremely helpful in understanding and describing both how addicts suffer and the complex adaptation they achieve when they adopt dependency on substances to relieve or cope with their distress.

Addicted individuals are acutely and chronically distressed and threatened because they reside in a "place," as Pat says, where affects constantly verge toward extremes, quantitatively and qualitatively. At times the distress or threat is the result of specific and intense affect such as rage, terror, or despair, and at other times (or even simultaneously) the quality of affects is a source of dis-ease and threat because they may be vague, absent, or confusing. Yet, with the schema she provides, Pat reminds us that it is even "scarier" because one may hover in a place between these extremes, with more palpable "panic—anger—and disappointment—and a lot of not understanding."

Pat, a 42-year-old mother of three, is employed in a private preparatory school as a special needs consultant. Despite her superior intelligence and her gifts as a teacher of the handicapped, she has had major difficulties overcoming her own developmental handicaps involving her experience with and expression of her feeling life. She typifies, albeit in the extreme, many of the unusual and extreme manifestations of affect with which addicts suffer. Over the course of her 12 years of treatment, but especially early on, the unusual qualities and intensities of her feelings have repeatedly bewildered, eluded, and overwhelmed her and me. Deficits and dysfunction in her affect life have been apparent during treatment hours, as have reports and evidence of subjective, global shifts and alterations in bodily temperature sensations, visual distortions, disintegration fantasies, and an array of atypical psychosomatic symptoms involving her skin, lungs, and musculoskeletal system. The association of being "addictively" driven with the psychosomatic symptoms is not uncommon in addicts. Within the realm of emotions, she has been pervasively unable to identify, name, tolerate, or express her feelings. In the treatment relationship, for two to three years, she could hardly speak. Most often, she grimaced with facial expressions of fear, anger, and confusion, shrugging away (e.g., hostilely thrusting out her left shoulder) my efforts to clarify, understand, or allay her enormous discomfort. Nevertheless, she meticulously kept all her appointments, usually arriving early and often in spite of extreme weather and other obstacles. Correspondingly, during the treatment, I had many reactions to her distress and problems related to me. I alternately or simultaneously experienced great distance, deadly boredom, a sense of burdensome responsibility, counterhostility, and a dysphoric, confusing sense of fragmentation that mirrored her own periodic fragmentation. Over the years, she has become less hostile and is more often friendly. She says that she knows better now what her feelings are ("I have names for the boxes") but is afraid to articulate them. She progressively and more readily talks freely but skirts threatening issues and feelings, instead filling the hours with circumlocutions about her work, family, and other activities.

Her poem "As a Child" hints at the developmental origins of Pat's distress and suggests that the intense and unusual qualities of her feeling life derive from a sense of being overwhelmed and unprotected from an early age. Her contemporary descriptions of her father as a volatile, angry person and her mother as an insensitive women make some of her reactions understandable. Memory fragments from her childhood years with them reveal that Father was physically and verbally abusive and

Mother was extremely ambitious for Pat's academic accomplishment but was otherwise impatient with her. Although reconstructing her history has been difficult, her past provides some basis for her poetic allusions to concerns about harshness and unresponsiveness. In the poem, Pat hints at traumatic abuse and neglect. She says, "I was shrieking in the wilderness"—[with] "terror," but nobody heard, saw, or believed her disharmony. She uses stampeding metaphors to convey that already there were failures and "defects in affect defense" (Wurmser, 1974). In the absence of (parental) controls or comfort, she describes being pulled into an undifferentiated swamp of despair and isolation ("sucking me down/pulling me away"). She juxtaposes heat to cold in search of comfort but laments that the "hell inside" makes it all elusive and impossible. She feels too overwhelmed and swept away and instead asks to drown, proclaiming she "deserve[s] suffering and death."

The addictions are often linked to near-death experiences, acutely apparent in extreme cases of intravenous use of addictive drugs, and recently in the smoking of free-base cocaine, and in alcoholism and other addictive behaviors that individuals practice despite physical, psychological, and social deterioration, often with devastating, if not fatal, consequences. Although Pat was not an addict in the narrow sense, as indicated, her painful sense of drivenness and the inability to control it were much like addicts' inability to control their substance use and related behaviors. Although her struggles are great to convey the nature of her distress, she suggests that courting (if not deserving) suffering and death is a better fate than the helplessness and boundlessness of her fear and despair. Her gifts as a poet and the absence of the disruptive influence of drug effects and aftereffects, I suspect, allow her to do with words what substance abusers do with action.

Pat's attraction to death has been mostly metaphorical (rarely has she been suicidal or a suicidal threat), but her absorption with death and deadly allusions has appeared to be on a continuum with actual near-death involvements of addicts. For Pat and for addicts, the threat of death and its near equivalents seems to be the ultimate expression of the terror and annihilation that must be endured, rather than a retreat and surcease from suffering that suicide or death represents for others. What I suggest is that pain and the threat involved in addictive behaviors are in part motivated behavior in response to passively felt distress that is experienced as confusing and out of control.

CONCLUSION

Addictive suffering has more to do with mastery and control of suffering than masochism, pleasure seeking, or the relief of pain alone. The drug of

choice or particular addictive attachment is probably the result of a
complex interaction of factors having to do with degrees of differentiation
or specificity in affect states, available addictive substances or solutions,
and the degree to which "self-care capacities" (Khantzian and Mack, 1983)
protect an individual from pursuing the most threatening or dangerous
involvements or attachments. As many patients who are not addicts
reveal, their choices of symptoms and behavioral patterns reveal many
commonalities with substance abusers. My experience with addicts and
alcoholics demonstrates how a range of compulsive and addictive involvements are expressions of individuals' attempts to cope with painful affect
states and troubled relationships, even though at the same time such
symptoms only perpetuate their difficulties. A psychodynamic study of
substance abusers' deficits in affect regulations and related difficulties in
object relations allows a more empathic appreciation of addictive suffering and can expand our understanding of human psychological suffering involving a range of symptoms and behaviors, which like the
addictions are repetitions, painful, and defensive at the same time as they
are self-injurious and self-defeating.

REFERENCES

Chein, I., Gerard, D. L., Lee, R. S. & Rosenfeld, E. (1964), *The Road to H.* New York: Basic
Books.
Ellinwood, E. H., Jr. (1967), Amphetamine psychosis. I. Description of individuals and
process. *J. Nerv. Mental Dis.*, 144:273–283.
Ewing, J. E. & Bakewell, W. E. (1967), Diagnosis and management of depressant drug
dependence. *Am. J. Psychiat.*, 123:909–917.
Fairbairn, W. R. (1944), Endopsychic structures considered in terms of object relations. In:
Psychoanalytic Studies of the Personality. London: Tavistock, 1952.
Fenichel, O. (1945), *The Psychoanalytic Theory of Neurosis*. New York: Norton.
Freud, S. (1920), *Beyond the Pleasure Principle*. *Standard Edition*, 18:7–61. London: Hogarth
Press.
Gawin, F. H. & Ellinwood, E. H., Jr. (1988), Cocaine and other stimulants: Actions, abuse, and
treatment. *New Engl. J. Med.*, 318:1173–1182.
Gedo, J. E. (1979), *Beyond Interpretation*. Hillsdale, NJ: The Analytic Press, 1993.
_____ (1986), *Conceptual Issues in psychoanalysis*. Hillsdale, NJ: The Analytic Press.
Greenberg, J. R. & Mitchell, S. A. (1983), *Object Relations in Psychoanalytic Theory*. Cam-
bridge, MA: Harvard University Press.
Greenspan, S. I. (1977), Substance abuse: An understanding from psychoanalytic development and learning perspectives. In: *Psychodynamics of Drug Dependence*, ed. J. D. Blaine
& D. A. Julius. *NIDA* Monograph 12. Rockville, MD: National Institute on Drug Abuse, pp.
73–87.
Jaffe, J. H. (1970), Drug addiction and drug abuse. In: *The Pharmacologic Basis of Therapeu-
tics*, ed. L. S. Goodman & A. Gilhman. London: Macmillan, pp. 276–313.
Khantzian, E. J. (1972), A preliminary dynamic formulation of the psychopharmacologic
action of methadone. *Proceedings of the Fourth National Methadone Conference*, San
Francisco, pp. 371–374.

_____ (1974), Opiate addiction: A critique of theory and some implications for treatment. *Amer. J. Psychother.*, 28:59–70.

_____ (1975), Self selection and progression in drug dependence. *Psychiat. Digest*, 10:19–22.

_____ (1978), The ego, the self and opiate addiction. *Internat. Rev. Psycho-Anal.*, 5:189–198.

_____ (1979), Impulse problems in addiction. In: *Working with the Impulsive Person*, ed. H. Wishnie. New York: Plenum, pp. 97–112.

_____ (1982), Psychological (structural) vulnerabilities and the specific appeal of narcotics. *Ann. N.Y. Acad. Sci.*, 398:24–32.

_____ (1985), The self-medication hypothesis of addictive disorders. *Amer. J. Psychiat.*, 142:1259–1264.

_____ (1990), Self regulation and self-medication factors in alcoholism and the addictions—similarities and differences. *Recent Dev. Alcohol.*, 8:255–271.

_____ & Khantzian, N. J. (1984), Cocaine addiction: Is there a psychological predisposition? *Psychiat. Ann.*, 14:753–759.

_____ & Mack, J. E. (1983), Self preservation and the care of the self—ego instincts reconsidered. *The Psychoanalytic Study of the Child*, 38:209–232. New Haven, CT: Yale University Press.

_____ & Treece, C. (1977), Psychodynamics of drug dependence: An overview. In: Psychodynamics of Drug Dependence, ed. J. D. Blaine & D. A. Julius. *NIDA* Monographs 12. Rockville, MD: National Institute of Drug Abuse, pp. 101–107.

Krystal, H. (1982), Alexithymia and the effectiveness of psychoanalytic treatment. *Internat. J. Psychoanal. Psychother.*, 9:353–378.

_____ (1988). *Integration and Self-Healing*. Hillsdale, NJ: The Analytic Press.

_____ & Raskin, H. A. (1970), *Drug Dependence*. Detroit: Wayne State University Press.

Lane, R. D. & Schwartz, G. E. (1987), Levels of emotional awareness. *Amer. J. Psychiat.*, 144:133–142.

Lichtenberg, J. D. (1983), *Psychoanalysis and Infant Research*. Hillsdale, NJ: The Analytic Press.

Luborsky, L. (1984), *Principles of Psychoanalytic Psychotherapy*. New York: Basic Books.

Mahler, M. S. (1968), *On Human Symbiosis and the Vicissitudes of Individuation*. New York: IUP.

Marty, P. & De M'Uzan, M. (1963), La Pensée Opératoire. *Rev. fr. psychanal.*, 27(suppl.):345–456.

McDougall, J. (1984), The "dis-affected" patient. *Psychoanal. Quart.*, 53:386–409.

Milkman, H. & Frosch, W. A. (1973), On the preferential abuse of heroin and amphetamine. *J. Nerv. Ment. Dis.*, 156:242–248.

Modell, A. H. (1984), *Psychoanalysis in a New Context*. New York: IUP.

Nemiah, J. C. (1970), The psychological management and treatment of patients with peptic ulcer. *Adv. Psychosom. Med.*, 6:169–173.

Rado, S. (1933), The psychoanalysis of pharmacothymia. *Psychoanal. Quart.*, 2:1–23.

Sashin, J. I. (1985), Affect tolerance. *J. Soc. Biol. Struct.*, 8:175–202.

Savit, R. A. (1954), Clinical communications: Extramural psychoanalytic treatment of a case of narcotic addiction. *J. Amer. Psychoanal. Assn.*, 2:494–502.

Sifneos, P. E. (1967), Clinical observations on some patients suffering from a variety of psychosomatic diseases. In: *Proceedings of the Seventh European Conference on Psychosomatic Research*. Basel: Karger.

Stern, D. N. (1985), *The Interpersonal World of the Infant*. New York: Basic Books.

Valenstein, A. (1973), On attachment to painful feelings and the negative therapeutic reaction. *The Psychoanalytic Study of the Child*, 28:365–392. New Haven, CT: Yale University Press.

Weider, H. & Kaplan, E. (1969), Drug use in adolescents. *The Psychoanalytic Study of the Child*, 24:399–432. New York: IUP.

Wikler, A. (1968), Diagnosis and treatment of drug dependence of the barbiturate type. *Amer. J. Psychiat.*, 125:758–765.

Woolcott, P. (1980), Addiction: Clinical and theoretical considerations. *Annual of Psychoanalysis*, 9:189–204. New York: IUP.

Wurmser, L. (1974), Psychoanalytic considerations of the etiology of compulsive drug use. *J. Amer. Psychoanal. Assn.*, 22:820–843.

_____ (1987), Flight from conscience: Experiences with the psychoanalytic treatment of compulsive drug users. *J. Subst. Abuse Treat.*, 4:157–179.

Chapter 12

STRESS AND EMOTION IMPLICATIONS FOR ILLNESS DEVELOPMENT AND WELLNESS

Daniel Brown

This chapter is about the relationship between affect and physical health. With the growing interest in body/mind therapies in medicine and behavioral medicine, this volume would be incomplete without some attempt to address health issues. Specifically, this chapter addresses the questions What is the relationship between affective development, illness development, and health maintenance? How does affective development contribute to physical wellness? and what constitutes optimal mental health or well-being?

DEFINITION OF STRESS

The contribution of affect to illness development is less understood, but many studies have clearly demonstrated the relationship between stress and illness development. To clarify how the concept of stress is defined in research, first, stress is usually associated with an externally perceived situation. Whereas Freud defined an affect, specifically anxiety, as a "response to an internal danger" (Freud, 1926), stress usually refers to an external event or situation, for example, life change, daily hassles, environmental pollution, and social isolation. Second, stress refers more to the perception of stress than to the stressful situation per se. Not all people react to the same situation in the same way; what is stressful for one may not be stressful for another. What is and is not perceived as stressful depends largely too on the range and adequacy of coping resources available to the individual (Roskies and Lazarus, 1980) and on the extent to which the person perceives his or her control over the situation (Marlatt and Gordon, 1985). Third, stress is primarily a biological construct, not an affect construct. Selye's (1956) pioneering work on the "general adaptation [or stress] syndrome" defines stress in terms of gross biological effects, meaning in terms of observable tissue change, for example, an enlarged adrenal cortex or a shrunken thalamus. The generally accepted understanding of the stress effects has been primarily either disregulation of the autonomic nervous system (Cannon, 1923; Gellhorn, 1967) or disregulation of specific organ systems (Schwartz, 1977, 1979; Weiner, 1975). Thus, the relationship between stress, or affect for that matter, and illness development pertains primarily to biological consequences, not to subjective experience.

STRESS AND ILLNESS DEVELOPMENT

The earliest work on stress and illness development focused on life change stress (Holmes and Rahe, 1967). Significant changes in the established routines of daily life such as loss, marriage, birth, change in work status, change in residence, and financial change were associated with the increased probability of subsequent illness. Current research on stress has shifted the emphasis to an understanding of daily hassles such as misplacing or losing things, having too many phone calls to return, getting stuck in traffic, and having to fill out forms (Kanner et al., 1981). These minor stressors accumulate and contribute to physiological disregulation and the development of physical symptoms. Other researchers have focused on the environment as a source of stress. Extreme temperature change (especially exposure to cold); barometric and weather changes; and exposure to toxic substances, radiation, and certain toxic foodstuffs also are associated with illness. In the social environment, extremes of isolation and chronic loneliness on one hand and overcrowding and lack of solitude on the other can contribute to the development of illness. The well-known Alameda County study clearly demonstrates that those who lack social support are at high risk and those with healthy social support systems are more resistant to illness development (Berkman and Syme, 1979).

MECHANISMS OF ILLNESS DEVELOPMENT

Two mechanisms by which stress can affect human physiology and contribute to illness development are disregulation of the nervous autonomic system, which in turn is associated with a variety of psychophysiological conditions, such as headache, hypertension, and asthma, and disregulation of the immune system, which in turn is associated with the development of a variety of immune-related conditions, such as infections, cancer, allergy, and autoimmune disease.

Autonomic Disregulation and Psychophysiological Disorders

Chronic stress results in repeated reactivation of the autonomic nervous system and, ultimately, in a condition of sustained sympathetic activation without intervening periods of rest. Chronic sympathetic activation without habituation contributes to a variety of harmful physiological changes in which the neurons in the autonomic nervous system may become sensitized and thereby stress reactive with little external provocation. Thus, high levels of sympathetic activation may occur readily and frequently, even in the absence of clear-cut external stressors. In this sense, sympathetic activation becomes conditioned as part of a chronic stress–response cycle. Furthermore, such readiness to activation is associated with a cascade of biochemical substances, namely catecholamines and corticosteroids, which are released into the tissues of the body.

The autonomic nervous system mediates the activity of the vasomotor system, the striate musculature, and other physiological systems. Chronic disregulation of the autonomic nervous system can lead to long-term disregulation of vasomotor and striate muscle activation, which in turn can contribute to the development of a variety of psychophysiological conditions. Autonomic hyperactivity is associated with bronchospasm in certain individuals with stress-reactive asthma (Magonet, 1960; Mathe and Knapp, 1971). Disregulation of normal cardiovascular response patterns is critical to the development of essential hypertension (Brown and Fromm, 1987; Fahrion, 1980). Autonomic hyperactivity (Bruyn, 1980; Sargent, Walters, and Green, 1973) with associated vasomotor disregulation (Dalessio, 1980; Graham and Wolff, 1938; Marshall, 1978) and chronic disregulation of striate muscle activation (Bakal and Kaganov, 1977; Budzynski, et al., 1973; Philips, 1977) contribute to a psychobiological predisposition to headache (Bakal, 1982).

Immune Disregulation

The immune system functions to protect the body from invasion by external agents like bacteria and viruses and to preserve the molecular integrity of the body over and against aberrant cell formations like tumors and cancer. This "complex recognition system" (Besedovsky and

Sorkin, 1981, p. 546) is composed of several categories of cells, a complex differentiation of labor between the cell types, and multiple regulatory processes: the humoral, or B-cell, system, which manufactures and secretes a variety of immunoglobulins or circulating antibodies that protect the body from infectious agents or antigens such as bacteria and viruses; the cell-mediated, or T-cell, system, which acts by "molecular touch" (Locke and Colligan, 1986, p. 58) on indigenous cells mistakenly transformed either by genetic mutation or by viral infection (Burnet, 1971); highly mobile natural killer (NK) cells, constituting the first line of defense, which search and destroy bacteria, viruses, and indigenous tumor and virus-infected cells when they first appear in the body and prior to involvement with B and T lymphocytes (Herberman and Holden, 1979); and a system of larger cells, the monocyte-macrophage system, which engulf bacteria, virus-infected tumor cells, and other antigens. The complex interactions between all of these systems function in the service of "immunological surveillance" to protect the organism from invasion by bacteria and viruses and from spontaneous mutations during reproduction of the body's own cells (Burnet, 1971).

The entire operation of the immune system is dependent on a complex biochemical signaling system consisting largely of neuropeptides (Pert, 1986; Toy, 1983). Biochemical messengers signal the general activation of the immune system in response to an antigen and also signal the specific activation and coordination of the B, T, and NK lymphocytes. Catecholamines (Crary et al., 1983), corticosteroids (Dennis and Mond, 1986), and certain opioid peptides (Shavit et al., 1984; Brown and Epps, 1985; Nair, Cilik, and Schwartz, 1986)—part of the stress response system—have the effect of suppressing immune functioning.

Stress is capable of affecting disregulation of the immune system. Research on animals has firmly established that a wide variety of acute and chronic stressors result in immunosuppression and illness development (Monjan, 1981; Monjan and Collector, 1977; Riley, Fitzmaurice, and Spackman, 1981). In humans, a number of studies have documented the relationship between stress, coping ability, immune functioning, and illness development (Dohrenwald and Dohrenwald, 1974; Holmes and Rahe, 1967; Levy, 1982; Locke et al., 1984). Other studies have suggested that bereavement (Bartrup et al., 1977; Linn, Linn, and Jensen, 1982; Stoddard and Henry, 1985), depression (Schleifer et al., 1980), and trauma (burns, accidental injuries, and surgery) (Goodwin, Bromberg, and Staszak, 1981; Munster, 1976) can affect immune functioning, yet these studies have been received with some skepticism because of methodological limitations (Stein, Miller, and Trestman, 1991).

Perhaps the most elegant research on the links between stress, immune functioning, and illness development has recently come from the laboratories of Kiecolt-Glaser and McClelland. Kiecolt-Glaser and associates studied the immune functioning of medical students throughout an academic year. Repeated measures of immune functioning such as NK activity, percentage of T cells, and helper–suppressor ratio were consistently lower around the time of academic examinations and higher during periods free from exams. When the population of medical students was further investigated along the dimensions of life change stress and social isolation, it became clear that immunosuppression around exams was greatest for the lonelier students and students who experienced life change stress (Kiecolt-Glaser, Garner, et al., 1984; Kiecolt-Glaser, Ricker, et al., 1984; Kiecolt-Glaser et al., 1986). In order to demonstrate the three-way association between stress, immunosuppression, and illness development, Kiecolt-Glaser examined the relationship between medical exam stress, loneliness, immune functioning, and illness incidence, such as incidence of upper respiratory infection and response to the Epstein-Barr virus and other herpesviruses in vitro (Glaser et al., 1985).

In other studies, Kiecolt-Glaser and associates investigated the relationship between stress, immunosuppression, and tumor/cancer vulnerability. Tumor development results from genetic mutation, or alteration of the genetic material of the cell. Normal cells are equipped with an enzyme system that repairs faulty replicated DNA. Psychiatric inpatients were subdivided into high-stress and low-stress groups. The high-distress groups had significantly poorer ability to repair the DNA of lymphocytes exposed to irradiation. Because the ability to repair DNA and the efficiency of NK activity are both necessary to control carcinogenesis and immunosurveillance of tumor cells, respectively, the researchers' findings suggest the possible mechanisms by which tumor or cancer cells may develop and proliferate in the stressed individual (Kiecolt-Glaser, Glaser, et al., 1985; Kiecolt-Glaser, Stephens, et al., 1985).

McClelland and associates have shed light on the enduring personality factors associated with immune functioning (McClelland et al., 1980; McClelland and Jemmott, 1980). Most of their work has centered on the notion of the inhibited power motive. Exam stress in students was associated with increases in catecholamine levels and decreases in immunoglobulin (IgA) activity as expected, but only in the subgroup of students who manifested an inhibited power motive (Jemmott et al., 1983; McClelland, Ross, and Patel, 1985). Another study clarified the link between immune functioning and illness development. High stress in people with high inhibited power motive but not in others was associated with decreased IgA and a greater incidence of upper respiratory infections (McClelland, Alexander, and Marks, 1982).

Various diseases associated with the immune system occur when the regulation of the complex functions of the immune system is disturbed.

One or another of the branches of the immune system may become dysfunctional (Solomon, Amkraut, and Kasper, 1974). According to Melnechuk (1986, personal communication), infections and cancer occur when immune functioning is hypoactive and therefore fails to recognize and destroy antigens. Allergies and autoimmune diseases occur when immune functioning is hyperactive. B-cell activity is not held in check by the suppressor T cells, and seemingly neutral targets are mistakenly recognized as antigens—external neutral stimuli (in the case of allergies), and internal normal cell populations (in the case of autoimmune disease). Figure 12.1 summarizes the various types of immune disregulation.

AFFECT AND ILLNESS DEVELOPMENT

The contribution of affect to illness development is becoming increasingly clear. In the case of asthma, for example, emotional stress can precipitate asthmatic episodes. Discussion of unpleasant memories and situations can increase bronchospasm and wheezing (Faulkner, 1941; Stevenson and Ripley, 1952). Dekker and Groen (1956) selected stressful emotional stimuli from the personal history of each of their patients and introduced those stimuli to induce attacks. When certain emotions become associated with asthmatic episodes, distinguishing cause from effect can be difficult. Does the emotion cause the episode, or is the emotion a consequence of the episode? On one hand, more often than not, anxiety, depression, frustration, and anger are the results of having an asthma attack, rather than its cause (Purcell and Weiss, 1970). On the other hand, emotions constitute a powerful class of triggers, at least for some people in whom the experience of certain emotions—fear, anger, excitement—may directly activate the autonomic nervous system, which, in turn, may trigger the bronchospasm (Purcell and Weiss, 1970). Moreover, the expressions accompanying certain emotions are associated with radical changes in air flow, for example, holding one's breath, crying, laughing, and gasping. These emotional expressions can trigger asthma attacks by means of mechanical irritation (Gold, Kessler, and Yu, 1972).

Antigen	Hyperactive immune functioning	Hypoactive immune functioning
endogenous	autoimmunity	cancer
exogenous	allergy	infection

Fig. 12.1. Classification of Diseases Associated with Disregulation of Immune-Functioning. (Adapted with permission from Theodore Melnechuk, 1986, personal communication.)

With respect to other psychophysiological disorders, the inhibition of emotional expression has been associated with symptom development. Suppression of emotion, notably anger, can trigger headaches in a subgroup of headache-prone individuals (Fromm-Reichmann, 1937; Harrison, 1975). Vascular headaches have been defined in terms of regional vasomotor disfunction (Dalessio, 1980). Anger, and especially the intentional inhibition of the expression of anger, is associated with pervasive cardiovascular changes. Anger suppression, therefore, can precipitate a headache in an individual whose vasomotor system has become sensitized.

Cancer Risk

The contribution of affect to illness development has been especially apparent in cancer research. Some researchers have identified that the habit of suppressing emotional expression, notably anger, is associated with rapid cancer growth in patients with breast cancer (Pettingale, Greer, and Dudley, 1977). Early researchers tried to identify a cluster of stable personality traits predictive of cancer risk, the so-called type C personality (Temoshok and Fox, 1983), but such work has been received with skepticism. Another area of personality research that has gained acceptance is on what has been called the "immunosuppression-prone personality" (Solomon, 1985).

In a series of prospective studies, Grossarth-Maticek and his associates have offered convincing support for the relationship between personality variables, specifically, style of emotional expression, and cancer vulnerability. The authors studied 1,353 people in a Yugoslavian village (Grossarth-Maticek et al., 1983) and then 2,563 subjects in Heidelberg, Germany (Grossarth-Maticek et al., 1988), over a 10-year-period. In the first study, the eldest person in every household in the Yugoslavian village of 14,000 participated in this study. Detailed psychosocial and medical data were collected on each participant, including standard risk factors, such as smoking, blood pressure, daily cholesterol level, and alcohol intake. The study also included personality inventories in an attempt to link personality variables to cancer, in an attempt to find evidence for a disease-prone personality (Eysenck, 1988). One questionnaire measured chronic hopelessness; another measured chronic irritation and anger; another contained questions related to the concept of rationality/antiemotionality. Participants, were asked, for example, "Do you try to overcome interpersonal conflicts with intelligence and reason, trying hard not to show any emotional response?" "Do you behave in almost all life situations so rationally that only very rarely is your behavior influenced by your emotions only?" Subjects were classified into those scoring high on rationality and antiemotionality (a total score of 10 or 11 on 11 items) or low (a total score of 0–9 on 11 items). The mean score on the inventory was 6.19 (SD = 2.38). Factor analytic studies confirmed rationality/antiemotionality to be the underlying construct. Intentional control of the expression of emotion, especially aggression, is the essential element of the questionnaire. Rationality/antiemotionality was shown to be negatively correlated with anger (van der Ploeg et al., 1989).

Details on the causes and circumstances of death were recorded during the next 10 years. Table 12.1 reproduces the data on a number of individuals who died of lung cancer and other types of cancer over the 10-year interval (Eysenck, 1988). When all other factors were controlled, rationality and antiemotionality were highly significant predictors of death from cancer over a 10-year period. Conversely, individuals who were freely expressive of their emotions and who used their feelings to guide their behavior had a relatively low incidence of cancer, especially lung cancer. Another inventory revealed that chronic hopelessness was an equally strong predictor of the incidence of cancer and lung cancer over the 10-year period. Expression of anger and irritation was associated with a significant decrease of cancer risk over the next 10 years (Grossarth-Maticek et al., 1983).

Table 12.2 reproduces the data on interaction of the personality variable for rationality/antiemotionality and smoking behavior (Eysenck, 1988). Nearly all of the individuals who died of lung cancer had high rationality/antiemotionality scores and smoked more than 21 cigarettes

Table 12.1.   Cancer and Scores on the Rationality/Anti-Emotionality Scales
of Grossarth-Maticek

	Low Score		High Score	
	Obs.	Exp.	Obs.	Exp.
Lung Cancer	0	26	38	12
Other Cancer	8	84	120	44

(Reprinted from Eysenck, 1988, with permission of the publisher and the author.)

Table 12.2. Lung Cancer Incidence by Smoking and Rationality/Anti-Emotionality in Males

Rationality and Anti-emotionality score	Smoking Habits			
	Never smoked	1-20 cigs/day	21+ cigs/day	Total
0	0/77	0/42	0/38	0/57
1-9	0/214	0/142	0/141	0/497
10-11	1/117	0/54	31/139	32/310
Total	1/408	0/238	31/318	32/964

(Reprinted from Grossarth-Maticek, Bastiaans, and Kanazir, 1985, with permission of the publisher.)

per day. Whereas smoking per se put the individual at risk for lung cancer and other types of cancer, it alone did not predict death from cancer. The research clearly demonstrated that rationality/antiemotionality was a much stronger predictor of lung cancer death than smoking per se. When standardized for age, the cancer incidence was about 40 times higher in individuals who scored high on rationality/antiemotionality when compared to those who scored low. Moreover, the combined effects of rationality/antiemotionality and smoking act synergistically to contribute to lung cancer death (Grossarth-Maticek, Bastiaans, and Kanazir, 1985). The study gains even more credibility when the findings were replicated on 2,563 individual studies during 10 years in Heidelberg, Germany (Grossarth-Maticek & Eysenck, 1990).

Cardiovascular Risk

The Yugoslavian and Heidelberg prospective studies also contained valuable data on cardiovascular risk and mortality. A fourfold personality topology of "psychosocial types" was developed, and participants in the Yugoslavian and Heidelberg studies were classified accordingly. Type I individuals were characterized as dependent on highly valued objects and goals but rarely finding satisfaction in their pursuits. Nevertheless, they persisted in seeking closeness to others or desirable goals. The affects characteristic of type I individuals were chronic hopelessness, helplessness, and frustration. These individuals typically remained distant from others, and they suppressed feelings, even when they tended to fail in their pursuits. Type II individuals tended to view others or external goals as the source of their dissatisfaction. They remained in a state of internal arousal due to their persistent dissatisfaction with others and with their achievement of life goals. The primary affect of this group was chronic anger. Type III individuals showed the characteristics of both type I and type II individuals. Type IV individuals were relatively healthy individuals who achieved relative autonomy as a condition for their psychological well-being. They were able to experience satisfaction in relationships and life goals (Eysenck, 1988; Grossarth-Maticek et al., 1988).

Figure 12.2 reproduces the data on cancer and cardiovascular risks according to personality type (Eysenck, 1988). In *both* the Yugoslav and Heidelberg 10-year prospective studies, type I individuals had significant risk for cancer mortality; and type II individuals had significant increased risk for cardiovascular mortality. The number of deaths related to other personality types was not significant (Eysenck, 1988; Grossarth-Maticek et al., 1988). A more recent, 13-year prospective study using a question-naire to measure these personality types replicated and confirmed the previous findings (Grossarth-Maticek and Eysenck, 1990).

The findings from these prospective European studies were highly consistent with the American studies on psychosocial factors and heart disease. Friedman and Rosenman (1959) pioneered research on the so-called type A personality. They found that individuals who had a pattern of behavior characterized by excessive competitive drive and a sense of time urgency (type A behavior pattern) had a greater risk of heart disease, in contrast to individuals who were relaxed and easygoing (type B be-havior pattern). To explore this relationship, they undertook an 8 1/2-year prospective study of 3,154 men aged 39–59, which was called the Western Collaborative Group Study. At follow-up, type A men were twice as likely as type B men to develop cardiovascular disease, when other risk factors such as smoking and hypertension were statistically controlled (Friedman and Rosenman, 1974). Numerous studies have since confirmed the find-ings. Extensive reviews now exist: Booth-Kewley and Friedman, 1987; Brand, 1978; Glass, 1977; Jenkins, 1976; Rowland and Sokal, 1977; and Zyzanski, 1978).

More recent research has attempted to refine our understanding of the essential components of the type A personality. The earliest research emphasized time urgency, intensity of involvement with one's job, impa-tience, ambitiousness, competitiveness, and hard-driving behavior. Based on this view, the Jenkins Activity Survey (JAS), a standardized inventory to assess type A behavior, contains three subscales: speed/impatience, job involvement, and hard-driving competitiveness (Jenkins, Zyzanski, and

YUGOSLAV STUDY

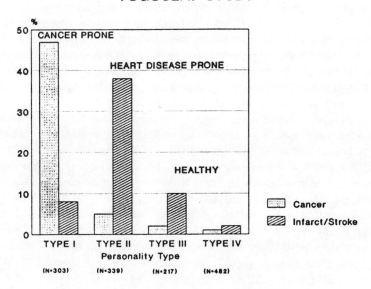

HEIDELBERG STUDY
(NORMAL GROUP)

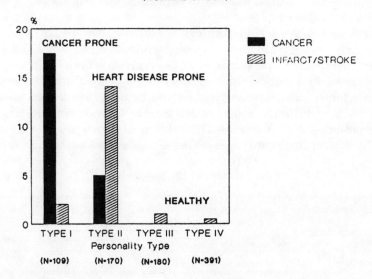

Fig. 12.2. Personality Cancer and Cardiovascular Risk. (Reprinted from Eysenck, 1988, with permission of the publisher and the author.)

Rosenman, 1971). Since 1975, research has emphasized aggressiveness and hostility (Lundberg, 1980; Price, 1982). Friedman, Brown, and Rosenman (1969) felt that type A behavior patterns represented a "struggle against people, objects in the environment and time" (Price, 1982, p. 18) and included such characteristics as bold determination and a readiness to argue in interpersonal relationships. Aggression/hostility is now thought to be a more significant predictor of cardiovascular risk than time urgency and impatience are.

More recent research has begun to make a distinction between an individual's expressive style and the aggression/hostility that is characteristic of type A behavior. Friedman, Hall, and Harris (1985) argued that genuine type A behavior and emotional expressivity are often confounded. Some individuals thought to be type A may not be. Healthy individuals who are vital and active in their expressive style may be mistaken for type A personalities. Moreover, some individuals thought to be type B may not be. Some individuals prone to cardiovascular disease may be mislabeled as type B if they have suppressed their hostility or drive and appear quiet, slow to speak, and nonaggressive. Friedman and Booth-Kewley (1987) used the Affect Communication Task (ACT) along with the JAS to study cardiovascular risk. The ACT measures the degree of nonverbal expressiveness. People who measured high on the ACT, for example, were animated, exhibitionist, and easily noticed. Figure 12.3 classifies individuals according to their response on both the ACT and the JAS. Individuals are classified in terms of both emotional expressiveness and type A or B behaviors.

Genuine type A's could be distinguished from false type A's based on their high JAS score but low scores on the ACT. In other words, it is the *combination* of type A personality—notably aggression/hostility—and little emotional expressiveness that predicts the possibility of cardiovascular disease. Individuals who scored high on type A traits, especially aggression/hostility, but who found healthy outlets for their aggression in the form of vigorousness and expressiveness (called "health charismatics") were not at risk for cardiovascular disease. Highly aggressive/hostile individuals

Coronary-Prone Behavior: Emotional Expressiveness:

Jenkins Activity Survey (JAS):	High Affective Communication (ACT)	Low Affective Communication (ACT)
High (Type A)	Healthy Charismatic	Genuine Type A
Low (Type B)	Alienated Type B	Genuine Type B

Fig. 12.3. Coronary-Prone Behavior and Emotional Expressiveness. (Graphically adapted from H. Friedman & Booth-Kewley, 1987, with permission of the publisher.)

who inhibited the expression of expressive feelings, who did not readily have the means to express aggressive feelings to others, and who instead redirected their aggression into hard-driving behaviors, overinvolvement in work, or time pressure were at a high risk for cardiovascular disease.

Genuine type B individuals (low ACT, low JAS) were not at risk for cardiovascular disease. They measure low on JAS and high on ACT and were the most interesting group of people. They were also the most depressed, anxious, hopeless, and unhappy individuals in the study. They felt alienated from themselves, from others, and from work. Their low score on the JAS suggested suppression of aggression/hostility. Their high score on the ACT suggested they wished to be popular. Taken in combination, the scores on both inventories suggested individuals who express aggression and frustration internally in the form of reproach and externally in the form of blame and the externalization of responsibility. These alienated type B's also significantly predicted for cardiovascular disease. Both genuine type A's and alienated type B's, which are the health-risk personalities, share the common factor of the inhibition of aggression. Genuine type A's do not appear to be able to freely verbalize aggressive-related feelings to others or to channel them into stable behavioral patterns; alienated type B's turn aggression both against the self and into complaints.

Overall, a consistent pattern emerges from research regarding the relationship between affect, psychophysiological change, cancer risk, and cardiovascular risk: *the inhibition of emotions is strongly associated with illness development.* Inhibition of emotions is meant to include both internal psychological defense against the conscious recognition of emotion and external expression or verbalization of emotions. To put it simply, a personality style associated with the consistent inhibition of affect is not healthy; it can contribute to a variety of biochemical changes such as excessive catecholamine release, which directly affects heart and other cardiovascular tissue (Price, 1982), and corticosteroid release, which causes suppression of the immune system (Brown and Fromm, 1987). These intervening biochemical changes contribute to disregulation of physiological systems, the outcome of which may be a degenerative disease such as coronary heart disease and cancer (Weiner, 1975).

HEALTHY AFFECT DEVELOPMENT AND WELLNESS

Inhibition is associated with illness development, but the question remains as to whether or not healthy affective development contributes to health and wellness. Lazarus and his associates (1991) have studied the ways individuals cope with stressful situations by developing a questionnaire to identify different coping strategies characteristically used to handle a variety of stressors. Subsequent factor analysis of the questionnaire resulted in an eightfold classification of coping strategies. First, coping strategies can be classified into adaptive and maladaptive. Each in turn can be subclassified into problem-focused and emotion-focused coping, each of which contains two subtypes: adaptive problem-focused coping, for example, consists of active problem-solving and cognitive restructuring. Maladaptive problem-focused coping comprises active avoidance of problems and magical thinking. Adaptive emotion-focused coping includes direct verbalization and seeking of emotional support from others. Maladaptive emotional-focused coping includes self/other blame and social withdrawal (Folkman and Lazarus, 1981; Tobin et al., 1982). With respect to health or illness development, the distinction between adaptive and maladaptive coping style correctly discriminated between individuals who had or did not have headaches (Holroyd et al., 1983) and depression (Tobin et al., 1985).

Kobasa and associates (Kobasa, Maddi, and Courington, 1981; Kobasa, Maddi, and Kahn, 1982) developed the concept of the hardy personality style, one that "encourages transformational coping" (Kobasa et. al., 1981 p. 368). The study involved 159 upper-level managers in a large utility company. Questionnaires were used to assess personality disposition, stressful life events, and symptoms of illness. A prospective study was conducted over five years. Stressful life events predicted illness, whereas hardiness predicted health, or the absence of illnesses. Interaction between stressful life events and hardiness also was found: individuals experiencing a high incidence of life change stress were less likely to become ill if they had a hardy personality. The concept of hardiness was defined by three characteristics: (1) perceived control: hardy individuals felt they had some influence over work and life events; (2) commitment: hardy individuals had a coherent philosophy of life and a sense of purpose that would get them fully involved in whatever they were doing; (3) challenge: hardy individuals did not see changes as threatening but as challenges. They welcomed and did not fear change; they were open and flexible. In contrast, individuals low in hardiness felt powerless, alienated, and insecure. Based on these findings, Kobasa and associates began introducing hardiness training seminars to high-risk groups in an effort to help people who have high-stress jobs.

Wellness training has also been applied to certain clinical populations. Grossarth-Maticek included prevention interventions in the Heidelberg prospective studies (Eysenck, 1988; Grossarth-Maticek et al., 1988). A total of 50 randomly selected subjects at high risk for cancer based on the previously mentioned personality tests were given 30 hours of cognitive-behavioral therapy. A total of 50 matched subjects were used as controls and did not receive the intervention. Table 12.3 shows the number of deaths in each group at 10-year follow-up. Those in the intervention group had significantly fewer cancer deaths (p > 0.001) than the controls did. Another sample involved 82 subjects prone to coronary heart disease. The intervention consisted of modifying the type 2 personality pattern associated with chronic anger. These subjects were taught means to express anger. Similarly, the intervention group relative to the control group showed a highly significant reduction in myocardial infarction and death.

Another prospective study was conducted by Spiegel and associates (1989). A total of 86 women with metastatic breast cancer were randomly assigned to a one-year treatment group or control group. The control group received routine oncological care. In addition, the treatment group received weekly supportive group therapy and self-hypnosis for pain control. At the 10-year follow-up, only three patients were alive. However, the survival rate was significantly different in each group. The women in the treatment group survived twice as long as the women in the control group. Although highly significant, it remained unclear exactly what had brought about the marked increased survival rate. Speigel et al. (1989) noted about the group therapy that "patients were encouraged to come weekly to therapy to express their feelings about the illness and its effect on their lives. . . . One major function of the leader was to keep the group directed towards facing and grieving losses" (p. 889).

These important prospective studies offer solid scientific support for the view that emotional expression can contribute to the prevention of serious illnesses like cancer and heart disease and to the maintenance of health and wellness. With these carefully designed prospective studies, research on illness development and health maintenance has moved far

Table 12.3. Deaths in Therapy and Control Groups

	Living	Died (cancer)	Died (other causes)	Total
Control groups	19	16	15	50
Therapy groups	45	0	5	50
				100

(Reprinted from Eysenck, 1988, with permission of the publisher and the author.)

beyond earlier anecdotal claims that expressively angry cancer patients had a longer survival rate than patients who suppressed anger (Pettingale et. al., 1977) and that the expression of humor can alter the course of immune-related illnesses (Cousins, 1979). These studies also invite the possibility that individuals with disease-prone personalities, or more specifically affect-inhibited personalities, might be identified and selected for specialized interventions. Can such individuals be taught to modify their characteristic mode of inhibiting affect? Based on what data are available, the answer seems to be yes. Wellness training has become increasingly popular in behavioral medicine clinics around the country.

WHAT RESEARCHERS CAN LEARN FROM EACH OTHER

The main limitation of research on illness development and health maintenance is the relatively unsophisticated constructs about affect associated with the research. Chapter 1 of this book describes the normal developmental line of affect with a number of development achievements along this continuum. According to this model, illness development would be associated with a developmental arrest in the middle of the continuum of eight developmental tasks, namely, with the developmental tasks of affect tolerance, verbalization, and recognition. As described in Chapter 1, the strongest relationship between level of psychopathology and psychosomatic conditions exists in personality-disordered and traumatized patients, especially those who have alexithymia or alexithymic features (McDougall, 1982, 1985; Krystal, 1979, 1982/83). Such patients manifest developmental arrests along a continuum of affect tolerance, verbalization, and recognition and are likely to deverbalize and resomatize affects (Krystal, 1974, 1975; Schur, 1955). Therefore, we might say that the development of physical illness is related primarily to problems in the area of affect tolerance, verbalization, and defense.

Grossarth-Maticek's important prospective data on the relationship of rationality/antiemotionality to cancer risk does not make it clear whether this construct of rationality/antiemotionality pertains to a verbalization of or recognition of affect or both. Friedman's data on the relationship of emotional expressivity to cardiovascular risk likewise fails to discriminate between affect verbalization and affect recognition. According to the descriptions of genuine type A's, they are low in emotional expressivity. They seem to be low in the free expression of feelings, especially aggressive feelings, and in expressing these in an appropriate and sensitive way toward others. Instead, they channel aggression into a behavioral style of hard-driving competitiveness. In other words, genuine type A's may have a problem with affect verbalization. Alienated type B's, who were high on emotional expressivity, seem to be lower in their capacity to recognize aggressive affects, which instead get expressed in complaints about self and others.

A number of questions remain, one of which is, are individuals who have accomplished each of the developmental tasks along the line of affect development physically healthier than those who show significant developmental arrests along the line of affective development? A prospective study would be valuable, and it is my hope that specific intervention methods will be refined to foster advancement along each stage of the continuum of affective development for adults. Other questions that future research must address are: Will affective education in primary schools also contribute to physical health over the life span? And will interventions and psychoeducational methods in the area of emotional development actually contribute to an ideal state of wellness or optimal health?

REFERENCES

Bakal, D. A. (1982), The Psychobiology of Chronic Headache. New York: Springer.
_____ & Kaganov, J. A. (1977), Muscle contraction and migraine headache: Psychophysiologic comparison. Headache, 17:208–215.
Bartrop, R. W., Luckhurst, E. & Lazarus, L. (1977), Depressed lymphocyte function after bereavement. Lancet, 1:834–946.
Berkman, L. F. & Syme, S. L. (1979), Social networks, host resistance and morality. Amer. J. Epidem., 109:186–204.
Besedovsky, H. O. & Sorkin, E. (1981), Immunologic-neuroendocrine circuits: Physiological approaches. In: Psychoneuroimmunology, ed. R. Adler. New York: Academic Press, pp. 545–574.
Booth-Kewley, S. & Friedman, H. S. (1987), Psychological predictors of heart disease: A quantitative review. Psycholog. Bull., 101:343–362.
Brand, R. J. (1978), An examination of the association between A-B behavior and coronary heart disease incidence. In: Coronary-Prone Behavior, ed. T. M. Debroski, S. M. Weiss, J. L. Shields, S. G. Haynes & M. Feinleib. New York: Springer, pp. 11–24.
Brown, D. & Fromm, E. (1987), Hypnosis and Behavioral Medicine. Hillsdale, NJ: Lawrence Erlbaum Associates.
Brown, S. L. & Epps, D. E. (1985), Suppression of T lymphocyte chemotactic factor production by both the opioid peptides B-endorphin and met-emkaphalin. J. Immun., 134:3384–3390.
Bruyn, G. W. (1980), The biochemistry of migraine. Headache, 20:235–256.
Budzynski, T. H., Stoyva, J. M., Adler, C. S. & Mullaney, D. J. (1973), EMG biofeedback and tension headache: A controlled outcome study. Psychosom. Med., 35:484–496.
Burnet, F. M. (1971), Immunological surveillance in neoplasia. Transplant Rev., 7:3–25.
Cannon, W. B. (1923), Traumatic Shock. New York: Appleton.
Cousins, N. (1979), The Anatomy of an Illness, as Perceived by the Patient. New York: Norton.
Crary, B., Hauser, S. L., Borysenko, M., Kutz, I., Hoban, C., Ault, K. A., Weiner, H. L. & Benson, H. (1983), Epinephrine-induced changes in the distribution of lymphocyte subsets in peripheral blood of humans. J. Immun., 131:1178–1181.

Dalessio, D. J. (1980), *Wolff's Headache and Other Pain*. New York: Oxford University Press.

Dekker, E. & Groen, J. (1956), Reproducible psychogenic attacks of asthma. *J. Psychosom. Res.*, 1:58–67.

Dennis, G. J. & Mond, J. J. (1986), Corticosteroid-induced suppression of murine B cell immune response antigens. *J. Immun.*, 136:1600–1604.

Dohrenwend, B. S. & Dohrenwend, B. P., eds. (1974), *Stressful Life Events: Their Nature and Effects*. New York: Wiley.

Eysenck, H. J. (1988), Personality, stress and cancer: Prediction and prophylaxis. *Brit. J. Med. Psychol.*, 61:57–75.

Fahrion, S. L. (1980), Etiology and intervention in essential hypnotension: A biobehavioral approach. Unpublished manuscript, The Menninger Foundation.

Faulkner, W. B. (1941), Influence of suggestion of the size of the bronchial lumen. *Northwest Med.*, 40:367–368.

Folkman, S. & Lazarus, R. S. (1981), An analysis of coping in a middle aged community sample. *J. Health Soc. Behav.*, 21:219–239.

Freud, S. (1926), Inhibitions, symptoms and anxiety. *Standard Edition*, 20. London: Hogarth Press, pp. 87–172.

Friedman, H. S., Hall, J. A. & Harris, M. J. (1985), Type A behavior, nonverbal expressive style, and health. *J. Person. Social Psychol.*, 48:1299–1315.

Friedman, M., Brown, A. E. & Rosenman, R. H. (1969), Voice analysis test for detection of behavior pattern. *J. Amer. Med. Assn.*, 208:828–836.

_____ & Booth-Kewley, S. (1987), Personality, type A behavior, and coronary heart disease: The role of emotional expression. *J. Pers. Soc. Psychol.*, 53:783–792.

_____ & Rosenman, R. H. (1959), Association of specific overt behavior pattern with blood and cardiovascular findings. *J. Amer. Med. Assn.*, 169:1286–1296.

Friedman, M. & Rosenman, R. H. (1974). *Type A Behavior and Your Heart*. New York: Knopf.

Fromm-Reichman, F. (1937), Contribution to the psychogenesis of migraine. *Psychoanal. Rev.*, 24:26–33.

Gellhorn, E. (1967), *Principles of Autonomic-Somatic Integrations: Physiological Basis and Psychological and Clinical Implications*. Minneapolis, MN: University of Minnesota Press.

Glaser, R., Thorn, B. E., Tarr, K. L., Kiecolt-Glaser, J. K. & D'Ambrosio, S. M. (1985), Effects of stress on methyltransferase synthesis: An important DNA repair enzyme. *Health Psychol.*, 4:403–412.

Glass, D. C. (1988), *Behavior Patterns, Stress, and Coronary Disease*. Hillsdale, NJ: Erlbaum.

Gold, W. M., Kessler, G. F. & Yu, D. Y. C. (1972), Role of vagus nerve in experimental asthma in allergic dogs. *J. Applied Physiol.*, 33:719–725.

Goodwin, J. S., Bromberg, S. & Staszak, C. (1981), Effect of physical stress on sensitivity of lymphocytes to inhibition by prostaglandin E2. *J. Immun.*, 127:518–522.

Graham, J. R. & Wolff, H. G. (1938), Mechanism of migraine headache and action of ergotamine tartrate. *Arch. Neurolog. Psychiat.*, 39:737–763.

Grossarth-Maticek, R., Bastiaans, J. & Kanazir, D. R. (1985), Psychological factors as strong predictors of mortality from cancer, ischaemic heart disease and stroke. *J. Psychosom. Res.*, 29:167–176.

_____ & Eysenck, H. J. (1990), Personality, stress and disease. *Psychol. Reports*, 66:355–373.

_____ Kanazir, D. T., Vetter, H. & Schmidt, P. (1983), Psychosomatic factors involved in the process of cancerogenesis. *Psychother. Psychosom.*, 40:191–210.

_____ Eysenck, J. H, Vetter, H. & Frentzel-Beyme, R. (1988), The Heidelberg prospective intervention study. In: *Primary Prevention of Cancer*, ed. W. J. Eylenbosch, N. van Larebeke & A. M. Deporter. New York: Raven Press, pp. 199–212.

Harrison, R. H. (1975), Psychological testing in headache. *Headache*, 14:177–185.

Herberman, R. B. & Holden, H. T. (1979), Natural killer cells and antitumor effector cells. *J. Natl. Cancer Inst.*, 62:441–445.

Holmes, T. H. & Rahe, R. H. (1967), The social readjustment rating scale. *J. Psychosom. Res.*, 11:213–218.

Holroyd, K. A., Tobin, D. L., Rogers, L. Hersey, K. G., Penzien, D. B. & Holm, J. E. (1983), Psychological coping strategies and recurrent tension headache. Paper presented at the Annual Meeting of the Society of Behavioral Medicine, Baltimore, MD.

Jemmott, J. B., Borysenko, J. Z., Borysenko, M., McClelland, D. C., Chapman, R., Meyer, D. & Benson, H. (1983), Academic stress, power motivation, and decrease in salivary immunoglobulin A secretion rate. *Lancet*, 1:1400–1402.

Jenkins, C. D. (1976), Recent evidence supporting psychologic and social risk factors for coronary disease, Part II. *New England J. Med.*, 294:1033–1038.

_____ Zyzanski, S. J. & Rosenman, R. H. (1971), Progress toward validation of a computer-scored test for the Type A coronary-prone behavior. *Psychosom. Med.*, 40:25–43.

Kanner, A. D., Coyne, J. C., Schaefer, C. & Lazarus, R. S. (1981), Comparison of two models of stress measurement: Daily hassles and uplifts versus major life events. *J. Nervous and Mental Disord.*, 125:181–201.

Kielcolt-Glaser, J. K., Garner, W., Speicher, C., Penn, G. M., Holliday, J. & Glaser, R. (1984), Psychosocial modifiers of immunocompetence in medical students. *Psychosom. Med.*, 46:7–17.

_____ _____ Strain, E. C., Stout, J. C., Tarr, K. L., Holliday, J. E. & Speicher, C. E. (1986), Modulation of cellular immunity in medical students. *J. Behav. Med.*, 9:5–21.

_____ _____ Williger, D. W., Stout, J., Messick, G., Sheppard, S., Ricker, D., Romisher, S. C., Briner, W., Bonnell, G. & Donnerberg, R. (1985), Psychosocial enhancement of immunocompetence in a geriatric population. *Health Psychol.*, 4:25–41.

_____ Ricker, D., George, J., Messick, G., Speicher, C. E., Garner, W. & Glaser, R. (1984), Urinary cortisol levels, cellular immunocompetency and loneliness in psychiatric inpatients. *Psychosom. Med.*, 46:15–23.

_____ Stephens, R. E., Lipetz, P. D., Speicher, C. E. & Glaser, R. (1985), Distress and DNA repair in human lymphocytes. *J. Behav. Med.*, 8:311–320.

Kobasa, S. C., Maddi, S. R. & Courington, S. (1981). Personality and constitution as mediators in the stress-illness relationship. *J. Health. & Soc. Behav.*, 22:368–378.

_____ Maddi, S. R. & Kahn, S. (1982), Hardiness and health. *J. Person. Social Psychol.*, 42:168–177.

Krystal, H. (1974), The genetic development of affects and affect regression. *The Annual of Psychoanalysis*, 2:98–126.

_____ (1975), Affect tolerance. *The Annual of Psychoanalysis*, 3:179–219. New York: IUP.

_____ (1979), Alexithymia and psychotherapy. *Amer. J. Psychother.*, 33:17–31.

_____ (1982–1983), Alexithymia and the effectiveness of psychoanalytic treatment. *Internat. J. Psychoan. Psychother.*, 9:353–378.

Lazarus, R. S. (1991), *Emotion and Adaptation.* New York: Oxford.

Levy, S. M. (1982), Biobehavioral interventions in behavioral medicine: An overview. *Cancer*, 50:1928–1935.

Linn, B. S., Linn, M. W. & Jensen, J. (1982), Degree of depression and immune responsiveness. *Psychosom. Med.*, (Abstract), 44:128.

Locke, S. & Colligan, D. (1986), *The Healer Within: The New Medicine of Mind and Body.* New York: Dutton.

_____ Kraus, L., Leserman, J., Hurst, M. W., Heisel, J. S. & Williams, M. (1984), Life change stress, psychiatric symptoms and natural killer cell activity. *Psychosom. Med.*, 46:441–453.

Ludenberg, U. (1980), Type A behavior and its relation to personality variables in Swedish male and female university students. Scand. J. Psychol., 21:133–138.

Magonet, A. P. (1960), Hypnosis in asthma. Internat. J. Clin. Exper. Hypno., 8:121–127.

Marlatt, G. A. & Gordon, J. R. (1985), Relapse prevention: Maintenance Strategies in the Treatment of Addictive Behaviors. New York: Guilford.

Marshall, J. (1978), Cerebral blood flow in migraine without headache. Research & Clinical Studies in Headache, 6:1–5.

Mathe, A. A. & Knapp, P. H. (1971), Emotional and adrenal reactions to stress in bronchial asthma. Psychosom. Med., 33:323–340.

McClelland, D. C., Alexander, C. & Marks, E. (1982), The need for power, stress, immune function, and illness among male prisoners. J. Abnor. Psychol., 91:61–70.

_____ & Jemmott, J. B. (1980), Power motivation, stress and physical illness. J. Human Stress, 6:6–15.

_____ Floor, W., Davidson, R. J., & Saron, C. (1980), Stressed power motivation, sympathetic activation, immune function & illness. J. Human Stress, 6:11–19.

_____ Ross, G. & Patel, V. (1985), The effect of an academic examination of salivary norepinephrine and immunoglobulin levels. J. Human Stress, 11:52–59.

McDougall, J. (1982), Alexithymia, psychosomatosis, and psychosis. Internat. J. Psychoanal. Psychother., 9:379–388.

_____ (1985), Theaters of the Mind: Illusion and Truth on the Psychoanalytic Stage. New York: Brunner/Mazel.

Monjan, A. A. (1981), Stress and immunologic competence: Studies in animals. In: Psychoneuroimmunology, ed. R. Ader. New York: Academic Press, pp. 185–228.

_____ & Collector, M. I. (1977), Stress-induced modulation of the immune response. Science, 196:307–308.

Munster, A. M. (1976), Post-traumatic immunosuppression is due to activation of suppressor T cells. Lancet, 1329–1330.

Nair, M. P. N., Cilik, J. M. & Schwartz, S. A. (1986). Histamine-induced suppressor factor inhibition of NK cells: reversal with Interferon and Interleukin 2. J. Immunol., 136:2456–2462.

Pert, C. B. (1986), The wisdom of the receptors: Neuropeptides, the emotions, and bodymind. Advances, 3:8–16.

Pettingale, K. W., Greer, S. & Dudley, E. H. T. (1977), Serum IgA and emotional expression in breast cancer patients. J. Psychosom. Res., 21:395–399.

Philips, C. (1977), A psychological analysis of tension headache. In: Contributions to Medical Psychology, ed. S. Rachman. New York: Pergamon, pp. 91–113.

Price, V. A. (1982), Type A Behhavior Pattern: A Model for Research and Practice. New York: Academic Press.

Purcell, K. & Weiss, J. H. (1970), Asthma. In: Symptoms of Psychopathology, ed. C. G. Costello. New York: Wiley, pp. 597–623.

Riley, V. M., Fitzmaurice, M. A. & Spackman, D. H. (1981), Psychoneuroimmunologic factors in neoplasis: Studies in animals. In: Psychoneuroimmunology, ed. R. Ader. New York: Academic Press, pp. 31–102.

Roskies, E. & Lazarus, R. S. (1980), Coping theory and the teaching of coping skills. In: Behavioral Medicine: Changing Health Lifestyles, eds. P. O. Davidson & S. M. Davidson. New York: Brunner/Mazel, pp. 38–69.

Rowland, K. F. & Sokol, B. (1977), A review of research examining the coronary-prone behavior pattern. J. Human Stress, 3:26–33.

Sargent, J. D. Walters, E. D. & Green, E. F. (1973), Psychosomatic self-regulation of migraine headaches. Seminars in Psychiat., 5:415–428.

Schleifer, S. J., Keller, S. E., McKegney, F. P. & Stein, M. (1980), Bereavement and lymphocyte function. Presented at the annual meeting of the American Psychiatric Association. San Francisco, CA.

Schur, M. (1955), Comments on the metapsychology of somatization. *The Psychoanalytic Study of the Child,* 10:119–164.

Schwartz, G. E. (1977), Biofeedback and the self-management of disregulation disorders. In: *Behavioral Self-Management: Strategies, Techniques and Outcomes,* ed. R. B. Stuart. New York: Brunner/Mazel, pp. 49–70.

——— (1979), Disregulation and systems theory: A biobehavioral framework for biofeedback and behavioral medicine. In: *Biofeedback and Behavioral Medicine.* New York: Aldine, pp. 27–56.

Selye, H. (1956), *The Stress of Life.* New York: McGraw-Hill.

Shavit, Y., Lewis, J. W., Terman, G. W., Gale, R. P. & Liebeskind, J. C. (1984), Opioid peptides mediate the suppressive effect of stress on natural killer cell cytotoxicity. *Science,* 233:188–190.

Solomon, G. F. (1985), The emerging field of psychoneuroimmunology. *Advances,* 2:6–19.

——— Amkraut, A. A. & Kasper, P. (1974), Immunity, emotions and stress. *Annals Clin. Res.,* 6:313–322.

Spiegel, D., Bloom, J. R., Kraemer, H. C. & Gottheil, E. (1989), Effect of psychosocial treatment of survival of patients with metastatic breast cancer. *Lancet,* 2:888–891.

Stein, M., Miller, A. H. & Trestmen, R. L. (1991), Depression, the immune system, and health and illness. *Arch. Gen. Psychiat.,* 48:171–177.

Stevenson, I. & Ripley, H. S. (1952), Variations in respiration symptoms during changes in emotion. *Psychosom. Med.,* 14:476–490.

Stoddard, F. J. & Henry, J. P. (1985), Affectional bonding and the impact of bereavement. *Advances,* 2:19–28.

Temoshok, L. & Fox, B. F. (1983), Coping styles and other psychosocial factors related to medical status and to prognosis in patients with cutaneous malignant melanoma. In: *Impact of Psychoendocrine Systems in Cancer and Immunity,* ed. B. H. Fox & B. H. Newberry. Toronto: C.J. Hogrefe, pp. 258–287.

Tobin, D. L., Holroyd, K. A. & Reynolds, R. (1982), The assessment of coping: Psychometric development of the Coping Strategies Questionnatire. Paper presented at the meeting of the Advancement of Behavior Therapy, Los Angeles.

Toy, J. L. (1983), The interferons. *Clin. & Exper. Immunol.,* 54:1–13.

Van der Ploeg, H. M., Kleijn, W. C., Mook, J., van Donge, M., Pieters, A. M. J. & Leer, J. H. (1989), Rationality and antiemotionality as a risk factor for cancer. *J. Psychosom. Res.,* 33:217–225.

Weiner, H. (1975), Are "psychosomatic" diseases, diseases of regulation? *Psychosom. Med.,* 37:289–291.

Zyzanski, S. J. (1978), Coronary-prone behavior pattern and coronary heart disease. In: *Coronary-Prone Behavior,* ed. T. M. Debroski, S. M. Weiss, J. I. Shields, S. G. Haynes & M. Feinleib. New York: Springer, pp. 25–40.

Part IV

TRANSFORMATIONS
OF AFFECT

With the maturation of formal operational thinking, affective experience for the adolescent adult is no longer bound to immediate situations and interactions but is transformed to the passion of ideas, ideology, and creative works.

Dan Jacobs, in his chapter, "Theory and Its Relation to Early Affective Experience," discusses our affective, often passionate attachment to our own theories, specifically, with respect to psychoanalytic theory-making. Jacobs believes that theory construction is an emotionally, never entirely scientific, process. He asserts that "theories develop out of and represent in symbolic form particular aspects of early object relations." Emotional attachment to theory derives from the affective tone of these early object relations. Depending on the quality of such object relations, some individuals may show a variety of attitudes toward their theories, from rigid adherence, to disillusionment about one's own theory, to striving to be free of any one theory. To illustrate this "passion transformed," Jacobs discusses several case vignettes regarding patients' interest in particular theories as this occurred in their psychoanalysis.

Jerome Sashin, in "Duke Ellington: The Creative Process and the Ability to Experience and Tolerate Affect," discusses the transformation of affect into the passion of musical creativity. According to Sashin, jazz is a musical medium by which emotions are known. Sashin sees Duke Ellington's musical genius in terms of Ellington's capacity to use total ambiguity and dissonance in integrative ways, his high capacity for affective tolerance being a crucial element. Sashin is particularly interested in the range of affective responses that individuals give affective-evoking stimuli: feeling feelings fully, not reacting to them, becoming overwhelmed by them, delaying the feeling, and experiencing sudden jumps to some other form of expression. He views each of these various responses as examples of discontinuous phenomena and uses catastrophe theory to explain the discontinuities in state caused by affective experience. Among these responses, feeling feelings with full intensity is the most desirable yet the most difficult to obtain. Those who are able to do so, like Duke Ellington, have a high capacity to fantasize, are able to verbalize affect, and have evolved psychic structures or "an inner container" for feeling. According to Sashin, from the perspective of affective development as described in chapter 1, we might say that Duke Ellington mastered the tasks of affective tolerance and verbalization.

The last chapter in this section, John Mack's "The Passions of Nationalism and Beyond: Identity and Power in International Relationships," illustrates how affect is transformed into the passions of ideological identifications—ethnonationalism. Mack tries to understand the often intense passion of ethnonationalistic identification in terms of fundamental needs for belonging, security, transcendence, personal and group identity, and self-worth. He shows how ethnonationalism and blind patriotism become intensified when people become threatened due to social disruption or economic decline. Under such conditions, people seek power through the creation of political alliances reinforced by military technology. According to Mack, the passion to dominate is an illustration of "secondary power." Newer and more constructive forms of power— "primary power"—come forth when individuals learn to transcend narrow ethnocentric identifications and to appreciate the interdependence of all groups in the larger community. Each form of power is rooted in the experiences of infancy, a time of intense needs and affects that are later transformed and become manifest in group identifications and associated ideologies.

Making theory, making art, and making political identifications are rarely purely cognitive but are rather illustrations of the intense affective experiences of early development that become transmuted into the products of culture, the history of ideas, works of art, and the passion of ideology or religion through a process of affective transformation.

Chapter 13

THEORY AND ITS RELATION TO EARLY AFFECTIVE EXPERIENCE

Daniel Jacobs

Human beings are, by nature, theory-making animals. Our heightened capacity for abstract, symbolic thinking distinguishes us from other forms of life, and infant research indicates just how early in life attempts to organize, synthesize, and make sense of stimuli begin (Greenspan, 1989; Stern, 1977, 1985; Talberg, Cuoto-Rosa, and O'Donnell, 1988). Stern (1985) notes that by three months of age infants form a schema of objects, events, and persons. The internal mental picture fosters in the infant an expectation of how things should sound, look, or smell.[1] The discrepancies between the infant's expectation (preverbal prototheories, if you will) and stimuli generate and maintain the infant's attention, provide cognitive stimulation, and allow for new learning and the development of new and more complex constructs. Piaget (1970) noted that the interchanges of the infant with the environment are, in essence, problem-solving arrangements designed to incorporate the new experiences into ever-enlarging cognitive and affective schemata. In describing cognitive development, he noted how the action-oriented thinking and "theorizing" of the preopera-

---

[1]Brenner (1982) has pointed out that in the same early stages of an infant's development, ideas and memories become associated with sensations of pleasure and unpleasure. The resulting complex of ideas and sensations (experienced, I would add, in the context of the mother–child relationship) constitute, according to Brenner, an affect. Harrison (1986), accepting this definition, feels that sufficient ego cohesion occurs by three to four months to justify the assertion that the infant is experiencing affect.

tional child (as far as sensorimotor intelligence) changes into a more
internal conceptual and socialized form of thinking and theorizing as the
child's mind develops. As Brown (this volume) points out, the development
of formal operational thinking in adolescence facilitates the incorporation
and integration of affect into elaborate philosophical, scientific, or religious belief systems. What Hartmann (1938) called the "synthetic function
of the ego" (which includes the capacity for the creation of increasingly
complex schema and for symbolization) seems inborn and to some degree
autonomous. Although we may accept the notion of inborn and autonomous ego energy wired for increasing integration and synthesis, the
extent to which this energy can, at any stage of development, be utilized
to fully develop synthesizing and explanatory functions is dictated not
only by an individual's innate capacities but also by environmental response. Learning, as Piaget noted, proceeds through attachment in
human relations. The caretaker helps or inhibits these synthesizing,
symbolic, and theory-making abilities. The manner in which she continuously shows the infant her own ways of organizing experience and affect
are part of the matrix in and from which the infant begins to organize
himself, his affects, and his relations with others.[2] As Winnicott (1971)
suggested, there is an overlap in this development between what the
mother supplies and the child can conceive. Clearly, the child learns and
begins to theorize about himself, about his mother, and about the world
she introduces within the affective ambience that mother and child
establish. The ambience is internalized by the infant and, in turn, influences its developing cognitive and affective schema. This aspect of mother–child interaction contributes to a quality of mind and spirit within
the child, which may provide the stimulus and space for her to play and
formulate—on whatever level of cognitive and affective development she
has attained—ideas about herself, her experiences, and her culture. The
child's developing and increasingly complex, interwoven affective and
cognitive schema and the associated mother–child relationship in which
they are created find combined expression in the developing child's
theories about herself and the world about her. Theories, psychoanalytic
ones included, develop out of and often continue to represent in trans-

---

[2]Daniel Stern (1977) described this interaction in the following way: "The infant's first
exposure to the human world consists simply of whatever his mother actually does with her
face, voice, body, and hands. The ongoing flow of her acts provides for the infant his
emerging experience with the stuff of human communication and relatedness. This chore-
ography of maternal behaviors is the raw material from the outside world with which the
infant begins to construct his knowledge and experience of all things human: the human
presence; the human face and voice; their forms and expressions that make up changes; the
units and meanings of human behaviors; the relationship between his own behaviors and
someone else's" (p. 9).

formed, symbolic form particular aspects of earliest object relations. These aspects of early object relations and their associated emotions, along with the defensive positions and creative possibilities that grew out of them, find sublimated expression in theories espoused and the emotional attachment to them.

Thus it is possible to state, as Adler (1980) has done, that our theories keep us company. Friedman (1988), as well, in noting how a theory may be used, has described its personification "as a chaperon" for some. In other words, our psychoanalytic theories, including the theories in this book about affect and its development—theories that serve important cognitive, synthesizing, and organizing functions—are also representations, displaced and sublimated, of early object relations (our first "company") and the affective states associated with them. Rangell (1982a) pointed out that egosyntonic attachments deriving from original object relations can focus on "institutions to which one is allied, to an alma mater, to one's country, to a psychoanalytic group or society, even to psychoanalytic theory" (p. 318). Of course, the holding of any theory is overdetermined and is developed, refined, and changed in relation to new experience, new knowledge, and, often, to new stages in the life cycle of the theorist.

Any psychoanalytic theory is based on a distinctive portrait of the human condition and the essential relationships between human beings and the world. The portrait is, in good part, a subjective one based on the inner interpersonal world of the theorist which has been translated into metapsychological hypotheses and schema (Stolorow and Atwood, 1979) and which may explain why attachment to particular theories may be so intense and why debate over theory has, at times, become so acrimonious. For what we are in disagreement about is not just empirical facts and their interpretation but personal, unconscious configuration of internal objects (Adler's "company") as well as the affects associated with them that theory symbolizes. As Leowald (1988) has pointed out, the work of art—in this case, one's own theory or that of another to which one becomes attached—gains "an existence of its own not unlike the transitional object of infancy; it becomes an embodiment of the engaging tensions [and, I would add, object relations] that have engendered it" (p. 75).

Obviously, theories may come to represent various affectively laden object relations that arise during the different stages of an individual's development. This explains, in part, the ability to hold contradictory theories simultaneously. This chapter deals with only one of many aspects of creating and holding theories, namely the relation of the affective experience of having a theory to early object relations. Sandler and Joffe (1987) have pointed out that in the content of sublimations (in this case, theory making or holding) are to be found not only symbolization of instinctual wishes but also representation of self and objects and that through such sublimation, "a love relationship may be created or reproduced" (p. 203).

Leowald (1988) points out how theory building and theory holding are intimately linked with the satisfactions that come with individuation from mother and the development of secondary-process functioning (associated with the acquisition of language) and are at the same time, through the choice of a theory, an expression of a wish to regain the oneness with her that has been lost. Thus, in the theory espoused and in the nature of the theorist's attachment to it, one can detect some aspect of the primary caretaker lost and refound and the nature of the theorist's emotional relation to her. Leowald has suggested that sublimation (which includes our choice of psychoanalytic perspective) is "passion transformed." Yet each therapist transforms (sublimates) or fails to fully transform that passion (about early object relations) into theory (including his or her theory of affects) in ways that are unique and specific to that therapist. For in one's theory, others can see the stamp of one's character and, if they know the theorist well enough, the working out of early object relations and their associated affects.[3]

We are all aware that different therapists have markedly different approaches to theory, as they have to passion. Some seem to date theories, going out with them until they grow tired and disappointed with their effect and then move on to a more attractive (and usually younger) theoretical companion. Others remain solidly monogamous, fending off any intrusion into their intense, if not always imaginative, attachment. For them, two's company, three a crowd. Some try to interchange theories, using whatever theory seems handy or useful at the moment, in a style reminiscent of the old song "When I'm Not Near the Girl I Love, I Love the Girl I'm Near." Still others try to remain doggedly free of theory, giving themselves over to the creative chaos of the therapeutic experience and resisting any conscious effort to organize it. In contrast, some seem to have turned their theories into well-oiled machines that provide them with the degree of comfort and certainty they need. Rangell (1982b) noted that psychoanalytic groups and institutions can be similarly characterized in terms of their attitudes toward theory. All approaches to theory—and we all have one, whether we are aware of it or not—have a profound

---

[3]Such an approach was attempted by Stolorow and Atwood (1979). They try to describe early life experiences and inner representational world of four psychoanalytic theorists (Freud, Jung, Reich, and Adler) and their effect on the development of each one's ideas. Their approach differs from my own in that they emphasize how theory helped each theorist maintain a psychic equilibrium. They do not stress, as I have tried to do, how the theory is a symbolic and sublimated representation of an early object in the theorist's life and that theorist's affective connection to that theory reflects something of the affective experience of that early object relationship.

effect on the nature of the therapeutic dialogue in which we engage. Therefore, we must analyze our relationship with and affective connection to psychoanalytic theories (including the theories in this book) and the "company" (affects embedded in early object relations) they symbolize. In so doing, we enlarge and make more sensitive the discourse we can have with ourselves and with others.

By proposing that we examine more closely our relationship to theory, I do not mean to suggest that the psychoanalytic theories to which we adhere are the result of only defensive operations or are, worse yet, indications of unresolved pathology. That Heinz Kohut's lonely childhood (Quinn, 1980), no doubt, made him sensitive to empathic failure and its consequences in no way detracts from his theory. Quite the contrary: although theories may have a defensive function in a way that any sublimation may be seen as a compromise formation, they are also the successful and creative transformations of early object relations and their associated affects into the ideas that now symbolize them. The purpose of analyzing our own or our patients response to a particular theory is not to demonstrate that it is either right or wrong or healthy or pathological but to make a link between the theory accepted or rejected and what it symbolizes for the individual; what it may grant him in terms of wish fulfillment and what it may protect him from in terms of defensive function.

Because we do not expect a high degree of self revelation at public meetings or in our literature, this tie of theory to our own early relationships often goes unmentioned. As a consequence, discourse about theory often remains cognitive in its approach, with special emphasis on being "scientific." It is, often, within this emphasis on Cartesian thinking and scientific materialism that some try to hide from themselves the infantile and affective roots of their theory building. Yet as Evelyn Fox-Keller has pointed out, theories are hardly ever constructed by way of clear-cut steps of induction, deduction, and clarification. Neither are they defended, rejected, or accepted in so straightforward a manner. Rank (1930) claimed "psychology is essentially a projective affair, as an individual's attempt to create his own comfort and consolation" (p. 131). Nevertheless, the developmental reasons for an affective attachment or aversion to particular theories are usually omitted from public discussion. We do not know how many theorists (and we all are theorists in our own way) ask themselves who is keeping them company in the form of the theory they choose and what affective purpose in terms of compromise formation that theory serves. Yet if we do not ask ourselves these questions, the foundations of our thought may remain unexplored.

Some years ago, I treated an unmarried man, fearful of commitment to women, who in the course of his analysis became extremely interested in the work of Donald Winnicott. As a member of the mental health field himself, he was able to talk over Winnicott's theories with his colleagues and to begin to take what he felt was a "Winnicottian approach" with his patients. In his mind, that meant paying attention to their false self-organization, allowing them the potential space they needed for creative solutions, and resisting any propensity for interpretations that might interfere with the patient's process of self-discovery. By all reports, his work was good and his patients seemed to do well under his care. During his analytic hours, he frequently focused on his own clinical work and its relation to Winnicott, occasionally stopping to wonder if I'd read Winnicott and what I thought of him. As the treatment progressed, the patient became increasingly preoccupied with whether or not I agreed with his (and Winnicott's) theoretical position. He suspected I did not, imagining me a strict Freudian, who had little tolerance for "romantic horseshit." He accompanied this image of me with tentative complaints about premature and intellectualized interpretations he felt did not allow him the creative space he needed. Such thoughts about potential differences between us and my intrusiveness as an analyst—his challenge to my "authority" and the retaliation from me he imagined—all induced in him feelings of intense anxiety that became so great that he frequently would have to change the subject after beginning to explore our relationship. The change in subject often involved turning from talking about him and me to an intellectualized account of a case in his own clinical practice and to his application of Winnicott's theories. Often his remarks seemed like a thinly disguised attempt to convince me of their value. After a while, I remarked that he seemed to turn to these theories at moments of intense anxiety about us. I wondered if he felt some comfort and protection when speaking of them. He agreed and went on to say how much he wanted me to see things as he did and to "meet him" like the good enough mother on some theoretical ground of his choice. He realized how he frequently evoked the "feeling" of that good mother through talking about Winnicott's theory whenever I had, in fact, disappointed him. He spoke of his fear that I would become (had, in fact, already become) his own mother whom he experienced as hardly good enough. On the contrary, she seemed to him a harsh, abrasive, and intrusive woman who stirred up arguments among family members and with whom he was constantly angry. His attachment to theory, which he used in his own work in a skillful way, began to have fuller meaning. It served as the good mother whom he desperately wanted (and had, in fact, to some degree experienced) instead of the mother of his conscious memory who sowed in him only confusion and anger. His frequent thoughts about potential space both in his own clinical work and in his analysis served to console him when, in the transference to me or in his patients' transferences to him, we became the intrusive and demanding mother from whom he need to distance himself in order to keep his own emotional equilibrium. In the face of his own rage toward her and his fears of retaliation from her, he comforted himself with the conscious images and unconscious memories of an idealized mother–child matrix, which, without being fully aware of it, Winnicott's theories had come to symbolize for him. The pleasure he derived from these theories, his interest in them, and the use of them in his practice symbolized for him his growth and his separateness from Mother and me in the transference, as well as a reunion with those aspects of Mother that were, in fact, good enough and of which he became aware later in his treatment. Obviously, the choice and use of this theory was overdetermined and had, as the analysis unfolded, many other meanings beside the preoedipal ones emphasized here.

In another instance, the persistent presence on the part of the patient of an atheoretical attitude toward his own problems revealed the repetition of an early mother–child relationship. Some years ago, a young single man came to see me, complaining of "having no feelings." He took no enjoyment in life and denigrated anything he undertook. He did well enough at his work; he found women with whom to have intercourse and who developed strong attachments to him, but he "felt nothing" for the women or for his work. This inability to affectively participate in his actions or thoughts left him with only one feeling: that he was "not really living." He was a second child, born at a time when his mother was depressed by the loss of her own father and embroiled both in endless family disputes with her mother and siblings and in other disruptions that followed her father's death. The patient reported that he always felt his mother's responses to him were stereotypic and devoid of any recognition of him as an individual. The patient never felt close to his mother or to his father, who died a slow death from cancer when the patient was twenty-two. Because during our sessions the patient frequently mentioned the circumstances of his father's death, I began to wonder whether his not feeling alive represented some identification with lost parents—one lost to depression, the other to death. When I finally broached the subject with the patient, he denied any connection with either parent and seemed uninterested in exploring the idea further. Any demonstration of interest on my part in trying to make sense of his experience was met with an equal lack of interest on his. Nor did he seem, furthermore, curious about the difficult nature of our interactions when I pointed them out to him. He remained adamantly "unpsychological" in his approach to himself. He seemed uninterested in psychodynamic explanations for behavior and showed a marked inability to develop what might be called an observing ego. Furthermore, he showed no interest in or curiosity about me. All the while, he clung to the treatment, feeling it was his only chance of changing, although he had no notion of how this change could be brought about.

After some years of analysis, the patient had made some small changes. He achieved a good deal of success at his work in terms of promotions and salary increases. He took some pleasure in a home he had bought and in the modern paintings he had begun to collect. He derived, however, very little pleasure from people and remained isolated and alone. He had, nevertheless, begun to show more feeling, namely, a great sensitivity to any perceived slight that brings with it fears of humiliation and intense and violent fantasies of revenge. Attempts on my part to help him further elaborate or understand his feelings were rebuffed.

The patient himself refused to speculate on what could have caused and continued to cause his painful condition in life. He tended only to describe repeatedly his unhappiness. He was not interested in whether the condition was biological or the result of early experiences. He had no idea as to how he would or could get better other than to keep coming to analysis, even though he had not found it very helpful. Any attempt to suggest exploring our relationship was met with seeming indifference, and any discussion about why he continued to come in the light of feeling no better was met with alarm at the thought I might tell him to leave. In turn, he offered me very little comfort as a therapist, often not responding to my comments at all or stating he found them meaningless. In a frustrated state, I returned to theory making in hopes of finding some understanding. How, for instance, could I best explain this man's condition? Had he genetically inherited a faulty pathway for object relations and the expression of affect? Would he as an infant have defied Tomkins's observations and not shown the usual motoric and facial responses indicative of early affect that Tomkins noted? Or is his limitation a manifestation of a failure in development arising in part from Mother's inability to provide genuine affective resonance to a developing infant, leaving him in a state of affective marasmus? Are we dealing with affects that are primarily preverbal and without psychic representation in word or image, thereby leaving them bereft of expression in a talking treatment? Had he, in other words, a "self-organization" based on infantile experience that is now represented by archaic behavior patterns in his life and in the transference that remain devoid of symbolic representation? Or is his state primarily a defensive one in which an ego threatened by overwhelming feelings of aggression depends on severe constriction and repression to maintain any sense of equilibrium? No doubt his state is a combination of the above, but although interesting, I found them all rather cold comfort as I daily confronted this man's distress and my own increasing feeling of therapeutic helplessness and thoughts of an interminable process. Having abandoned even the little comfort that theory making provided, I fell into a phase of helplessness, silently agreeing with him when he said that even though the analysis was of little help, it would probably end only when one of us died, probably of old age. As I listened without theory or direction, I found images of my own childhood surfacing, images of being alone or of returning as a child to an empty house and of waiting for my mother to come home. I began to realize that his atheoretical position was, in effect, an important idea about himself which contained repressed affects. It stated that he was very different from others; that he was someone to whom the usual theories did not apply; that there was no matrix from which to organize his sense of self; that the stereotypic responses his mother offered, like my interpretations, were of no help; and that in being atheoretical he was in his own way stating he was a motherless child, unable to create theories, helpless and enraged at being abandoned, but identified with and clinging to the absent mother through the absence of any ideas about himself. I decided not to offer an interpretation of his atheoretical position but instead merely to accept his feelings of loneliness and separateness without any expectation of his willingness to explore or "understand" them.

Slowly, over time, as I abandoned any wish that he change or gain from what we discussed, I noticed the patient began to tentatively theorize about himself. First, it came in the container, "You would say I was . . ." He seemed pleased when I said that it might well be what I might say, had I thought of it, but it was he who had the idea. He would then dismiss his idea as though it were of no use, fearful, I thought, that I might forget to understand how motherless a child he still was and that he could count on no one and no idea that was their symbolic representation. I replied I did not know whether the idea was useful or not; it did not appear so to him right now, but I noted that he seemed to abandon quite quickly his own conceptions. In this case, the abandonment of any idea or theory about himself, the subsequent and necessary temporary giving up on theory on my part, led to a deeper understanding of the role that ideas about himself (theories) played in psychodynamics of this patient. He was the abandoned infant and at the same time the abandoning mother who offered no meaningful notions of how he might begin to organize or understand himself.

I present these examples not to demonstrate that affective connections to theory or seeming lack of it are necessarily pathological but as a way of showing how the connections and some of the function they serve can be better understood. This example and others like it led me to look more closely at some aspects of my own propensity for one psychoanalytic theory over another. Through a recent experience, my relation to a theory and its connection to early affective experiences of my own became clear. For some years, I had found myself resistant to some of the ideas of Melanie Klein, particularly her insistence on the infant's early struggle with the death instinct through paranoid and projective mechanisms. I marshaled the now familiar objections of many who disagree with her view of the infant's paranoid-schizoid position. In coming back to Klein's work as part of the preparation for a course on theory that I would be teaching, I noticed in reading her theories that I experienced a profound sense of discomfort I could not fully explain or describe. I noticed, too, that this feeling seemed to keep me from deeper involvement in Klein's theoretical contributions. At first, I attributed it to a strong identification with my psychoanalytic teachers who had looked with some disdain on her work. But why was this identification still so necessary and from what might it be protecting me? I had been musing off and on about the matter, when I went for a massage, part of my weekly routine at that time. That day, the masseuse suddenly put her fingers behind my ears on the spots where at age two part of my mastoid bones had been removed because of a life-threatening infection in them. The actual position of being under a sheet while the area behind my ears was being vigorously rubbed—a physical reminder of the early surgical experience—awakened in me long-repressed affects of sadness, anxiety, and helplessness as well as anger with my mother, whom as a toddler I blamed for the pain of the surgery as well as the separation from her that was inflicted upon me. When I went back to my reading of Klein that evening, it was clearer to me what my resistance to her theories about the infant's paranoid position and the projection of the death instinct had, on the level of my own early affect and object relations, been about. I had used my identification with admired teachers (including my training analyst) and their theoretical orientation as protections against the overwhelming affects aroused by this life-threatening early separation which undermined my sense of well-being. In that way, my strong identification with the teachers and their theories represented a return to a protective caring oneness with Mother, as well as a separation from the more frightening aspects of her care (represented by Klein and her theories).

It was the intensely painful aspects of this separation from Mother and my intense anger with her as a result of it, which Klein's theory, without my being conscious of it, had come to symbolize. Klein's general lack of attention in her theories to what Winnicott was later to call "the holding environment" inadvertently awakened in me echoes of my own early experience which I wanted to avoid. This bit of self-exploration into my relationship to a psychoanalytic theory has not made me a Kleinian, but it helped me to be more open to a fuller and less encumbered appraisal of her contribution.

In this chapter, I have focused on the earliest aspects of attachment to theory. Affective connection to theories is multidetermined, and, to be complete, I would have to trace in my vignettes how particular attachments to theory were linked not only to the mother–child relationship, but also to the sublimations and attempted resolutions of conflicts arising from the oedipal period and later stages of development. That remains, perhaps, for another paper. These vignettes, limited as their focus may be, nonetheless constitute examples of how, in the work of self-analysis and the psychoanalysis of others, "sublimation turns upon itself, as it were, against itself—to unmask itself" (Leowald, 1988, p. 43). Otto Rank put it a different way: "If the world is my projection, so is becoming conscious of this projection, my birth" (Taft, 1958, p. 41). Theory can lose its vitality if it becomes too remote, if we do not unmask its origins and its transference meanings and so put it, as Einstein suggested, sympathetically in touch with experience, ours and our patients'. In some cases, theories that don't interest us may simply have no resonance with our experience; in others, as I've tried to show, too much. In our clinical work, our teaching, our supervising, and our writing, it is useful to seek in the holding of any psychoanalytic theory, that vital symbolic connection to earliest object relations and their associated affects. Certainly sublimation in the form of interest in theory making and holding extends well beyond the mother–child dyad. But I have chosen to emphasize that dyad because that is where sublimation and the capacity to symbolize begin and where theory like a transitional object begins to takes the form of created "company." It is those, no doubt, who can tolerate for a while the aloneness and uncertainty of going beyond relating to theory as old companions and who can forge new and imaginative encounters with it who contribute most to our psychoanalytic growth.

REFERENCES

Adler, G. (1980), Transference, real relationship and alliance. *Internat. J. Psycho-Anal.*, 61:547–558.

Brenner, C. (1982), *The Mind in Conflict.* New York: IUP.

Friedman, L. (1988), *The Anatomy of Psychotherapy.* Hillsdale, NJ: The Analytic Press.

Greenspan, S. (1989), *The Development of the Ego.* Madison, CT: IUP.

Harrison, I. (1986), A note on the nature and the developmental origins of affects. In: *Psychoanalysis: The Science of Mental Conflict,* ed. A. Richards & M. Willick. Hillsdale, NJ: The Analytic Press.

Hartmann, H. (1938), *Ego Psychology and the Problem of Adaptation.* New York: IUP, 1958.

Keller Fox, E. (1983), *A Feeling for the Organisms.* New York: Freeman.

Leowald, H. (1988), *Sublimation.* New Haven, CT: Yale University Press.

Piaget, J. (1970), *Structuralism,* trans. C. Moschler. New York: Basic Books.

Quinn, S. (1980), Interview with Heinz Kohut. *New York Times* Magazine. November 9, pp. 120–131.

Rangell, L. (1982a), The object in psychoanalytic theory. *J. Amer. Psychoanal. Assoc.*, 33:301–344.

_____ (1982b), Transference to theory. *The Annual of Psychoanalysis,* 10:29–57. New York: IUP.

Rank, O. (1930), *Psychotherapy and the Soul.* New York: Barnes.

Sandler, J. & Joffe, W. G. (1987), On sublimation. In: *From Safety to Superego: Selected Papers of Joseph Sandler,* ed. J. Sandler. New York: Guilford Press.

Stern, D. (1977), *The First Relationship.* Cambridge, MA: Harvard University Press.

_____ (1985), *The Interpersonal World of the Infant.* New York: Basic Books.

Stolorow, R. & Atwood, G. (1979), *Faces in a Cloud.* New York: Aronson.

Taft, J. (1958), *Otto Rank.* New York: Julian Press.

Talberg, G., Cuoto Rosa, J. & O'Donnell, M. (1988), Early affect development. *Internat. J. Psycho-Anal.,* 69:239–261.

Winnicott, D. W. (1971), *Playing and Reality.* London: Tavistock.

Chapter 14

DUKE ELLINGTON
The Creative Process and the Ability to Experience and Tolerate Affect

Jerome I. Sashin

Duke Ellington, described as being the first, and perhaps the only great, creative composer of jazz, was repeatedly acclaimed as one of the giants of music. As Lawrence (1987) points out, composers Igor Stravinsky, Aram Khachaturian, Percy Grainger, and Leonard Bernstein publicly affirmed Ellington's genius, as did conductors Arturo Toscanini, Paul Whiteman, André Previn, Leopold Stokowski, Arthur Fiedler, and Sir Thomas Beecham. In 1932, the European public was comparing Ellington's compositions with Bach, Debussy, and Delius. In 1934, the English composer Constant Lambert compared Ellington's work to that of Franz Liszt. In 1987, Lawrence said:

> The real interest of Ellington's records lies not so much in their color, brilliant though it may be, as in the amazingly skillful proportions in which the color is used. I do not only mean skillful as compared with other jazz composers, but as compared with so-called highbrow composers. I know of nothing in Ravel so dexterous in treatment as in the varied solos in the middle of the ebullient "Hot and Bothered"' and nothing in Stravinsky more dynamic than the final section. The combination of themes at this moment is one of the most ingenious pieces of writing in modern music.

In 1936, *The Gramophone Record Shop Encyclopedia of Record Music* stated, "He has incomparable powers of rhapsodic invention and an instinct for tonal nuances and orchestral ingenuities equal to the most brilliant flights of Rimsky-Korsakov's or Richard Strauss's imagination" (Lawrence, 1987). They further commended Ellington for some of his compositions that were of "unique significance for their poly-timbres, their complex textures, the spontaneous and rhapsodic flow of their melodies, the homogeneity of style and above all for their sensitive and poignant revelation of pure feeling in tone." Aaron Copland, reviewing Ellington's recording of "Diminuendo in Blue" and "Crescendo in Blue" in 1938 for *Modern Music,* compared him with other musicians writing jazz music and noted, "The master of them all is Duke Ellington. . . . Ellington is a composer, by which I mean, he comes nearer to knowing how to make a piece hold together than the others" (Lawrence, 1987).

From 1916, when at the age of 17 he wrote "Soda Fountain Rag" and "What You Gonna Do When the Bed Breaks Down," he wrote thousands of compositions, including "Mood Indigo," "Solitude," "Sophisticated Lady," and "I Let a Song Go out of My Heart"; music for films, ballet, musical comedy, stage productions, and symphony orchestra; and three major sacred works, and he was working on an opera at the time of his death nearly 60 years later (Lawrence, 1987).

What were some of the components of Ellington's musical greatness? According to Duke (Ellington, 1976), the first person in the parade of those who could do all that they could for him and his advancement was Oliver "Doc" Perry. Perry taught him a system of reading the lead and recognizing the chords so that he could have a choice in the development of his ornamentation. Then came Henry Grant, who taught him harmony and gave him a music foundation that lighted the direction to more highly developed composition. But the one who gave him "one of the best semesters I ever had in music" was Will Marion Cook. Cook was one of the two foremost black musicians of the times—he had studied with Antonin Dvorak and had an international reputation.

> Several times after I'd played some tune I'd written but not really completed, I'd say, "Now, Dad, what's the logical way to develop this theme? What direction should I take?" "You know you should go to the conservatory," he'd answer, "but since you won't, I'll tell you. First, you find the logical way, and when you find it, avoid it and let your inner self break through and guide you. Don't try to be anybody else but yourself."

Feel the feeling!
Duke goes on to say,

> Painting a picture, or having a story to go with what you were going to play was of vital importance in those days. The audience didn't know anything

about it, but the cats in the band did. Today the music has grown up and become quite scholastic, but this was au naturel, close to the primitive where people send messages in what they play, calling somebody, or making facts and emotions known.

Making emotions known! Feeling the feelings! He did all that but much more too. A look at some of his compositions will explain.
As Fox (1981) points out,

> The 1920s saw the appearance of three of his most important pieces: "The Mooche," "Black and Tan Fantasy," and "Creole Love All." The early version (Miley—Baby Cox) of "The Mooche" is the most successful in sounding the weird atmosphere of this fierce blues. No other jazz composer has so thoroughly achieved and mastered the atmosphere of sounding of the sinister and the occult as has Ellington.

Bellerby (1979) adds:

> The first downward swirl of the clarinet set against Miley's swaying trumpet and Greer's temple blocks at once sense the macabre; the wordless chant of Baby Cox adds a strange hue to the bizarre coloring, Johnny Hodges's saxophone seizing this atmosphere with occult tension [p. 148].

Collier (1978) points out:

> "Black and Tan Fantasy" of 1927 signifies a racial mixture. It mixes diverse moods. It begins with dirgelike blues in B flat major, played in harmony by muted trumpet and trombone. Then follows a 16-bar melody in B flat major, "pretty" and rather florid by the alto saxophone. Next are solos by trumpet and trombone, all muted and growly, carrying out the minor feeling of the opening strain, although this section is in fact an ordinary blues. The minor feeling is produced by a heavy use of the blue third. The record ends with a brief quote from the famous Chopin funeral march.

According to Collier, in 1927, this mixture was something brand new. "Here was a piece that was true jazz set into the framework of a worked out composition. Listeners sensed that behind this work was more than a skilled arranger; they were aware of the presence of an imaginative artist who knew exactly what he was about."

As the 1930s approached, Ellington's compositions began to impose a pattern on his soloists. By the time "Creole Rhapsody" was recorded on January 20, 1931, it was completed. As Fox (1979) states:

Collective improvisation can be vigorous, sometimes it even achieves a transitory profundity; but if an artistic creation is to possess either breadth or depth it must be the work of one man, the concept of an imagination that can hold its several parts together [p. 124].

Fox (1979) adds:

"Creole Rhapsody" stands out today not only as one of Ellington's finest and most completely integrated works but also as a landmark in his musical development. . . . There was even a gentle attempt to evade the convention that jazz must split up into four-bar phrases. As Gunther Schuller, the American horn-player, has pointed out: "In 'Creole Rhapsody' he experimented with a 16-bar phrase made up of a pattern of 5 plus 5 plus 4 plus 2" [p. 126].

Fox (1979) asserts, "[D]uring the 1930s, he took on the stature of a composer, becoming increasingly concerned with the problems of harmony and form, yet never losing the essential impetus of jazz" (p. 137).

Percy Grainger, during a lecture at New York University, compared Ellington's music to that of Bach and Delius and pointed out that in "Rude Interlude," comparisons with Delius and Ravel take on genuine substance: heavy in texture, reflective in mood; no tangible melody; only a somber harmonic sequence (Lawrence, 1987).

Bellerby (1979) states, " 'Echoes of the Jungle' (1932) is of tremendous importance, great music in itself and a significant piece. . . . In *Echoes* we have an uncanny intermingling of solo and ensemble passages. From the first growls of the brass to the last wails of the clarinet choir, an imaginative mood of fear is seized and wonderfully explored" (pp. 148–149). And Collier (1978) points out:

"Ko-Ko" of 1940, considered by many critics to be his finest accomplishment, is a mixture not of moods but of tonalities. It is basically a 12-bar blues in E minor, with an excursion into the relative major—G major—after the trombone passage by Nanton. However, Ellington uses throughout certain chords, at the time advanced for jazz, which produce a good deal of ambiguity about which key is in fact intended. According to Edward Bonoff, a musician who has studied the piece carefully, "This piece is shot through with minor eleventh chords, rarely used in jazz in that day." Ellington here is making use of the lessons Will Marion Cook gave him. . . . The main point, however, is the ambiguous tonality.

Much of Ellington's writing, as we see, was devoted to the exploitation of moods. His son Mercer (Ellington and Dance, 1978) put it this way: "Where Ellington led and was different almost from the beginning was that he sought a sensuality in the way his music was expressed; there was always an motion attached to the sound." And Collier (1978) states, "Duke Ellington did not, like most jazz musicians, create from the hot feelings of the moment, but, following Wordsworth's precept, worked from emotion recollected in tranquility."

What did Ellington's musical genius consist in? What are the qualities of his music that gave it its greatness? According to Collier (1978), in *The Making of Jazz*, four things:

First—a keen sense of tone palette. Duke said often, "I think of music in terms of color." In the creation of sheer sound he had few peers in music of any kind. For example, he took the simplest of melodies and voiced it for muted trumpet, muted trombone, and clarinet to make his classic "Mood Indigo." This is an unusual combination and the problem becomes which notes to give to which instruments to make the three instruments blend into a distinct, unified sound. How, in other words, do you mix red, yellow, and white to obtain a particular shade of orange? Ellington's ability to solve this sort of problem left fellow arrangers like Henderson, Redman, and Bill Challis awed. Second—an extraordinary command of dissonance management of internal harmonics so that even extremes of dissonance were never painful but had genuine musical meaning. For example, in the 1943 recording of "The Saddest Tale"—Harry Carney's bass clarinet solo is behind muted trumpets playing some extremely close harmonics, which never become harsh or irritating. Third—he was the finest writer of short melody in 20th century America; in the master of melody is the hand of Will Marion Cook. And a fourth aspect of the genius of his work, which was much commented upon by the musically educated people who began to admire him early, was his effort to break out of the 4-square mold of 8- 12- 16- 32-bar forms in which virtually all jazz—indeed, all popular music—was played. "Baby, When You Ain't There," recorded in 1932, is primarily a blues, but it begins and ends with a 20-bar segment created by a stretching out of the blues a few bars longer than is customary. "East St. Louis Toodle-oo" includes 18-bar segments among the 8- and 16-bar pieces. "Birmingham Breakdown" is built on a 20-bar theme. The examples are numerous and so neatly does he bring the parts together that few musicians noticed at first that he was departing from the standard forms, and he had hardly any imitators in this practice for a decade. As important as these skills were, was his ability to find and develop the instrumentalists who could array his music in the sounds he wanted. He was always very conscious of the differences in sounds from one trumpet or saxophone player to the next. Rather than bring into the band men who adhered to a common sound, as most leaders did, he deliberately sought out men who produced a sound different from what he already had. For example, trombonists Joe Nanton, Juan Tizol, and Lawrence Brown played so differently that they might as well have been using different instruments. Ellington's genius lay not in a single insight, but in a mastery of many facets of music.

Here we see the crucial importance that feeling played in his work—the ability to feel feelings, to express feelings, to evoke feelings. But we also see other key features of his work: he could break out of the current conventions of the times, venture into new domains, and make impressive use of tonal ambiguity and dissonance while always holding things together in an integrated whole. These features reveal to another important capacity Duke had—what Keats (1817) called negative capability—the ability to tolerate uncertainty and ambiguity.

Ellington could work up to the last minute of a deadline, keeping things open. In fact, he said he needed to have such a deadline to impose a degree of essential stress and stimulation and, as Mercer says, just in case a better ending appeared in his mind. Duke could immerse himself, allow himself to descend—into himself—into what he described as the four descending levels of the self. He could tolerate the unknown, ambiguity, without resorting to premature closure or flight.

Both the ability to feel feelings and his capacity to keep things open while venturing into the new and unknown, to tolerate ambiguity and uncertainty—this negative capability—can be included under the general term of affect tolerance.

Thus Ellington clearly had high affect tolerance, which was extremely important in his creative process. How can we understand it? Where did it come from? What enabled him to have it? Let us begin by looking more closely at affect tolerance as we try to understand Ellington's musical greatness.

First of all, when I say affect tolerance, what do I mean by affect? I mean subjectively felt feelings. And what is the ability to experience and tolerate affect? I mean the ability to respond to a stimulus which we would ordinarily expect to evoke feelings, such as would a surgical operation, a school exam, or the death of a loved one, with feelings. Although these kinds of stimuli—which can be called affect-evoking stimuli and which include internal events such as thoughts, memories, wishes, and external events like the ones just mentioned—ordinarily evoke feelings in most people most of the time, they don't always. Some people don't have the ability to feel feelings.

In response to an affect-evoking stimulus, some people experience subjectively, that is, they feel feelings. In response to a loss, they feel sad. In response to anticipated surgery, they feel scared. But others respond differently.

Deutsch (1937) described four fascinating cases: the first was of a young man of 19, who had an affectionate and undisturbed attachment to his mother and no special neurotic difficulties. When she died, he showed no grief whatsoever. Within the family, this apparently "heartless" behavior was never forgotten. Another characteristic of his behavior was particularly striking; he could break off friendships and love relationships with amazing ease and without feeling any regret or pain. The second case was of a 30-year-old man. When the news of the death of his very dearly loved mother reached him in a distant university city, he departed at once for the funeral but found himself incapable of any emotion whatsoever, either on the journey or at the funeral. He was possessed by a tormenting indifference despite all efforts to bring forth some feeling. The third man, in his early 30s and without apparent neurotic difficulties, came into analysis for nontherapeutic reasons. To all kinds of experiences, he showed the same dull apathetic reactions. There were no reactions of grief at the loss of individuals near to him, no unfriendly feelings, and no aggressive impulses. Deutsch's fourth case was a middle-aged woman without symptoms but with a curious disturbance in her emotional life. In actual situations that should produce sadness, she showed emotionless behavior; a direct emotional reaction was impossible. These cases describe a form of nonfeeling response, which we can label "an apparent nonreaction."

In another example, Pulver (1971) describes the case of a businessman in analysis. At one point in a session, he asked the analyst a specific question regarding what he should do in regard to a marital problem he'd been talking about. The analyst said nothing. The patient suddenly began hitting the wall with his fist. The analyst asked how he was feeling. "OK." Pulver then asked if he was angry. "No, why should I be?" "Because you got no answer to your question," said Pulver. "No, you were doing the right thing; you're not supposed to answer questions," said the patient. Pulver says that it was not until more than three months later that the patient could speak of actually feeling anger when he relived that incident.

I used to see a similar kind of response in patients in our local VA hospital. Often they would tell me about "Dear John" letters from girlfriends ending relationships with them while they were in Vietnam. When I asked how they had felt, they would often say, "Fine, it didn't bother me; I didn't care." But when I asked, "What happened then?" they would tell me they got into fights, wrecked property such as cars, or did drugs. In other words, these G.I.'s, like Pulver's businessman, responded with action—often sudden and impulsive, sometimes destructive or self-destructive, or chaotic—but in any case, a motor discharge without felt feelings.

There is a third common form of nonfeeling affect-response, such as happened in a friend of mine. She was eagerly anticipating the gathering of her whole family for Thanksgiving. Wednesday evening her favorite son called to say he could not come. She began to scratch her hands. I asked what happened and how she felt. She told me the message and kept scratching. How did she feel? Her only response was, "I don't know. I don't know!" Her skin was itching and the scratching was causing her pain, but she was unable to describe feeling disappointed, unhappy, annoyed, irritated, or even upset.

In the 1870s, Henry Maudsley, in a beautiful series of lectures, fortunately still available in a book called *Body and Mind* (Maudsley, 1884), described the same phenomenon, capturing it so well in his famous statement: "Sorrow which has no vent in tears shall cause other organs to weep." What he meant, of course, was that sorrow-evoking stimuli, that is, stimuli we would expect to evoke sorrow but that do not evoke that affect—the feeling—of sorrow—often lead to somatic dysfunction. What Maudsley was describing, then, is a third form of nonfeeling affect-response—somatic dysfunction.

Here is a fourth: Tolpin (1974) recently wrote of a researcher who, whenever he was criticized, would become very tired and have to take a nap for 10 or 15 minutes. He did not feel upset, angry, hurt, ashamed, or anxious—no, just tired. In exploring these incidents carefully, Tolpin gradually learned that when this man was criticized, his mind would become all mixed up. He could not think clearly or organize his thoughts, and then he would feel tired and need to sleep. Others have described similar reactions. Goldberg (1981) describes Mr. I's reaction to separations: "My head was up on the ceiling, my body on the floor; I was disconnected." We can label these types of disorganization as cognitive disorganization. And we can group together somatic dysfunction, impulsive action, and the cognitive disorganization reaction into the single category of overload discharge reactions, or, simply, overloads.

So, one feature of affect-response is that it can have different forms: feelings, apparent nonreactions, and overload discharge reactions, including impulsive actions, somatic dysfunction, and cognitive disorganization.

Affect-response has other features as well. Nemiah, Freyberger, and Sifneos (1975) describe the following:

> A patient with hypertension, for example, gave a detailed account of a struggle with his son. On three successive days he calmly asked his son to remove a bag of garbage from the kitchen. Each day his request was ignored. On the evening of the third day, the patient came home from work to discover that the cat had spread rotting food all over the floor. In a trice, without warning, he smashed the bannister of the stairs leading to the second floor. This impulsive outburst was without premonitory affect or fantasy, and was accompanied only by a vague inner sense of upset that the patient could in no way define as anger or other specific affect [pp. 432–433].

Note that the steadily increasing stimulus over three days—which we might label level of provocation—has scarcely any effect on feelings; but it triggers an impulsive outburst—a motor discharge—from what appeared to be an apparent nonreaction—calm—state. This incident illustrates not only the absence of feelings as a form of affect-response but also the sudden shift from an apparent nonreaction on the first two days to the violent motor action of smashing the bannister.

Fenichel (1945) writes about another feature of affect-response with respect to several different affects such as shame, fear, grief, and disgust, and illustrates it with the example of the man who comes home to find a telegram saying his mother died and puts it on the table saying, "Oh what a shock this'll be in the morning!" That is, affect-response can have delays. It is so common that Hollywood has a special name for it: the double take.

Khantzian (1979) describes a characteristic seen commonly in people suffering from addictions and alcoholism. These people often do not have moderate responses to moderate stimuli. Instead they often show extremes—either very little anger or sudden, massive rage, which can lead to all kinds of maladaptive behavior and cognitive disorganization that interferes with self-care functioning. But this is true of other emotions in other people as well. We quite naturally speak of sudden bursts of anger and of anxiety attacks.

The characteristics of the abnormal affect-response (i.e., of low affect tolerance) include:

1. The possibility of several different states such as apparent non-reactions, impulsive action, somatic dysfunction, and cognitive disorganization rather than feelings.
2. Sudden jumps between states.
3. Delays.
4. Extremes of feeling responses without access to moderate levels.

Lawrence (1987) shows that Duke Ellington did not respond to affect-evoking events with any of the aforementioned overload discharge patterns. Ellington was very much a feeling person. Once, when asked, "How do you feel when you sit down at the piano on stage?" he answered, "Scared! You have to enjoy a little stage fright to get that extra punch" (Ellington, 1976).

For more than 20 years, I have been interested in high affect tolerance in general, not only with respect to Ellington and what enabled him to have it but also what determines the particular form of the response to an affect-evoking stimulus? Why is it that some people respond by feeling feelings, and others respond with apparent nonreactions, overloads, delays, or sudden jumps?

To try to answer this question, I developed a model of affect-response. Unfortunately, for many years there were no methods available to model phenomena in which sudden jumps occurred between differing states. In 1976, however, a new field emerged that was designed precisely for such situations. Discovered by the Frenchman René Thom, catastrophe theory (Thom, 1976) studies discontinuous phenomena in nature. The term "catastrophe" in the title does not refer only to disasters such as the sudden collapse of a bridge or of the stock market but includes any situation when sudden changes occur, such as the abrupt bursting of a bubble, the discontinuous transition from water at its freezing point to ice at its melting point, or the sudden qualitative shift in our minds when we "get" a pun or a play on words. Catastrophe theory provides a catalog of models to describe phenomena in nature when multiple states are possible, sudden jumps can occur between states, delays can occur, and certain states can be inaccessible. The models vary in complexity depending on the number of factors that are involved in the phenomenon being studied. As we have just seen, affect-response has these characteristics; it seemed to me that catastrophe theory would be ideally suited to model it.

When I looked into the catastrophe theory catalog for models that effectively described situations such as the one we treat here with affect-response, namely, the three different states of apparent nonreactions, feelings, or overloads, along with sudden jumps and delays, I found just one model, but it gave two important pieces of information. It told how large the number of underlying factors was that were controlling the situation, and it gave the way the factors were interrelated. That is, according to catastrophe theory, it turns out that any phenomenon in nature with these characteristics, such as the phenomena of affect-response, is being controlled/determined/influenced by four—not merely one or two or even three but also not 10 or 100 or 1,000—but four underlying factors that are interrelated in one particular way, which is given by this one specific catastrophe theory model. Because of its geometric shape, the model is called the butterfly model.

What catastrophe theory didn't say, of course, was just what those underlying factors were in the specific case of affect-response. The psychiatric literature said affect-response was not merely a result of stimulus intensity but was also determined by three additional mediating factors. One was the capacity to fantasize. According to Freud (1911), the normal person uses the capacity to fantasize in order to cope with the delays and frustrations of everyday life so as to bear painful, stressful affects without having to resort to impulsive action or dissolve into a state of helpless despair." In the 1960s, Parisian psychoanalysts Marty and De M'Uzan (1963) focused on this as well.

Another factor was the ability to verbalize affect. Freud (1915) again was one of the first to mention this. He wrote that in order for feelings to be experienced (i.e., for affects to become conscious, words had to be linked to them), it was the linkage with word representations that allowed the affect to cross the repression barrier and become conscious. Anna Freud (1936) emphasized this factor too, as did Furman (1974), who found that if young, impulse-ridden children put their feelings into words, they could feel their feelings and decrease their impulsivity.

The third factor (Brazelton and Als, 1979; Kohut, 1971; Mahler, Pine, and Bergman, 1975) has to do with the early mother–child relationship or the mother–child–father envelope. Via the process of internalization of the good aspects of the relationship with a parent or parents who can tolerate their own as well as their child's feeling states, the child develops an inner psychological structure that enables him or her to feel, modulate, and contain feelings.

Plugging the butterfly model from catastrophe theory in these four clinical factors reveals that, indeed, this clinical model of affect-response does effectively describe many of the clinical phenomena and seemed to have predictive power (Sashin, 1985).

Can this model help us to understand Ellington's impressive affect tolerance? Let's see. Just how good were Ellington's inner container, ability to verbalize affect, and capacity to fantasize? To assess the intactness of the inner container, strictly speaking we should have information abut Duke's self-representation and object representations—the kind of data that generally can be obtained only by the free associative process such as occurs during the course of psychoanalysis or by projective tests like the Rorschach or Thematic Apperception Test. But we can make certain inferences by considering his parents and the quality of Duke's relationship with them. What kind of people were they? How well did they tolerate affect? How close were they to their son? Lawrence (1987) provides rich information.

Duke's mother, Daisy, was a very strong woman. She was quite beautiful, from a prominent family, and the favorite of her parents. According to her younger sister, Florence (Lawrence, 1987), "Daisy was full of life and the 'belle of the ball' until she got married; then she changed, but once Edward was born, she was alive again." Sonny Greer, a longtime member of Duke's band, told Lawrence, "Whenever Duke walked into her house, she'd light up." His father, James, was a grandiloquent man, full of charm and a successful, powerful figure who encouraged grandeur. According to Duke (Ellington, 1976), "He was a party man, a great dancer, a connoisseur of vintages, and unsurpassed in creating an aura of conviviality, and his vocabulary was what I always hoped mine to be." Duke's parents had married in their teens and were only 20 years old when Duke—their only child for 18 years—was born. They remained very close to Mother's large, extended family in which she was one of 10 children; Duke, as the first male grandchild, was very special to them all. As one of his cousins told Lawrence, "We thought he was the grandest thing in the world."

Ellington (1976) stated, "I was pampered and spoiled rotten by all the women in the family—aunts and cousins, but my mother never took her eyes off of precious little me, her jewel, until I was four years old." Duke opens his autobiography as follows.

> Once upon a time, a beautiful young lady and a very handsome young man fell in love and got married. They were a wonderful and compatible couple and God blessed their marriage with a fine baby boy, 8 pounds, 8 ounces. They loved their little boy very much, they raised him, nurtured him, coddled him, spoiled him, gave him everything he wanted. Finally when he was about 7 or 8 they let his feet touch the ground.

He added, "My mother would say, 'Edward, you are blessed. You don't have anything to worry about, Edward, you are blessed.' " Duke felt that sharing deep religious experiences with his mother gave him an extraordinary feeling of security. He always mentioned throughout his life that he was guided by a mysterious light. Daisy continually reinforced in him the idea that he was "special."

Thus a definite impression emerges of two strong parents—both with the definite capacity to tolerate their own as well as their son's feelings. There is no evidence of any kind of pathology that would indicate impaired affect tolerance, such as psychoses, tendencies toward severe somatic dysfunction, chaotic or impulsive behavior, alcoholism, or drug abuse. Instead, there was a close, warm, consistent, reliable tie between them and between them and their son. Indeed, it seems that Duke was fortunate in having even more than "good-enough" parenting; theirs was more like an ideal mother–father–child envelope. Therefore, it can be inferred reasonably confidently that his inner container was intact, strong, and healthy.

Now what about Duke's ability to verbalize affect? Some of his lyrics give evidence. Although the lyrics for most of his songs were written by others, he did write some himself. Mercer (Ellington and Dance, 1978) gives an example of an unfinished lyric he wrote for a song about women—"Shame on You—Suffer":

(A)   (C) (Choir) First Act
and Finale

Suffer, suffer,
You beautiful witch!
Suffer, suffer,
Till you're down in the ditch.

(B)
If you have never suffered
And hoped in vain,
How will you appreciate
Love without pain?

If it don't fit, then force it
You beautiful wretch!
Suffer, suffer,
'Cause you ain't got nothin' that won't stretch!

I know you hate to suffer,
You know I know you're proud,
So you have your tantrum, but suffer,
And let me hear you crying out loud!

As Mercer points out, this song eloquently describes feelings of contempt and hatred.

Another example of Duke's ability to express feelings in words appears in the opening pages of his autobiography (Ellington, 1976), where Duke includes a song, "Music," which ends with these lines:

Music is the woman
You follow day after day;
Music is the woman
Who always has her way.

The topless chick—
You like to see shake it—
No matter how hard you try,
You never quite make it.

When you don't hear her
You desperately miss her,
And when you embrace her,
You wish you could kiss her.

There are many more examples such as in the lyrics of "Me and You" of 1940, "Oh Baby . . . Maybe Someday" of 1936, and "I Don't Know What Kind of Blues I've Got" of 1942. Clearly, Duke had an excellent ability to verbalize affect—to express feelings in words.

Ellington's capacity to fantasize is nothing short of remarkable, and it can best be seen in two aspects of his composing. Tom Whaley—eight years his senior and a highly respected musician in his own right— worked for Duke for many years, often copying his scores for him. Whaley (Dance, 1970) once said,

Years ago when I was playing, I used to make some funny chords, and to me they sounded good. "What kind of chords you playing?" they'd ask. "I don't know," I'd say, "but keep on listening." They were all squares 'way back then. They didn't know anything about augmented fifths. [He added that

Duke's methods were unorthodox] because he goes against all the rules of music. He says if it sounds good, that's all that matters.

Whaley went on to compare Duke with Billy Strayhorn, composer of "Take the A Train" and a very close colleague of Duke's. Dance (1970) wrote:

> Billy always had a very good idea—a picture. The way he pictured music, when you looked at the chord, you could hear it, right in your mind. Sometimes, with Duke's, you'd have to stop—he has all those notes in there! The first time I was copying his music, I said "Duke, you got an E natural up there against an E flat." He said, "That's all right. Put it down." After you hear it, it sounds great. On paper, you think it won't. Just like Wild Bill Davis saying at the record date the other day, "Hey, you got an F sharp down there and an F up here." I said, "That's right." I've gotten used to it. It took time. At first some of the things he'd do seemed so fantastic, but they always sounded great. When you get used to that sound, you know it's Ellington. He's able to hear it. He knows it before he puts it down.

Mercer (Ellington and Dance, 1978) similarly stated, "He liked to show he could break rules successfully—like ending compositions in a key unrelated to the rest of the piece or devoting a whole composition to making the seventh chord rise instead of resolve downward." Schuller (1968), too, points this out. Referring to "Misty Mornin'," he says, "The unique inner voicings that helped make *Mood Indigo* so special are tried out very briefly. Such voicings were unorthodox and wrong, according to the textbooks. But Ellington did not know or care about the textbooks" (p. 342).

But they both do work! That's the point. In his mind's ear, Duke could hear the sounds as they sound when played, something that others could not do. This is an important component of the capacity to fantasize—to be able to elaborate auditory imagery. He would also often use visual imagery in composing. As aforementioned, he said, "I often think of music in terms of color" (Ellington, 1976). The tones would become colors in his mind's eye, and he would work with them that way, drawing on his own early background as a painter.

The second way this capacity shows itself in his work is in Duke's ability to hear and distinguish subtle differences between instrumentalists and hence to write for individuals, not instruments. He said, "You can't write music unless you know how the man who plays it, plays poker" (Ellington, 1976). He knew the qualities of his musicians both on their instruments and personally, so much so that the orchestral parts early in his career were not labeled "trumpet," "trombone," "saxophone," and so on but "Cootie," "Tricky," and "Barney." Billy Strayhorn told Lawrence

(1987), "Each member of his band is to him a distinctive tone color and set of emotions which he mixes with others equally distinctive to produce a third thing called the Ellington effect."

Thus Ellington was an individual with amazing musical output—in quantity and quality—who was, as Westry and Harrison (1984) say, "The Greatest Musical 'Colorist' in Jazz History"—and whose creative process was clearly related to a high affect tolerance—meaning a capacity to experience, feel, modulate, contain, and express his feelings and a capacity to tolerate ambiguity and uncertainty, keeping things open as he ventured into the new and unknown.

And this high affect tolerance, in turn, seems related to three underlying strengths: a healthy, intact inner container; an excellent ability to verbalize affect, and a truly remarkable capacity to fantasize, especially to hear auditory images in his mind's ear as well as see visual images in his mind's eye. Each of these can be assessed and also improved. Sometimes, what appears to be a deficit is an inhibition, a block caused by conflict; sometimes even a deficit can be improved by the proper approach. Clinicians should keep this in mind, especially those of us who see individuals in treatment for problems related to composing and maybe even creativity in general. We should think about individuals' affect tolerance, inner container, ability to verbalize affect and capacity to fantasize. How good are they? And how can they be improved? In this way we shall be able not only to increase our understanding of these talented people and their difficulties but also to offer them help in actualizing their creative potential.

REFERENCES

Bellerby, V. (1979), Duke Ellington. In: *The Art of Jazz*, ed. M. T. Williams. New York: DeCapo Press, pp. 123–138.

Brazelton, T. B. & Als, H. (1979), Four early stages in the development of mother–infant interaction. *The Psychoanalytic Study of the Child*, 34:349–370. New Haven, CT: Yale University Press.

Collier, J. L. (1978), *The Making of Jazz*. New York: Dell.

Dance, S. (1970), *The World of Duke Ellington*. New York: DaCapo Press.

Deutsch, H. (1937), *Neuroses and Character Types*. New York: IUP, pp. 226–236.

Ellington, D. (1976), *Music Is My Mistress*. New York: DeCapo Press.

Ellington, M. & Dance, S. (1978), *Duke Ellington in Person*. New York: DeCapo Press.

Fenichel, O. (1945), *The Psychoanalytic Theory of Neurosis*. New York: Norton.

Fox, C. (1979), Duke Ellington in the nineteen-thirties. In: *The Art of Jazz*. New York: DeCapo Press, pp. 123–138.

Freud, A. (1936), *The Ego and the Mechanisms of Defense*. New York: IUP.

Freud, S. (1911), Formulations of the two principles of mental functions. *Standard Edition*, 12:213–226. London: Hogarth Press.

_____ (1915), Repression. *Standard Edition*, 14:141–158. London: Hogarth Press.

Furman, R. A. (1978), Some developmental aspects of the verbalization of affects. *The Psychoanalytic Study of the Child*, 33:87–211. New Haven, CT: Yale University Press.

Goldberg, A., ed. (1981), *The Psychology of the Self—A Casebook*. New York: IUP.

Keats, J. (1817), *Letters of John Keats, Selected by F. Page*. London: Oxford University Press, 1954, p. 53.

Khantzian, E. J. (1979), Impulse problems and drug addiction. In: *Working with the Impulsive Person*, ed. H. A. Wishnie & J. Nevis-Olesen. New York: Plenum, pp. 97–112.

Kohut, H. (1971), *The Analysis of the Self*. New York: IUP.

Lawrence, A. (1987), Duke Ellington, unpublished manuscript.

Mahler, M. S., Pine, F. & Bergman, A. (1975), *The Psychological Birth of the Human Infant*. New York: Basic Books.

Marty, P. & De M'Uzan, M. (1963), *Rev. fr. psychanal.*, 27(suppl.):345–356.

Maudsley, H. (1884), *Body and Mind*. New York: Appleton.

Nemiah, J. C., Freyberger, H. & Sifneos, P. E. (1975), Alexithymia: A view of the psychosomatic process. In: *Modern Trends of Psychosomatic Medicine*, Vol. 3, ed. O. W. Hill. London: Buttersworth, pp. 430–439.

Pulver, S. E. (1971), *Int. J. Psycho-Anal.*, 52:347–354.

Sashin, J. (1985), *J. Soc. Biol. Struct.*, 8:175–202.

Schuller, G. (1968), *Early Jazz*. New York: Oxford University Press, pp. 318–357.

Thom, R. (1976), *Structural Stability and Morphogenesis*. Reading, PA: Benjamin.

Tolpin, P. H. (1974), *The Annual of Psychoanalysis*, 2:150–177. New York: IUP.

Westry, J. A. & Harrison, F. (1984), *The New College Encyclopedia of Music*. New York: Norton.

Chapter 15

THE PASSIONS OF NATIONALISM AND BEYOND

Identity and Power in International Relationships

John E. Mack

Human life contains certain dimensions that are so much with us that we have come to take them for granted, rarely if ever asking ourselves, "Why really is it that way?" or "Does it have to be like that?" Striking among them is the passion of ethnonationalism, that intensity of feeling that attaches to an ethnic group or a nation state, and a force of such emotional power that once caught in its spell, human beings will sacrifice everything, may kill one another, or can order the killing of others without many feelings of hesitation or regret.

The habits of nationalistic violence, which sometimes reach genocidal proportions, seem at times so ingrained that it seldom occurs to us that they are driven by energies we hardly begin to comprehend. In partial explanation of conduct that a visitor from another planet might find quite bizarre, we may offer rational historical or contemporary justifications, usually involving a story of genuine hurt or threat, and not pause to wonder whether such explanations adequately account for the magnitude or power of the phenomenon. An initial attitude that there is a mystery here that needs exploration could yield unexpected insight and might even lead to additional knowledge about the sources of affective intensity itself. At the very least, acknowledgment of not knowing in addition to greater openness to the human complexities past and present that are contained in all ethnonational conflict situations, could make room for examination and appreciation of the powerful emotional forces that block constructive change.

The breakup of the Soviet Union has led to an upsurge in nationalistic passions. Long-repressed desires and hatreds have emerged as groups that were formerly contained both geographically and emotionally within the empire strive to reassert their identities and settle old scores. In the fall of 1991, cries of independence against the central authority that began with the breaking away of the countries of Eastern Europe spread to the republics within the Soviet Union itself and then extended to a largely Muslim region in the Caucasus called Chechen-Ingushetia, which sought to separate from the Russian Republic. Chechen nationalism had become heightened during World War II, when Stalin deported the Chechens to Siberia, from which they were not allowed to return until 1957 (*New York Times*, 1991).

Waves of nationalistic passion are not, of course, limited to the Soviet Union or Eastern Europe. They have force in the struggles between Serbs and Croats, Palestinians and Israelis, northern and southern Irish, ethnic French and English Canadians, and Tamil and Sinhalese or Hindus and Sikhs in Sri Lanka and India. The growing power of the drive for self-determination among peoples all over the world and the decline of central political authority are part of a single process that has at its core the human yearning for self-fulfillment. The process offers a great opportunity and at the same time poses terrible dangers for humankind. Opportunity lies in the possibility that new reverence for the lives of individual human beings in an ecologically sustainable and politically secure environment might emerge. Danger resides in the very real chance that hostile passions—aggravated by fear and fueled by the sale of weapons for profit—might lead to Hobbesian chaos, a war of all against all that could, in turn, through the use of nuclear weapons, ultimately lead to extinction of life as we know it.

Current world conditions make the dangers especially great. So-called "conventional" weapons have become more deadly, and their means of delivery have been facilitated by improved transportation and communication systems. Meanwhile, government and nongovernment arms suppliers seem, so far, all too willing to meet the demand until a countervailing worldwide revulsion and resistance to this practice bring it to a halt. The earth's delicate life-sustaining physical environment has become increasingly threatened by violence itself, as demonstrated so dramatically by both pollution of the sea and the oil fires that raged during and after the Persian Gulf war of January–February, 1991. Finally, the drive of peoples for self-determination is occurring at a time of relatively diminishing physical resources such as water, oil and other forms of energy, and, especially, land, which the human species in its arrogance believes can be owned or exploited for the exclusive benefit of one or another of its subgroups.

The idea of "national sovereignty," like "economic growth," has, until recently, possessed a kind of sacred solemnity, as if the vital interests of one or another national group were not the business of other groups or the human community as a whole. But a moment's thought enables us to see that respect for a particular nation's autonomy or sovereignty has been quite arbitrary, depending almost entirely on the tolerance and ambitions of other state powers and nationalistic forces. And perhaps this is as it must be, for life on this planet is maintained in a profoundly connected and delicate structure. Human groups are genuinely interdependent, not only with each other but with all of the planet's living systems. From this fact it follows that the destructive power of ethnonational aggression and fear is the entire planet's business and that the interests of one or another group must be reconciled with the larger interest of the whole human community. It is necessary, therefore, that we deepen our understanding of the roots of such violence and build upon the forms of nonviolent intervention that are beginning to be brought to the resolution of interethnic and international conflict.

We live in paradoxical times. It seems as if each day we learn of another human group that is seeking to break away from a parent group or central authority. Simultaneously, however, powerful forces are creating new connections, "commonwealths," confederations, and regional economic and political arrangements for survival and security. At times, we seem not too far from the beginnings of a genuine worldwide human community that is more than merely a new internationalism with its connotation once again of borders and national separatism. Is it vain to imagine that the deeper knowledge of the human psyche, which has been applied in this century to our understanding of individuals and groups, might be brought to bear upon the problem of ethnonationalism and contribute to the restraint of violent passions and the healing of historical wounds? The inner world—the landscape of human feeling—appears to be the uncharted frontier that now confronts us in our struggle to live in peace with one another.

FUNCTIONS OF NATIONALISTIC IDENTIFICATION

In an attempt to understand the emotional strength of nationalistic identifications, it seems natural to begin with the psychological functions that the ethnonational group serves for individual human beings (Mack, 1983). British historian Berlin (1979), using the first person singular to capture subjective intensity, writes of the all-consuming power of nationalistic emotions in human social life.

> My nation [intones his nationalist] apart from which I am . . . a leaf, a twig, broken from the tree, which alone can give it life; so that if I am separated from it by circumstance or my own wilfulness, I shall become aimless, I shall wither away, being left, at best, with nostalgic memories of what it once was to have been truly alive and active and performing that function in the pattern of the national life, understanding of which alone gave meaning and value to all I was and did [p. 346].

That passage captures the basic functions of nationalistic feeling and identification. First, there is the need to belong, to be connected, to be a part of something larger than oneself without which one feels painful emptiness and aloneness in a life without meaning. Russian historian Tsipko, in a 1990 conference on ethnic conflict resolution in the Soviet Union, said, "A root condition of spiritual health is a sense of belonging" (Esalen, 1990). Second is the function of security and protection, of survival itself. The world, however its perimeters may be defined for particular people, is an unsafe place. Only the nation state, with its military forces and weapons, or the ethnic group as it strives for state-hood, seems to protect us from the violence of others and, unconsciously, from our own fears of uncertainty and the unknown. Third is the quest for transcendence that is implicit in Berlin's words, a kind of spiritual depth or power that goes beyond simple survival. Kelman (1987), in a lecture at the International Society of Political Psychology, noted the "blending of self-protection with self-transcendence" that loyalty to a nation represents. Church and state may be separated by law, but religious-style emotion and language surround the relationship to the nation state and are regularly invoked by national leaders when they wish to inspire loyalty and sacrifice among their followers. O'Brien (1988) invented the term "Godland" to denote the contemporary deification of the nation state. Fourth is the function of the ethnonational group in securing a sense of personal and group identity, which is for establishing and maintaining the sense of self. Ethnonational struggles are fought as much over com-peting claims to national identity as they are over land or other physical resources. It is common now for spokespersons representing an ethno-national group in an arena of international political conflict to attempt to discredit the legitimacy of another group's claim to statehood, or even "peoplehood," on the grounds that the other group has not lived in a particular territory very long or cannot justly defend itself as a historical entity. Conversely, the tremendous power associated with official and unofficial acknowledgment or recognition of a national group's right to exist or its legitimacy, as lent by other nations or significantly placed individuals, is directly related to the overriding importance of the nation state for a sense of personal and group identity (Montville, 1989). Finally, emotional connection with the nation state or ethnonational group is strongly tied to the sense of personal worth or value and power. It is not an exaggeration to say that for countless individuals, self-esteem and personal power seem to rise and fall with the fate of the ethnonational group. The link between identity and power brings us close to the core of the problem of nationalism

THE QUESTION OF IDENTITY

Identity, the core sense of self, is profoundly subjective and personal. It is for this reason that if a competitive or adversarial group raises doubt about of the legitimacy of a group's identity, it is particularly offensive and inflammatory. But the sense of identity does not exist in isolation. It grows out of all that we feel ourselves to be a part of or connected with—family, peer and professional groups, a tribe or nation, a spiritual community, the earth, or, in mystical experience, all of creation. Therefore, threats to the dimensions of self that constitute our primary identification jeopardize more than physical survival: they threaten the deepest sense of one's being or very existence over time.

At the same time, the resorting to blind nationalism, or its more exalted cousin, patriotism, can be, if not Samuel Johnson's last refuge of scoundrels, at least a relatively facile way to claim or experience a sense of identity when social structures or institutions seem to be crumbling and economic hardship creates uncertainty about the future. In November 1990, as the Soviet empire was beginning to come apart, Russian historian Gassan Gussejnov, who is a small part Azerbaijani, observed that in the context of deprivation and threatened identity, "People opt for nationalism. Local vulgar patriotism prospers. It is the right to be someone without effort. You don't have to do anything to become a Russian, like to study to be a doctor" (Esalen, 1990).

The history of ethnonational groups is the history of the threats to the sense of self of a people. Beyond the partisan rhetoric, the opening speech of Haidar Abdel-Shafi, head of the Palestinian delegation, at the October-November 1991 Arab-Israeli conference in Madrid, expresses the tight linkage of historical woundedness and identity (New York Times, 1991).

> We, the people of Palestine, stand before you in the fullness of our pain, our pride, and our anticipation for we have long harbored a yearning for peace and a dream of justice and freedom. For too long, the Palestinian people

338   PASSIONS OF NATIONALISM

have gone unheeded, silenced and denied, our identity negated by political
expedience, our rightful struggle against injustice maligned, and our
present existence subsumed by the past tragedy of another people.

That other people is, of course, the Jewish people. My most recent
encounter with the Jewish people's "past tragedy" occurred in July 1991,
when my wife and I traveled to Lithuania in search of her roots in the
village of her father's birth (Mack, 1991). Most disturbing to us, even more
than the alacrity with which some Lithuanians had participated in Hitler's
project for the extermination of the Jews, were the elimination of even
traces of former Jewish communities and the obliteration of evidence that
Jewish people had ever existed there at all when, in fact, there had once
been a prosperous and rich Jewish culture in Lithuania. Between peoples
who have shared a common geography, struggles over land or other
resources are more profoundly about historical wounds and tragedies
that cannot be acknowledged because of a mechanism I have called the
egoism of victimization (Mack, 1979), meaning the inability of a people to
grow beyond the constrictions of the group self that have constituted the
group's long-term adaptation to historic wounds and that prevent it from
empathizing with the pain or needs of another people.

"Self-determination" is the term that is most often used to capture a
people's drive for national statehood. But the term carries a broader
implication than its specific political meaning: it connotes personal realization or fulfillment and the sense of agency or control. As social psychologist Ronen (1979) puts it, "Individual self-determination, to rule one's self,
to control one's own life, is a basic given of the human existence" (p. 55). It
is here that power becomes a central force. The importance of personal
identification with a nation's power cannot be overestimated, yet this
dynamic has been little studied in the psychology of nationalism and
international relations. In discussions of political psychology, power is
generally taken to mean military or, nowadays, economic power. We
choose leaders who we think will be "strong" or "tough" and protect us or
be ready to demonstrate power militarily.

Many of us were surprised by the joyous celebrations that followed the
military successes of the Persian Gulf war, despite the failure to dislodge
Saddam Hussein from power, the ghastly one-sidedness of the actual
conflict, the terrible slaughter of Iraqi soldiers and civilians, and the
bloody crushing of the uprising of Shiite and Kurdish minorities after a
formal cease-fire has been declared. We should not have been surprised,
for it is apparent from this and other historical examples that the intensity
of the exhilaration and self-satisfaction that accompany the expression of
a nation's military prowess will, for most people, carry greater psychological weight, at least in the short run, than empathy for the suffering of

another national group or the achievement of useful political or humanitarian results as judged by objective criteria. Identification with naked power will, at least in the short run, tend to override other values and the consideration of consequences.

There is a great need to understand the dynamic relationship between power and the sense of self. This subject, so fundamental to an appreciation of the intensity of nationalistic passions, has been relatively neglected in psychoanalysis and it the dynamic and self psychologies that have derived from it.

THE PSYCHOLOGY OF POWER

Freud (1900) used the quotation from Virgil's *Aeniad*, "If I cannot bend the Higher Powers, I will move the Infernal Regions" (p. 608*n*) as a motto for *The Interpretation of Dreams* and had earlier proposed it for a chapter on symptom formation for a book on the neuroses, which was never completed (Masson, 1985). He intended the quote to refer to "repressed instinctual impulses"; "Higher Powers" is generally interpreted to refer to the ego or the intellect. But another, more political, interpretation is possible.

Schorske (1980) analyzes dreams of Freud's that show his feelings of frustration and impotence in the arena of Viennese power politics and the competing forces of Austrian, Hungarian, and German nationalisms in the 1890s. Prevented from entering that political world either by reason of his being Jewish and the climate of anti-Semitism in Vienna or by elements of his own temperament, Freud, in Schorske's words, "sought to exhume his own political past through dream analysis" (p. 202). Nevertheless, Schorske finds, for example, in the "Dream of Irma's Injection," that "a political wish was found to lie as a deeper reality beneath the professional one" (p. 187). Freud consistently avoids political interpretations of his dreams so that "politics could be reduced to an epiphenomenal manifestation of psychic forces" (p. 183). The "Higher Powers" could also be political forces and authorities, leaders like the Austrian minister/president Count Franz Thun, about whom Freud dreamt and whom he would not or could not cultivate. In his revelation of universal instinctual forces and family psychodynamics, presumed to lie deeper than the political forces themselves, Freud would do politics and the politicians one better, reducing them, in effect, to their personal motivations: "Patricide replaces regicide; psychoanalysis overcomes history. Politics is neutralized by a counterpolitical psychology" (p. 197).

A story that Harvard psychologist Goethals tells of his colleague Professor Henry Murray's two-hour visit with Freud in 1926 provides further support for the idea that Freud avoided the psychology of power. Murray told Goethals that he could not understand "how a man of your genius" could put forth such a "puerile" theory of human motivation (referring to the libido theory). According to Murray, Freud agreed and said that he had originally defined three basic human motivating forces—sexuality, power, and aggression—but that he had come under such attack for his sex theory that he was taken up with defending it against his critics and never got around to developing the others. In his later years Freud did, of course, explore the role of aggressive motivations, but he never took up the study of power.

Finally, there is the evidence of Freud's complex attraction and resistance to the study of Nietzsche's works, in which, of course, the psychology of power played a central role (Mack, 1990a, 1993). On one hand, Freud expressed an "excess of interest" in Nietzsche (Nunberg and Federn, 1962, p. 359) and spent a considerable amount of money collecting his works. On the other hand, as his biographer Gay (1988) observes, "Freud treated Nietzsche's writings as texts to be resisted far more than to be studied" (p. 45). We do not know exactly what it was in Nietzsche that Freud resisted, but Nietzsche leaves no doubt that power in its various manifestations was central to his worldview. In an 1897 note, for example, Nietzsche wrote, "There is nothing to life that has value, except the degree of power—assuming that life itself is the will to power" (p. 37).

Nietzsche's universe, psychological and physical, is different from Freud's, more chaotic and less civilized, "a monster of energy, without beginning, without end . . . a sea of forces flowing and rushing together, eternally changing, eternally flooding back" (Nietzsche, p. 550). It is dominated by great cycles of death and rebirth, of creativity and destructiveness. Freud's world, however tragic, seems more manageable, more humanly boundaried. The psyche in Freud's universe seems separate from the great archetypal forces of the Nietzschean cosmos, in which human motivation and behavior seem more embedded, more congruent, and more participatory in the cosmic flow and forms. Indeed, the experience of the twentieth century has been profoundly Nietzschean in the sense that the human enterprise, especially as manifested by the behavior of large groups, appears to have been driven at least as much by the archetypal polarities of Nietzsche's "monster of energy" as by the more personal psychological force of individual psyches projected onto a larger collective canvas. The psychodynamic understanding of this enterprise, if it is to contribute as it must to the knowledge of the functioning of the human psyche in large groups, can no longer avoid the exploration of power, however much we may have been diverted from this study by Freud's and our own personal and scientific priorities and resistances.

To understand the place of power in human psychology and political life, it is useful to define the basic meaning of the word. In its political sense, power is customarily taken to mean some form of control or domination by one person or group over others, usually through military strength. But the fundamental meaning of power is more general, having to do with any capacity to do or accomplish something, to influence or affect others or the world around us. In this second sense, power becomes an essential dimension of human psychology, one of its bedrocks. For without the capacity to affect our surroundings, we are by definition powerless or helpless, a condition that is, at least in its extreme form, more disturbing than any other known to humankind. The ultimate Orwellian nightmare, as in *1984* itself, is to be in a state of utter helplessness in the face of a danger that is uniquely threatening. For this reason, all living creatures, including of course human beings, develop strategies to ward off powerlessness, to *be* powerful. It is in the individual and collective development of these strategies for achieving and experiencing power in the evolution of our political selves that psychology and politics become linked.

In its meaning, power is close to spirit, to the fundamental energies that inhabit the universe. Native peoples through time have had many words to define these energies, the forces in nature and in ourselves with which we must come to terms (Mack, 1990a, 1993). In the West, we have relied heavily on material technology to harness the universe's primal energies and to dominate or conquer nature and ourselves in order to feel powerful and secure. This strategy is proving to be a failure on a scale never known before, as exemplified best by the threat of the nuclear weapons competition and the worldwide reign of terror that has been its result and by the slow death of the planet's life systems in the wake of our unlicensed efforts to dominate and exploit nature. It is for these reasons, I expect, that more and more people in the West are turning to traditional Native American and Eastern religious understandings of nature through which human beings have evolved painstakingly their ways of existing in harmony with other living creatures and the inanimate world.

A newborn infant embodies the paradoxes of power. It is uniquely vulnerable, requiring our protection and care, but at the same time it has a special ability, perhaps because of its closeness still to the world of spirit and the primal creative energies of nature, to bring forth the love and power of others on its behalf (Erikson and Erikson, 1953). Sensing perhaps in some deep intuitive way the capricious or precarious nature of their world, infants do not rely long on the exclusive power of others to protect and take care of them. The core sense of self, which is thought to develop in the period between 3 and 6 months (Stern, 1985), includes a sense of agency or authorship, the capacity to initiate action on one's own behalf. It is from this capacity for agency that the strategies for achieving power and for countering helplessness and vulnerability, develop.

PASSIONS OF NATIONALISM

Each stage of human development from infancy through adult life has its characteristic strategies for securing power and offsetting the sense of vulnerability from which we are never entirely free. For we are destined always to live with the inescapable knowledge that our lives are under our own control only to a very limited extent and that we are fated to die, returning to a kind of nothingness. It is when individuals or groups, either inside or outside the international political order, desperately seek a kind of total, risk-free safety, security, or control that the greatest dangers to human and other forms of life arise.

The small infant's first strategy for achieving power resides in its very helplessness and charm, the precursor of seductiveness and manipulation of the feelings of others on which so many older children and adults rely. This capability shows up in more sophisticated forms in political diplomacy and negotiation. Indeed, each strategy we learn as individuals in order to gain power and overcome our helplessness has its counterpart or is carried forward in the feelings and forms of human group and political life. Stubbornness and the need to exercise control are not far behind charm among the infant's power stratagems, followed soon by tyranny itself. I have seen children in the second year of life—including one 21-month-old boy who would sit behind his doctor father's desk giving orders—acting like willful corporate executives or political officials while their parents reacted with amusement, confusion, or anger. The two kinds of power embodied in the infant's earliest strategies for securing it—either to be with, connect, charm, persuade, and invite or, alternatively, to dominate, coerce, and control—remain possible avenues or options that human beings cultivate in various admixtures throughout life. These alternative courses are clearly apparent in styles of negotiation and in the ways of conducting relationships in the international political arena (Saunders, 1985, 1991).

Another basic strategy for gaining power, which children learn at their parents' knee, is the creation of dependency in others in order to maintain our hold over them by making ourselves, in effect, indispensable. Like drug pushers, we learn to cultivate an inescapable need for us. The fierce, counterdependent battle that adolescents and some adults wage to free themselves of the hold that parent figures have maintained over them is better understood than the more subtle means that we have used to maintain the dependence and relative helplessness of our children.

Mature adults spend their life developing inner strength or power and relative freedom from the reach of the power of others over us. But we are destined to be forever social creatures, interdependent within the framework of society's institutions. Knowing this, we appreciate from an early age that the most essential means whereby we gain power is in the formation of alliances. Beginning within the family, we learn to ally ourselves with other individuals, starting with our parents, siblings, and other relatives in order to extend our power, offset our helplessness, and be protected from the threats of others and the whims of fate. Later we attach ourselves to groups and institutions, or to the leaders who represent them so as to experience a range of our power that exceeds what we can achieve on our own. Each developmental stage of life has its characteristic group and political identifications, beginning with early childhood play groups and extending to adolescent clubs and gangs and eventually to trade and professional societies and academic, scientific, religious, military, and political institutions. Our political selves evolve throughout our lives. The extraordinary emphasis placed on the loyalty and trustworthiness of individuals within an organization or, conversely, the fear of betrayal or too much individualism derives from the role of the organization in providing a sense of power and security for its members and offsetting their conscious and unconscious experience of vulnerability.

The ethnonational group, or nation as it is called when the group achieves state sovereignty, is a particularly effective and quintessentially modern political institution, designed to give its members a sense of personal power and protection in a world in which helplessness before nature has been replaced by the threat of other, proximate human groups. Modern nationalism feeds on the vulnerability it itself creates. National leaders, self-selected in the first place at least in part by their inordinate drive for power and fear of helplessness, command a political and scientific elite whose principal function has been to develop a set of political alliances and a technologically sophisticated military force in the pursuit of power and security. This method of achieving power began to be fundamentally questioned in the late 1980s, when the absurdity of trying to feel safe through the acquisition of weapons of mass destruction that were ultimately as dangerous to their possessors as to a putative enemy became obvious even to the leading nuclear countries themselves. Nevertheless, in the early 1990s, we are witnessing once again the rise of new nationalisms and tribalisms and the resurgence of old ones, as human groups, having liberated themselves from imperial control, find little to stop them from avenging historical hurts or expressing their drive for self-realization by forming new states or extending their boundaries at the expense of other groups. The war between Serbs and Croats is a characteristic example of this process.

Modern technology is obviously intimately tied to the ways we now achieve a feeling of power and self-worth. In the United States, we take great pride in the "smart" bombs that helped to destroy Iraq, but we cannot afford to educate or take care of our children or house our people. Yet there are great paradoxes associated with contemporary technology. We revel in the superior technology that allowed the United States and its

PASSIONS OF NATIONALISM

allies to win the Persian Gulf war relatively easily. Special bomb "sights" allowed us to kill the enemy without having to see him at all while centralized control of television information protected us from having to see the beseeching eyes of orphaned Iraqi children. Republican candidate for president Buchanan (1992) blatantly declared that what we need in a president is an "American nationalist who would put America first." At the same time, however, technology connects us profoundly to one another. Intercontinental ballistic missiles underscore our common security and total interdependence. Television satellites in the heavens allow us to see for the first time other members of the human family in all parts of the globe. Advanced military technologies have added to the fear that impels the drive toward statehood. But technology also offers the possibility of overcoming our fear of the other through the sharing of its benefits and the facilitation of communication. Technology virtually creates ethnonationalisms; yet it can enable us to move beyond their straitjackets.

MENTAL DUALISM

A proclivity for dualistic thinking and feeling—a tendency to divide the world into dichotomies or polarities—represents another fundamental quality or potential of the human psyche that is essential to an understanding of nationalism. In the Freudian tradition, dualism is seen to be rooted in the primitive forces of the individual unconscious, where love and hate, Eros and Thanatos, and narcissism and object relationships grow out of the psychobiological conditions of personal development. In Jungian psychology, the dualities expressed in concepts such as the persona and the shadow or anima and animus or in our notions of good and evil or darkness and light are archetypal, reflecting broad patterns of nature in which the human psyche participates. In the transpersonal schools of thought, the roots of dualism lie beyond human biography, or even group life, but are traceable to the phases of birth and death, to the transpersonal, Nietzschean forces of creation and destruction in the universe of which human individual and group life partakes (Garrison, 1988).

Whatever may be our theoretical starting point, it seems clear that the dualism of the human psyche—its tendency to create difference, separation and fragmentation on the one hand and connection, oneness, or wholeness on the other—is played out in a constant ebb and flow in the political arena. At the same time as empires come apart and separate, states emerge, new forms of regional cooperation and internationalism begin, and the new states themselves discover conflicting ethnonational forces and identities that may divide them from within (Weiner, 1991).

Some of the great spiritual traditions, deriving from the consciousness of a transcendent unity residing in and beyond nature, know the apocalyptic power of dualism and the overwhelming danger of collective hate and pride. The traditions are naturally distrustful of nationalisms, which arrogate to man rather than God the ultimate responsibility for political arrangements. Theologian Tinder (1989) writes that "In the Christian view, while every individual is exalted, society is not" (p. 82). In this view, the creation of nation states is an idolatrous and dangerous arrangement, the self-serving exaltation of one group's interest at the expense of another's, and "Nationalism or some other form of collective pride becomes virulent, and war unrestrained" (Tinder, 1989). Native American texts, which are getting more attention now as the failures of traditional nationalistic arrangements mount in scope and intensity, express bewilderment at the idea that human groups could believe that they own the earth, which so patently, in their experience, belongs to the Great Spirit. One of the most terrible wars of this century was fought in the Persian Gulf at the beginning of 1991 on the pretext that national boundaries—in this case that of a small, oil-rich sheikdom whose border was arbitrarily drawn by the withdrawing British but 30 years before—are more sacred (the word actually used by New York State Representative Steven Solarz in supporting the resolution authorizing the war) than human lives.

There are peculiarities of ethnonational history and nationalistic power that favor dualistic thinking. First, political leaders find it valuable to concentrate a people's attention on an outside enemy in order to maintain group cohesion and their own power (Mack, 1990b). The primitive psychological structures that divide the world into polarities of good and evil translate easily into self and other, us and them (Group for the Advancement of Psychiatry, 1987), friend and enemy. By way of an obliging and relatively uncritical mass media, the communication of fear of another state that is armed with modern weaponry is a potent device available to a contemporary leader who consciously or unconsciously seeks to recruit these dichotomizing tendencies of the psyche in the service of a political agenda. With the collapse of the Soviet Union, there has been a good deal of debate about whether the United States needs a new enemy to hold itself together as a society. President Bush anxiously reassured NATO that the organization could somehow be maintained without the Soviet enemy. What I have called elsewhere the "ideologies of enmity" (Mack, 1986, 1990b) are the collective habits of thought that freeze these political dualisms and divisions in place.

The need of a national group to deny the darkness of its own history and the costs in lives and suffering of others in establishing its identity builds a powerful dualistic base into the structure of ethnonationalistic thought. Glorious myths of national origin exalt the conquests and victories of one's own group and show little empathy for the devastation on the other side. But to do this the humanity of the other peoples must be denied, or they must be depicted as so savage or "barbaric"—a favorite word applied to the aggressive acts of the other but never to one's own— that the national conquest or expansion is justified. Serbs in their recent killing of Croatians express only their hatred and recall the horrors of Croatian complicity with the Nazis, omitting from their consciousness any redeeming value in their neighbors as human beings (Henricson-Cullberg et al., 1991).

Finally, the immediate and long-term impacts of hurts, threats, humiliation, and loss in relation to an outside adversary breed fear and distrust, leading to constriction of the sense of self for the individuals within an ethnonational group and for the group itself. Further separateness and the desperate search for security, power, and control through acquisition of military weapons inspire more fear and distrust and start an intensifying process that often results in war. The narrowed scope of the group, together with its limited capacity to identify beyond its own needs and those of other nations that serve its perceived immediate interests, reduces political dialogue to a primitive survival level in which worst-case scenarios and bizarre military schemes for achieving security that are unrealistic in the nuclear age come to predominate. If historical wounds are still fresh, as is so often the case among neighboring peoples who have lived in strife-filled proximity through the centuries, the desire for and the acting out of motives of revenge or retribution may consciously or unconsciously contribute to the political chemistry. A wounded leader linked to a wounded people is a particularly deadly combination in these times.

The cycles of fear and dualism feed upon themselves, bringing ever greater separateness and constriction unless interrupted, at least temporarily, by some outside force such as a war whose cost is unbearable or, more rarely, by new expressions of psychologically mindful diplomacy or of enlightened leadership that can transcend the habits and traditions of conventional power politics (Mack, 1990c). Although American political analysts have credited our military strength and resolve for the end of the cold war and reduction of the nuclear threat, I suspect that the perception on the part of Gorbachev and his followers of the paramount need to break the cycle of fear and mistrust was a more important factor.

NEW FORMS OF POWER

As we have seen, power in its human expressions derives from the energies that are immanent in nature. In striving to have or experience power, we are participating in the vitality that is inherent in the physical universe. The fateful questions for the human future reside not in whether power will remain central in our psychology but in the forms of power that are to be expressed. The Sioux Indian medicine man John (Fire) Lame Deer eloquently describes power as it is inherent in nature:

> The Great Spirit pours a great, unimaginable amount of force into all things—pebbles, ants, leaves, whirlwinds—whatever you will. Still there is so much force left over that's not used up, that is in his gift to bestow, that has to be used wisely and in moderation if we are given some of it . . . all animals have power, because the Great Spirit dwells in all of them, even a tiny ant, a butterfly, a tree, a flower, a rock. The modern white man's way keeps that power from us, dilutes it. To come to nature, feel its power, let it help you, one needs time and patience for that. Time to think, to figure it all out. You have so little time for contemplation; it's always rush, rush, rush with you [Lame Deer and Erdoes, 1972 pp. 103, 116].

Power in Lame Deer's sense, what I have called "primary power" (Mack, 1989), exists in nature in virtually unlimited supply. Even the forms of energy available on the earth to satisfy our basic physical needs are adequate if creative solutions are pursued, conservation were to become an accepted value, and our materialistic appetites were appropriately governed.

But the power about which Lame Deer is speaking is not simply physical. It is the power that is experienced in the spirit of living beings and objects and in our own psyches. We saw earlier that the alternative directions for expressions of power are apparent in earliest childhood. One line of development leads us to the experience of wholeness and of emotional and spiritual connection with one another, and it enables us to extend our identities beyond our own family to other groups, peoples, and life forms—even to the earth itself. It is this form of power, which is inner directed and grows with the psychological and spiritual growth of the individual, that enables us to overcome personal and political divisions and to transcend our wounds and frustrations without violence (Ikeda, 1991). It is the feeling that our life can make a difference, that we can create something worthwhile, even influence events. It is also the power of joy, play, and music. This form of power is nourished by the experience of being cared for, loved, and valued. The other kind of power, which I have called "secondary power," also begins its developmental line in childhood. This is the power of domination, coercion, and control. It brings resentment and fear and separates children from their parents, leaders from their citizens, and peoples from one another. It is the psychological source of war.

It is secondary power that is usually meant—especially military force—when we speak of power in the context of politics and international relations ("power politics") and in the striving to gain hegemony or to be "number one." Secondary power in its manifestations by both individuals and groups feeds on fear, loss, and wounds in groups, just as for individuals painful, frustrating, and wounding experiences force reliance on tactics of domination and control in our personal life. These wounds must be understood and addressed if we are to bring about the profound shifts in the forms of power that will be required if there is to be a future for the human species on this planet.

IMPLICATIONS

It follows from this discussion that the task that faces psychologists, or diplomats and officials *as* psychologists, is one of healing wounds at a collective level, of bringing about a shift in the political conversation from exclusively secondary power to primary power considerations. During the first days of the Madrid conference that began the negotiation of the Arab-Israeli conflict, news commentators seemed to become impatient with the delegation representatives, pressing them to get "beyond" the stories of suffering and the seemingly endless setting forth of claims based on their peoples' respective histories of pain and victimization and on to the "substantive" matters of territory, security, and economic resources. But the path to these "substantive" issues lies through the emotional forest, for it is precisely those unhealed historical wounds that breed suspicion and distrust, prevent meaningful dialogue, and bring about reliance on coercive military strategies to achieve security and maintain power.

It is not, of course, merely the exchanging of stories of suffering that ever leads to the overcoming of past hurts. The wounded parties must be enabled to see and hear one another, overcoming the inevitable egoism, the exclusive focus on one's own suffering, and the lack of empathy for the other's that constitute the inevitable outcome of historical victimization. Recognition of the other, acknowledgment of one's own responsibility for the other's plight, and apology for past crimes against an adversary represent powerful forces for healing and political change. Anwar Sadat's personal assumption of responsibility for Arab isolation of Israel, Canon John Baker's apologies to Catholic Ireland for British historical crimes, and Soviet admission of guilt for the massacre in the Katyn forest are well-known contemporary examples of expressions of moral responsibility. They are indeed dramatic acts by states or internationally prominent political leaders, but there are countless smaller efforts that less known or less prominently placed citizens can undertake in the process of healing and expanding political responsibility, which has been called citizen or "Track II" diplomacy (Chasin and Herzig, 1988; Davidson and Montville, 1981–82; Warner and Shuman, 1987).

Joseph Montville, former U.S. State Department Foreign Service officer and astute political psychologist, demonstrated the methods and power of acknowledgment and apology in a controversial plenary speech in 1986 at the American Psychoanalytic Association. After reviewing the history of the persecution of Jews by Christians, Montville (1989) offered a symbolic apology to the audience, which contained many Jews, in order to enhance, ultimately, his ability to serve as a more trusted broker in future negotiations between Arabs and Jews in the Middle East:

> I ask as a private, individual Christian the forgiveness of the Jewish people for the hurts inflicted on them by Christendom. I ask to be permitted to mourn Jewish losses with Jews and then work in brotherly alliance with Jews and Arabs to mourn unjust hurts suffered by some Arabs as Jews fleeing Christian brutality in Europe established a homeland in Palestine and ultimately the State of Israel. And I ask to work with Jews and Arabs to establish a relationship which assures a secure and just future for them and their children [p. 317].

The audience was deeply moved and expressed its appreciation of Montville's act of courage by giving him a standing ovation, a rare occurrence in that otherwise restrained group.

A promising expansion of the possibilities of Track II diplomacy lies in the use of facilitators and mediators who are knowledgable about the emotional forces that permeate all situations of ethnonational conflict (McDonald and Bendahmane, 1987). Psychologically trained mediators or facilitators who have earned the trust of the embattled parties can help to hold and bear the tensions that inevitably arise between the groups, be sensitive to the powerful feeling currents beneath manifest communications, and can translate meanings across cultural and ideological divides (Gutlove, 1990) in order to bridge differences between or among the parties. Track II approaches alone or in combination with official diplomacy have been fruitfully applied to Franco-German relations after World War II, Turkish-Greek conflict in Cypress, intergroup conflict in the Dominican Republic, the Arab-Israeli conflict, the U.S.–Soviet relationship, and other divided groups.

Former Assistant Secretary of State for the Middle East Harold Saunders observed at the 1991 conference of the International Society of Political Psychology (ISPP) that the development of nonviolent political means of dealing with leaders like Saddam Hussein, who seem to set no limits on the destructiveness they will wreak in the service of their power, represents a particularly important challenge in the coming years (Saunders, 1991). As psychiatrist Jerome Frank (1991) has written, "Blood-thirsty leaders may well become the greatest threat to human survival." Preventing such leaders from achieving great power by our diagnosing their inclinations along the way, and forgoing the short-term nationalistic advantage of backing them politically and militarily when they seem to serve a short-term nationalistic interest, may become the central dimension of the international diplomatic process.

CONCLUSION

Psychologists are engaged in an expanding dialogue with the world. The boundaries between the private and the public are becoming less distinct. Our individual and group selves are increasingly connected. Through television and other, more subtle, webs of information and communication the Persian Gulf war, the breakup of the Soviet Union, the Middle East peace process, and the destruction of the living environment have become part of therapeutic conversation (Conn, 1991; Gerber, 1990; Mack, 1988). Like sexuality in another era, the power of political issues to affect the emotional state and lives of our patients may become apparent only when we ask (Gerber, 1990). At the same time, psychologists and psychotherapists are coming to appreciate that we have something to contribute, not just as private citizens but as members of a profession whose responsibility it is to recognize the play of emotional forces and psychodynamic principles in group life of which international relationships is one example. If we do not participate directly, we can support those who do and insist that diplomatic efforts conducted on our behalf take advantage of the increasing knowledge from social psychology, psychoanalysis, group dynamics, negotiation theory, and the social sciences that applies to the understanding of intergroup conflict. ISPP, whose 1992 theme was "bringing political psychology to public policy," is a multidisciplinary organization, one of whose purposes is to bring together all who wish to participate in the understanding of international political processes and resolution of intergroup conflict. An expanded, active membership could make the group more effective.

The major threats facing the earth today cannot be understood or approached at the level of the nation state acting simply in its own interest. The pollution and death of the ocean's life forms, the destruction of the rain forest, the warming of the earth's surface, the puncturing of the ozone layer, the inequitable distribution of resources among the world's peoples, and the epidemics and famines that may be sources of future wars are all global in scale, and the victories involved in solving them cannot accrue to one nation acting alone. Yet if, as I have contended here, personal worth and power, even a basic sense of identity for so many people, are tied to the fate of a particular ethnic group or nation state, then the task of expanding identity to the level of the larger human community is formidable indeed.

It is not yet clear whether we Americans, who reveled in the techno-logical prowess demonstrated in the Gulf war but who show a tendency to retreat into isolationism when faced with domestic economic problems, will be able to gain sustained satisfaction from cooperative solution of global problems. Surely it will require a kind of leadership we have not yet seen, on the part of statesmen and others who are willing to speak truthfully about the planetary crises and the new alliances necessary to solve them. It is often asked whether we need an outside enemy to maintain cohesion as a nation. I would state the question differently. Can we find ways of integrating the aggressive, fearful dimensions of our psyches and discover personal worth, security, and power through new alliances and partnerships and new forms of identity that reach beyond ethnonational definitions and the boundaries of nation states and that are better suited to protecting the earth's life systems and more equitably distributing the planet's diminishing material resources.

There is some evidence that the nation state as we know it is largely a male invention, which has emerged out of patriarchal tribal structures. It certainly has been dominated by archetypal male values and habits. The progressive Catholic theologian Berry (1989) has captured the male ag-gressiveness of nationalism:

> The nation state might be considered the most powerful institution ever invented for organizing human societies. Above all, the concept of national sovereignty came into being. This concept might be considered a supreme expression of what we are here designating as patriarchy, the aggressive use of power in pursuit of male values of conquest and dominion. In virtue of this concept, each nation declared itself an independent entity subject to no other power on earth [p. 153].

One of the forms of separateness yet to be overcome is the one that exists between the males and the females of our species and the male and female dimensions of our individual nature. One of the partnerships yet to be forged in the search for new forms of power may be that one between men and women, as men expand their protective roles beyond the nation and tribe to the earth itself and women move toward full participation in the manifestations of leadership that can sustain the human future and the planet's other life systems. Our lives will be immensely enriched thereby intellectually, affectively, and spiritually.

REFERENCES

Berlin, I. (1979), Nationalism: Past neglect and present power. *Partisan Rev.*, 3:337–358.

Berry, T. (1988), *The Dream of the Earth*. San Francisco: Sierra Club Books.

Buchanan, P. (1992), National Public Radio, January 4.

Chasin, R. & Herzig, M. (1988), Correcting misperceptions in Soviet-American relations. *J. Humanistic Psychol.*, 28, 3:88–97.

Conn, S. A. (1991), When the Earth Hurts, Who Responds? Psychotherapy in a Global, Earth-Centered Context. Unpublished manuscript.

Davidson, W. D. & Montville, J. V. (1981–82), Foreign policy according to Freud. *Foreign Policy*, 45:145–157.

Erikson, E. & Erikson, J. (1953), The power of the newborn. *Mademoiselle*, June, p. 2.

Esalen Institute, Soviet-American Exchange Program (1990), Ethnic Conflict Resolution in the Soviet Union: The Heritage of Stalinism. Conference, November 4–9, 1990. Big Sur, CA.

Frank, J. (1991), Hard Thoughts on the Gulf War: The Dilemma of the Bloodthirsty Enemy. Unpublished manuscript.

Freud, S. (1900), *The Interpretation of Dreams. Standard Edition*, 5. London: Hogarth Press, 1959.

Group for the Advancement of Psychiatry (1987), The committee on international relations of the group for the advancement of psychiatry. In: *Us and Them*. New York: Brunner/ Mazel.

Garrison, J. (1988), The darkness of God: Theology after Hiroshima. In: *Human Survival and Consciousness Evolution*, ed. S. Grof. New York: State University of New York Press, pp. 151–176.

Gay, P. (1988), *Freud, A Life for Our Time*. New York: Norton.

Gerber, L. A. (1990), Integrating political-societal concerns in psychotherapy. *Amer. J. Psychother.*, 44:471–483.

Gutlove, P. F. (1990), Facilitating dialogue across ideological divides: Techniques, strategies and future directions. Conference April 20–22, Pocantico Hills Estate, Tarrytown, NY.

Henricson-Cullberg, M., Schierup, C., Sommelius, S. & Oberg, J. (1991), After Yugoslavia, What? Report by a conflict-mitigation mission to Croatia, Slovenia and Serbia. *Politika*. Production of the Transnational Foundation for Peace and Future Research, Lund, Sweden.

Ikeda, D. (1991), The age of "soft power" and inner-motivated philosophy: For developing a new Japan–U.S. relationship. Presented at the Kennedy School of Government, Harvard University, Cambridge, MA.

Kelman, H. (1987), On the sources of attachment to the nation. Presented at panel on patriotism, International Society of Political Psychology, San Francisco, CA.

Lame Deer, J. (Fire) & Erdoes, R. (1972), *Lame Deer*. New York: Pocket Books.

Mack, J. E. (1979), Foreword. *Cyprus—War and Adaptation* by V. Volkan. Charlottesville, VA: University Press of Virginia.

———(1983), Nationalism and the self: An essay on the collective narcissism of everyday life. *Psychohistory Rev.*, 2:47-69.

——— (1986), National security reconsidered: New perspectives generated by the prospect of a nuclear winter. In: *The Long Darkness: Psychological and Moral Perspectives on Nuclear Winter*, ed. L. Grinspoon. New Haven, CT: Yale University Press, pp. 103–140.

——— (1988), The threat of nuclear war in clinical work: Dynamic and theoretical considerations. In: *Psychoanalysis and the Nuclear Threat*, ed. H. B. Levine, D. Jacobs & L. J. Rubin. Hillsdale, NJ: The Analytic Press, pp. 189–214.

——— (1989), Reflections of two kinds of power. *Center Rev.*, 3:1–10.

_____ (1990a), Changing Models of Psychotherapy: From Psychological Conflict to Human Empowerment. Center for Psychological Studies in the Nuclear Age, Cambridge, MA.

_____ (1990b), The enemy system. In: *The Psychodynamics of International Relationships I*, ed. V. D. Volkan, J. A. Julius & J. V. Montville. Lexington, MA: Lexington Books, pp. 57–69.

_____ (1990c), Leadership for politics of transcendence. *Center Rev.*, 4:12–14.

_____ (1991), A Baltic memoir. *Center Rev.*, 2:13.

_____ (in press), Power, powerlessness and empowerment in psychotherapy. *Psychiatry.*

Masson, J. M., ed. (1985), *The Complete Letters of Sigmund Freud to Wilhelm Fliess*. Cambridge, MA: Harvard University Press.

McDonald, J. W. & Bendahmane, D. B. (1987), *Conflict Resolution*. Washington, DC: Foreign Service Institute, U.S. Department of State.

Montville, J. V. (1989), Psychoanalytic enlightenment and the greening of diplomacy. *J. Amer. Psychoanal. Assn.*, 37:297–318.

New York Times (1991), November, Sec. A, p. 10.

Nietzsche, F. (1968), *The Will to Power*. New York: Vintage Books.

Nunberg, H. & Federn, E., ed. (1962), *Minutes of the Vienna Psychoanalytic Society*, Vol. I. New York: IUP, pp. 1906–1908.

O'Brien, C. C. (1988), *God Land*. Cambridge, MA: Harvard University Press.

Ronen, D. (1979), *The Quest for Self-Determination*. New Haven, CT: Yale University Press.

Saunders, H. H. (1985), *The Other Walls*. Washington, D.C.: American Enterprise Institute for Public Policy Research.

_____ (1991), Discussion at panel on political psychology and the Gulf war. Presented at International Society of Political Psychiatry Conference, Helsinki, Finland.

Schorske, C. E. (1980), *Fin-de-Siècle Vienna*. New York: Knopf.

Stern, D. N. (1985), *The Interpersonal World of the Infant*. New York: Basic Books.

Tinder, G. (1989), Can we be good without God? *Atlantic Monthly*, December, pp. 69–72, 76–77, 80, 82–85.

Tsipko, A. (1990), Esalen Institute Soviet American Exchange Program, Ethnic Conflict Resolution in the Soviet Union: The Heritage of Stalinism. Conference, November 4–9, 1990. Big Sur, CA.

Warner, G. & Shuman, M. (1987), *Citizen Diplomats*. New York: Continuum.

Weiner, M. (1991), The impact of nationalism, ethnicity and religion on international conflict. Lecture to Peoples and States Seminar. Massachusetts Institute of Technology, Cambridge, MA.

Part V

NEW DIRECTIONS

In chapter 1 the developmental task for normal adults is described in terms of the consciousness of the vicissitudes of everyday affective experience and the dimensions of affective processing by which affect comes into experience. Throughout this volume psychotherapy has been used as an example of one vehicle to foster adult affective development. This section addresses how altered states of consciousness have been used throughout history to explore the workings of the mind, in general, and to access affects and to understand the processing of affects, in particular.

John Mack, in "Nonordinary States of Consciousness and the Access of Feelings" discusses how psychoanalysis traces its origins to the use of hypnosis as an altered state of consciousness in order to explore the workings of the mind. Although Freud became uncomfortable with authoritative hypnosis and favored instead the free association method, permissive hypnosis has become popular in the past three decades and once again is used as a primary means to access affective experiences, largely traumatic, that are not easy to access with conventional verbal psychotherapy. Mack also discusses Grof's means to access intense affective states, notable through the use of psychedelic drugs and more recently through holotropic breathwork. These are powerful vehicles to access affective states not otherwise accessible to ordinary consciousness, for example, birth trauma, early childhood trauma, and transpersonal experiences. Use of powerful altered-state-inducing methods became primary ways to access traumatic experiences recorded by means other than normal memory, such as the somatic memory that van der Kolk described in Chapter 9.

Daniel Brown, in "The Path of Meditation: Affective Development and Psychological Well-Being," discusses classical accounts of the path of meditation in the Eastern contemplative tradition, whose systems consist of disciplined means to cultivate attention and result in a systematic progression of altered states of consciousness, each with it's own characteristic experiences (including affective experiences). The goal is to gain insight into the workings of the mind at every level of its operation and in so doing to permanently change ordinary perception. This goal is traditionally referred to as enlightenment, and Brown argues that enlightenment results in both a continuous awareness of the levels of affective processing and an enduring shift in affective processing. According to Brown, enlightenment is said to permanently eradicate the appetitive-aversive dimension of affect from the ongoing processing of experience, which implies a fundamental rearrangement in ordinary affective information processing so that one is less immediately reactive to experience as it unfolds and therefore one experiences a profound sense of psychological well-being.

Chapter 16

NONORDINARY STATES OF CONSCIOUSNESS AND THE ACCESSING OF FEELINGS

John E. Mack

We are seeing lately an expanded interest in psychotherapies, human growth-promoting workshops, and spiritually focused methods of inner exploration, which have in common the use of nonordinary states of consciousness to access deeper and more intense experience and emotion. At first glance, these approaches may appear new, deviant, or even radical. In actuality, however, they represent means of rediscovering access to realms of the psyche that have been familiar to ancient peoples and non-Western societies from the beginning of recorded time. Shamanic healing, mysticism, kundalini yoga, naturally growing hallucinatory plants, meditation methods, and ecstatic religious experiences are but a few of the ways that human beings throughout history have opened themselves to the deeper regions of the psyche.

The imbalanced rationalism of the Western mind has succeeded in separating us from this fuller knowledge of ourselves and the universe in which we are embedded. Freud's work might be considered in this light as a beginning effort to reacquaint our culture with these lost domains of knowledge. But in his almost exclusive focus on individual biographical development and experience, Freud turned away from the staggering implications of what he was discovering, leaving it to others to map more fully the virtually infinite reaches of the human psyche.

FREUD AND THE HISTORICAL USE OF HYPNOSIS

Psychoanalysis traces its origins to the use by Freud (1925) of Western medicine's most familiar nonordinary state of consciousness, hypnosis, to explore the unconscious origins of neurotic symptoms (p. 19). Freud extended the use of hypnosis from its limited application by Liebeault and Bernheim as a means of removing symptoms by suggestion to its fuller use as an investigative method. It is striking that these words are being written almost exactly a century after Freud gave up the therapeutic use of hypnosis in favor of the concentration method and then free association, which led to the development of psychoanalysis itself. Although he abandoned hypnosis for complex reasons, including that he did not consider himself adept in it, Freud continued throughout his life to acknowledge his debt to hypnosis for opening to him the vistas of the human unconscious. "We psycho-analysts may claim to be its legitimate heirs and we do not forget how much encouragement and theoretical clarification we owe to it" (Freud, 1917, p. 462), Freud wrote, 25 years after he had stopped using hypnosis with his patients.

A reconsideration of the principal reasons why Freud gave up hypnosis can help us to understand why therapists and patients are returning a century later to the use of nonordinary states of consciousness, including hypnosis, for treating a variety of emotional disorders and for the deeper exploration of unconscious psychological forces. In view of the way that hypnosis was used in Freud's time (i.e., to suggest away symptoms through the use of the doctor's authority while the patient was in an altered state of consciousness), it is not surprising that many patients "relapsed" and that the method appeared to be therapeutically ineffectual.

In Freud's emerging view of the therapeutic process in psychoanalysis, the figure or role of the doctor was of central importance. Therapeutic change would come to be seen as the result of many forces, but of greatest importance was the analysis of transference—the meanings and distorted attributions from the patient's past upon the person of the analyst. The hypnotic connection, as viewed by Freud, was a highly erotized relationship whose effectiveness depended on the physician's authority and hardly allowed detailed examination of the patient's feelings and thoughts directed toward the doctor, on which psychoanalytic treatment came increasingly to depend.

During the time that Freud was still using hypnosis therapeutically, his illustrations of how he would work indicate the peremptory and radically nonanalytic way he might speak to patients: "You are not asleep, but you are hypnotized, you are under my influence; what I will say to you now will make a special impression on you and will be of use to you" (Freud,

1891, p. 110). More than a decade after he stopped using it, and had developed the free association method, Freud (1905) still viewed hypnosis in this authoritarian light.

> The hypnotist says: "You see a snake; you're smelling a rose; you're listening to the loveliest music," and the hypnotic subject sees, smells and hears what is required of him by the idea that has been given. . . . outside hypnosis and in real life, credulity such as the subject has in relation to his hypnotist is shown only by a child towards his beloved parents . . . an attitude of similar subjection on the part of one person towards another has only one parallel, though a complete one—namely in certain love-relationships where there is extreme devotion [p. 296].

The idea that hypnosis necessarily required a virtually slavish attitude of the patient toward the hypnotist may have been a carryover of 19th-century beliefs from the days of Mesmer, Puysegar, Braid, Charcot, and others. It surely was inconsistent with the emphasis on the analysis of resistance that became central in Freud's therapeutic method. "The objection to hypnosis," Freud wrote in a 1904 essay on psychoanalytic procedure, "is that it conceals the resistance and for that reason has obstructed the physician's insight into the play of psychical forces. Hypnosis does not do away with the resistance but only evades it and therefore yields only incomplete information and transitory therapeutic success" [p. 252].

Freud's repudiation of hypnosis as a therapeutic technique is based on the idea that the very nature of the hypnotic process necessitates the bypassing of the patient's observing self and the surrender of executive ego functioning to the hypnotist. The belief that the patient must be a more or less passive agent, surrendering his or her will to the authority of the hypnotist to whom he or she is emotionally bonded, Svengali-like, has, I believe, prejudiced the professional view of hypnosis and perhaps our attitude toward the therapeutic use of other nonordinary states of consciousness as well.

In spite of the negative associations, it was perhaps inevitable that interest in using nonordinary states of consciousness in general and hypnosis in particular for exploring the depths of the psyche and treating emotional disorders would be revived. For with the discoveries of psychoanalysis, together with evolving interest in this century in the richness and complexity of human emotional life, we have also learned the limitations of purely verbal methods for investigating unconscious mental content and processes. Hypnotic trance states facilitate (almost by definition) the suspending of attention to the stimuli of ordinary waking consciousness and enable the intricately layered affective and cognitive domains of the inner world to emerge.

Gill and Brenman (Brenman and Gill, 1947; Gill and Brenman, 1961), Hilgard (1965), Frankel (1976), Spiegel and Spiegel (1978), Brown and Fromm (1986), and Fass and Brown (1990) have established the extraordinary value of hypnosis as an investigative tool both for exploring human perception, trance, dissociative states, and ego functioning and for treating a variety of clinical conditions. Contemporary therapeutic applications of hypnosis are far more sophisticated than the methods applied in Freud's time. Evolving from the techniques of Milton Erickson, Erika Fromm, and others, the approaches used now are largely "permissive" rather than authoritative, permitting the patient's own creative energies and directions to guide the process, with the hypnotist functioning primarily as a facilitator who provides a safe, structured context in which the work can proceed (Fass and Brown, 1990, p. 46).

Accessing, tolerating, expressing and integrating emotionally powerful experience are of central importance in the therapeutic use of hypnosis, for the vicissitudes of human development have for countless individuals included a wide range of encounters, stimuli, excitements, disappointments, and wounds whose pathogenic energies persist until their source can be identified and the affectively charged memories recovered and reworked. Hypnosis is perhaps the classically structured nonordinary state of consciousness, for it comprises both verbal and nonverbal techniques to facilitate and organize the emergence of affectively laden memories and to control the regressive intensity of the investigative and therapeutic processes.

Fromm (1972), Spiegel (1981), and Haley (this volume) have shown how hypnosis can be used to enhance the patient's sense of being in charge or in control of the mind and the therapeutic process itself while affectively disturbing memories emerge. This focus on the patient's sense of agency and empowerment is consistent with shifting contemporary notions of transference and of the therapist–patient relationship. The therapeutic enterprise in general is being perceived increasingly in nonhierarchical terms, with the analyst or therapist functioning as a facilitator in a collaborative process or dialogue. Transference attributions naturally arise, but in contemporary mutual or collaborative approaches, the distortions of perception of the figure of the analyst, whose examination once constituted the backbone of the treatment endeavor, are less likely to be encouraged. The figure of the doctor or therapist himself, including the hypnotist, is becoming less central, as authority is increasingly given over to the patient's own self-exploration and self-functioning (Gray, 1990).

This shift in our view of the nature of the therapeutic enterprise (Mack, 1990, 1992, 1993) has great implications for the use of nonordinary states of consciousness in clinical work. In the Grof holotropic breathwork method, for example, which is discussed later, the role of the figure of the leader is that of a facilitator, the transference elements are minimized, and great trust is placed in the patient's inner wisdom during the self-discovery process (Grof, 1988, 1992).

TRAUMA, AFFECT, AND NONORDINARY STATES
OF CONSCIOUSNESS

Recognition and understanding of trauma have been central in the evolution of psychoanalytic and psychodynamic theory and practice. Early use of hypnosis by Charcot, Liebeault, Bernheim, and Freud led to the recognition that experiences that derived from some action or event in the outside world and that overwhelmed the ego's defenses would produce a state of unbearable and unmanageable tension, which could not be discharged except through symptom formation, pathological character development, destructive (including self-destructive) actions, or ego fragmentation. At the core of all theories of trauma are a fundamental state of helplessness and vulnerability and an inability to define, experience, express, or integrate disturbing affects that are brought about by such hurtful or threatening events. Trauma is thus the outcome of a relationship between the intrapsychic and the external worlds.

In view of the intensity with which the ego strives to ward off the distress associated with traumatic memories, it is not surprising that use of a powerful therapeutic tool like hypnosis, which can overcome defensive barriers, would have led to the recovery of traumatic memories. As Freud gave up hypnosis and developed the psychoanalytic method, he also turned to the exploration of the intrapsychic world and, to a great extent, left behind the study of trauma, especially the pathological effects of incestuous sexual seduction on the young women he was treating.

Gradually and inescapably, mental health clinicians have returned to the study and treatment of emotional trauma if for no other reason than that the pervasive, hurtful effects of physical and sexual abuse, war and the threat of war, refugee problems, racial injustice, economic inequality and losses, family breakup and instability, and separations of all kinds have forced us to reshape our theoretical formulations and reorder our clinical priorities.

Several chapters in this book address the relationship between acute and persistent trauma and affective disturbances, and the renewed attention to trauma is enabling us both to discover the complex biological, psychological, and social forces involved in it and to discover new treatment approaches while returning to and rediscovering older methods that were left behind in the development of psychoanalysis.

It is in this context—the return of our attention to trauma—that the renewed interest in the therapeutic power of nonordinary states of consciousness can be best understood. For it is through the use of such states of consciousness that clinicians can most effectively recover buried memories and the associated feelings that could not be recognized, felt, or expressed at the time when the trauma was occurring. For example, Haley (this volume) describes the use of hypnosis to access feelings and memories of deeply troubling actions on the part of Vietnam veterans that so overwhelmed the soldiers' emotional defenses and so deeply violated basic personal values at the time they occurred that the very capacity to feel itself—that which, above all, makes us human—was severely damaged. Hypnosis is used here effectively to identify, uncover, and work through traumatic memories and associated powerfully disturbing affects that were inaccessible at the time that the traumatic event occurred (Brown and Fromm, 1986). In contrast to the early use of hypnosis primarily for undoing repression and for symptom removal through suggestion, contemporary applications to the treatment of trauma involve a systematic treatment process in which hypnosis is used in conjunction with other therapeutic methods such as self-hypnotic relaxation, guided imagery and hypnoprojective techniques, and various supportive and ego adaptive approaches (Brown and Fromm, 1986, p. 277). In these approaches, the therapeutic objectives include not only the uncovering and working through of troubling affects but also ego integration, self-development, and even "learned psychophysiological control" to enable the traumatized person to react less sensitively to future triggering of traumatic experiences (Brown and Fromm, 1986; van der Kolk, this volume).

GROF HOLOTROPIC BREATHWORK

Therapeutic application of a nonordinary state of consciousness is central to the holotropic breathwork method developed by Stanislav and Christina Grof (Grof, 1988, 1992), the former, a physician trained as a Freudian psychoanalyst in Prague in the 1950s. In 1956, he became one of the first physicians to experiment with LSD soon after it was discovered by Albert Hofmann at Sandoz Laboratories in Switzerland (Hofmann, 1983). Grof's personal experiences with this psychedelic agent radically changed his view of the human psyche, the therapeutic process, and his understanding of humankind's place in the cosmos. He found that there were vast ("transpersonal") realms of the unconscious beyond what he had found to be accessible through the free association method. Intense emotions and powerful images associated with early experiences, his own birth, and domains outside of biographical history were opened up to consciousness with the use of LSD (Grof, 1975).

During the next two decades, Grof conducted approximately 4,000 research and therapeutic sessions with LSD in Czechoslovakia and the United States. In the 1970s, he found that sessions using deep and rapid breathing with evocative music and taking place in a supportive and secure setting could access the same personal and transpersonal realms of experience as he was encountering with LSD. Over the past 15 years the Grofs have conducted thousands of holotropic breathwork sessions in small groups and workshops and have trained several hundred breathwork practitioners who are now applying their method in the United States and Europe.

My own first direct experience with holotropic breathwork occurred in 1987 with the Grofs in a small-group setting at the Esalen Institute in California. During the two-hour session, I experienced intense feelings of loss associated with the death of my biological mother when I was $8\frac{1}{2}$ months old, as well as a profound sense then and in subsequent sessions of both her suffering with peritonitis before she died and my father's grief following her death—emotions about which I had spoken extensively during my two personal analyses but which I had never been able to access in such an immediate way. During that session, in which two Soviets were also participating, I had my own introduction to the transpersonal realms of the unconscious, namely, a powerful experience of identification with a person, other being, object in nature, or force that lay outside of my personal history. I "became" a Russian father (in what seemed to be the 15th century) who was unable to protect his four-year-old son from being beheaded by the Mongols. Out of this experience, my capacity to identify with Soviet fears, and seemingly unrealistic political defensiveness, increased greatly, enabling me to become more effective in the psychopolitical work on the Soviet-American relationship in which I was then engaged. Subsequent sessions of my own involved equally powerful and valuable biographical, birth-related, and transpersonal experiences.

Drawing upon his experience with LSD and holotropic breathwork, Grof has developed a new topography, or "cartography," of the human psyche: memories and feelings related to the perinatal, postnatal, and transpersonal levels of experience mingle in complex ways and can be accessed through nonordinary states of consciousness, including, in addition to breathwork and psychedelics, hypnosis, mystical experiences, profound meditative states, yoga, shamanic journeys, and religious ecstasies. Buried biographical memories and feelings return with special vividness and power. Birth-related experiences that can be traced to the stages of the birth process itself (Grof has identified four birth phases he calls matrices) are relived with great power (Grof, 1985). Experiences of birth, death, and rebirth open the breather's consciousness to realms of experience beyond familiar conscious and unconscious material. Finally, the breather is able to discover affinities outside of hitherto known interpersonal relationships, experiencing profound encounters or identifications with mythic figures and potentially all of the human and non-human elements in the cosmos. The collective unconscious that is often largely a theoretical construct in Jung's theories becomes a living reality in breathwork experiences.

The transpersonal dimension of the work has a powerful spiritual impact, reconnecting the breather with primary religious experiences, a sense of sacred awe from which he or she may have been cut off since childhood. Powerful heart-openings and uplifting, luminous, or transcendent experiences bring the breather to a higher sense of value and purpose and of connection with the universe. Nature itself becomes imbued (or reimbued) with deep and ineffable sacred beauty and wonder, and the destruction being wrought by technology and material desire become intolerable. Perhaps the most fundamental difference between the breathwork method and psychoanalysis—or the psychoanalytically derived psychotherapies—lies in the role of the therapist. In the psychodynamic therapies, at least as traditionally practiced, the clinician's role is central, either as a transference figure or through providing in his or her own person or interpretation some sort of corrective experience or new relationship model. In the breathwork, intense feelings in relation to the figure of the leader or facilitator, or to other supporting figures, naturally arise, and such a figure may even be distorted, idealized or devalued. But the fundamental process is not based primarily on transference or even on the actual relationship with the clinician. Instead, a kind of inner radar searches the unconsciousness in a process of opening and discovery facilitated or enabled by the therapist/leader but not focused on him or her.

As practiced in individual work or groups, a safe and secure space is found that provides enough room for the breather(s) to move around freely in response to bodily impulses or strong feelings that come up in the session. Each breather is paired with a "sitter," who attends to his or her basic needs and safety, such as providing water, tissues, and protection from bumping into or being bumped by other breathers or accompanying the breather to the bathroom. The leader is supported by other facilitators, one of whom attends to the music. A ratio of one facilitator to four to six pairs seems to be ideal. The sessions begin in a somewhat darkened room with the breathers lying on their back in a comfortable, open position, sometimes covered with a blanket or using eyeshades so as to block out light. The breathers are instructed to put aside expectations and not to try to solve any identified problem or focus on a particular conflict or "issue" but to trust that their inner wisdom will take their consciousness where it needs to go. A brief relaxation exercise starts the process of turning inward, and instruction is given to breathe more deeply and rapidly, after which the music begins—loud and driving at first, eventually more steady, and heartful or celestial, with variations according to the choices of the facilitator.

As the turning inward process deepens, and the busy-mind activity we ordinarily associate with everyday consciousness is left behind or allowed to pass by (as also occurs in meditation), powerful emotions, body sensations and impulses, and strong images come into consciousness, which may relate to biographical or perinatal experiences or to transpersonal realms that have little to do with the known history of the individual. It is difficult to generalize, but from an ontological standpoint, the quality of the experience at its height tends to lie somewhere between fantasizing and being fully present to a new reality. One may, for example, be fully engaged in a struggle with a god or other mythic being or become quite completely a fish swimming under water. At the same time, however, a small but steady, observing ego is recording what is being experienced and can usually report on it later.

From an affective standpoint, the intensity and range of feelings are greater than I have generally noted in therapies that do not use a nonordinary state of consciousness. This is especially true when repositories of warded off feeling have been identified and brought into full consciousness and expression by effective bodywork techniques (Grof with Bennett, 1992, p. 16). The sessions generally last from two to three hours and are concluded by completing a mandala drawing, which may express central elements of the experience, even when breathers consider themselves inept as an artist.

The breathwork leader functions as a facilitator, enabling the value of the experience to take place by overseeing the physical space, making sure that each breather's basic safety is ensured, noting that the music is moving the energy in the room in a positive direction (a judgment that is largely intuitive), and performing focal bodywork as needed (Grof with Bennett, 1992, p. 16). Again, transference elements may arise: the facilitator may appear to a breather as a loving or threatening father or mother figure or be confused with a god, goddess, or other mythic being. But this dimension is secondary. The therapeutic, healing, or growth-promoting work is largely the result of the psyche's own direction, the inner radar (Grof with Bennett, 1992) that identifies the places that our consciousness needs to go. In this way, theoretical constructs or preconceptions about "what I should work on today" are put aside in favor of an unconscious knowledge of the inner realms that need to be explored at the time.

Remarkably, in later discussion or through sharing in small groups, the relevance of what has occurred in the session to the breather's ongoing life becomes apparent, sometimes with startling clarity.

HOLOTROPIC BREATHWORK, TRAUMA, AND AFFECT

The holotropic breathwork method can evoke a wide range of profound emotions and bring the breather in touch with a rich world of images and sensations whether the individual is choosing the experience for therapeutic reasons or for purposes of personal growth. The breathwork underscores, however, the important pathogenic role of trauma in human development. Trauma, as Herman (this volume) discusses, may range from a single severe physical assault to complex, chronic, and catastrophic physical and psychological affliction. Grof distinguishes traumas of commission, such as parental cruelty, childhood surgery, rape, varieties of physical and sexual abuse, war and refugee experiences, or the birth process itself, from those of omission, which are associated with deprivation, loss, or unmet emotional needs. In both instances, the therapeutic power lies in the capacity of the breather to access in the altered state of consciousness past experiences that had originally occurred under conditions in which the experience often could not even be defined and feelings could not be identified, felt, or expressed.

The traumatic history may be quite well known to the breather. In my first breathwork session, another breather, a man in his mid-50s, was screaming in fear and rage as he relived an attempt by his mother to choke him as a baby. In this first breathwork session, he told me months later, he felt in the nonordinary state of consciousness associated with this experience more relief from the fear and anger than he had felt during many years of talking about the event through other forms of therapy. Through this method, many patients are enabled to discover childhood surgery or parental relational neglect. They can obtain relief from disabling symptoms or constricting affects—emotions that have been walled off or frozen since the time of the trauma.

The memories of many forms of trauma, such as infant and early childhood surgery and accidents or acute and chronic experiences of physical and sexual abuse, are stored in the body and locked away, it would appear, as much in the tissue cells themselves as in the brain. The process of accessing or reaccessing emotions in a nonordinary state of consciousness such as occurs in the holotropic breathwork method may be related to the emotions recovered through autonomic arousal as van der Kolk discusses in this volume. Memories that seem inaccessible through associative techniques may have been recorded initially as unexpressed or even unfelt physiologically anchored energies and may require a new context and means of accessing them in order to bring about relief of symptoms and integration of the crippling pathological impact of the original experiences. As traumatic memories and associated powerful feelings become accessed during nonordinary states, intense energies expressed through body tensions, shaking, sobbing, loud vocalization, and other emotional expressions may come to the surface. Sometimes tensions become "stuck" in the musculature, requiring focal bodywork performed by skilled facilitators, to move the energy along. The facilitors provide physical resistance to the experiencer's effort, as he or she is encouraged, paradoxically, to exaggerate the tension or strain in the involved muscle groups. The expression of a full sound, such as a groan or scream, also helps to discharge the painfully stored emotion.

In the case of situations of personal deprivation and loss, the reliving of personal wounds in a setting of caring and protection may be powerfully therapeutic. A sensitive sitter can provide comforting and holding, especially at the conclusion of the session, when the breather is most open and needy. It is important that the sitter recognize the special vulnerability and openness brought about by the altered state of consciousness in the breathwork session and not intrude his or her own emotional need to heal or rescue the breather. Above all, the safety provided and the opportunity to reaccess and tolerate by means of the altered state of consciousness the original loss and associated painful affects constitute the core of the therapeutic or healing process.

Following the breathwork session, in which a great deal of affectively powerful material may have come forth, it is important that breathers be given the opportunity to integrate the experience of what they have undergone by sharing in small-group discussion and individual sessions with clinicians who are familiar with the therapeutic use of nonordinary states of consciousness and with the perinatal and transpersonal realms of the unconscious. This process may be similar to the "working through" that occurs in traditional psychoanalysis except that the primary therapeutic or healing work occurs in the nonordinary state of consciousness while the talking serves to consolidate and integrate the intense feelings and personal discoveries that have occurred during the breathwork sessions. More traditional psychotherapies or "talking treatments" are particularly important following breathwork sessions in order to explore the changes and future decisions to be made concerning human relationships and work choices. After one explores the psyche through holotropic breathwork or other kinds of nonordinary states of consciousness, profound changes in worldview, values, and personal priorities are likely to occur. This can leave one feeling quite alone and "unmet" unless one has a community of friends or colleagues who have also discovered holotropic realms in their own therapeutic work or spiritual paths.

COMMON ELEMENTS AND DIFFERENCES

There are, of course, a great variety of ways of bringing about nonordinary states of consciousness in addition to hypnosis and holotropic breathwork (aforementioned) and meditation (Brown, this volume). Most of these can be used therapeutically or for personal growth work and include shamanic journeys, psychedelic substances, religious ecstatic states, yoga, relaxation techniques, therapeutic touch, bodywork (alone or in combination with psychological methods), various energy therapies and massage, and some types of music, poetry reading, and other forms of artistic experience and expression. Psychoanalysis and free association create to a certain degree a nonordinary state of consciousness, especially when dreams and associated affects are worked with intensively. But the reliance on verbalization, the interactive or ongoing relational dimension, and the interpretive process tend to limit the extent to which the method facilitates the creation of an altered state or can provide access to the deeper realms of the unconscious.

Freud (1895) wrote of the "withdrawal of the cathexis of attention" from the outside world that occurs in hypnosis (p. 337). In his view, which he continued to express as late as 1921 and which was consistent with his emphasis on the centrality of transference, this shift in the "distributions of mental energies" occurs as a result of the patient's directing attention onto the person of the analyst (Freud, 1921, p. 126). The perspective being offered here for hypnosis and other altered states, including meditation ("reducing the amount of sensory in-put," Brown, this volume), also stresses the shift of attention away from the outside world but places less emphasis on the role of the leader or therapist, who functions more as a guide or facilitator to support the patient or client in redirecting attention to the inner world.

When the person's energies are effectively withdrawn from the out-side world, and attention and perception shift to inner feelings, thoughts, and sensations, a nonordinary state naturally occurs. Its depth depends on the person's ability to simultaneously note and "let go of" distracting products of mental activity as they pass through awareness. This "mind-fulness" or turning inward is the common characteristic of therapeutic modalities such as hypnosis and Grof breathwork and the meditation techniques and processes described by Brown (this volume). Therapeutic nonordinary states and meditation also have in common the eliciting of thoughts and feelings from the deeper levels of the psyche and the creation of a new awareness of the unconscious and the inner world. As Brown writes of the preliminary stage of meditation, "Amongst the flow of thoughts, memories, fantasies, percepts, bodily sensations and other events in the stream of consciousness the meditator also will observe the ebb and flow of emotional states."

But the experiencing of affects, however therapeutic it may be or central to the use of nonordinary states of consciousness in a healing context, is not the purpose of advanced states of meditation. Here the focus is on awareness itself and the process of self-observation. The self itself as the instrument of knowing dissolves, and the pure experience of interconnectedness or oneness can emerge. Affects, even when fully experienced, are allowed to be held in consciousness, but only so that the perception of them, like all other perceptions, can be allowed to pass. The ultimate goal of meditation is not therapeutic, or even to bring about healing. Rather it is to bring enlightenment by gaining control of and changing the very structure of perception and information processing so that egoistic concerns can be relinquished and the experience of love, compassion, and oneness may emerge. Stated differently, nonordinary states, when used therapeutically, seek to bring the deeper realms of the psyche into consciousness in order to expand self-knowledge and to integrate memories and experiences from which we have been cut off or which afflict us through their actions outside of awareness. A skilled meditator, on the other hand, as Brown (this volume) writes, changes his view of reality itself, gaining access to expanded awareness by breaking "the code of the time–space structure of ordinary perception."

SUMMARY

Through nonordinary states of consciousness we can be brought into connection with the cycles of birth, death, and rebirth; with powerful feelings from early childhood; and with the transpersonal realms in which each individual can discover the capacity to identify with beings and forces in nature outside of personal biographical experience—a physical and emotional reification of Jung's idea of the collective unconscious.

When we are able to access, or reaccess, emotions that have been warded off in the body cells or in autonomic regulatory systems, then the human organism's previously blocked natural healing powers can become available. It is in this working through or integrative process that the greatest therapeutic value of nonordinary states may reside.

Finally, nonordinary states of consciousness have value beyond their therapeutic applications for personal growth and the expansion of consciousness. As Brown discusses in Chapter 17, the turning of attention from outer stimuli to the inner processes of thought and feeling, as occurs among experienced meditators, permits the questioning of the structure of perception itself and makes available information from a realm of being in which the distinctions between inside and outside or between psyche and nature lose their power and in which a deeply fulfilling extension of the range of human consciousness can occur.

REFERENCES

Brenman, M. & Gill, M. M. (1947), *Hypnotherapy: A Survey of the Literature.* Menninger Foundation Monographs Series 5. New York: IUP.

Brown, D. & Fromm, E. (1986), *Hypnotherapy and Hypnoanalysis.* Hillsdale, NJ: Lawrence Erlbaum Associates.

Fass, M. & Brown, D., ed. (1990), *Creative Mastery in Hypnosis and Hypnoanalysis.* Hillsdale, NJ: Lawrence Erlbaum Associates.

Frankel, F. H. (1976), *Hypnosis: Trance as a Coping Mechanism.* New York: Plenum Medical Books.

Freud, S. (1891), Hypnosis. *Standard Edition,* 1:103–114. London: Hogarth Press, 1966.

———— (1895), Project for a scientific psychology. *Standard Edition,* 1:283–397. London: Hogarth Press, 1966.

———— (1904), Freud's psycho-analytic procedure. *Standard Edition,* 7:249–256. London: Hogarth Press, 1953.

———— (1905), Physical (or mental) treatment. *Standard Edition,* 7:283–304. London: Hogarth Press, 1953.

———— (1917), Introductory Lectures on Psycho-Analysis. Part III. *Standard Edition,* 16:243–463. London: Hogarth Press, 1963.

———— (1921), Group psychology and the analysis of the ego. *Standard Edition,* 18:67–143. London: Hogarth Press, 1955.

———— (1925), An autobiographical study. *Standard Edition,* 20:7–70. London: Hogarth Press, 1959.

Fromm, E. (1972), Ego activity and ego passivity in hypnosis. *Internat. J. Clin. Exp. Hypn.,* 20:238–251.

Gill, M. M. & Brenman, M. (1961), *Hypnosis and Related States.* New York: IUP.

Gray, P. (1990), The nature of therapeutic action in psychoanalysis. *J. Amer. Psychoanal. Assn.,* 38:1083–1097.

Grof, S. (1975), *Realms of the Human Unconscious.* London: Souvenir Press (E&A).

———— (1985), *Beyond the Brain.* Albany: State University of New York Press.

———— (1988), *The Adventure of Self-Discovery.* Albany: State University of New York Press.

———— with Bennett, H. Z. (1992), *The Holotropic Mind.* San Francisco: Harper.

Hilgard, E. R. (1965), *Hypnotic Susceptibility.* New York: Harcourt, Brace & World.

Hofmann, A. (1983), *LSD My Problem Child,* trans. J. Ott. Los Angeles: Tracher.

Mack, J. E. (1990), Changing Models of Psychotherapy: From Psychological Conflict to

Human Empowerment. Center for Psychological Studies in the Nuclear Age. Cambridge, MA.

_____ (1992), Power: An Overview. Presented at symposium of the Boston Psychoanalytic Society and Institute. "Power: Empowerment and Abuse in Clinical Practice and Everyday Life," March 14 & March 15, 1992.

_____ (in press), Power, powerlessness and empowerment in psychotherapy. *Psychiatry*.

Speigel, D. (1981), Vietnam grief work using hypnosis. *Amer. J. Clin. Hypn.*, 24:33–40.

Speigel, H. & Speigel, D. (1978), *Trance and Treatment*. New York: Basic Books.

Chapter 17

THE PATH OF MEDITATION
Affective Development and Psychological Well-Being

Daniel Brown

The normal adult is faced with the task of understanding the workings of the mind. In terms of affective development, the two developmental tasks for relatively healthy adults are to recognize the vicissitudes of affective experience in everyday life and to observe and discriminate the various levels of affective processing. I argued in Chapter 1, however, that many normal adults fail to ever address the issues of understanding the workings of the mind and becoming conscious of affective processes, because for many normal adults, mastery of the stages along the continuum of affective development remains incomplete. Therefore, the question of disciplined self-observation was raised as a means to facilitate both progression along the normal line of affective development and mastery of its phase-specific tasks.

The view taken was that affective development for the normal adult can take many forms. The individual, for example, may observe the context of the stream of consciousness, become aware of shifts in mood and emotional state, observe the stream of negative self-talk, free associate, reflect on conscious and unconscious motivation, reflect on the subjective meaning of events and behavior, distinguish between fantasy, feeling, and action, and observe mind–body connections. Some individuals become engaged in disciplined self-observation, which can also take many forms: In Chapter 1, psychoanalytic psychotherapy was briefly discussed as an example of one model. And a number of other chapters in

this book have fleshed out our understanding of psychoanalytic psychotherapy as a vehicle of affective development. Although psychotherapy
has become an important tradition of disciplined self-observation in the
West, it is not the only form available. Historically, philosophical reflection and disciplined contemplation have represented the primary means
to understand the workings of the mind.

Another form of disciplined self observation will be explored here,
namely, the path of meditation. Again, within the great contemplative
traditions of East and West, many forms of meditation each detail their
own unique progression of stages of development (Brown, 1977, 1981;
Wilbur, Engler, and Brown, 1986). It is not possible to review the great
variety and richness of these traditions, but I have argued elsewhere that
the various descriptions of stages of development in meditation across
contemplative traditions in vastly different cultures, although seemingly
quite different, may all have the same underlying path-structure (Brown,
1977, 1986). Thus, whereas this chapter presents one model—a Buddhist
meditation model—for the path of meditation in some detail, description
of the progression of stages of development in Buddhist meditation is also
fairly representative of the stages (but not content) of meditation development in general.

If Western psychoanalytic psychotherapy is one form of disciplined
self-observation that fosters growth along the continuum of affective
development, what is the primary goal of such development? In other
words, what is the ideal view of the person who has successfully completed psychotherapy or psychoanalysis? This doesn't mean an outcome
in terms of symptom relief or better adjustment to life circumstances. In
psychoanalytically oriented psychotherapy or psychoanalysis—in which
the focus is on disciplined self-observation in the context of the therapeutic relationship—what is the endpoint? Chapter 1 discussed two possible endpoints with respect to affect. First is the capacity to fully recognize the vicissitudes of affective experience in everyday life. This may also
include: accurate recognition of affects (without disavowal); an understanding of the personal meaning of affective experiences; a reflection on
conscious and unconscious motivation; and some ability to distinguish
between an emotional state, its meaning, and the response, or action-
tendency that arises from it. Second is the ability to discern various levels
of affective processing and to become conscious of the processes by
which affects come into immediate conscious experience.

Whereas Western psychotherapy's main contribution is in fostering
recognition of affective experiences, it is somewhat limited in enabling
individuals to discern the various levels of affective processing, many of
which operate outside of conscious awareness. Most individuals who
complete psychotherapy or psychoanalysis, no matter how extensive

their understanding of subjective meaning, unconscious motivation, and the like may be, still have little conscious awareness of the rapid processing levels in the affective-response system, especially the more immediate preattentive expressive-motor and schematic or appetitive/aversive levels of processing that Arnold (1960) and Leventhal (1980) describe. The reason that Western psychotherapy rarely leads to awareness of these high-speed levels of affective processing is that Western psychotherapy does not emphasize disciplined, rigorous attention or awareness training to the same degree that it is emphasized in the great contemplative traditions. Attention/awareness training is the cornerstone of any meditation tradition. Precisely because so much emphasis and care are devoted to attention/awareness training in meditation, meditation becomes a vehicle to open up awareness to the rapid-processing levels of the human information processing system normally operating outside of conscious awareness. In this sense, meditation contributes something to our understanding of adult affective development that is rarely found in Western psychotherapy.

Moreover, the endpoint of development in meditation is profoundly different from that of psychotherapy (Brown, 1986). By gaining insight into the workings of the mind on every level through disciplined meditation, the meditator experiences a profound and enduring transformation of the structures of the mind. This relatively permanent new development is called enlightenment. What does enlightenment inform us about optimal development and specifically about affective development? In a sense, this chapter is about exceptional human abilities. The classical descriptions of the path of meditation and enlightenment raise the possibility of relatively enduring psychological well-being for the remainder of the life span.

BACKGROUND

Conducting these studies has necessitated living within two worlds—the world of the meditation practitioner and the world of the scientist-clinician. Both perspectives were required in order to understand meditation properly. The work began with more than 10 years' study of the authoritative texts and commentaries of the great Eastern meditation traditions, focusing primarily on the Tibetan Mahayana Buddhist tradition (Brown, 1981), the Burmese mindfulness tradition (Thera, 1962), and the Hindu yogic tradition (Mishra, 1973). Every effort was made to study these from the perspective of how the individual cultures understand themselves, which necessitated learning the canonical languages, translating classical meditation texts, interviewing contemporary practitioners and their teachers, and practicing the meditations directly. The main difficulty in studying classical meditation literature is its use of a highly sophisticated technical language for internal experience. To properly understand such technical language use, a detailed semiotic analysis was conducted of the classical descriptions of meditation experience (Brown, 1977, 1981, 1986; Brown and Engler, 1980) This chapter gives a summary of the experiences of each stage of meditation according to what the authoritative texts agree upon as being characteristic of the main stages in the path of meditation.

Ten years of scientific research was conducted on highly skilled contemporary practitioners of meditation in order to investigate systematically the effects of meditation on cognition, perception, personality, experience, and relationships. These studies constituted a kind of outcome study comparable to the outcome studies utilized in psychotherapy. We have tried to understand the salient effects of meditation to ascertain the validity of the truth claims regarding meditation experience described in these classical texts.

The studies used several types of skilled meditators: first, intensive retreatants at an American center (Insight Meditation Society, Barre, Massachusetts) in the Burmese tradition of mindfulness meditation. Once a year, an intensive (16 hrs. per day) three-month-long retreat is offered to about 100 meditators. For 10 years, predata and postdata have been collected on these retreatants. Second, a data base was compiled on American meditators within that tradition. As part of the data base, the teachers designated which meditators reached certain levels of attainment in an effort to develop specific criterion groups of skilled meditators within that tradition. It became clear that duration of practice alone was not an adequate measure of skill development, because meditators progressed at very different rates. The method of teacher nomination allowed us to specify which meditators in the overall pool were likely to have reached certain levels of proficiency according to the criteria of attainment established by the tradition itself. Third, the teachers themselves were used as subjects. Because the earliest phase of the research consisted of practicing meditation and translating meditation texts, many of the great teachers gained increasing confidence in our motives for conducting the research, and they volunteered to participate in it. As a result we were in the unique position of being able to test highly skilled and often exceptional meditators both in America and in South Asia. On occasion this included bringing some of the contemporary masters or saints into the laboratory or studying them in the field. Thus we were able to investigate by laboratory means such attainments as deep concentrative states (known as samadhi states) and enlightenment.

ATTENTION AND AWARENESS TRAINING

Research has demonstrated meditation to be a type of attentional and awareness skill training and a systematic application of focused attention to, sustained concentration on, or moment-by-moment awareness of certain events in the stream of consciousness (Brown, 1977; Goleman, 1975). Such attentional skill development results in significant alterations in cognition and perception. Whereas most of the research on meditation in the West has emphasized psychophysiological changes, most of the classical texts on meditation in the East emphasize cognitive and perceptual changes. Therefore, most of our research has addressed the cognitive and perceptual effects of intensive meditation practice. But we will see that that research has important implications for understanding the experience of affect in meditation.

STAGES OF MEDITATION DEVELOPMENT

Such rigorous attention deployment results in a variety of altered states of consciousness, which unfold in an invariant sequence (Brown, 1977, 1986). Meditation is best viewed as an example of adult development along a path not normally available to individuals but indeed readily available to one who engages in the disciplined training of attention and awareness. The sequence of changes that occur in states of consciousness is predictable, describable, and measurable. Most of the great texts on the so-called path of meditation pertain to experiences of states of consciousness.

According to our comparisons of the texts about the path of meditation from many traditions, there is general agreement that meditation development occurs in three broad stages: the preliminary stage; the concentration stage; and the insight stage (Brown, 1977, 1986). The final outcome is said to be a stable and enduring alteration in perception, known as enlightenment. This chapter studies meditation at each of these three stages both from the perspective of the indigenous classical descriptions of meditation experience and from the perspective of Western scientific inquiry.

Preliminary Stage—Classical Descriptions

Meditation begins with a period of preliminary training, in which the meditator intentionally reduces the amount of sensory input and thereby changes the context of everyday activity. He or she adopts simplified daily behavioral routines—usually in the form of an intensive meditation re-

treat. The meditator creates a suitable context in order to begin awareness training (called "mindfulness") not only during periods of formal
sitting meditation but also throughout daily activities such as eating and
walking. The goal of mindfulness practice in general is to attain without
lapses a state of continuous awareness throughout all daily activities and
in particular to cultivate observation of how events in the stream of
consciousness constantly change as the patterns of behavior and sensory
stimuli change (Brown, 1986).

As a means to sharpen this inward focus, the meditator trains one or
more stable meditation postures. He or she learns to reduce bodily activity
by holding effortfully a number of body points steady and immovable for
extended periods of time: the back, straight; the eyes, fixed; the feet,
cross-legged, and so on, until the body "settles" and the posture can be
maintained in a relaxed and alert way without discomfort or pain. The
goal of postural training is not relaxation per se but an even distribution
and regular output of muscle activity, which results in a comfortable
alertness as much as in relaxation (Brown, 1977; Ikegami, 1970).

Awareness and postural training serve to introduce the meditator to
the internal world, a world that at first emerges in a "blooming buzzing
confusion" (James, 1901/1961). In many traditions, the meditator is given
instructions to focus on the breath as a way to steady awareness during
the introduction to a stormy internal world. As the meditator continues to
train awareness inwardly upon events in the stream of consciousness, he
or she is easily distracted by incessant thoughts, fantasies, spontaneously
occurring memories, intense emotions, and uncomfortable bodily states—
a process that has been called "unstressing" (Goleman, 1975). Nevertheless, the skilled meditator does not become too distracted by the content
of the stream of consciousness but turns awareness to the process of
change itself, regarding the ever-changing events in the stream of consciousness. The objective is to maintain steady awareness upon the breath
and to recover quickly when distracted. With practice, events come forth
in a successive manner in the stream of consciousness. There is a rearrangement in the stream of consciousness, wherein events seem to come
forth in a more orderly manner. The meditator is now capable of alertly
attending to each and every event exactly as it occurs (Brown, 1977, 1986).

Preliminary Stage—Scientific Inquiry

The research conducted on meditators during the preliminary stage of
training is consistent with descriptions in the classical texts. To discover
whether contemporary practitioners of meditation have comparable experiences, we constructed an instrument called the Trance, Imagery, and
Meditation Experience profile (TIME), revised it on several occasions, and

administered it to various populations of meditators matched for demographic characteristics but not for amount of meditation experience. The questionnaire was given to U.S. practitioners of Burmese mindfulness meditation at different levels of experience—immediately after two-day, two-week, and three-month retreats of 16 hours per day of intensive meditation. A discriminant function analysis was used to construct models for the dimensions along which the three groups significantly differed according to differences in amount of meditation experience. The most experienced meditators (three months) relative to the least experienced (two days) differed significantly along two attentional dimensions: attentional equanimity, which is the ability to maintain the focus of attention amid internal and external distractions, and attentional dexterity, which is the ease of recovery of the focus of attention once distracted. Note that the least experienced, relative to the more experienced meditators, reported spending a lot of time thinking, specifically planning how to go about the meditation (proaction), and anticipating what would occur next in the stream of consciousness (anticipation). The least experienced, relative to the most experienced, meditators reported a greater preoccupation with certain events in the stream of consciousness: spontaneously occurring memories, changes in the body image, and changes in the vividness, size, shape, and surface of perceived visual objects (new perception). The intermediate group, relative to the others, tended to become fascinated with personal memories, demonstrated greater awareness of simple visual changes, and showed greater sensitivity to changes in the bodily state, such as tingling, numbness, and pain. The most experienced group relative to the others, reported greater imagery sequences or fantasy and strong emotions (emotional intensity) yet was not distracted from the focus of meditation when emotional states occurred (emotional equanimity). The group also experienced a lot of changes in the breath when meditating upon it. Furthermore, the most experienced meditators, relative to the others, did not typically use the self as a reference point to the experience (frame of reference) or perceive the events in the stream of consciousness as belonging to the self (disidentification) (Forte, Brown, and Dysart, 1987/88a).

In sum, the more experienced meditators showed greater attentional skill and less concern with certain contents in the stream of consciousness, especially thinking and memories. They did, however, experience stronger emotions and a variety of bodily states. The goal of meditation for them was to resist distraction and continue training attention in the midst of many internal changes. Experienced meditators who do this learn to disidentify with the content of the stream of consciousness over time. An independent study by an associate used Gutman scaling to study changes in meditation experience over time (Kim-Ling, 1981). The main finding was that skilled meditators developed a quality of nonreactive awareness to events in the stream of consciousness.

Concentration Stage—Classical Descriptions

Having stabilized awareness amid distractions, the mediator is ready to begin the second series of meditations, the concentration training, which is a means to develop considerable skill in selective attention and in sustaining attention. According to classical accounts, the meditator trains by using an object of awareness as a support to develop concentration. The object of awareness may be the movement of the breath, an intentionally generated sound (mantra) or a visual object, such as an icon. Many of the meditators in our research used visual objects (Brown, 1986).

The meditator first adopts a stable posture and fixes the gaze steadily upon the image. Every time attention wanders from the object of awareness, the mediator effortfully holds fast to the object and bringing attention back until achieving the goal of having attention stay on the object for the greater part of the meditation session. The meditator repeats the practice many times until able to sustain concentration for a full session without being distracted by thoughts, fantasies, bodily states, or emotions.

As a result of intensive concentration, the meditator experiences a rearrangement in the stream of consciousness, in which the field of concentration becomes reduced to a compact little seed floating in space (Brown, 1977, 1986). The seed condenses information from the various sense systems and is experienced in a similar form regardless of whether the object of awareness was originally a visual, auditory, or kinesthetic object. Specific images, colored lights, bodily sensations, and even fragrances emanate from the seed during concentrative meditation. Eventually, these specific perceptual patterns disappear, and the seed becomes more luminous than before. The skilled meditator then enters a state of consciousness known as samadhi (Brown, 1986).

The classical texts define samadhi in terms of both the point of observation and the observable event. From the perspective of the observer, samadhi is a state in which awareness stays one-pointedly, meaning it is not interrupted by events ordinarily experienced in the stream of consciousness such as thoughts, memories, fantasies, bodily sensations, emotions, and even perceptions. From the perspective of the observable event, samadhi is defined as a noncognitive state of consciousness, in which gross cognitions such as thoughts, fantasies, and perceptual patterns simply do not occur for the duration of the samadhi state. The Burmese teachers have a very clear criterion for attaining samadhi: the meditator should be able to sit for an hour of meditation, experience no more than five distracting thoughts, recognize each thought immediately upon arising, dissipate it immediately by becoming aware of it, and not have it interrupt concentration upon the object of awareness at all. The meditator in samadhi is said to be so absorbed in the object of awareness that all activity of the senses is temporarily suspended during the samadhi state. The *Yogasutras* gives the classic definition of samadhi as follows: "Awareness stays upon that, penetrates into that, and takes on identity with that object [of-awareness]" (Mishra, 1973).

Concentration Stage—Scientific Inquiry

The first perceptual experiment utilized Rorschach inkblots as a perceptual instrument (instead of a personality test) and was given prior to, immediately after, and one year after a three-month 16-hour-per-day intensive meditation retreat by U.S. practitioners of Burmese mindfulness meditation. Responses to the TIME and ratings by the meditation teachers were used as independent criteria to discriminate which retreatants achieved some degree of proficiency in samadhi. The staff facilitating the meditation retreat, who meditated less intensively (2 hrs./day) but who shared the same beliefs and expectation of gain from the practice, were used as a control group. The inkblots typically remind normal nonmeditating subjects of different images or percepts, such as a butterfly or a person. Figure 17.1 shows the typical response of a normal subject just

CARD VIII.

1. Looks like two rats on each side...some kind of being like that...an animal.

2. Upside down it looks like an old fashioned...parts of a woman's dress...the top of a corset.

INQUIRY

1. [Rats?] Rodents, actually [Describe?] Long tails...short faces...and their legs

2. [Dress?] This looks like the top...this corset (points to the gray). I can't figure out what this is...it's got some ruffles...frills...then, it's cut into a tight vest underneath the breast area...looks very uncomfortable.

Fig. 17.1. Typical Rorschach Response—Prior to Meditating

prior to meditating. Figure 17.2 shows the same subject's response to the same card upon completing three months of intensive meditation and having attained samadhi. This response is typical across all 10 cards within each subject and across all subjects in the samadhi group. Rorschach data collected during samadhi are characterized by a paucity of associative elaborations as well as a relative lack of production of images or percepts such as animals or butterflies. Card VIII is the easiest of all the cards on which to see an image (typically animals), because the ink is shaped closely like an animal on the side of the card. The rodent was the only image produced by this subject on all ten cards. Yet, this subject, like all the subjects in the samadhi group, spent as much time as other subjects who responded to what they "saw." What they "saw" was not butterflies and people but what was actually there; they responded with the pure perceptual features of the inkblot, with an accurate description of stimulus characteristics, such as the interesting shapes, edges, colors, and shading. These responses are highly unusual and are not seen on the normal or clinical Rorschachs to any degree. The results are consistent

CARD VIII.

1.   Well, the colors...all of it...colors against the white color...they're striking.

2.   Rodents climbing...They look exactly like rodents.

INQUIRY

1.   Colors? yah, all the colors. [Form?] all the different forms of the color...each shading of the color has a certain form to it...[what might it look like?] Nothing...nothing at all...last time I was struck very much with this one...I tried to find something...and turned it around and around...Once somebody told me that you were real bright if you turned it around...I never forgot that so I did...[This time?] This time, the colors were enough...very pleasant, pretty...It doesn't look like anything to me...but there's part of it that takes on a very distinct form.

2.   I remember the rodents climbing from last time. They look exactly like rodents to me [How so?] The shape...the feeling I get of the way they're climbing...moving their feet...tail...faces.

Fig. 17.2. Rorschach Response—Samadhi Group

with the classical descriptions of very concentrated meditators. Samadhi is a state relatively free of thinking and fantasy productions (Brown and Engler, 1980).

In another series of experiments investigating the perception of intensive meditators, we used a tachistoscope (T-scope), which is an electronic instrument capable of presenting stimuli at very high speeds, say, thousandths of a second, to a subject who views the stimuli on a screen through a stationary viewing hood designed to stabilize vision so as to reduce artifacts caused by head and eye movements.

The first T-scope experiments were conducted using simple flashes of light as stimuli. Subjects were given time to adapt to a background field of fixed luminance and then viewed stimulus presentations through a stationary viewing hood. The detection threshold experiment consisted of a series of trials of single flashes of light superimposed on the background field, the duration of which was randomly varied for each stimulus presentation. The subject was asked to report detection of the flash. Flashes of very brief duration could not be seen; flashes of longer duration could be seen.

The discrimination threshold experiment consisted of a series of trials of two successive flashes of light at a duration well above threshold. The interval between each flash was randomly varied. The subjects were asked to report whether they saw one or two flashes. If the two successive flashes were presented at a very close interval, they were "seen" as a single flash due to a summation effect in ordinary perception. Both experiments were conducted until each subject achieved 70% detection accuracy. Dummy trials in which no flash (detection experiment) or only one flash (discrimination experiment) was presented were interspersed randomly into the stimulus presentations.

In one study using a predesign/postdesign, the T-scope detection and discrimination experiments were conducted just prior to and immediately after three months with a group of U.S. practitioners of Burmese mindfulness meditation and with a group of staff controls at the retreat center (Brown, Forte, and Dysart, 1984a). There were significant decreases in both detection and discrimination thresholds over the course of the meditation retreat for the intensive meditators but not for the staff controls. Because the groups were matched for demographics, prior meditation experience, and expectation of gain from meditation, these differences were most likely due to the practice of intensive mindfulness. In another comparative study, the tachistoscopically determined detection and discrimination thresholds of three meditation groups (intensive meditators, staff controls, and meditation teachers) were compared to a control group of nonmeditators of similar demographics. The meditators had significantly lower detection thresholds (p < .007) but not discrimination thresholds than the nonmeditators (Brown, Forte, and Dysart, 1984b).

The results of these experiments taken together suggest that meditators show enduring improvements in visual sensitivity to light stimuli (lower detection thresholds) and state-dependent increases in the ability to discriminate rapid, successive events in the stream of consciousness while intensively meditating. Even though the experiments were not conducted with subjects proficient in samadhi, they do suggest that intensive meditation results in a lowered threshold to light stimuli. Thus, when the *Yogasutras* states that samadhi is the "shining forth of only light . . . devoid of its own form" (Mishra, 1973), the text may be describing not simply a subjective state but an objectively measurable change in visual sensitivity to light under a condition of fixed luminance. The mind of the meditator "sees" with greater internal luminance.

Perhaps our most unusual studies of samadhi were conducted with subjects highly proficient in samadhi. The Dalai Lama personally selected four highly accomplished meditators from the Tibetan Buddhist tradition to participate in a T-scope study. Each of these exceptional meditators lived in a secluded dwelling in the mountains, and the three subjects in the first experiment were skilled in samadhi practice. The research was conducted nearby in Upper Dharamsala, India, one of the main Tibetan refugee centers. The experiment used a T-scope driven by a portable IBM PC whose power was supplied by a portable generator. In this study, stimulus forms were used instead of light flashes, namely, the letters s, x, and z, which pilot studies showed to have an equal probability of recognition accuracy according to the stimulus characteristics of the letter (Brown et al., 1988).

In the first experiment on recognition accuracy, a single-subject, repeated-measures block design was used in which each of the three subjects was tested successively in an alternating sequence of nonmeditation (NM) and meditation (M) trials during the same experimental day. Each block consisted of a two-minute period to adapt to the fixed luminance of the background field followed by an experimental trial of one of three randomly presented stimulus forms—s, x, or z—at the center of the visual field in one of four randomly assigned stimulus durations for a minimum of 125 observations per trial. Dummy observations were inserted into each trial, in which no letters were presented. A portal on the viewing hood was used to ensure that the subject kept the eyes open throughout the M as well as the NM trials. Figure 17.3 shows an example of the results of one subject, using a two-way analysis of variance (ANOVA) (condition [NM vs. M] and time). There was a significant main effect for the M vs. NM condition for all three lamas in the study. On NM

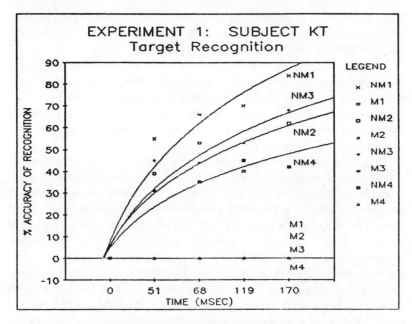

Fig. 17.3.   Target Recognition—Subject KT

trials, recognition accuracy is a function of stimulus duration: the greater
the duration, the greater the accuracy. On M trials, two subjects made no
correct identification of any stimulus letters, a performance significantly
less than chance. A third subject made correct identifications in one but
not the other of two M trials, but his overall performance was significantly less than in the NM condition. No subject ever misidentified a
dummy display, which attests to the accuracy of reporting according to
what was actually "seen" or not seen, not according to what may have
been expected. No subject closed the eyes during any part of the experiment.

   In a second experiment with an advanced tantric meditation master
(one of the very best in the Tibetan tradition), we repeated the experiment
with some modifications. The same stimulus forms—s, x, and z—were
used, but their color (black, blue, red, and green) and location (left or right
side of the screen) were varied. The same single-subject repeated-
measures block design was used with two M and two NM trials of 125
randomly presented stimulus observations each. A two-way ANOVA—
condition (NM vs. M) and time—was conducted for each of the three
dependent variables: accuracy of target recognition, color recognition,
and left/right position. The study replicated the results of the former
experiment, wherein target recognition accuracy significantly decreased
in the meditation condition. There was also a significant decrease in

color recognition during the M condition and a significant decrease in position recognition during the M condition. Once again, this subject kept the eyes open and did not misidentify any dummy trials.

These findings demonstrate an important feature of samadhi: the temporary suspension of pattern recognition ability during meditation. The finding cannot be explained entirely in terms of expectation effects (as indicated by responses to the dummy trials). While keeping their eyes open, these meditators do not "see" the stimulus forms during samadhi. Nor do they recognize the color or position of the form.

Taken together, the Rorschach and T-scope experiments illustrate some of the essential parameters of the samadhi state. We are reminded from the Rorschach data that the meditator in samadhi does not generate thoughts or images. From the T-scope studies of target recognition, we learn that samadhi is a state in which the mind has stopped—at least in terms of such functions as higher perceptual processing like pattern recognition. And from the T-scope experiments on light flashes, we learn that samadhi is a state in which the meditator has greater light sensitivity. The exceptional meditator "stops the mind," at least in the sense of voluntarily suspending gross cognitive activity, and holds awareness on a more subtle level of ordinarily preattentive mental activity, namely the subtle high-speed movements in which the stream of consciousness is experienced as a flow of light. The meditator is now more aware of the stream than of the objects that float in it.

Insight Stage—Classical Descriptions

Skill in suspending gross cognitive/perceptual activity during meditation is not considered in and of itself to be a goal of meditation practice. The purpose of gaining voluntary control over perceptual processes is to stabilize a new point of observation by which to gain fundamental insight into the processes by which the self and the world are constructed in ordinary perception. The meditator begins the insight series of meditations, a series of further refinements of samadhi. Having "stopped the mind," at least in terms of gross cognitions, the meditator now takes the subtle flow of light as the object of awareness. This practice is called concentration without support because the flow of light, considered a subtle object, cannot support concentration in the same way as, say, an icon or the breath can. The skilled meditator becomes aware of the moment-by-moment changes in the flow of light occurring at very high speeds and is able to observe these changes without the slightest distraction in a balanced way. Moreover, the meditator begins to gain insight into how the ordinary point of observation—the self-representation and sense of self-agency—introduces subtle biasing factors into moment-by-moment perception. By searching for the source of this self-representation within the subtle changes that occur, the meditator experiences a profound rearrangement in the stream of consciousness. Ordinary self-representation drops away, and only pure awareness remains as the point of observation of ongoing experience (Brown, 1977, 1986).

Having stabilized this new point of observation, the meditator attempts to apply the insight to a new context through a practice known as reverse samadhi. The meditator voluntarily shifts awareness from the subtle flow of light to gross cognitions once again during meditation. At high speeds, the skilled meditator's pure awareness automatically tracks whatever happens to arise in the stream of consciousness. In so doing, the meditator gains insight into the way the ordinary sense of self and world are constructed from these simpler high-speed events. The meditator also comes to understand that this ordinary sense of self is a mere representation without inherent existence (Brown, 1977, 1986).

With further experience, the meditator gets less interested in the content of the stream of consciousness and more interested in the very way events come forth. The skilled meditator is said to be aware of the exact moment of impact of each event in the stream of consciousness prior to its construction as some form of gross cognition such as a thought or a percept. The meditator also notes the brief duration of the event and also the exact moment that the event passes from awareness. This attainment is called clear comprehension.

Eventually, a shift occurs. The meditator experiences events coming forth and going very quickly like intense flashes of light. This is called arising and passing away samadhi. The meditator now searches to discover the way events come forth in the stream of consciousness, which leads to an understanding of the time–space structure of ordinary perception. Is the seeming arising and passing of events itself another subtle form of perceptual bias? Another construction? Apparently so. The skilled meditator is said to crack the code of the time–space structure of ordinary perception. As a result, the meditator opens to a new transcendent dimension of experience in which all potential events of the universe and the fabric of potential interactions between such events come forth simultaneously. Within this undivided interconnectedness, interactions occur not by causal laws but by relative relationship to everything else. Awareness no longer tracks the successive events in the stream of consciousness as in earlier samadhi states but like an explosion "pervades" the vast interconnectedness of the potential universe. These samadhi experiences are called the extraordinary samadhis because of the profound shift in consciousness that occurs (Brown, 1986).

Insight Stage—Scientific Inquiry

The Rorschachs collected from a group of U.S. meditators in the Burmese mindfulness tradition skilled in the insight series of practices yielded results nearly opposite to those of the samadhi group described earlier. The Rorschachs were characterized by increased productivity and a richness of associative elaborations. Whereas normal nonmeditating subjects typically produce one or two responses per card, these subjects consistently gave 10 or more per card and claimed that their productivity was unlimited. Whereas repeated administration of the Rorschach either days or years later yields many of the same responses for normal nonmeditating subjects, a number of meditation subjects given the Rorschach repeatedly over several days produced nearly all new responses the second time. Figure 17.4 illustrates how each response was richly elaborated. It appears that the skilled meditator is unusually open to the flow of internal associations. This Rorschach finding is consistent with the classical description of reverse samadhi in which awareness tracks the gross cognitions that arise in the stream of consciousness at very high speeds without interruption (Brown and Engler, 1980).

CARD VIII.

1.   This is a wonderful one, too...Sideways, this is...again...the red figure is a four-legged animal...like a mountain lion...and now he's running, leaping over a real rocky and difficult terrain...There's a sense of great energy and power in him, but the most wonderful thing of all is how sure-footed he is...a great sense of flight...He always lands on just the right crop of rock...never misses...always instinctively sure of his footing so he'll be able to go on like that...Wonderful mastery and wonderful fit between the animal and his world...kind of perfect harmony between them, even though it's very dynamic...Leaping...He always does it...Here, he's in flight...just landed with the front paw and the back paw is still in the air and he's feeling, not very reflective...Just doing it spontaneously. He's feeling the great energy and lightness and challenge. He loves the challenge because he's equal to it...But it's always keeping him out there on his limit...With this is another wonderful thing...It has to do with the colors again...a progression in his progress from warm, wonderful colors to colder, finally, very cold colors. He is starting from a place of warmth and security and as he started from there, he can carry it out and conquer the cold, insecure place because he himself is the pink, the color of the heat, light, energy and warmth...and so he can go out and master the cold of the world again.

Fig. 17.4.   Rorschach Response—Insight Group

Another T-scope study was suggestive of the skilled meditator's insight into the way events come forth in the stream of consciousness. That study compared phenomenological reports of advanced U.S. meditators in the Burmese mindfulness tradition to nonmeditating simulators at visual threshold. The seven meditators were nominated by their teachers as being highly skilled. The three simulating nonmeditator controls were asked to describe their experiences on perceptual tasks using a level of sophistication about perception and knowledge of how the mind works comparable to that of experienced meditators; namely, they were asked to simulate being a meditator to an experimenter blind of these instructions. (Simulator designs have been utilized in psychological research on states of consciousness to separate out that portion of the overall variance motivated by the wish to comply with the experimenter's expectations from that portion unique to advanced meditation practice per se.) The stimulus presentations consisted of single and successive light flashes at randomly presented durations and interstimulus intervals until a critical stimulus duration and a critical interstimulus interval were determined respectively for each subject. Then, the critical stimulus duration and critical interstimulus interval were held at threshold on a series of repeated observations. Subjects were asked to describe everything they were aware of during the act of perceiving the target (Forte, Brown, and Dysart, 1987/88b).

The skilled meditators gave very unusual reports relative to the simulators. First, whereas the nonmeditating simulators saw two flashes, the meditators reported seeing the moment of arising of the first flash, its brief duration, the moment of its disappearance, the gap between the flashes, the moment of arising of the second flash, its brief duration, and finally, its disappearance—an event that typically occurred in less than 100 msec. in objective time. Second, the meditators also reported that the visual field was constantly moving in a subtle way and that the flash was simply "movement within movement" that created the illusion of a separate event or flash. Third, meditators described a shift in perspective in which the flash of light did not seem to occur as an external event on the visual screen but rather as a "blip in the mind," namely, a subtle movement in the internally perceived stream of consciousness. These reports suggest that skilled meditators are aware of perceptual mechanisms normally outside of conscious awareness and are especially sensitive to the way events come forth temporally in the stream of consciousness. They do seem to report "clear comprehension" of the arising and passing of these normally very quick and largely preattentive events. Once again, the meditators' performance is consistent with the classical descriptions of insight meditation.

We unfortunately do not have any conclusive experimental data on

subjects in extraordinary samadhi. We did, however, conduct two independent, backward-masking experiments using the T-scope with skilled
meditators from the Tibetan and Burmese traditions. After determination
of the recognition threshold for each subject, the subject was presented a
stimulus letter above threshold followed by a randomly varying interval
of time before the presentation of a masking stimulus such as a ring
surrounding the letter. If the interstimulus interval between the stimulus
letter and the masking stimulus is short, the mask cancels out or masks
recognition of the stimulus letter. In a typical perceptual experiment with
normal subjects, recognition accuracy drops. If the interstimulus interval
is long, the mask does not interfere with target recognition. In each of two
separate experiments—one with U.S. meditators in the Burmese mindfulness tradition and the other with the Tibetan lamas—we failed to demonstrate a stable masking effect. This failure may indeed be an artifact of the
experiment and the limitations of the equipment, but it suggests that
skilled meditators may show an equal probability of recognition accuracy
across interstimulus intervals. In other words, recognition of the target
no longer operates according to the usual constraints of time. Information
for the exceptional yogi may be processed simultaneously instead of
sequentially over time. Although inconclusive, these data are consistent
with the classical descriptions of extraordinary samadhi in which awareness operates outside of the time–space structure of ordinary information-
processing.

Enlightenment—Classical Descriptions

As pure awareness pervades the vast interconnectedness of the potential
universe and has nothing further to alight upon, it eventually turns back
upon itself. This practice of awareness of awareness sets up a profound
shift known as enlightenment, which occurs as a series of three instanta-
neous shifts in awareness. During the first shift, called basis enlightenment or cessation, all events, content, and activity suddenly cease. Vast
awareness remains, with no sense of activity in the mind. The locus of
awareness is said to shift or "go to the other shore." Following cessation
comes path enlightenment, in which the activity of the interconnected
universe suddenly returns, as if awareness were linked up to its path
through all the potential universes of experience. Following this comes
fruition enlightenment, in which the meditator's stream of consciousness
is permanently rearranged. Following this shift, the meditator returns to
an ordinary state of consciousness with some recognition that a profound
change has occurred. Enduring trait changes are said to characterize
enlightenment. The meditator must then learn how to gain voluntary
control over the enlightened state and how to intentionally produce the

state of awareness experienced at the initial moment of enlightenment, even if only for brief durations. This attainment is called maturity of fruition. There are also further refinements of enlightenment or further paths to attain. The nature of these varies according to tradition. In the Burmese tradition, for example, there are four levels of enlightenment, each resulting in a more radical rearrangement in ordinary experience (Brown, 1986).

Prior to enlightenment, ordinary perception carries with it an inherent limitation, notably a subtle reactivity. For any given event that occurs in the stream of consciousness, there is a reaction to it that either clings to it or averts from it. Awareness and the events in the stream of consciousness are inextricably bound up with each other for the unenlightened individual. This reactivity is considered to be the basis of suffering. A second limitation to ordinary perception is the discontinuity of awareness. A fair amount of the richness of the everyday world is missed due to significant lapses in awareness.

Enlightenment is said to eradicate such limitations. During enlightenment, awareness shifts its locus; it goes somewhere else, "to the other shore," as the texts describe. After enlightenment when the ordinary events in the stream of consciousness reoccur, awareness, now no longer affected by lapses, looks upon these events without the slightest bit of reactivity. Enlightenment does not alter the events in the stream of consciousness; it alters the quality of awareness. The exceptional meditator finds the middle ground between the extremes of keeping the events of the stream of consciousness out of awareness as is reflected in the operation of psychological defenses on one hand, and the compulsion to react to the events on the other hand. The enlightened meditator simply is fully and immediately aware. This awareness is described as "still," namely, without reactivity. While this shift in the locus of awareness, together with the changes in the association between awareness and the events in the stream of consciousness, is what primarily characterizes the first level of enlightenment, the highest levels of enlightenment are characterized by further changes, namely a significant alteration of the nature of the stream of consciousness itself. According to traditional accounts, the highest enlightenment is characterized by an absence of any kind of suffering (Brown and Engler, 1980).

Enlightenment—Scientific Inquiry

A number of Rorschachs were collected from advanced meditators in the Burmese tradition of mindfulness, both in the United States and in South Asia, who were nominated by the authoritative teachers in that tradition as possibly having attained at least the first of the four stages of enlightenment. We also collected a few Rorschachs from those likely to have attained the last two stages of enlightenment. The samples represent the most exceptional meditators—the contemporary saints of their tradition. Figure 17.5 shows the Rorschach response of a subject in the initial enlightenment group. At first glance, these Rorschach protocols were not obviously different from the Rorschachs collected from nonmeditators or beginning meditators. These subjects saw butterflies, people, and the like. However, 5–20% of the total responses on each Rorschach had to do with the interaction of form and energy or form and space. These subjects tended to view their own internal imagery in response to the shape of inkblots as merely manifestations or "emanations" of energy/space within the mind. They had a unique perspective in which they were aware of the moment-by-moment process by which movement, energy, or space in the stream of consciousness became organized into forms and images in response to the inkblots. However, the remainder of the Rorschach protocol for each subject was quite varied depending on the personality of

CARD X.

1.   Sort of like, just energy forces, and um...like molecules...something like the energy of molecules...very much like a microscopic view. In some way there are more patterns of energy. There are different energies in the different colors. It looks like it's a view into the body where there's energy...there's movement, but it's steady because it's guided by a life-force. There is arising and passing away of these different elements.

INQUIRY

1.   The colors seemed very alive and suggested life, and they seemed very basic or elemental--both the shapes and the size. They don't have heavy substance, you know...They each, um...are relatively fragile. [Different colors suggested different elements?] Yeah...and then it started to seem just like a vibration...really not a swelling movement but a pulsation...just coming and going of...um...kind of elemental bits (laughs at word choice) of life (laughs some more). [Arising and passing away of elements?] It was very far out when it happened...I can't um...some of that was because of the suggestion of a spinal column (response from previous administration of Rorschach)...um...It reminded me somewhat of those electron microscope pictures of the body and I just had this sense of the movement of it all.

Fig. 17.5. Rorschach Response—Initial Enlightenment Group

the subject. According to their Rorschachs, these allegedly enlightened subjects were not without intrapsychic conflict. Using the Holt scoring system for drive-dominated content and defenses, we found an increase in drive manifestations but a decrease in defensive operations. In other words, these subjects manifested various psychological conflicts in an open way and with less reactivity in the form of psychological defense. Initial enlightenment did not eradicate their conflicts, such as struggles with dependency, sexuality, and fear of destructiveness. Initial enlightenment did make them significantly less reactive to those conflicts (Brown and Engler, 1980).

These Rorschachs are consistent with the classical accounts of enlightenment. Enlightenment is characterized by a return of the ordinary events in the stream of consciousness along with a shift in the locus of awareness and the relationship between awareness and the events in the stream of consciousness. The enlightened meditator is less reactive to the moment-by-moment events in the stream of consciousness, although the events themselves do not change. The Rorschach content of the initially enlightened subject is fairly ordinary except for the qualifications that the responses or images were simply moment-by-moment emanations arising from energy or movement in the stream of consciousness in response to perceiving the inkblot. As the Rorschachs suggest, initial enlightenment does not eradicate intrapsychic conflict, only reactivity to it. Conflictual themes occur, but they occur with greater awareness and with less psychological defendedness. Because the reactivity inherent in ordinary perception has been eradicated, the enlightened individual does not suffer in the ordinary sense. Perception has been permanently changed.

The higher stages of enlightenment are characterized by a significant alteration in the stream of consciousness itself. At the third stage of enlightenment, the meditator is said to be no longer influenced by sexual or aggressive impulses or by painful affects. At the fourth and final stage, the fully enlightened master is said to have perfected the mind and is free of any kind of conflict or suffering. Meditation is a vehicle by which the meditator permanently alters perception and in so doing is permanently freed from suffering.

We have collected several Rorschachs from meditators alleged to have mastered one of the final two stages of enlightenment, wherein this profound reorganization in the stream of consciousness occurs. Each of these Rorschachs was strikingly similar to the others. Each master used the Rorschach as an occasion to teach us about the workings of the mind. One subject used the cards to explain various states of mind. Another subject described various subtle levels of perception unknown to the ordinary individual. Each of the subjects exemplified the remarkable shift in perspective that is characteristic of enlightenment. Whereas most normal subjects unquestioningly accept the physical reality of the inkblot and project images onto it, these masters saw the inkblot itself as a projection of the mind (Brown and Engler, 1980).

Figure 17.6 is a typical example of a response to card VII from one of the masters. The subject produced a total of 32 responses, 13 of which pertained to specific states of mind (41%) and 3 to states of the ordinary and nonordinary world (9%). The most unusual feature of this Rorschach, and of all of the Rorschachs of the masters for that matter, was the integrative style of response. Ordinary subjects typically respond to each of the 10 Rorschach cards independently. Rarely do subjects refer to other cards when giving a response to a particular card. Each of the masters was an exception. Each of the 10 cards, as presented, was utilized in the service of a systematic discourse on teachings about the nature of ultimate reality and the path to alleviate human suffering. Thus, for example, the subject in Figure 17.6 began in card I with images of humans and animals suffering in everyday life. Card II depicted angered states of mind, and card III the hellish consequences of such states of mind. Cards IV and V depicted ignorance and craving, believed to be the two root causes of suffering in Buddhism. Card VI described the way the body and mind could be used to gain liberation. Card VII as shown in the figure depicted the results of the meditation practice. Cards VIII to X depicted the beneficial results of having mastered the meditation practice as well as the harmful consequences of not practicing. Integrating all the Rorschach cards into a single associative theme is an extremely rare finding. I know of no Rorschachs from either normal or clinical populations on which such a finding has been reported. Yet, each master in our sample produced the same integrative style of response.

Elsewhere (Brown and Engler, 1980) we have argued that this integrative style is a function of the profound reorganization of perception and

CARD VII.

1. I see a body [here, which reminds me of] a temple (D6). The mind, here, is like a cavern. I can also call this (with the portion identified as "mind" inside it) the physical body.

2. From it, wings have spread...the impulses, too (D10).

3. Ultimately, this body has gone up to the temple (identifies a second temple, D8). At the end of spiritual practice, the mind can travel in two temples (i.e., the first temple is the human body, once the source of impulses, but now the master of them; the second is the temple at the end of spiritual practice).

Fig. 17.6. Rorschach Response—Master's Group

therefore of the stream of consciousness that occurs in the final stage of enlightenment. The awareness of these unusual masters is said to operate simultaneously on all levels of reality; so, seeing how all the Rorschach cards hang together would not represent an unusual feat from that perspective. Furthermore, when these Rorschachs were scored for drive-dominated material, we found them to be absent of drive conflicts. The implication of this finding is profound: the masters in our sample don't seem to evidence any signs of ordinary conflict; it is as if some profound intrapsychic reorganization has occurred. Completely devoid of the signs of ordinary suffering, these exceptional individuals stand out as genuine saints in the modern world. The single most striking feature of this sample was their kindness. Each was distinctly loving and considerate throughout the testing situation (Brown and Engler, 1980).

Two of the masters were tested with the T-scope. Each produced results similar to those already described, such as an increase in acuity to light flashes and a decrease in recognition accuracy to stimulus forms. The sample, however, produced one additional finding: both subjects reported that the target stimulus, and indeed even the background screen, episodically "disappeared" during the testing. These exceptional meditators presumably had mastered what is called maturity knowledge, that is, the capacity to produce voluntarily the cessation experience characteristic of the initial moment of enlightenment. In other words, they could enter that extraordinary state at will. In the transition, the target, the screen, everything dropped away for a brief duration. As one of the masters said,

> My awareness goes to the other side. Every time the light flashes on the screen, the awareness must return and respond in terms of phenomenal reality. But you are not testing what happens to the awareness, only phenomenal reality. Tell me, can your machine measure what happens to awareness?

We agreed that only practice could tell us that (Forte, Brown, and Dysart, 1987/88b).

AFFECT DEVELOPMENT AND THE PATH OF MEDITATION

The Preliminary Stage of Meditation

The primary goal of the preliminary stage of meditation is the development of relatively continuous awareness (mindfulness) of the moment-by-moment events in the stream of consciousness while one remains in a stable, undistracted state of attentiveness. During this early stage of meditation, the meditator is introduced to his or her inner world. Among the flow of thoughts, memories, fantasies, percepts, bodily sensations, and other events in the stream of consciousness, the meditator also will observe the ebb and flow of emotional states. According to traditional accounts of meditation, the emotions experienced at the onset of practice are largely negative. They are called afflictive emotions (Tibetam *nyon mong*) because their very intensity often serves as a distraction from the primary goal of training continuous, undistracted mindfulness (Brown, 1981; Ngawang Dhargyey, 1974).

Our research using the TIME profile with meditators in the Burmese mindfulness tradition is consistent with the classical accounts of the preliminary stage with respect to affect. More experienced as compared to less experienced meditators differed significantly along two dimensions of affect—affect intensity and affect equanimity. The more experienced meditators reported experiencing intense emotions, either pleasant or unpleasant, but mostly unpleasant (affect intensity). They also reported, however, being relatively undisturbed by the emotions in the sense that such intense emotional states usually did not distract them from maintaining their focus of attention on whatever the object of meditation happened to be (Forte et al., 1987/88a).

Independent research on a clinical population of psychotherapy patients practicing Burmese mindfulness meditation as an adjunct to their psychotherapy reported similar findings (Kutz, Borysenko, and Benson, 1985). Ongoing psychotherapy patients who attended a short-term adjunctive meditation group experienced an intensification of the psychotherapy process in several respects. Meditation resulted in enhanced availability of emotions, an increase in primary process thinking, and the development of detached observation of internal states. Thus, as mindfulness meditators learned to become aware of the moment-by-moment events that arose and passed in the stream of consciousness, they experienced discrete emotional states more clearly and more intensely, without the defensive disavowal characteristic of ordinary waking experience and sometimes of psychotherapy. Moreover, they learned simply to observe these emotional states from a nonreactive perspective of self observation.

Concentration Stage

The primary goal of the concentration stage of meditation is to achieve a stable samadhi state, in which awareness stays one-pointedly on its object and in which the meditation object has become transformed from its gross form (perceptual pattern, thought, bodily sensation) to a subtle form (flow of light). Three technical terms are used to describe this state: noncognition (Tibetan *mi rtog ba*), clarity (*gsal ba*), and bliss (*bde ba*) (Brown, 1981). The technical term "bliss" refers to a nonordinary affective state that arises as a concomitant to intense concentration once the meditation session is relatively free from the occurrence of ordinary afflictive emotional states (*nyon mong*). Nonordinary means that these intense emotions are typically not part of everyday emotional experience.

According to the classical descriptions of concentration meditation, there is a progression of four substages of deep concentration called absorptions, which occur after the meditator has attained samadhi (Buddhaghosa, 1976; Lati Rinbochay et al., 1983). Nonordinary affective states arise in conjunction with the first absorption. The first absorption is characterized by two nonordinary affective states—lightheartedness and bliss. The first, lightheartedness, is described as a mental quality. The meditator is able to deploy attention in a highly skillful and flexible manner and can essentially use it in anyway he or she intends. Concentration is so refined that it is as if every atom in the body could be perceived. The main feeling is incredible lightness and buoyancy as if floating. Thus the meditator is able to apply concentration at a very refined level for long periods without becoming tired. The greater the concentration, the greater the lightheartedness and therefore the less the fatigue. This seeming unceasing energy and lightness are actually by-products of the success of meditation. The second, bliss, is described primarily as a bodily state. It may occur as a momentary state, like a flash of intense ecstasy or thrill of rapture. It may build up slowly and wash over the meditator, as if waves of bliss were washing through the body. However bliss occurs, it is always intensely uplifting and is said to consume any residual negative emotional states, mental agitation, or fatigue.

During the second absorption, lightheartedness and bliss persist, but the meditator is able to refine concentration even further.

During the third absorption, lightheartedness drops away, but blissful states persist. At this stage, the meditator begins to realize that even lightheartedness and bliss can serve as a source of attachment. By applying awareness to the growing attachment to these nonordinary states, lightheartedness begins to subside. A new nonordinary state emerges, called equanimity. Equanimity is described as an affective state in which awareness is undistracted and in which there is no reactivity (no attachment or aversion) to the events arising in the stream of consciousness. Affective equanimity is the fundamental affective experience of the advanced meditator.

During the fourth absorption, affective equanimity becomes the dominant experience. By applying awareness to the very attachment to intensely blissful states as they occur, these more intense bodily states subside in the fourth absorption, just as the less intense mental state of lightheartedness subsided in the third absorption. The only remaining nonordinary affective state in future meditation practice is likely to be affective equanimity. Affective equanimity is described as freedom from the five main afflictive emotions: attachment, aversion, lack of awareness, doubt/fear, and pride. It is also described as freedom from the extremes of pleasure and pain, joy and grief, hope and fear, and praise and blame.

Insight Stage

The primary goal of the insight stages of meditation is to develop a stable perspective of awareness (samadhi) by which to continuously observe the workings of the mind at every level. Specifically, the meditator tries to gain insight into how the mind constructs ordinary experience. The first objective is to replace ordinary self-representation with pure awareness as the point of observation. The meditator comes to see ordinary self-representation as "empty" (Tibetan *stong ba*), that is, as a constructed representation separate from "pure awareness' (*rang rig*). Then, the meditator uses this awareness to examine each level in the information processing system—the subtle flow, the gross content of the stream of consciousness, and, eventually, the very process of how events arise and pass, moment by moment. The meditator also comes to realize that the temporal foundation of experience is also "empty," meaning it is a mere construction. As the meditator comes to understand this, a profound shift in perspective occurs, namely, the experience of interconnectedness (Brown, 1986).

   During this stage, the full range of affect is available. If the meditator voluntarily holds awareness at the level of the gross content of the stream of consciousness, a full range of ordinary affects or discrete emotional states arise in the stream of consciousness. If the meditator voluntarily holds awareness at the level of the subtle flow of light during deep concentration, the nonordinary affective states arise (lightheartedness, bliss, and equanimity). If the meditator holds awareness at a very refined level to observe the temporal process by which events arise and disappear, moment by moment, only affective equanimity occurs. That which changes during the insight stage has less to do with the type and range of affect experienced than with the perspective of self-observation with respect to affects and other experiences that occur. The advanced meditator experiences a progression of shifts in the perspective of self-observation: (1) awareness embedded within the ordinary self representation is replaced by (2) pure awareness of the stream of consciousness, which in turn is replaced by (3) awareness embedded within the experience of interconnectedness.

Enlightenment—An Enduring Shift in the Structure of Experience

Enlightenment is characterized by two essential transformations: eradication of any lapses or discontinuities in moment-by-moment awareness and eradication of the reactivity inherent in ordinary moment-by-moment experience. The shift in the locus of awareness that occurs with enlightenment constitutes an enduring trait change.

How do we understand enlightenment in terms of affective development? First, the enlightened individual is said to have achieved permanent continuity of awareness, without lapses. From the perspective of ordinary, temporally unfolding experience, the meditator is continuously aware of the events in the stream of consciousness, without interruption. In other words, the construct of disavowal or psychological defense against conscious recognition no longer applies to any type of experience. Moreover, the enlightened meditator's awareness operates on a number of levels simultaneously. In each moment of experience, the meditator is aware of the very processes by which events arise and cease in experience. Viewed from the perspective of information processing theory, the enlightened individual is capable of voluntarily holding awareness at the level of input, or at the earliest levels of information processing, normally operating at high speeds, beyond the conscious awareness of the ordinary person (Brown et al., 1988). The advanced meditator has a thorough comprehension of what has been called action-tendencies in the information processing theories of affect (Arnold, 1960). In Buddhism, the terms "attachment" and "aversion" are very similar to Arnold's (1960) and Leventhal's (1980) appetitive-aversive dimension of affective information processing. The difference between the Eastern and Western perspectives on these action-tendencies, or, better, reaction tendencies, is that the Eastern contemplatives have applied the theory as a system of soteriology, that is, as a practical means to liberation from the limiting and biasing factors inherent in the way the mind ordinarily operates. During advanced insight meditations, the skilled meditator learns to hold awareness upon the very reactive tendencies (attachment and aversion) that accompany each event in the stream of consciousness, moment by moment. Upon enlightenment, these reaction tendencies disappear.

Second, a reorganization is said to occur during enlightenment in the structure of experience, so that these ordinary reaction tendencies permanently disappear. What is affective experience like for the enlightened individual? At the earliest level of enlightenment, discrete emotional states still occur in ongoing experience. What changes are the awareness and the reactive tendency that accompany emotional states or any other event in the stream of consciousness. As an emotional state arises in the stream of consciousness, it is experienced with full awareness and without any reactivity. The enlightened individual allows the anger, sadness, or joy to remain in full awareness without trying to avert from it or hold on to it, until, like all other experience, it passes. This is another way of saying that enlightenment is a way of finding the middle ground between the extremes of failing to consciously recognize the affective state (disavowal) and the compulsion to act on the affective state.

At the very refined level of enlightenment, a fundamental and permanent structural transformation occurs. According to classical descriptions of full enlightenment, all afflictive emotional states permanently disappear. Full enlightenment implies the absence of suffering and emotional conflict. The only nonordinary affective state that characterizes full enlightenment is a stable and enduring condition of affective equanimity.

Full enlightenment is one example of an endpoint made possible through rigorous disciplined self-observation. Individuals who practice along the path of meditation learn to cultivate relatively continuous awareness of ongoing experience and then to investigate the operations of the mind at each level of the information processing system. They skillfully learn voluntary control over the levels of processing in their ability to temporarily suspend higher cognitive/perceptual operations so as to allow awareness to track high-speed processes normally out of conscious awareness. It is as if the meditator takes the mind apart with awareness to see how it works at each level and then puts it back together differently so that it works better.

The path of meditation offers two things that other methods of disciplined self-observation like psychotherapy do not. First, the skilled meditator is thoroughly conscious of all the levels of affective processing, an attainment rarely achieved in psychotherapy. Second, the enlightened meditator experiences a profound structural reorganization so that the action or reaction tendencies inherent in ordinary experience permanently disappear, including eventually the experience of ordinary afflictive emotional states. The fully enlightened individual is said not to experience any negative affect or pain. The resultant nonordinary trait of affective equanimity is a vision of psychological well-being not heretofore described in the Western psychotherapy literature. Freud (1930) stated that the best that psychoanalysis could offer to civilization was a means to transform neurotic conflict into ordinary everyday unhappiness. Western psychotherapeutic methods are very useful when working with psychopathology; they offer little in the way of relief for ordinary everyday unhappiness. In contrast, meditation is a method designed specifically to change ordinary everyday unhappiness. Meditation is not a method designed to alter psychopathology. Meditation changes everyday unhappiness by addressing its source: the operations of ordinary perception. Meditation is a method by which an individual can become aware of, gain voluntary control over, and permanently reorganize the operations of the information processing system at every level of its operation. Enlightenment is an enduring reorganization of perception, a reorganization of the reactivity inherent in ordinary perception, and as a result, a reorganization of emotional experience.

The fully enlightened individual simply does not experience ordinary everyday unhappiness. The enlightened one has found the Noble Truth at the foundation of the Buddhist tradition: the truth of the end of suffering in this lifetime (Wilbur et al., 1986). The enlightened one also has a direct experience of the interconnectedness of all potential events in the universe. Such an experience inevitably leads to an ethical and compassionate outlook on life. When the meditator directly realizes that each event in the stream of consciousness and each instance of behavior are interconnected with everything in the potential universe, it is impossible to think and act in isolation from this context. Realizing that each thought or behavioral act has an influence on everything else, the meditator becomes sensitized to the consequences of thought and action. Through this realization, his or her thought and action necessarily become ethical and compassionate. Thus the meditation traditions arrive at a conclusion very different from Freud's. Freud in his pessimism could not see a civilization "beyond discontent" (Freud, 1930). But Freud's psychoanalytic, free associative method was aimed largely at the content in the stream of consciousness. The meditation traditions—which put forth a rather different method, namely a tool to permanently change ordinary perception—therefore are able to draw a very different and largely optimistic conclusion: psychological well-being *is* a possibility. It is possible to create a civilization beyond ordinary everyday unhappiness, beyond discontent.

REFERENCES

Arnold, M. B., ed. (1960), *Emotion and Personality* (2 vols.). New York: Columbia University Press.
Brown, D. P. (1977), A model for the levels of concentrative meditation. *Internat. J. Clin. Exp. Hypn.*, 25:236–273.
_____ (1981), Mahamudra meditation stages and contemporary cognitive psychology: A

study in comparative psychological hermeneutics. Unpublished doctoral dissertation, University of Chicago.

_____ (1986), The stages of meditation in cross-cultural perspective. In: *Transformations of Consciousness*, ed. K. Wilbur, J. Engler & D. P. Brown. Boston: New Science Library/ Shambhala, pp. 219–283.

_____ & Engler, J. (1980), The stages of mindfulness meditation: A validation study. *J. Transpers. Psychol.*, 12:143–192.

_____ Forte, M. & Dysart, M. (1984a), Differences in visual sensitivity among mindfulness meditators and non-meditators. *Percept. Mot. Skills*, 58:727–733.

_____ _____ _____ (1984b), Visual sensitivity and mindfulness meditation. *Percept. Mot. Skills*, 58:775–784.

_____ _____ Goodale, R., Dysart, M., Glissen, M. & Cohn, C. (1988). "Stopping the mind": Recognition of visual information by exceptional meditators. Unpublished manuscript.

Buddhaghosa, B. (1976), *Visuddhimagga [Path of Purification]* (trans. B. Nyamamoli). Berkeley, CA: Shambhala.

Forte, M., Brown, D. & Dysart, M. (1987/88a), Differences in experiences among mindfulness meditators. *Imaginat., Cognit., Personal.*, 7:47–60.

_____ _____ _____ . (1987/88b), Through the looking glass: Phenomenological reports of advanced meditators at visual threshold. *Imaginat., Cognit., Personal.*, 4:323–338.

Freud, S. (1930), *Civilization and Its Discontents. Standard Edition*, 21:64–145.

Goleman, D. (1975), Meditation and consciousness: An Asian approach to mental health. *J. Appl. Physiol.*, 33:719–725.

Ikegami, R. (1970), Psychological study of Zen posture. In: *Psychological Studies on Zen*, ed. Y. Akishige. Tokyo: Zen Institute of Kamazawa University, pp. 105–153.

James, W. (1901/1961), *The Varieties of Religious Experience*. New York: Colliers.

Kim-Ling, P. (1981), Intensive Buddhist meditation and the self. Unpublished doctoral dissertation, Boston University.

Kutz, I., Borysenko, J. & Benson, H. (1985), Meditation and psychotherapy. *Amer. J. Psychiat.*, 142:1–8.

Lati Rinbochay, D. L., Locho Rinbochay, Zahler, L. & Hopkins, J. (1983), *Meditative States in Tibetan Buddhism*. London: Wisdom.

Leventhal, H. (1980), Toward a comprehensive theory of emotion. *Adv. Exp. Soc. Psychol.*, 13:139–207.

Mishra, R. (1973), *Yogasutras [The Textbook of Yoga Psychology]*, (trans. Patanjali). Garden City, NY: Anchor Press.

Ngawang Dhargyey, G. (1974), *Tibetan Tradition of Mental Development*. Dharmsala, India: Library of Tibetan Works and Archives.

Thera, N. (1962), *The Heart of Buddhist Meditation*. New York: Weiser.

Wilbur, K., Engler, J. & Brown, D. (1986), *Transformations of Consciousness*. Boston: Shambhala.

INDEX

416

INDEX

Hurt, expression of, gender differences in, 101
Husbands, response to wives' emotions, 117
Hussein, S., 349
Hyde, J. S., 101, 119
Hyperarousal, 228, 236
Hypertension, essential, stress-reactive, 283
Hypnosis, 355, 363: Freud and, 358–360, 368; historical use of, 358–361; as investigative tool, 360; passive, 248; for posttraumatic stress disorder in Vietnam veterans, 250–255, 256, *See also* under Posttraumatic stress disorder: return to, 358; trauma, affect and, 361–362

I

Idea(s): affects as sum total of, 81; infant, 305n
Idealization, 151
Ideation, 82
Identity feelings, 190: lack of, 212; pathological and devalued, 176
Ikeda, D., 347, *352*
Ikegami, R., 378, *402*
Illness development: affect and, 281, 286–287; cancer risk, 287–289; cardiovascular risk, 289–293; developmental arrest related to, 296–297; mechanisms of, 282–286; stress and, 219, 282, 296–297
Imagery, in hypnotherapy for posttraumatic stress disorder in Vietnam veteran, 253
Imaginary television, use in hypnosis of trauma patient, 251
Immune system: disregulation of, illness development and, 283–286; operation of, 284
Immunoglobulin (IgA) activity, 285
Immunosuppression-prone personality, 287
Impulses, instinctual, repressed, 339
Inagaki, K., 18, *60*
Inappropriate affect, in schizophrenic, 45
Incest survivors, 252
Incongruity hypothesis, 10
Infant affect behavioral interchanges with mother, 76; affect sequence, relation-

ship to affects in older persons, 206–207; confidence in communication, 14; discrete affect states in, 73; emotional expressiveness of, language and, 111; expectations, 305, 305n; experience of affect, 82; facial expressions of, 70; falling in love with, 13; interchanges with environment, 305; normal, affective expression in, 6–9; paradoxes of power and, 341; paranoid-schizoid position, 314; strategy for achieving power, 342
Infant–caregiver interactions: affective displays and, 16; specific affect profile and, 74
Infant–caregiver system: good-enough, 14, 15; regulation of, 11
Infant research, application to research on elderly, 205–206, 214
Infantile experience, 312
Infantile objects, inner, break with, 162
Infection, immune system and, 286
Information processing, 10–11, 41: action-tendencies in, 399; affects interfering with, 221; enlightenment and, 399; gender differences in, 109
Information processing theories of affect, 36, 41
Ingram, R., 105, *119*
Inhelder, B., 164, *179*
Inhibition, illness development and, 293
Inner experience of affect, 18
Inoff-Germain, G., 110, *121*
Input dysfunction theory, 10–11
Insight, 142
Integration, enhancement of, 142
Integrative psychoanalytic theory, 5
Intense feelings, gender differences in, 97
Interest, xvi: affect of, 206; affective development and, 9–12
Internal feeling, 53
Internal sensory perception, 30
Internal states, self-regulation of, 21
Internal visceral experience, 17, 18
Internalization, transmuting, 21, 192
Internalizers of emotion, 88
International Society of Political Psychology (ISPP), 349, 350
Interpersonal dimension of affects, 73
Interpretation: clarification and, 135; primary, 129

matic stress disorders, 241; traumatic, 266: uncovering and working through of, use of hypnosis for, 362

Memory, 36, 76: age changes in, 231; emotions' effects on, 218, 221, 226–228, 237; hippocampus and, 229–230; impairment of, trauma and, 236; infant, 305n; toddlers', 21; visceral, 221

Mental activity, distracting products of, 368

Mental energies, distributions of, shift in, 368

Mental flexibility, in elderly, 204–205

Mental representations, linked with affect states, construction of, 75

Messick, G., 285, *299*

Metadialogue, 142

Methadone, 267

Meyer, D., 285, *299*

Meyer, G. J., 29, *63*

Meyers, M. B., 110, *120*

Milkman, H., 262, 263, 265, *278*

Miller, A. H., 284, *301*

Miller, J. B., 101, 102, *120*

Miller, P. A., 31, *59*

Miller, R. E., 28, *58*, 88, *118*

Mills, L. L., 102, *118*

Millsap, R. E., 204, *216*

Mind, functions of, 237

Minuchin, S., 148, *156*

Mishra, R., 375, 381, 384, *402*

Mitchell, D., 233, *239*

Mitchell, S. A., 266, *277*

Modell, A. H., 20, 23, 26, 49, *63*, 68, *85*, 163, *179*, 196n, *199*, 266, *278*: views on manic defense, 163; on unconscious guilt, 69

Models of the Mind (Gedo and Goldberg), 34–35, *55*

Modern Music, 318

Mond, J. J., 284, *298*

Monjan, A. A., 284, *300*

Monocyte-macrophage system, 284

Montville, J. V., 337, 349, *352*, *353*

Mood(s), 72: continuity of, 72–73; development, early affective experience and, 15–16; self-management of, 164

Mood, D. W., 30, *63*

Mook, J., 288, *301*

Moore, B. E., 78, *85*

Morgan, G. A., 23, *64*

Moriarty, A., 16, *63*

Morrier, E., 249, *257*

Moss, H. A., 24, *61*

Mother, *See also* Caregiver; Parent: death of, feelings toward, in young child, play and, 136–140; dual-paycheck, emotional expressiveness in, 104; good, theory as, 310; idealized, 174; images of, in affect tolerance problems in adolescent girl, 174; responsibility to infant emotion, gender differences and, 98–99; self-denying behavior, 152; separation from, 314; theory choice and, 311; unavailable, 153

Mother–child–father envelope, affect-response and, 327

Mother–child interaction: child's theory making ability and, 306, 306n; gender differences and, 98

Mother–child matrix, idealized, 311

Mother–child relationship: affect-response and, 327; in affect tolerance problems in adolescent girl, 165–166, 167–168, 171, 172–173; attachment to theory and, 311

Mother–son dyad, synchrony in, 99

Mothering, thinking required in, 101–102

Motivation: acquired, 234; affect function as, 70, 75

Motor phenomena, in play, 142

"Mourning and Melancholia" (Freud), 77

Mourning process, *See also* Grief: during adolescence, 162, 163

Mullaney, D. J., 203, *297*

Munn, P., 99, *119*

Munson, M., 233, *238*

Munster, A. M., 284, *300*

Murphy, J. M., 224, *240*

Murphy, L. B., 13, 14, 16, 20, *63*

Murray, M. A., 31, *66*, 93, *121*

Music, power of, 347

Mutalipassi, L. R., 224, *239*, 242, *257*

My Lai, 244

Myelinization, 227

Myers, K. M., 92, 102, *118*

Mystical experiences, 363

Mythic figures, encounters or identifications with, 364

iencing of affect states and, 75–76; theories and, 5, 307–308, 398n, 315: representational world construction and, 18
Object removal, 172
Object representations, 164: affective expe-
rience and, 22; maturation of, 18–19
Object ties, earliest, painful attachments to,
266
Observer, young child as, 135
Obsessions, 54
Occupation, sex-role stereotypic, fear and,
105–106
Oedipal behavior, affective challenge in,
152–153
Oedipal stage conflict, 151: family support
for, child's effort in finding, 146–158;
development and resolution of, 145;
unresolved, 124
Oedipal themes, play theory and, 135
Ogden, T. H., 141, *144*
Ohrenstein, L., 31, *63*
Ollendick, T. H., 33, *63*
Olson, S. L., 21, *63*
Olthof, T., 29, 30, *60*
Omission, traumas of, 366
Operation Phoenix, 244–245, 248, 254
Opiate(s), 284: effects on emotions, 263
Opiate system, endogenous, 227: in post-
traumatic stress disorder, 224, 225;
trauma and, 235, 236
Oppenheim, D., 102, *120*
Oppositional behavior, 156
Organ systems, disregulation of, 282
Organization, capacity for, 14, 141
Organizer, affect as, 145
Orlofsky, J. L., 105, *120*
Ornstein, P. D., 5, 43, *63*
Orr, S. P., 224, 235, 236, *239*
Ortiz, A., 224, 227, *239*
Ortony, A., 7, *63*
Osborne, E. W., 233, *239*
Osofsky, J., 146, *158*
Other, self-regulating, 11
Overloads, affect-response and, 326

P

Pain, 24, 224: numbing and recovery,
236–237; perception of, dampening of,
227; pleasure benefits of, 234–235;
state of mind and, 246

Painful affects, child's, 130
Pajer, K. A., 16, *58*
Pallmeyer, T. P., 224, *238*
Pancer, S. M., 31, *63*
Panic, 181, 232: continuous and discontinuous models for, 187f, 187, 188f, 188
Papousek, M., 10, *63*
Paranoid-schizoid position, infant's 314
Parent, *See also* Caregiver; Mother; Father:
abandoning, 152; of adolescent,
including in analytic session, 172, 173,
174, 177, 178; affect tolerance and, 328;
affective displays of, children's relatedness to, 145–146; affective reactions to
young children, 146; behavior of,
child's perception of, 165; communication of message by, 27; emotional development and, gender differences and,
2–3; fear responses, modeling of, 27;
lost, identification with, 311; same-sex,
displacements of love toward, 163
Parent–child dyad, gender differences in,
99–100
Parker, K. D., 102, *120*
Parnell, K., 98, *120*
Parson, E. R., 242, 243, 244, 251, 255, 256,
257
Participant, young child as, 135
Pascucci, N. J., 243, *256*
Passive-aggressive struggles, in young
child, 136
Past, feelings from, reexperiencing of, 132
Patel, V., 285, *300*
Patient, response to therapist, 184
Pawlby, S., 13, *63*
Payne, E., 251, *257*
Peer relationships: expression of emotions
and, gender differences in, 115; same-
sex, gender differences in, 97–98
Pelcovitz, D., 221, 223, 231, *240*
Penn, G. M., 285, *299*
Pennebaker, J. W., 30, 40, 45, *63*
Penzien, D. B., 294, *299*
Perception: ordinary, limitation to, 391;
time-space structure of, in meditation,
387
Perceptual-affect-action patterns, 269
Perceptual development, maximization of,
12
Perceptual motor theory of emotion, 40
Perceptual samplings, 10